PENGUIN CLASSICS

# WEBSTER: THREE PLAYS

There is very little factual information remaining about John Webster. He is thought to have been born in London in 1580 and to have died in 1634. In 1598 he entered the Middle Temple but, like several of his contemporaries, gave up his study of the law for literature. His legal expertise is nevertheless very much in evidence in *The Devil's Law-Case* (1620). Webster's collaboration with Middleton, Drayton and others on a play called *Caesar's Fall* is the first documentary evidence we have of the playwright, and he is later listed as a collaborator on a play called *Ladey Jane*. He wrote two comedies with Dekker, *Westward Ho!* and *Northward Ho!*, but these read more as Dekker's works than Webster's.

When *The White Devil* was first performed in 1612 it was not a great success, a fact which Webster blamed on the ignorance of the audience and the poor theatrical setting. Consequently, when he completed *The Duchess of Malfi* in 1614, he offered it to the King's Men rather than the Queen's Men and the play proved a good deal more popular, moving to the Globe to end its run. With these two tragedies, now frequently revived, Webster achieved a reputation second only to Shakespeare's.

David Gunby is Reader in English at the University of Canterbury, Christchurch, New Zealand. A great admirer of Webster, he is the author of several article-length studies of the plays, as well as a monograph on *The White Devil*.

# JOHN WEBSTER·THREE PLAYS

## THE WHITE DEVIL
## THE DUCHESS OF MALFI
## THE DEVIL'S LAW-CASE

Introduction and Notes
by D. C. Gunby

PENGUIN BOOKS

PENGUIN BOOKS

Published by the Penguin Group
Penguin Books Ltd, 27 Wrights Lane, London W8 5TZ, England
Penguin Books USA Inc., 375 Hudson Street, New York, New York 10014, USA
Penguin Books Australia Ltd, Ringwood, Victoria, Australia
Penguin Books Canada Ltd, 2801 John Street, Markham, Ontario, Canada L3R 1B4
Pengun Books (NZ) 182–190 Wairau Road, Auckland 10, New Zealand

Penguin Books Ltd, Registered Offices: Harmondsworth, Middlesex, England

This collection first published in the Penguin English Library 1972
Published in Penguin Classics 1986
7 9 10 8 6

Introduction and notes copyright © D. C. Gunby, 1972
All rights reserved

Printed in England by Clays Ltd, St Ives plc
Set in Monotype Bembo

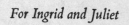
*For Ingrid and Juliet*

# CONTENTS

# INTRODUCTION

## I

To some readers and critics (fewer now than formerly) John Webster is one of the most overrated figures in English literature, equipped with flashes of poetic genius, but morally chaotic and dramaturgically inept. To others (myself among them), he is one of the greatest English dramatists. The three plays contained in this volume represent the peak of Webster's achievement: the work by which he must be judged. Two of them, *The White Devil* and *The Duchess of Malfi*, have in recent years enjoyed notable stage successes. The third, *The Devil's Law-Case*, has not yet been revived, yet for all the difficulties that the tragicomic mode creates for a modern audience, it contains much that is very good, and one scene, the trial, which is among the finest in Jacobean drama. Read together, the three plays will, I hope, win further support for the growing critical conviction that Webster is a great poet and dramatist, a comic writer of real distinction, and a tragedian second only to Shakespeare – nor always to him.

## II

Until recently we knew little for certain about Webster's life. Even the dates usually given for his birth and death, 1580 and 1634, represented no more than intelligent guesses. The situation has improved considerably with the discoveries of Mary Edmond (published in *The Times Literary Supplement*, 24 December, 1976, pp. 1621–2), but there are still large gaps in our knowledge, exemplified by our continuing uncertainty about the dramatist's birth and death dates, so that

9

what is known has, as before, to be supplemented by conjecture.

We have always known, because Webster himself remarks on the fact in the dedication to his civic pageant, *Monuments of Honour* (1624), that he was a Londoner, 'born free' of the Merchant Taylors' Company. We now know with certainty what was previously only conjectured: namely that this link with the Merchant Taylors derived from his father's membership of the Company. We also know that John Webster senior, who was made free of the Merchant Taylors' Company in 1571, was by trade a coachmaker, and that he built up a large and prosperous business, hiring as well as building wagons, carts and coaches, before his death, probably in 1615.[1] Thereafter the family business, which was situated in Cow Lane, Smithfield, near the cattle market and in a street which was a recognized centre for coach- and harness-makers, was run (equally successfully, it seems) by his son Edward until the latter's death in 1644.

Of the private as well as the business lives of Edward Webster and his father we now know a good deal, thanks largely to Miss Edmond. Of John junior, the dramatist and elder (or eldest) son, we know for certain much less. His parents probably married in 1577, so that a birthdate of 1580 for the first son is not improbable. Nor is it improbable that the 'Master John Webster, gentleman, son and heir apparent of John Webster of London, gentleman', entered as a student at the Middle Temple in 1598, was the future dramatist. A period as a law-student, even if ill-spent, would certainly help to explain Webster's considerable knowledge

---

1. Until a separate Coachmakers' Company was founded in 1677, it was usual for members of this trade to join the Merchant Taylors, with whom – e.g. in the provision of trappings and hearses for funerals – they had some community of interest.

of the law, and the vehemence with which, in *The Devil's Law-Case*, he affirms his belief that 'Bad suits, and not the law, bred the law's shame'. The temptation to identify the law-student with the dramatist becomes stronger when we learn that the same Master John Webster did not complete his course of studies. It may be that Webster, following the lead of another poet and dramatist, John Marston, who had also been a student at the Middle Temple, found his inclinations ran contrary to his calling, and deserted law for literature.

This, however, is speculation. For facts we must wait until May 1602, when an entry in the diary of Philip Henslowe, the theatrical entrepreneur, reveals that 'antoney monday & mydleton mihell drayton, webester & the rest' were working on a play called (by Henslowe, whose spelling is wildly individual, even for his day) 'sesers ffalle'. For this work, now lost, Webster and his colleagues received an advance of £5. A week later Henslowe records 'fulle paymente' of £3 to the same team for a work he refers to as 'too shapes' (i.e. two ghosts), which is probably the same play as *Caesar's Fall*. In October of the same year, Webster is mentioned again, this time working with five others on a two-part history play, *Ladey Jane*, while in November he and Thomas Heywood were advanced £3 'in earneste of a playe called cryssmas comes bute once ayeare'. The latter is lost: the former survives only in a compressed and corrupted form as *Sir Thomas Wyatt*. In 1607 it was published: reading it now, one wonders why.

During 1603 or the spring of 1604 Webster produced his first unaided work, an Introduction to Marston's very popular tragicomedy, *The Malcontent*. Though competent, it indicates nothing of what he was later to achieve. Nor, for that matter, do *Westward Ho!* and *Northward Ho!*, the city comedies which Webster wrote in collaboration with

Dekker during 1604-5. The two were well received at the time, and make pleasant entertainment still, but they read more as Dekker's work than Webster's. Clearly the younger man was still following the older's lead.

Since it is on his two great tragedies, *The White Devil* and *The Duchess of Malfi,* that Webster's reputation ultimate y rests, it may seem that so much attention to the dramatist's early career is unnecessary. Yet unless we take account of Webster's undistinguished service as a hack-writer and collaborator, we cannot fully appreciate the amazing achievement that these two plays represent. It is as if Shakespeare had written nothing between *The Taming of the Shrew* and *Hamlet* or *Macbeth.*

Though *The White Devil* (1612) was acclaimed by Dekker for its '*Braue Triumphs* of *Poesie, and Elaborate Industry*', it does not seem, initially, to have been enthusiastically acclaimed in the theatre. Webster himself, confident of the play's worth, put this failure down to the setting for the production – 'so dull a time of winter' and 'so open and black a theatre' – and to the inadequacies of the audience, who he felt resembled 'those ignorant asses (who visiting stationers' shops, their use is not to inquire for good books, but new books)'. His low opinion of the audience was probably justified, for the *habitué* of the Red Bull at Clerkenwell generally dined on rough-and-ready fare – jingoistic history plays, gory tragedies and knock-about farce – and his taste was, in consequence, unsophisticated. Whatever the reason for the failure, Webster took no chances with his next play. Switching his allegiance, he offered *The Duchess o, Malfi* not to the Queen's Men, but to their rivals, the King's Majesty's Servants. The move seems to have been justified, for the King's Men presented the play with considerable success, first at their indoor theatre, the Blackfriars, in the spring of 1614, and afterwards at the Globe.

*The White Devil* and *The Duchess of Malfi* together represent the peak of Webster's achievement as poet and dramatist. Certainly nothing he wrote thereafter (unless it were his lost comedy, *Guise* [c. 1616], which he himself mentions in the same breath as his two tragedies) quite measures up to them. Nevertheless, it would be a mistake to see his later career simply as a decline into mediocrity, and to ignore all the work, dramatic and non-dramatic, for which he was responsible after 1614. If we dismiss as unworthy of attention the plays written in collaboration during the early 1620s – one of them, *Keep the Widow Waking* (1624), a pot-boiler based on contemporary London trials, got Webster and his fellow-dramatist, John Ford, into difficulties with the law – we are still left with four works of more than passing value. One is *A Monumental Column*, an elegy on the death of Henry, Prince of Wales, written in 1613, and invaluable as an aid to understanding Webster's tragic vision, particularly as expressed in *The Duchess of Malfi*. Another is the group of thirty-two prose 'characters' added to the third (1615) edition of Sir Thomas Overbury's *Characters* – an edition that Webster himself probably saw through the press. A third is *Appius and Virginia* (c. 1627), probably Webster's last work, and generally believed to have been written in collaboration with Thomas Heywood; straightforward and relatively unsubtle, it has a simplicity and vigour which are not unsuited to its theme. The last of the four is *The Devil's Law-Case* (1620). A deeply serious play, though in the tragicomic mode, it is Webster's most undervalued work, one whose full worth is only now being recognized. It alone is sufficient to refute the charge, often made, that in creating *The White Devil* and *The Duchess of Malfi*, Webster burnt himself out.

So much of John Webster the dramatist. But what of John Webster the man? What meagre evidence there is tells us that his wife was named Sara (without telling us when they married or where) and that they had a not inconsiderable family, including John (possibly born early 1606), Elizabeth, Sara and others. Where the dramatist lived, however, remains a mystery, as does all else about him. It may be surmised, from what we know of the prosperity of the family business, that John Webster was financially independent and had no need to supplement in other ways the minuscule income that would have derived from his literary work. Given his proverbial slowness in composition, this combination of leisure and financial security was no doubt crucial to his achievement.

We do not know when Webster died. He may have been the John Webster buried at St James's, Clerkenwell, on 3 March 1638, though the fact that in 1634 Heywood's *Hierarchy of the Blessed Angels* refers to him, as to other dramatists then dead, in the past tense, has led scholars to conclude that he died earlier than this. As with so much of his biography, we can do no more than conjecture. And tantalizing though this state of affairs is, the uncertainty is not inappropriate. Webster's hero-villains die, characteristically, 'in a mist'. The dramatist does the same.

### III

In the address to the reader which prefaces *The White Devil*, Webster lists those dramatists whose work he particularly admires:

Detraction is the sworn friend to ignorance. For mine own part I have ever truly cherish'd my good opinion of other men's worthy labours, especially of that full and height'ned style of Master Chapman, the labour'd and understanding works of Master Jonson: the no less worthy composures of the both worthily excellent Master Beaumont, and Master Fletcher: and lastly (without wrong last to be named) the right happy and copious industry of Master Shakespeare, Master Dekker, and Master Heywood, wishing what I write may be read by their light.

The statement is significant not only for the names it includes, but also for the order in which they are listed, and the comments made on each. Shakespeare, it will be noted, is praised, along with lesser lights, for his 'happy and copious industry', but primacy is given to art of a different kind, to the 'full and heighten'd style' of George Chapman, and the 'labour'd and understanding works' of Ben Jonson.

Webster's preferences are understandable, for he was himself a deliberate and conscious artist. An enemy, Henry Fitzjeffrey of Lincoln's Inn, has recorded a vivid, if malicious, impression of 'crabbed (Websterio) / The play-wright, cartwright' in the throes of composition:[2]

> Was ever man so mangl'd with a poem?
> See how he draws his mouth awry of late,
> How he scrubs: wrings his wrists: scratches his pate.
> A midwife! Help? By his brain's coitus,
> Some centaur strange: some huge Bucephalus,
> Or Pallas (sure) engendred in his brain, —
> Strike Vulcan with thy hammer once again.

Though hostile, the caricature is not without a ring of truth. Webster himself provides confirmation of this in his address to the reader, where he defends himself against 'those who report I was a long time in finishing this tragedy' with a confident assertion of his worth as a poet and dramatist. With Euripides, he claims that slowness is justified if the results endure.

2. In a poem called 'Notes from Blackfryers', printed in *Certain Elegies done by Sundry Excellent Wits* (London, 1617).

Speed of composition and literary merit are not always mutually exclusive, of course, as the 'happy and copious industry' of Shakespeare demonstrates. To explain Webster's slowness, therefore, we must look elsewhere. One factor is undoubtedly his temperament, the deliberative cast of mind which leads him again and again to rethink and rephrase from play to play. This predisposition is further revealed in Fitzjeffrey's portrait of Webster the critic:

> This is the critic that (of all the rest)
> I'd not have view me, yet I fear him least,
> Here's not a word cursively I have writ,
> But he'll industriously examine it.
> And in some twelve months hence (or there about)
> Set in a shameful sheet, my errors out.

To a critical faculty as serious and painstaking as this, the journey between a first draft and a final version must have been a long and arduous one, strewn with discarded alternatives.

Another cause of his slowness is Webster's dependence on borrowing as a method of composition. The technique he employed was the standard one of his age – an age, it should be remembered, when no stigma attached to what is now called plagiarism, when on the contrary rhetorical tradition encouraged imitation both as an aid to good writing and as a form of literary flattery. Into a commonplace book he copied anything in his reading which appealed to him, either for its content or its turn of phrase. With this commonplace book before him, he wrote his plays. Or perhaps it would be truer to say 'constructed', for Webster's reliance on borrowed materials was so extensive, even for a Jacobean, that the process of composition became a long and complex building operation, with materials of very diverse kinds being brought together from all sides, and worked with great skill and enormous labour into a unified whole.

To emphasize Webster's borrowing, it should be stressed, is not to decry his artistry. On the contrary, what he borrowed he generally bettered by reworking, and always made his own. In the last scene of *The Duchess of Malfi*, for example, the Cardinal reflects in soliloquy:

> When I look into the fishponds in my garden,
> Methinks I see a thing, arm'd with a rake
> That seems to strike at me. V.v. 5–7

Webster's source was probably Lavater's *Of Ghostes and Spirites Walking by Night* (1596), where it is reported 'that Pertinax for the space of three days before he was slain by a thrust, saw a certain shadow in one of his fishponds, which with a sword ready drawn threatened to slay him, and thereby much disquieted him'. Pertinax's dream is interesting, but the Cardinal's foreboding has a haunting quality about it. The magic lies in the rephrasing and tightening of the passage, as well as in the force introduced by the substitution of 'thing' for 'shadow', 'rake' for 'sword', and 'strike' for 'slay'.

Ben Jonson told Drummond of Hawthornden 'that Donne for not keeping of accent deserved hanging'. At times it is tempting to say the same of Webster, to join Rupert Brooke in proclaiming that 'Webster probably had a worse ear for metre. at least in blank verse, than any of his contemporaries'. But one only has to read the lyrics scattered through the plays, Cornelia's dirge in *The White Devil* or Romelio's in *The Devil's Law-Case*, for example, to realize that Webster has a very fine ear, that he can, when he wishes, write a line as smooth and mellifluous as any. The point is that like Donne (to whom he was obviously related stylistically) Webster deliberately avoids smoothness, finding a less regular kind of blank verse, close to the rhythms of ordinary speech, more to his purpose. For though his verse may at times seem metrically lame or halting, it allows the dramatist to run the full gamut of expression from high tragedy to broad comedy, from bitter conflict to tender lovemaking. It enables him to satirize quite mercilessly those aspects of his age which seem to him evil or false, and to provide *sententiae*, or moral tags, for its enlightenment. It enables him to build up intensity and then, in a line, to release it. It is, in short, perfectly adapted to the varied demands of drama, and to the expression of Webster's peculiarly individual view of the world.

## IV

What is Webster's view of the world? To a remarkable degree, considering the smallness and homogeneity of his unaided output, critics have from the first failed to agree. George Bernard Shaw, disgusted by what he regarded as gratuitous horrors and empty melodrama, crowned the dramatist 'Tussaud Laureate'. T. S. Eliot, who knew enough about Jacobean dramatic conventions to admire Webster's dramaturgical skill, none the less shared Shaw's view that Webster's underlying philosophy is characterized by confusion and morbidity. 'The case of John Webster, and in particular *The Duchess of Malfi*,' he says in his essay, 'Four Elizabethan Dramatists', 'will provide an interesting example of a very great literary and dramatic genius directed towards chaos.'[3] Earlier, in 'Whispers of Immortality', he had given imaginative expression to this chaos when he wrote:

> Webster was much possessed by death
> And saw the skull beneath the skin;

3. T. S. Eliot, *Selected Essays* (London, 1951), p. 117.

And breastless creatures under ground
Leaned backwards with a lipless grin.

Daffodil bulbs instead of balls
Stared from the sockets of the eyes!
He knew that thought clings round dead limbs
Tightening its lusts and luxuries.[4]

Unfortunately for Webster, some of his most ardent admirers have praised him in terms which seem to justify the strictures of Shaw and Eliot. Rupert Brooke, for instance, believes that 'the chief characteristic of Webster's two plays and of many things in those plays, is that they are good; and the chief characteristic of Webster is that he is a good dramatist'.[5] Yet he also describes a Webster play as 'full of the feverish and ghastly turmoil of a nest of maggots', and sees 'the world called Webster' as one where life 'seems to flow into forms and shapes with an irregular abnormal and horrible volume'. Reading Brooke without reading Webster, one might well conclude with Eliot and Shaw that he was morbid, and perhaps not read him at all.

It is characteristic of early Webster criticism – and all the quotations so far predate 1925 – that it tells us more about the critic's world-view than the dramatist's. By more recent critics Webster has been more objectively served. Even so, there remains a gulf between those who claim for Webster a place second only to Shakespeare, and those who consider him grossly overrated. Foremost amongst the latter are Ian Jack and L. G. Salingar. Jack's view is that Webster is a 'decadent', one who, lacking 'a profound hold on any system of moral values', uses horrors to 'no deeper purpose than to make our flesh creep'.[6] Salingar is equally emphatic

4. T. S. Eliot, *Collected Poems 1909–1936* (London, 1936), pp. 53–4.
5. R. Brooke, *John Webster and the Elizabethan Drama* (London, 1916), pp. 157–8.
6. I. Jack, 'The Case of John Webster', *Scrutiny* XVI (1949), pp. 38–43.

about sensationalism and lack of direction. To him the emotions in *The White Devil* and *The Duchess of Malfi* are chaotic: 'every sensation is inflamed, every emotion becomes an orgy'. 'Webster is sophisticated,' he says, 'but his sophistication belongs to decadence. The poet's solemnity and his groping for a new basis for tragedy only serve to expose his inner bewilderment.'[7]

In countering these charges, Webster's supporters agree on some points, but not on others. They agree that he is no decadent, gratuitously exciting the emotions. They agree, too, that Webster's own views are not necessarily those of his cynical and amoral protagonists. They disagree, however, about the values embodied in the plays, and as to what, in the last analysis, the dramatist is trying to say. Some see courage, divorced from morality, as his central concern. Others, modifying this view, find him preoccupied with 'integrity of life', with the individual's struggle to remain true to himself. Others again (and this point of view has enjoyed considerable popularity in recent years) conclude that he is more or less existentialist in outlook, presenting, as one critic puts it, 'a unity of empirical, responsible, sceptical, unsurprised, and deeply perceptive concern for the characters and society portrayed'.[8] Yet another, in flat contradiction, finds in Webster 'a study of the working of sin in the world', a rigorous didacticism which affirms that before they die, the wicked are forced to acknowledge 'the supremacy of that Divine Law against which they have offended'.[9]

7. L. G. Salingar, 'Tourneur and the Tragedy of Revenge', in *A Guide to English Literature. Vol 2: The Age of Shakespeare*, ed. Boris Ford (Harmondsworth, 1955), p. 349.

8. John Russell Brown, in his introduction to the Revels Plays edition of *The Duchess of Malfi* (London, 1964), p. xlix.

9. Lord David Cecil, 'John Webster', in *Poets and Storytellers* (London, 1949), pp. 30 and 33.

Since great literature is timeless in its significance, we may accept these differing interpretations as a tribute to Webster, and proof of the perennial relevance of the plays. Yet at the same time we need, if any sort of critical perspective is to be maintained, to distinguish between those readings of Webster which chiefly reflect the preoccupations of our own age, and those which may, with some certainty, be grounded in the ideas and attitudes of the Jacobeans. An existential reading of *The White Devil* and *The Duchess of Malfi* is perfectly possible, while a Freudian interpretation, particularly of *The Duchess of Malfi*, brings valuable insights. Yet an understanding of the half-medieval, half-modern amalgam of thought and belief which constitutes the Jacobean world-view is essential if we are to see the plays more or less in their original colours.

History is a record of constant change, but not of change at a constant rate. The first half of the seventeenth century was, as our own age is, a period of accelerated change, a time when the impact of new ideas and attitudes was felt particularly severely. Socially and economically, the nation was unsettled by the fundamental changes involved in moving from a corporate feudal order (however degenerate) to the greater individualism of the capitalist system. Jacobean England was prosperous, but the prosperity was unevenly spread, and subject to violent fluctuation. With prices rising faster than rents or wages, the urban middle class of merchants, bankers, shipowners, entrepreneurs and the like, flourished, but the landowners (and this included the King) and the masses, both urban and rural, suffered. Even in good times unemployment was widespread, and vagrancy a serious problem. In the country the rate of change was, as always, slower, and the disruption less acute. Yet the enclosure movement brought discontent along with increased agricultural productivity, while the drift of the nobility to London and the court (a movement which James I tried vainly to halt) and the steady purchase of estates by wealthy citizens unwilling to continue the same feudal and paternalistic patterns of behaviour, led to a decline in the traditional activities of the nobility and gentry: the dispensation of hospitality, charity, and patronage, and the local administration of justice. Politically there was also unease, as the rights of King and Parliament came into conflict, and men wondered how the two were to be reconciled, and the exercise of the royal prerogative related to the continued operation of the common law. In religion, too, there were upheavals, as the Church of England walked a narrow (sometimes impossibly narrow) path between the conflicting pressures of Catholicism and radical Protestantism. Clashes between the Anglican and Puritan wings of the established Church over aspects of church government and liturgy were accompanied by disagreements over theological issues which, seemingly abstruse, in fact bore fundamentally on the two parties' views of man and society, as well as on the eternal issues of salvation and damnation.

Another source of confusion and unease, though not as profound a one as has often been asserted, or as widespread, was the cosmological impact of the new astronomy. Medieval (and, largely, Jacobean) man's world-picture derived from the Ptolemaic theory of the universe, geocentric, hierarchic, and immutable. Copernicus and Kepler showed the earth to be but one planet orbiting one star. Such a world-view contradicted Christian dogma, Biblical authority, and the evidence of the senses, as well as Ptolemy and his precursor, Aristotle. Allied to the view, widely held in Jacobean England, that the world was in its old age, the last stage of a steady process of degeneration begun at the Fall (it was generally agreed that the end of the world would occur in the year 2000), this cosmological upheaval provided a powerful reinforcement of the pessimism, the sense of the 'brevity, misery, and vanity of life', as Douglas Bush puts it,[10] which has always haunted man, but did so with particular intensity during the Jacobean age.

This world of change, confusion, shifting standards and, above all, pessimism, is clearly reflected in Webster's plays. Douglas Bush has said that for seventeenth-century man the fundamental question was 'What do I know?' The answers which their lives imply reveal that most of his leading characters – and many of the minor ones – are morally and spiritually adrift. Gunnar Boklund, observing this fact, particularly in *The White Devil*, concludes that Webster portrays 'a world without a centre', 'a world where mankind is abandoned, without foothold on an earth where the moral law does not apply, without real hope in a heaven that allows this predicament to prevail'.[11] This, it seems to me, is profoundly untrue. It is a more or less accurate description of the way Flamineo, Bosola or Romelio see things, but it is not the way that Webster does. On the contrary, his is a strictly moral universe, watched over by a God willing and able to intervene in human affairs, and to direct the apparently haphazard towards the fulfilment of the divine will. It is a world in which God and the Devil struggle for mastery, just as, microcosmically, they do within every Christian soul.

Nor is this surprising, once one considers the intensity and depth of Jacobean religious belief. Attempts have been made to show that religious belief in early seventeenth-century England was confined largely to the unthinking, that among the intellectually sophisticated, Christian

10. D. Bush, *English Literature in the Earlier Seventeenth Century* (Oxford, 1952), p. 278.

11. G. Boklund, *The Sources of The White Devil* (Uppsala, 1957), pp. 179–80.

orthodoxy was obsolete. For this twentieth-century reading of a seventeenth-century situation there is no real evidence. A few noted sceptics apart, Jacobean intellectuals were as religious as their unthinking fellows. Sir Francis Bacon might be laying the foundations of modern scientific method, but his Confession of Faith is that of an essentially medieval man. Sir Walter Raleigh could entertain at Sherborne a group of free-thinkers, yet begin his *History of the World* with an assertion of God's divine purpose and providential care, and an account of the Creation and the Fall. What we find in Webster is not, therefore, unusual, but rather the orthodoxy of his age. Like his fellows, he believes in the existence of an indivisible entity embracing both the physical and the spiritual, the seen and the unseen. Those of his characters who recognize this fact, and live in harmony with the moral laws which sustain the universe, enter their reward, after death if not before. Those who disregard these truths, whether out of confusion, indolence or depravity must, sooner or later, pay for their sins. In Webster's plays, salvation and damnation are ever-present realities.

Baldly summarized in this way, Webster's plays sound like dramatized versions of Thomas Beard's *Theatre of God's Judgements*, that simple-minded and nastily dogmatic compendium of sin and retribution gorily exacted. The briefest look at the plays themselves, however, or at the complexities of Webster criticism, will serve to dispel such a misapprehension. Webster is a didactic writer; his aim, in the best Renaissance tradition, is to instruct as he delights. But he is also a great poet and dramatist, possessed of a deep and rich tragic vision, and the dramaturgical skills required to body it forth. And so in offering his answers to the spiritual problems of his age, in charting the progress of the proud towards humility and self-knowledge, or the materialistic towards disillusionment, disorientation, and the mists of death, he goes far beyond didacticism to produce, in *The White Devil*, *The Duchess of Malfi* and, to a lesser extent, *The Devil's Law-Case*, highly subtle and coherent works of art, in which all the resources of poetic drama are directed towards the embodiment of a complex, moving, and deeply religious vision of human existence.

## V

As part of the additional notes to the plays (see pp. 415–59), I include critical comments on each scene. Because the plays are complex, and the space available limited, I can deal there only with salient features and crucial points of interpretation. To put such a discussion in perspective, I need here to make some brief general observations.

Both *The White Devil* and *The Duchess of Malfi* belong to that dramatic genre known as revenge tragedy, a genre itself part of a larger group under the heading of the tragedy of blood. Together, these titles suggest the main features of such plays. They centre (outwardly at least) upon murder, and murder in revenge for murder. They depict these murders in violent and bloody detail. In the poorer examples of the genre, the dramatist seeks to do no more than that: violence is an end in itself. Generally, however, the plays go far beyond this – to mine the rich vein of interest, social, political, and religious, which L.G. Salingar summarizes so well in his 'Tourneur and the Tragedy of Revenge':[12]

The theme of revenge [the 'wild justice' of Bacon's essay] was popular in Elizabethan tragedy because it touched important questions of the day; the social problems of personal honour and the survival of feudal lawlessness; the political problem of tyranny

12. op. cit., p. 334.

and resistance; and the supreme question of providence, with its provocative contrasts between human vengeance and divine.

In presenting their revenge plots, with all the implications they carry, the dramatists almost invariably – the great exception is *Hamlet* – set their plays in Italy or (and to an Englishman the two were scarcely distinguishable) Spain. In doing so, they embodied the typical Englishman's attitude to these distant lands: a mixture of fear and fascination born partly of ignorance and religious prejudice and partly of a reading of historians like Guicciardini, who furnished the sober Protestant mind with horrendous examples of papists, politicians and poisoners at work. The 'Italy' thus created was, as G. K. Hunter has remarked, 'a mode of human experience rather than ∴ a country'.[13] Inasmuch as it reflected a real world, it was, however, an English one. For the strong satiric elements to be found in most Italianate revenge plays indicate a deep concern for a society under stress and felt, for reasons referred to earlier, not to be changing but degenerating.

As mouthpieces for this satiric concern, the dramatists use the character type known as the malcontent. Often, as with Flamineo and Bosola, a graduate embittered by his inability to find suitable employment in a highly stratified society, the malcontent is a man divided within himself. On the one hand he is a blunt moralist, ruthlessly exposing the vices and follies of mankind. On the other he participates in the viciousness and self-seeking of the world he rails against. He is, if you like, a Becky Sharp in his certainty that he could live virtuously on £5000 a year. But unlike Thackeray's amoral heroine, he goes about denouncing those who, on such an income, perversely refuse to espouse honesty.

13. 'English Folly and Italian Vice', in *Jacobean Theatre*, ed. J. R. Brown and B. Harris (London, 1960), p. 103.

If as a moralist the malcontent is the natural mouthpiece for the dramatist's satiric purposes, as a self-seeking adventurer he is the perfect agent of the revenger. The latter, who usually plans murders but hires others to carry them out, is generally portrayed as a stage Machiavel. As such he in no way resembles the great Italian historian and political theorist. Rather he is a travesty of Machiavelli's ideas, based on his opponents' distorted views of what Machiavelli was saying, grafted on to the native English stage-figure of the morality vice. As Richard III, he can be entertaining, and even amusing. As Francisco, Ferdinand, and the Cardinal, he is a compelling embodiment of evil, whose destruction is essential if the power of the Devil is to be controlled, and God's will done on earth.

Though *The Devil's Law-Case* is a tragicomedy, and concerned therefore, as the Italian critic Guarini puts it, with 'the danger not the death', it has a very great deal in common with the two tragedies which preceded it. Indeed, it could, without distortion, be termed a tragicomic, bourgeois version of the tragedy of blood. It is set in Italy. It features revenge and (attempted) murder. Its hero differs from those in the tragedies, but only in that he is a conflation of the Machiavel and the malcontent. In a suitably frugal, middle-class manner, Romelio both plans and carries out his own revenge, as well as providing the bulk of the play's satiric comment. And as the form of *The Devil's Law-Case* is related to that of the tragedies, so is its meaning. The richness of significance which L. G. Salingar finds in revenge tragedy, and which is certainly present in Webster's two tragedies, informs his one tragicomedy also.

Given such similarities, it may be wondered why Webster chose, in *The Devil's Law-Case*, to work in the tragicomic mode at all. The answer lies, I think, in what this volume seeks to provide – a reading of the three plays in chronological order. What emerges from such a reading – for me at least – is a sense of the development of Webster's thinking, as well as its continuity. The premisses from which Webster works remain the same in all three plays. What he says changes, and the way he says it must change also. In *The White Devil* the emphasis is primarily upon the evil-doer. Though we are provided with positive norms, both through the language and through characters like Cornelia, Isabella, Giovanni and, at last, Monticelso, our attention is focused mainly upon Vittoria, Flamineo, Brachiano and Francisco, and their downhill journey to damnation. In *The Duchess of Malfi* the balance of interest is more even. We are still fascinated by the evil-doers, Bosola, Ferdinand and the Cardinal, but their power to attract is more than matched by the warm and luminous figure of the Duchess. Watching her progress from pride to humility and hence to salvation through a providential care which not even Bosola, the agent through whom it is provided, recognizes, we are introduced to a positive element greater than the implied values of *The White Devil* can reveal. In *The Devil's Law-Case* this movement from the implicit to the explicit is taken further still. The Duchess is redeemed by the providential use of Bosola's divided nature, but only in death. Romelio, on the other hand, is saved from the consequences of pride and despair without having to enter heaven's gates. The greater optimism implied by Romelio's survival, as well as by the active co-operation of men and institutions, Ariosto (the law) and the Capuchin (the Church), in the workings of providence demands a change in dramatic genre. *The Devil's Law-Case* is not tragedy manqué, a tragic plot with a comic conclusion incongruously grafted on to it, as some critics would seem to infer. It is planned from the first with a tragicomic dénouement in mind. Yet as tragicomedy it stands in direct descent from *The White Devil* and *The Duchess of Malfi*, its explicit justification of the ways of God to man an outgrowth of the implied theodicies of the two great tragedies.

# SELECT BIBLIOGRAPHY

Unless otherwise stated, the place of publication is London.

E. B. Benjamin, 'Patterns of Morality in *The White Devil*', *English Studies*, xlvi, 1965, pp. 1–15.

Travis Bogard, *The Tragic Satire of John Webster*, Berkeley, 1955.

Gunnar Boklund, *The Sources of The White Devil*, Uppsala, 1957.

Gunnar Boklund, *The Duchess of Malfi: Sources, Themes, Characters*, Harvard, 1962.

M. C. Bradbrook, *Themes and Conventions of Elizabethan Tragedy*, Cambridge, 1935.

Rupert Brooke, *John Webster and the Elizabethan Drama*, 1916.

R. W. Dent, *John Webster's Borrowing*, Berkeley, 1960.

Inga-Stina Ekeblad, 'The Impure Art of John Webster', *Review of English Studies*, ix, 1958, pp. 253–67.

D. C. Gunby, '*The Devil's Law-Case*: An Interpretation', *Modern Language Review*, xliii, 1968, pp. 545–58.

D. C. Gunby, *Webster: The White Devil*, Studies in English Literature Series, 1971.

G. K. and S. K. Hunter, *John Webster*, 1970.

James Hurt, 'Inverted Rituals in Webster's *The White Devil*', *Journal of English and Germanic Philology*, lxi, 1962, pp. 42–7.

Ian Jack, 'The Case of John Webster', *Scrutiny*, xvi, 1949, pp. 38–43.

Clifford Leech, *John Webster: A Critical Study*, 1951.

Clifford Leech, *Webster: The Duchess of Malfi*, 1963.

Brian Morris (ed.), *John Webster: A Critical Symposium*, 1970.

Hereward T. Price, 'The Function of Imagery in Webster', *Publications of the Modern Languages Association*, lxx, 1955, pp. 717–39.

# TEXTS

THE three plays contained in this volume were published a total of nine times during the seventeenth century: *The White Devil* and *The Duchess of Malfi* four times each; *The Devil's Law-Case* only once. For present purposes, however, only the First Quartos of each are of any significance. These have served as copy-texts for the present edition. All the evidence points to Webster's active participation in the production of the Quartos, which are well printed and, save over the lineation of *The Devil's Law-Case*, present the editor with few problems.

In keeping with the general principles of this series, I have modernized spelling, except where doing so would entail the loss of a rhyme or second meaning, and emended the punctuation where Jacobean methods of pointing dramatic speech present difficulties for the modern reader. In past participles and preterites the distinction between 'd for unstressed and *ed* for stressed final syllables has been maintained, this involving regularization in parts of *The Devil's Law-Case*. I have also retained such contractions and elisions as seem to be required rhythmically. I have been conservative in my handling of stage directions, but have not hesitated to add to them where it seemed necessary. All such additions are given in square brackets. Brief notes, largely glossarial, appear at the foot of each page. The longer notes appear, together with a commentary on each scene, at the back of the book. A brief account of sources and influences is also given.

The neglect which attended *The Devil's Law-Case* in the seventeenth century has attended it in the twentieth also, and in preparing this edition I have had no modern spelling texts available for consultation. I have, however, benefited greatly from the following editions of the tragedies: *The White Devil*: ed. Elizabeth Brennan, New Mermaid Series, 1966; ed. J. R. Brown, The Revels Plays, 2nd ed. 1966; and ed. Gamini Salgado in *Three Jacobean Tragedies*, The Penguin English Library, 1965. *The Duchess of Malfi*: ed. Elizabeth Brennan, New Mermaid Series, 1964; ed. J. R. Brown, The Revels Plays, 1964. Like them, and like all who have subsequently worked upon the plays, however, I am above all indebted to the late F. L. Lucas, whose four-volume, old-spelling edition of *The Complete Works of John Webster* (1927, republished 1966), with its voluminous and marvellously wide-ranging notes, remains essential reading for those who love scholarship and, more, love the plays of John Webster.

# THE
# WHITE DIVEL,

## OR,

The Tragedy of *Paulo Giordano Ursini*, Duke of *Brachiano*,

With

The Life and Death of Vittoria Corombona the famous Venetian Curtizan.

*Acted by the Queenes Maiesties Seruants.*

Written by IOHN WEBSTER.

*Non inferiora secutus.*

*LONDON,*
Printed by *N.O.* for *Thomas Archer*, and are to be sold at his Shop in Popes head Pallace, neere the Royall Exchange. 1612.

# DRAMATIS PERSONAE

MONTICELSO, a Cardinal; afterwards Pope PAUL IV.

FRANCISCO DE MEDICI, Duke of Florence; in the fifth act disguised as MULINASSAR, a Moor.

BRACHIANO, otherwise PAULO GIORDANO URSINI, Duke of Brachiano; Husband of ISABELLA and in love with VITTORIA.

GIOVANNI, his son by ISABELLA.

LODOVICO (or LODOWICK), an Italian Count; in love with ISABELLA.

ANTONELLI } his friends; later fellow-conspirators.
GASPARO

CARLO } BRACHIANO's attendants, secretly in league with FRAN-
PEDRO } CISCO.

CAMILLO, husband of VITTORIA, and nephew of MONTICELSO.

HORTENSIO, one of BRACHIANO's officers.

MARCELLO, a soldier, follower of FRANCISCO, and brother of VITTORIA.

FLAMINEO, his brother; secretary to BRACHIANO.

CARDINAL OF ARAGON.

JULIO, a physician.

*CHRISTOPHERO, his assistant.

*GUID-ANTONIO.

*FERNEZE.

*JAQUES, a Moor, servant to GIOVANNI.

ISABELLA, sister to FRANCISCO, and wife to BRACHIANO.

VITTORIA COROMBONA, a Venetian lady; first married to CAMILLO, afterwards to BRACHIANO.

CORNELIA, mother to VITTORIA, MARCELLO, and FLAMINEO.

ZANCHE, a Moor; servant to VITTORIA.

MATRON of the House of Convertites.

Ambassadors, armourer, attendants, chancellor, conclavist,

* non-speaking parts, or 'ghost characters'.

35

conjuror, courtiers, lawyers, officers, page, physicians, register.
Ladies.

*The action takes place in Italy, first at Rome,*
*but in the final act, at Padua.*

# TO THE READER

IN publishing this tragedy, I do but challenge to myself that liberty, which other men have tane before me; not that I affect praise by it, for *nos haec novimus esse nihil*: only since it was acted, in so dull a time of winter, presented in so open and black a theatre, that it wanted (that which is the only grace and setting out of a tragedy) a full and understanding auditory: and that since that time I have noted, most of the people that come to that playhouse, resemble those ignorant asses (who visiting stationers' shops, their use is not to inquire for good books, but new books) I present it to the general view with this confidence:

> *Nec rhoncos metues, maligniorum,*
> *Nec scombris tunicas, dabis molestas.*

If it be objected this is no true dramatic poem, I shall easily confess it, – *non potes in nugas dicera plura meas: ipse ego quam dixi,* – willingly, and not ignorantly, in this kind have I faulted: for should a man present to such an auditory, the most sententious tragedy that ever was written, observing all the critical laws, as height of style, and gravity of person; enrich it with the sententious *Chorus,* and as it were lifen death, in the passionate and weighty *Nuntius:* yet after all this divine rapture, *O dura messorum ilia,* the breath that comes from the uncapable multitude is able to poison it, and ere it be acted, let the author resolve to fix to every scene, this of Horace,

> – *Haec hodie porcis comedenda relinques.*

7. *auditory*: audience.
16. *have I faulted*: have I fallen short of a desired standard.
21. *Nuntius*: messenger in classical drama.

To those who report I was a long time in finishing this tragedy, I confess I do not write with a goose-quill, winged with two feathers, and if they will needs make it my fault, I
30 must answer them with that of Euripides to Alcestides, a tragic writer: Alcestides objecting that Euripides had only in three days composed three verses, whereas himself had written three hundred: 'Thou tell'st truth', quoth he, 'but here's the difference: thine shall only be read for three days,
35 whereas mine shall continue three ages.'

Detraction is the sworn friend to ignorance. For mine own part I have ever truly cherish'd my good opinion of other men's worthy labours, especially of that full and height'ned style of Master Chapman, the labour'd and understanding
40 works of Master Jonson: the no less worthy composures of the both worthily excellent Master Beaumont, and Master Fletcher: and lastly (without wrong last to be named) the right happy and copious industry of Master Shakespeare, Master Dekker, and Master Heywood, wishing what I write
45 may be read by their light: protesting, that, in the strength of mine own judgement, I know them so worthy, that though I rest silent in my own work, yet to most of theirs I dare (without flattery) fix that of Martial:

– *non norunt, haec monumenta mori.*

32. *verses:* lines.

# [ACT ONE]

## [SCENE ONE]

*Enter Count* LODOVICO, ANTONELLI *and* GASPARO.

LODOVICO: Banish'd?

ANTONELLI:      It griev'd me much to hear the sentence.

LODOVICO: Ha, ha, O Democritus thy gods
That govern the whole world! Courtly reward,
And punishment! Fortune's a right whore.
If she gives ought, she deals it in small parcels,     5
That she may take away all at one swoop.
This 'tis to have great enemies, God 'quite them:
Your wolf no longer seems to be a wolf
Than when she's hungry.

GASPARO:           You term those enemies
Are men of princely rank.

LODOVICO:        O I pray for them.     10
The violent thunder is adored by those
Are pash'd in pieces by it.

ANTONELLI:      Come my lord,
You are justly doom'd; look but a little back
Into your former life: you have in three years
Ruin'd the noblest earldom –

GASPARO:        Your followers     15
Have swallowed you like mummia, and being sick
With such unnatural and horrid physic
Vomit you up i'th' kennel –

---

5. *in small parcels:* in small portions.

7. *'quite:* requite.     12. *pash'd:* smashed.

16. *mummia:* a medicinal preparation made originally from Egyptian
mummies; but later from corpses generally.

18. *kennel:* channel, gutter.

39

ANTONELLI:  All the damnable degrees
Of drinkings have you stagger'd through; one citizen
20 Is lord of two fair manors, call'd you master
Only for caviare.

GASPARO:  Those noblemen
Which were invited to your prodigal feasts,
Wherein the phoenix scarce could scape your throats,
Laugh at your misery, as fore-deeming you
25 An idle meteor which drawn forth the earth
Would soon be lost i'th' air.

ANTONELLI:  Jest upon you,
And say you were begotten in an earthquake,
You have ruin'd such fair lordships. ·

LODOVICO:  Very good,
This well goes with two buckets, I must tend
The pouring out of either.

30 GASPARO:  Worse than these,
You have acted certain murders here in Rome,
Bloody and full of horror.

LODOVICO:  'Las they were flea-bitings:
Why took they not my head then?

GASPARO:  O my lord
The law doth sometimes mediate, thinks it good
35 Not ever to steep violent sins in blood;
This gentle penance may both end your crimes,
And in the example better these bad times.

LODOVICO: So; but I wonder then some great men 'scape
This banishment; there's Paulo Giordano Orsini,
40 The Duke of Brachiano, now lives in Rome,
And by close panderism seeks to prostitute
The honour of Vittoria Corombona:
Vittoria, she that might have got my pardon

24. *fore-deeming*: prejudging.
29. *tend*: attend.      41. *close*: secret, private.

40

For one kiss to the Duke.

ANTONELLI:              Have a full man within you.
We see that trees bear no such pleasant fruit                45
There where they grew first, as where they are new set.
Perfumes the more they are chaf'd the more they render
Their pleasing scents, and so affliction
Expresseth virtue, fully, whether true,
Or else adulterate.

LODOVICO:          Leave your painted comforts.        50
I'll make Italian cut-works in their guts
If ever I return.

GASPARO:        O sir.

LODOVICO:            I am patient.
I have seen some ready to be executed
Give pleasant looks, and money, and grown familiar
With the knave hangman; so do I, I thank them,        55
And would account them nobly merciful
Would they dispatch me quickly.

ANTONELLI:                    Fare you well,
We shall find time I doubt not, to repeal
Your banishment.

    [A sennet sounds.]

LODOVICO:        I am ever bound to you:
This is the world's alms; pray make use of it:        60
Great men sell sheep, thus to be cut in pieces,
When first they have shorn them bare and sold their
    fleeces.
    Exeunt.

44. *Have a full man within you:* 'Be complete in yourself.'
47. *render:* give out, emit.
49. *expresseth:* presses out.
50. *painted:* artificial, unreal.
59. S.D. *sennet:* a trumpet call.

## [SCENE TWO]

*Enter* BRACHIANO, CAMILLO, FLAMINEO, VITTORIA
COROMBONA [*and attendants*].

BRACHIANO: Your best of rest.

VITTORIA:                         Unto my lord the Duke.
The best of welcome. More lights, attend the Duke.
[*Exeunt* VITTORIA *and* CAMILLO.]

BRACHIANO: Flamineo.

FLAMINEO:             My lord.

BRACHIANO:                         Quite lost Flamineo.

FLAMINEO: Pursue your noble wishes, I am prompt
5      As lightning to your service, O my lord!
[*Whispers*] The fair Vittoria, my happy sister
Shall give you present audience. Gentlemen
Let the caroche go on, and 'tis his pleasure
You put out all your torches and depart.
[*Exeunt Attendants.*]

BRACHIANO: Are we so happy?

10   FLAMINEO:                         Can't be otherwise?
Observ'd you not tonight my honour'd lord,
Which way so e'er you went she threw her eyes?
I have dealt already with her chamber-maid
Zanche the Moor, and she is wondrous proud
15     To be the agent for so high a spirit.

BRACHIANO: We are happy above thought, because 'bove
merit.

FLAMINEO: 'Bove merit! We may now talk freely: 'bove
merit! What is't you doubt? Her coyness? That's but the
20     superficies of lust most women have; yet why should
ladies blush to hear that nam'd, which they do not fear to

7. *present:* immediate.    8. *caroche:* large coach.    10. *Can't:* can it?
20. *superficies:* exterior, outward appearance.

handle? O they are politic! They know our desire is in-
creas'd by the difficulty of enjoying; whereas satiety is a
blunt, weary and drowsy passion; if the buttery-hatch at
court stood continually open there would be nothing so    25
passionate crowding, nor hot suit after the beverage –
BRACHIANO: O but her jealous husband.
FLAMINEO: Hang him, a gilder that hath his brains perish'd
with quicksilver is not more cold in the liver. The great
barriers moulted not more feathers than he hath shed hairs,    30
by the confession of his doctor. An Irish gamester that will
play himself naked, and then wage all downward, at
hazard, is not more venturous. So unable to please a
woman that like a Dutch doublet all his back is shrunk
into his breeches.    35
Shroud you within this closet, good my lord;
Some trick now must be thought on to divide
My brother-in-law from his fair bed-fellow.
BRACHIANO: O should she fail to come –
FLAMINEO: I must not have your lordship thus unwisely    40
amorous: I myself have loved a lady and pursued her with
a great deal of under-age protestation, whom some three
or four gallants that have enjoyed would with all their
hearts have been glad to have been rid of. 'Tis just like a
summer bird-cage in a garden: the birds that are without,    45
despair to get in, and the birds that are within despair and
are in a consumption for fear they shall never get out.
Away, away my lord,

---

24. *buttery-hatch:* half-door over which provisions, especially drinks,
    are served from the buttery, where they are stored.
29. *the liver:* the supposed seat of the passions; *great barriers:* waist-high
    barriers preventing dangerous close fighting during tournaments.
30. *shed hairs:* through the treatment of venereal disease.
34. *Dutch doublet:* a Dutch doublet was close-fitting, its breeches wide;
    *back:* virility.

*Enter* CAMILLO.

See, here he comes.

   [*Exit* BRACHIANO.]

   [*Aside*]        This fellow by his apparel

50 Some men would judge a politician,
But call his wit in question you shall find it
Merely an ass in's foot-cloth. [*to* CAMILLO] How now,
   brother,
What, travelling to bed to your kind wife?

CAMILLO: I assure you brother, no. My voyage lies
55 More northerly, in a far colder clime;
I do not well remember, I protest,
When I last lay with her.

FLAMINEO:         Strange you should lose your count.

CAMILLO: We never lay together but ere morning
There grew a flaw between us.

FLAMINEO:         'T had been your part
To have made up that flaw.

60 CAMILLO:        True, but she loathes
I should be seen in't.

FLAMINEO:     Why sir, what's the matter?

CAMILLO: The Duke your master visits me. I thank him,
And I perceive how like an earnest bowler
He very passionately leans that way,
He should have his bowl run.

65 FLAMINEO:        I hope you do not think -

CAMILLO: That noblemen bowl booty? 'Faith his cheek
Hath a most excellent bias; it would fain
Jump with my mistress.

FLAMINEO:     Will you be an ass
Despite your Aristotle or a cuckold

50. *politician:* crafty person.
52. *foot-cloth:* an ornamental cloth which covered the horse's back and
   hung down to the ground. It was considered a sign of dignity.

Contrary to your ephemerides 70
Which shows you under what a smiling planet
'You were first swaddled?

CAMILLO: Pew wew, sir tell not me
Of planets nor of ephemerides.
A man may be made cuckold in the day-time
When the stars' eyes are out.

FLAMINEO: Sir God boy you, 75
I do commit you to your pitiful pillow
Stuff'd with horn-shavings.

CAMILLO: Brother?

FLAMINEO: God refuse me,
Might I advise you now your only course
Were to lock up your wife.

CAMILLO: 'Twere very good.

FLAMINEO: Bar her the sight of revels.

CAMILLO: Excellent. 80

FLAMINEO: Let her not go to church, but like a hound
In leon at your heels.

CAMILLO: 'Twere for her honour.

FLAMINEO: And so you should be certain in one fortnight,
Despite her chastity or innocence,
To be cuckolded, which yet is in suspense: 85
This is my counsel and I ask no fee for't.

CAMILLO: Come, you know not where my nightcap wrings
me.

FLAMINEO: Wear it o'th' old fashion, let your large ears

70. *ephemerides:* almanac or calendar containing daily astrological or
meteorological predictions.
75. *God boy you:* 'God be with you'.
77. *horn-shavings:* shavings from the horns supposed to grow on the
foreheads of cuckolds.
77. *God refuse me:* 'May God cast me off' (an oath).
81. *but:* except.    82. *leon:* leash.
87. *wrings:* pinches (because of the cuckold's horns on Camillo's
forehead).

45

90 come through, it will be more easy; nay, I will be bitter:
bar your wife of her entertainment: women are more
willingly and more gloriously chaste, when they are least
restrained of their liberty. It seems you would be a fine
capricious mathematically jealous coxcomb, take the
95 height of your own horns with a Jacob's staff afore they
are up. These politic enclosures for paltry mutton makes
more rebellion in the flesh than all the provocative electuaries doctors have uttered since last Jubilee.

CAMILLO: This does not physic me.

100 FLAMINEO: It seems you are jealous. I'll show you the error
of it by a familiar example: I have seen a pair of spectacles
fashion'd with such perspective art, that lay down but one
twelve pence o'th' board, 'twill appear as if there were
twenty; now should you wear a pair of these spectacles,
105 and see your wife tying her shoe, you would imagine
twenty hands were taking up of your wife's clothes, and
this would put you into a horrible causeless fury.

CAMILLO: The fault there sir is not in the eyesight.

FLAMINEO: True, but they that have the yellow jaundice,
110 think all objects they look on to be yellow. Jealousy is
worser, her fits present to a man, like so many bubbles in
a basin of water, twenty several crabbed faces; many times
makes his own shadow his cuckold-maker.

*Enter* [VITTORIA] COROMBONA.

See she comes; what reason have you to be jealous of this
115 creature? What an ignorant ass or flattering knave might

95. *Jacob's staff*: a measuring instrument.
96. *politic*: cunning. *mutton*: loose women (slang). There is also a reference
to the enclosure of land for sheepfarming by rich landowners.
97. *provocative electuaries*: aphrodisiacs.
98. *uttered*: put forth for sale.
101–102. Perspective spectacles were made from glass cut into facets so
that one image was made to seem many.
112. *several*: different.

46

he be counted, that should write sonnets to her eyes, or
call her brow the snow of Ida, or ivory of Corinth, or
compare her hair to the blackbird's bill, when 'tis liker the
blackbird's feather. This is all. Be wise; I will make you
friends and you shall go to bed together; marry look you,      120
it shall not be your seeking, do you stand upon that by any
means; walk you aloof, I would not have you seen in't.
Sister, (my lord attends you in the banqueting-house)
your husband is wondrous discontented.

VITTORIA: I did nothing to displease him, I carved to him      125
at supper-time.

FLAMINEO: (You need not have carved him in faith, they say
he is a capon already. I must now seemingly fall out with
you.) Shall a gentleman so well descended as Camillo (a
lousy slave that within this twenty years rode with the       130
black-guard in the Duke's carriage mongst spits and
dripping-pans.)

CAMILLO: Now he begins to tickle her.

FLAMINEO: An excellent scholar, (one that hath a head fill'd
with calves' brains without any sage in them) come            135
crouching in the hams to you for a night's lodging (that
hath an itch in's hams, which like the fire at the glass-house
hath not gone out this seven years). Is he not a courtly
gentleman? (When he wears white satin one would take
him by his black muzzle to be no other creature than a        140
maggot.) You are a goodly foil, I confess, well set out (but
cover'd with a false stone, yon counterfeit diamond).

CAMILLO: He will make her know what is in me.

125. *carved:* served at table; made advances to ('a sort of digitary ogle' –
    Lucas).
127. *carved:* castrated.
131. *black-guard:* kitchen menials. *carriage:* baggage train.
135. *calf:* young fool.
137. *hams:* thighs and buttocks; *glass-house:* glass factory. There was one
    near the Blackfriars theatre.
141. *foil:* setting for a jewel; *cover'd:* a double entendre.

FLAMINEO: Come, my lord attends you; thou shalt go to
145  bed to my lord.

CAMILLO: Now he comes to't.

FLAMINEO: With a relish as curious as a vintner going to
taste new wine. [To CAMILLO] I am opening your case
hard.

CAMILLO: A virtuous brother, o' my credit.

150  FLAMINEO: He will give thee a ring with a philosopher's
stone in it.

CAMILLO: Indeed I am studying alchemy.

FLAMINEO: Thou shalt lie in a bed stuff'd with turtles' feathers, swoon in perfumed linen like the fellow was
155  smothered in roses. So perfect shall be thy happiness, that
as men at sea think land and trees and ships go that way
they go, so both heaven and earth shall seem to go your
voyage. Shalt meet him, 'tis fix'd, with nails of diamonds
to inevitable necessity.

160  VITTORIA [aside to FLAMINEO]: How shall's rid him hence?

FLAMINEO: I will put breese in's tail, set him gadding
presently. [To CAMILLO] I have almost wrought her to it,
I find her coming, but might I advise you now for this
night I would not lie with her; I would cross her humour
165  to make her more humble.

CAMILLO: Shall I? Shall I?

FLAMINEO: It will show in you a supremacy of judgement.

CAMILLO: True, and a mind differing from the tumultuary
opinion, for *quae negata grata*.

147. Flamineo refers to Brachiano; but Camillo thinks Flamineo speaks
of him.
148. *case*: a triple pun: a legal case; a case of wine; double entendre.
153. *turtles'*: turtle doves, which were proverbial for devotion to their
mates.      160. *shall's*: shall us.
161. *breese*: gadflies. *presently*: immediately
168. *tumultuary*: hastily formed.
169. *quae negata grata*: 'what is denied is desired'.

48

FLAMINEO: Right: you are the adamant shall draw her to     170
you, though you keep distance off.

CAMILLO: A philosophical reason.

FLAMINEO: Walk by her o' the nobleman's fashion, and tell
her you will lie with her at the end of the progress.

CAMILLO: Vittoria, I cannot be induc'd or as a man would     175
say incited –

VITTORIA: To do what sir?

CAMILLO: To lie with you tonight; your silkworm useth to
fast every third day, and the next following spins the
better. Tomorrow at night I am for you.     180

VITTORIA: You'll spin a fair thread, trust to't.

FLAMINEO: But do you hear, I shall have you steal to her
chamber about midnight.

CAMILLO: Do you think so? Why look you brother, because you shall not think I'll gull you, take the key, lock     185
me into the chamber, and say you shall be sure of me.

FLAMINEO: In troth I will, I'll be your jailer once;
But have you ne'er a false door?

CAMILLO: A pox on't, as I am a Christian tell me tomorrow
how scurvily she takes my unkind parting.     190

FLAMINEO: I will.

CAMILLO: Didst thou not mark the jest of the silkworm?
Good night: in faith I will use this trick often.

FLAMINEO: Do, do, do.

   *Exit* CAMILLO.

So now you are safe. Ha ha ha, thou entanglest thyself in     195
thine own work like a silkworm.

---

170. *adamant:* loadstone, and (by faulty etymology) the hardest metal
or stone.
174. *progress:* state journey.
181. *You'll spin a fair thread:* a proverbial phrase, usually applied
ironically to a badly performed action.
190. *scurvily:* sourly.

*Enter* BRACHIANO.

Come sister, darkness hides your blush; women are like
curs'd dogs, civility keeps them tied all daytime, but they
are let loose at midnight; then they do most good or most
200    mischief. My lord, my lord.

BRACHIANO: Give credit: I could wish time would stand
    still
And never end this interview, this hour,
But all delight doth itself soon'st devour.
    ZANCHE *brings out a carpet, spreads it and lays on it two*
    *fair cushions. Enter* CORNELIA [*listening, behind*].
Let me into your bosom happy lady,
205    Pour out instead of eloquence my vows;
Loose me not madam, for if you forgo me
I am lost eternally.

VITTORIA:        Sir in the way of pity
I wish you heart-whole.

BRACHIANO:        You are a sweet physician.

VITTORIA: Sure sir a loathed cruelty in ladies
210    Is as to doctors many funerals.
It takes away their credit.

BRACHIANO:        Excellent creature.
We call the cruel fair, what name for you
That are so merciful?

ZANCHE:        See now they close.

FLAMINEO: Most happy union.

215    CORNELIA [*aside*]: My fears are fall'n upon me, O my heart!
My son the pander: now I find our house
Sinking to ruin. Earthquakes leave behind,
Where they have tyrannized, iron or lead, or stone,
But, woe to ruin! violent lust leaves none.

BRACHIANO: What value is this jewel?

198. *curs'd*: vicious.
220–27. *jewel*: used here with an extended double entendre.

VITTORIA:               'Tis the ornament    220
Of a weak fortune.

BRACHIANO: In sooth I'll have it; nay I will but change
My jewel for your jewel.

FLAMINEO:           Excellent,
His jewel for her jewel; well put in Duke.

BRACHIANO: Nay let me see you wear it.

VITTORIA:               Here sir.    225

BRACHIANO: Nay lower, you shall wear my jewel lower.

FLAMINEO: That's better; she must wear his jewel lower.

VITTORIA: To pass away the time I'll tell your Grace
A dream I had last night.

BRACHIANO:        Most wishedly.

VITTORIA: A foolish idle dream:    230
Methought I walk'd about the mid of night,
Into a church-yard, where a goodly yew-tree
Spread her large root in ground; under that yew,
As I sat sadly leaning on a grave,
Checkered with cross-sticks, there came stealing in    235
Your Duchess and my husband; one of them
A pick-axe bore, th'other a rusty spade,
And in rough terms they 'gan to challenge me,
About this yew.

BRACHIANO:      That tree.

VITTORIA:           This harmless yew.
They told me my intent was to root up    240
That well-grown yew, and plant i'th' stead of it
A withered blackthorn, and for that they vow'd
To bury me alive: my husband straight
With pick-axe 'gan to dig, and your fell Duchess
With shovel, like a fury, voided out    245

238. *'gan:* began.     241. *stead of:* in the place of.
243. *straight:* immediately.     244. *fell:* cruel.
245. *voided out:* emptied out.

The earth and scattered bones. Lord how methought
I trembled, and yet for all this terror
I could not pray.

FLAMINEO:    No the devil was in your dream.

VITTORIA: When to my rescue there arose methought
250 A whirlwind, which let fall a massy arm
From that strong plant,
And both were struck dead by that sacred yew
In that base shallow grave that was their due.

FLAMINEO: Excellent devil.
255 She hath taught him in a dream
To make away his Duchess and her husband.

BRACHIANO: Sweetly shall I interpret this your dream:
You are lodged within his arms who shall protect you,
From all the fevers of a jealous husband,
260 From the poor envy of our phlegmatic Duchess.
I'll seat you above law and above scandal,
Give to your thoughts the invention of delight
And the fruition; nor shall government
Divide me from you longer than a care
265 To keep you great: you shall to me at once
Be dukedom, health, wife, children, friends and all.

CORNELIA [advancing]: Woe to light hearts, they still forerun our fall.

FLAMINEO: What fury rais'd thee up? Away, away!
Exit ZANCHE.

CORNELIA: What make you here my lord this dead of
night?
270 Never dropp'd mildew on a flower here,
Till now.

FLAMINEO: I pray will you go to bed then,
Lest you be blasted?

260. *phlegmatic:* of a cold, dull temperament.
272. *blasted:* blighted; cursed.

52

CORNELIA:  O that this fair garden,
Had with all poison'd herbs of Thessaly,
At first been planted, made a nursery
For witchcraft; rather than a burial plot  275
For both your honours.
VITTORIA:  Dearest mother hear me.
CORNELIA: O thou dost make my brow bend to the earth,
Sooner than nature; see the curse of children!
In life they keep us frequently in tears,
And in the cold grave leave us in pale fears.  280
BRACHIANO: Come, come, I will not hear you.
VITTORIA:  Dear my lord.
CORNELIA: Where is thy Duchess now adulterous Duke?
Thou little dream'd'st this night she is come to Rome.
FLAMINEO: How? Come to Rome –
VITTORIA:  The Duchess –
BRACHIANO:  She had been better –
CORNELIA: The lives of princes should like dials move,  285
Whose regular example is so strong,
They make the times by them go right or wrong.
FLAMINEO: So, have you done?
CORNELIA:  Unfortunate Camillo.
VITTORIA [*kneeling*]: I do protest if any chaste denial,
If anything but blood could have allayed  290
His long suit to me –
CORNELIA [*kneeling*]:  I will join with thee,
To the most woeful end e'er mother kneel'd,
If thou dishonour thus thy husband's bed,
Be thy life short as are the funeral tears
In great men's.
BRACHIANO:  Fie, fie, the woman's mad.  295

273. *herbs of Thessaly:* Thessaly, in Northern Greece, was renowned
    for poisonous herbs.  279. *frequently:* incessantly.
285. *dials:* sundials.  290. *blood:* life-blood; bloodshed; sexual desire.
295. *In great men's:* In great men's lives.

CORNELIA: Be thy act Judas-like, betray in kissing;
 May'st thou be envied during his short breath,
 And pitied like a wretch after his death.
VITTORIA: O me accurs'd.
 *Exit* VITTORIA.
300 FLAMINEO: Are you out of your wits, my lord?
 I'll fetch her back again.
BRACHIANO:    No I'll to bed.
 Send Doctor Julio to me presently.
 Uncharitable woman, thy rash tongue
 Hath rais'd a fearful and prodigious storm,
305 Be thou the cause of all ensuing harm.
 *Exit* BRACHIANO.
FLAMINEO: Now, you that stand so much upon your
  honour,
 Is this a fitting time o' night think you,
 To send a duke home without e'er a man?
 I would fain know where lies the mass of wealth
310 Which you have hoarded for my maintenance,
 That I may bear my beard out of the level
 Of my lord's stirrup.
CORNELIA:    What? Because we are poor
 Shall we be vicious?
FLAMINEO:   Pray what means have you
 To keep me from the galleys, or the gallows?
315 My father prov'd himself a gentleman,
 Sold all's land, and like a fortunate fellow,
 Died ere the money was spent. You brought me up,
 At Padua I confess, where, I protest,
 For want of means, (the university judge me,)
320 I have been fain to heel my tutor's stockings
 At least seven years. Conspiring with a beard
 Made me a graduate, then to this Duke's service;

302. *presently:* immediately. 304. *prodigious:* ominous. 316. *all's:* all his.

I visited the court, whence I return'd
More courteous, more lecherous by far,
But not a suit the richer. And shall I,                          325
Having a path so open and so free
To my preferment, still retain your milk
In my pale forehead? No, this face of mine
I'll arm and fortify with lusty wine
'Gainst shame and blushing.                                      330
CORNELIA: O that I ne'er had borne thee!
FLAMINEO:                                          So would I.
I would the common'st courtezan in Rome
Had been my mother rather than thyself.
Nature is very pitiful to whores
To give them but few children, yet those children               335
Plurality of fathers; they are sure
They shall not want. Go, go,
Complain unto my great lord cardinal,
Yet may be he will justify the act.
Lycurgus wond'red much men would provide                        340
Good stallions for their mares, and yet would suffer
Their fair wives to be barren –
CORNELIA:                            Misery of miseries.
    *Exit* CORNELIA.
FLAMINEO: The Duchess come to court? I like not that;
We are engag'd to mischief and must on.
As rivers to find out the ocean                                 345
Flow with crook bendings beneath forced banks,
Or as we see, to aspire some mountain's top
The way ascends not straight, but imitates
The subtle foldings of a winter's snake,
So who knows policy and her true aspect,                        350
Shall find her ways winding and indirect.
    *Exit.*

346. *crook:* crooked; *forced:* artificial.     347. *aspire:* reach.

# [ACT TWO]

## [SCENE ONE]

*Enter* FRANCISCO DE MEDICI, *Cardinal* MONTICELSO,
MARCELLO, ISABELLA, *young* GIOVANNI, *with little*
JAQUES *the Moor.*

FRANCISCO: Have you not seen your husband since you
    arrived?

ISABELLA: Not yet sir.

FRANCISCO:          Surely he is wondrous kind.
    If I had such a dove house as Camillo's
    I would set fire on't, were't but to destroy
5    The pole-cats that haunt to't, – my sweet cousin!

GIOVANNI: Lord uncle you did promise me a horse
    And armour.

FRANCISCO: That I did my pretty cousin.
    Marcello see it fitted.

MARCELLO:         My lord, the Duke is here.

FRANCISCO: Sister away, you must not yet be seen.

10  ISABELLA: I do beseech you
    Entreat him mildly, let not your rough tongue
    Set us at louder variance; all my wrongs
    Are freely pardoned, and I do not doubt
    As men to try the precious unicorn's horn
15    Make of the powder a preservative circle
    And in it put a spider, so these arms
    Shall charm his poison, force it to obeying
    And keep him chaste from an infected straying.

---

5. *pole-cats:* fetid-smelling animals related to the stoats and ferrets;
also prostitutes (slang); *haunt to't:* resort to it; *cousin:* generally
kinsfolk, but often applied to nephew or niece.

FRANCISCO: I wish it may. Be gone.
    *Exit* [ISABELLA].
    *Enter* BRACHIANO *and* FLAMINEO.
                             Void the chamber.
    [*Exeunt* FLAMINEO, MARCELLO, GIOVANNI *and*
    JAQUES.]
  You are welcome, will you sit? I pray my lord       20
  Be you my orator, my heart's too full;
  I'll second you anon.
MONTICELSO:         Ere I begin
  Let me entreat your grace forgo all passion
  Which may be raised by my free discourse.
BRACHIANO: As silent as i'th' church – you may proceed.   25
MONTICELSO: It is a wonder to your noble friends,
  That you that have as 'twere ent'red the world,
  With a free sceptre in your able hand,
  And have to th'use of nature well applied
  High gifts of learning, should in your prime age     30
  Neglect your awful throne, for the soft down
  Of an insatiate bed. O my lord,
  The drunkard after all his lavish cups,
  Is dry, and then is sober; so at length,
  When you awake from this lascivious dream,      35
  Repentance then will follow; like the sting
  Plac'd in the adder's tail: wretched are princes
  When fortune blasteth but a petty flower
  Of their unwieldy crowns; or ravisheth
  But one pearl from their sceptre: but alas!      40
  When they to wilful shipwreck loose good fame
  All princely titles perish with their name.

19. *Void:* empty.
31. *awful:* commanding awe.
36–7. *the sting . . . adder's tail:* the adder was popularly believed capable
    of stinging with its tail as well as its mouth.
42. *name:* reputation.

BRACHIANO: You have said my lord –

MONTICELSO:             Enough to give you taste
How far I am from flattering your greatness?

45   BRACHIANO: Now you that are his second, what say you?
Do not like young hawks fetch a course about;
Your game flies fair and for you –

FRANCISCO:             Do not fear it:
I'll answer you in your own hawking phrase.
Some eagles that should gaze upon the sun

50   Seldom soar high, but take their lustful ease
Since they from dunghill birds their prey can seize.
You know Vittoria?

BRACHIANO:         Yes.

FRANCISCO:           You shift your shirt there
When you retire from tennis.

BRACHIANO:          Happily.

FRANCISCO: Her husband is lord of a poor fortune
Yet she wears cloth of tissue –

55   BRACHIANO:           What of this?
Will you urge that my good lord cardinal
As part of her confession at next shrift,
And know from whence it sails?

FRANCISCO:          She is your strumpet –

BRACHIANO: Uncivil sir there's hemlock in thy breath

60   And that black slander; were she a whore of mine
All thy loud cannons, and thy borrowed Switzers
Thy galleys, nor thy sworn confederates
Durst not supplant her.

FRANCISCO:         Let's not talk on thunder.
Thou hast a wife, our sister; would I had given

65   Both her white hands to death, bound and lock'd fast

46. *fetch a course about:* turn tail, refuse to fly to the mark.
52. *shift:* change.     53. *Happily:* haply, perhaps.
57. *shrift:* confession.     61. *Switzers:* Swiss mercenaries.

In her last winding-sheet, when I gave thee
But one.
BRACHIANO: Thou hadst given a soul to God then.
FRANCISCO:                                        True:
Thy ghostly father with all's absolution,
Shall ne'er do so by thee.
BRACHIANO:              Spit thy poison –
FRANCISCO: I shall not need, lust carries her sharp whip     70
At her own girdle; look to't for our anger
Is making thunder-bolts.
BRACHIANO:              Thunder? in faith,
They are but crackers.
FRANCISCO:              We'll end this with the cannon.
BRACHIANO: Thou'lt get nought by it but iron in thy
    wounds,
And gunpowder in thy nostrils.
FRANCISCO:                        Better that              75
Than change perfumes for plasters –
BRACHIANO:                          Pity on thee,
'Twere good you'ld show your slaves or men condemn'd
Your new-plough'd forehead. Defiance – and I'll meet
    thee,
Even in a thicket of thy ablest men.
MONTICELSO: My lords, you shall not word it any further    80
Without a milder limit.
FRANCISCO:              Willingly.
BRACHIANO: Have you proclaimed a triumph that you bait
A lion thus?
MONTICELSO: My lord!
BRACHIANO:              I am tame, I am tame sir.
FRANCISCO: We send unto the Duke for conference

68. *ghostly:* spiritual.
76. *change perfumes for plasters:* change sexual indulgence for its results:
    disease.

85 'Bout levies 'gainst the pirates; my lord Duke
Is not at home; we come ourself in person,
Still my lord Duke is busied; but we fear
When Tiber to each prowling passenger
Discovers flocks of wild ducks, then my lord
90 ('Bout moulting time I mean,) we shall be certain
To find you sure enough and speak with you.

BRACHIANO:                                        Ha?

FRANCISCO: A mere tale of a tub, my words are idle,
But to express the sonnet by natural reason,
When stags grow melancholic you'll find the season.
*Enter* GIOVANNI.

95 MONTICELSO: No more my lord; here comes a champion,
Shall end the difference between you both,
Your son the prince Giovanni. See my lords
What hopes you store in him; this is a casket
For both your crowns, and should be held like dear:
100 Now is he apt for knowledge; therefore know
It is a more direct and even way
To train to virtue those of princely blood
By examples than by precepts: if by examples
Whom should he rather strive to imitate
105 Than his own father? Be his pattern then,
Leave him a stock of virtue that may last,
Should fortune rend his sails, and split his mast.

BRACHIANO: Your hand boy – growing to a soldier?

GIOVANNI: Give me a pike.

89. *wild ducks:* prostitutes (Lucas).
90. *moulting time:* when the mating season is over; when hair is falling
through venereal disease.
92. *tale of a tub:* cock-and-bull story; with an allusion to the use of the
sweating-tub in the treatment of venereal disease.
93. *express . . . natural reason:* put it simply.
95. *champion:* i.e. Giovanni, in his new suit of armour.
101. *even:* straightforward.          106. *stock:* line of ancestors; store.

FRANCISCO: What, practising your pike so young, fair coz?　110
GIOVANNI: Suppose me one of Homer's frogs, my lord,
　　Tossing my bullrush thus. Pray sir tell me
　　Might not a child of good discretion
　　Be leader to an army?
FRANCISCO:　　　　　　Yes cousin, a young prince
　　Of good discretion might.
GIOVANNI:　　　　　　Say you so?　115
　　Indeed I have heard 'tis fit a general
　　Should not endanger his own person oft,
　　So that he make a noise, when he's a horseback
　　Like a Dansk drummer. O 'tis excellent!
　　He need not fight; methinks his horse as well　120
　　Might lead an army for him; if I live
　　I'll charge the French foe, in the very front
　　Of all my troops, the foremost man.
FRANCISCO:　　　　　　　　What, what!
GIOVANNI: And will not bid my soldiers up and follow
　　But bid them follow me.
BRACHIANO:　　　　　　Forward lapwing.　125
　　He flies with the shell on's head.
FRANCISCO:　　　　　　Pretty cousin.
GIOVANNI: The first year uncle that I go to war,
　　All prisoners that I take I will set free
　　Without their ransom.
FRANCISCO:　　　　Ha, without their ransom?
　　How then will you reward your soldiers　130
　　That took those prisoners for you?
GIOVANNI:　　　　　　　Thus my lord:
　　I'll marry them to all the wealthy widows
　　That falls that year.

110. *practising your pike:* a double entendre.
113. *discretion:* good judgement.　115. *discretion:* prudence.
119. *Dansk:* Danish.　　125. *lapwing:* a symbol of precocity.

FRANCISCO:       Why then the next year following
You'll have no men to go with you to war.

135 GIOVANNI: Why then I'll press the women to the war,
And then the men will follow.

MONTICELSO:           Witty prince.

FRANCISCO: See a good habit makes a child a man,
Whereas a bad one makes a man a beast:
Come, you and I are friends.

BRACHIANO:         Most wishedly;

140 Like bones which broke in sunder and well set
Knit the more strongly.

FRANCISCO: [*calls*]     Call Camillo hither.
You have received the rumour, how Count Lodowick
Is turn'd a pirate?

BRACHIANO:     Yes.

FRANCISCO:         We are now preparing
Some ships to fetch him in.
    [*Enter* ISABELLA.]
                Behold your Duchess;

145 We now will leave you and expect from you
Nothing but kind entreaty.

BRACHIANO:         You have charm'd me.
   *Exeunt* FR[ANCISCO], MON[TICELSO], GIOV[ANNI].
You are in health we see.

ISABELLA:         And above health
To see my lord well.

BRACHIANO:      So! I wonder much,
What amorous whirlwind hurried you to Rome.

ISABELLA: Devotion my lord.

150 BRACHIANO:        Devotion?
Is your soul charg'd with any grievous sin?

ISABELLA: 'Tis burdened with too many, and I think
The oft'ner that we cast our reck'nings up,
Our sleeps will be the sounder.

BRACHIANO:                              Take your chamber.

ISABELLA: Nay my dear lord, I will not have you angry;     155
  Doth not my absence from you two months
  Merit one kiss?

BRACHIANO:        I do not use to kiss.
  If that will dispossess your jealousy,
  I'll swear it to you.

ISABELLA:                    O my loved lord,
  I do not come to chide; my jealousy?                      160
  I am to learn what that Italian means;
  You are as welcome to these longing arms,
  As I to you a virgin.

BRACHIANO:                    O your breath!
  Out upon sweetmeats, and continued physic!
  The plague is in them.

ISABELLA:                        You have oft for these two lips   165
  Neglected cassia or the natural sweets
  Of the spring violet; they are not yet much withered.
  My lord I should be merry; these your frowns
  Show in a helmet lovely, but on me,
  In such a peaceful interview methinks                     170
  They are too too roughly knit.

BRACHIANO:                          O dissemblance!
  Do you bandy factions 'gainst me? Have you learnt
  The trick of impudent baseness to complain
  Unto your kindred?

ISABELLA:              Never my dear lord.

BRACHIANO: Must I be haunted out, or was't your trick      175

---

157. *I do not use to:* I am not in the habit of.
161. *I am to learn:* i.e. I am yet to learn; *Italian:* Italians were proverbially
  jealous.
166. *cassia:* a kind of cinnamon; also used more loosely to refer to any
  fragrant or expensive perfume.
172. *bandy factions:* form leagues (Lucas).

To meet some amorous gallant here in Rome
That must supply our discontinuance?
ISABELLA: I pray sir burst my heart, and in my death
Turn to your ancient pity, though not love.
180 BRACHIANO: Because your brother is the corpulent Duke,
That is the great Duke, 'sdeath I shall not shortly
Racket away five hundred crowns at tennis,
But it shall rest upon record. I scorn him
Like a shav'd Polack; all his reverent wit
185 Lies in his wardrobe; he's a discreet fellow
When he's made up in his robes of state –
Your brother the great Duke, because h'as galleys,
And now and then ransacks a Turkish fly-boat,
(Now all the hellish Furies take his soul,)
190 First made this match, – accursed be the priest
That sang the wedding mass, and even my issue.
ISABELLA: O too too far you have curs'd!
BRACHIANO:                   Your hand I'll kiss:
This is the latest ceremony of my love,
Henceforth I'll never lie with thee, by this,
195 This wedding ring: I'll ne'er more lie with thee.
And this divorce shall be as truly kept,
As if the judge had doom'd it: fare you well,
Our sleeps are sever'd.
ISABELLA:             Forbid it the sweet union
Of all things blessed; why the saints in heaven
Will knit their brows at that.

---

177. *supply our discontinuance:* make up for our discontinuance of sexual
    intercourse.
179. *ancient:* former.
181. *great Duke:* a pun; Francisco was Grand Duke of Tuscany; *'sdeath:*
    [By] God's death!
187. *h'as:* he has.
188. *fly-boat:* a pinnace or small fast boat.
193. *latest:* last.

BRACHIANO:                    Let not thy love                    200
  Make thee an unbeliever; this my vow
  Shall never on my soul be satisfied
  With my repentance: let thy brother rage
  Beyond a horrid tempest or sea-fight,
  My vow is fixed.

ISABELLA:                    O my winding sheet,                    205
  Now shall I need thee shortly. Dear my lord,
  Let me hear once more what I would not hear:
  Never?

BRACHIANO: Never!

ISABELLA: O my unkind lord may your sins find mercy,
  As I upon a woeful widowed bed                    210
  Shall pray for you, if not to turn your eyes
  Upon your wretched wife, and hopeful son,
  Yet that in time you'll fix them upon heaven.

BRACHIANO: No more; go, go, complain to the great Duke.

ISABELLA: No my dear lord, you shall have present witness    215
  How I'll work peace between you; I will make
  Myself the author of your cursed vow.
  I have some cause to do it, you have none;
  Conceal it I beseech you, for the weal
  Of both your dukedoms, that you wrought the means    220
  Of such a separation; let the fault
  Remain with my supposed jealousy,
  And think with what a piteous and rent heart
  I shall perform this sad ensuing part.

    *Enter* FRANCISCO, FLAMINEO, MONTICELSO, MAR-
    CELLO.

BRACHIANO: Well, take your course. My honourable
  brother!                                                      225

FRANCISCO: Sister! – this is not well my lord – why sister!
  She merits not this welcome.

215. *present*: immediate.

BRACHIANO: Welcome, say?
She hath given a sharp welcome.

FRANCISCO: Are you foolish?
Come dry your tears; is this a modest course?
230 To better what is nought, to rail, and weep?
Grow to a reconcilement, or by heaven,
I'll ne'er more deal between you.

ISABELLA: Sir you shall not,
No though Vittoria upon that condition
Would become honest.

FRANCISCO: Was your husband loud,
Since we departed?

235 ISABELLA: By my life sir no.
I swear by that I do not care to lose.
Are all these ruins of my former beauty
Laid out for a whore's triumph?

FRANCISCO: Do you hear?
Look upon other women, with what patience
240 They suffer these slight wrongs, with what justice
They study to requite them; take that course.

ISABELLA: O that I were a man, or that I had power
To execute my apprehended wishes,
I would whip some with scorpions.

FRANCISCO: What? turn'd fury?

245 ISABELLA: To dig the strumpet's eyes out, let her lie
Some twenty months a-dying, to cut off
Her nose and lips, pull out her rotten teeth,
Preserve her flesh like mummia, for trophies
Of my just anger. Hell to my affliction
250 Is mere snow-water: by your favour sir –
Brother draw near, and my lord cardinal –
Sir let me borrow of you but one kiss,

227. *say?*: say you?     234. *honest*: virtuous.
243. *my apprehended wishes*: the desires I feel.

Henceforth I'll never lie with you, by this,
This wedding-ring.

FRANCISCO:         How? ne'er more lie with him?

ISABELLA: And this divorce shall be as truly kept,     255
As if in thronged court, a thousand ears
Had heard it, and a thousand lawyers' hands
Seal'd to the separation.

BRACHIANO: Ne'er lie with me?

ISABELLA:               Let not my former dotage
Make thee an unbeliever; this my vow     260
Shall never on my soul be satisfied
With my repentance: *manet alta mente repostum.*

FRANCISCO: Now by my birth you are a foolish, mad,
And jealous woman.

BRACHIANO:         You see 'tis not my seeking.

FRANCISCO: Was this your circle of pure unicorn's horn,     265
You said should charm your lord? Now horns upon thee,
For jealousy deserves them; keep your vow,
And take your chamber.

ISABELLA: No sir I'll presently to Padua,
I will not stay a minute.

MONTICELSO:         O good madam.     270

BRACHIANO: 'Twere best to let her have her humour,
Some half-day's journey will bring down her stomach,
And then she'll turn in post.

FRANCISCO:             To see her come
To my lord cardinal for a dispensation
Of her rash vow will beget excellent laughter.     275

ISABELLA: *Unkindness do thy office, poor heart break,*
*Those are the killing griefs which dare not speak.*
    *Exit.*

---

272. *bring down her stomach:* reduce the swelling caused by hysterical
    passion (the mother).
273. *turn in post:* return post-haste.

*Enter* CAMILLO.

MARCELLO: Camillo's come my lord.

FRANCISCO: Where's the commission?

280 MARCELLO: 'Tis here.

FRANCISCO: Give me the signet.

FLAMINEO [*to* BRACHIANO]: My lord do you mark their whispering; I will compound a medicine out of their two heads, stronger than garlic, deadlier than stibium; the

285 cantharides which are scarce seen to stick upon the flesh when they work to the heart, shall not do it with more silence or invisible cunning.

*Enter Doctor* [JULIO].

BRACHIANO: About the murder.

FLAMINEO: They are sending him to Naples, but I'll send

290 him to Candy; here's another property too.

BRACHIANO: O the doctor –

FLAMINEO: A poor quack-salving knave, my lord, one that should have been lash'd for's lechery, but that he confess'd a judgement, had an execution laid upon him, and

295 so put the whip to a *non plus*.

DOCTOR: And was cozen'd, my lord, by an arranter knave than myself, and made pay all the colourable execution.

FLAMINEO: He will shoot pills into a man's guts, shall make them have more ventages than a cornet or a lamprey; he

300 will poison a kiss, and was once minded, for his masterpiece, because Ireland breeds no poison, to have prepared a deadly vapour in a Spaniard's fart that should have poison'd all Dublin.

282. *do you mark:* pay attention to.
284. *stibium:* antimony, used as a poison; *cantharides:* Cantharis vesicatoria or Spanish fly, a powerful irritant poison.
290. *property:* tool.
292. *quack-salving knave:* rogue acting as a quack doctor.
296. *cozen'd:* cheated.
297. *colourable:* plausible.

BRACHIANO: O Saint Anthony's fire!

DOCTOR: Your secretary is merry my lord.                                305

FLAMINEO: O thou cursed antipathy to nature! Look his
eye's bloodshed like a needle a chirurgeon stitcheth a
wound with. Let me embrace thee toad, and love thee, O
thou abhominable loathsome gargarism, that will fetch up
lungs, lights, heart, and liver by scruples.                          310

BRACHIANO: No more; I must employ thee honest doctor,
You must to Padua and by the way,
Use some of your skill for us.

DOCTOR:                                   Sir I shall.

BRACHIANO: But for Camillo?

FLAMINEO: He dies this night by such a politic strain,               315
Men shall suppose him by's own engine slain.
But for your Duchess' death?

DOCTOR:                                   I'll make her sure.

BRACHIANO: Small mischiefs are by greater made secure.

FLAMINEO: Remember this you slave; when knaves come
to preferment they rise as gallowses are raised i'th' Low            320
Countries: one upon another's shoulders.

*Exeunt* [BRACHIANO, FLAMINEO *and Doctor* JULIO.]

MONTICELSO: Here is an emblem nephew, pray peruse it.
'Twas thrown in at your window –

CAMILLO:                                   At my window?
Here is a stag my lord hath shed his horns,
And for the loss of them the poor beast weeps.                       325
The word *Inopem me copia fecit.*

---

304. *O Saint Anthony's fire!*: erysipelas; but here, perhaps, slang for
   breaking wind.
307. *bloodshed*: bloodshot. *chirurgeon*: surgeon.
309. *gargarism*: gargle.
310. *by scruples*: in small quantities.
315. *politic strain*: cunning method; spraining of a muscle.
316. *engine*: contrivance.                320. *gallowses*: gallows-birds.
322. *emblem*: emblematic picture.

MONTICELSO:                    That is:
Plenty of horns hath made him poor of horns.
CAMILLO: What should this mean?
MONTICELSO:                    I'll tell you: 'tis given out
You are a cuckold.
CAMILLO:          Is it given out so?
330    I had rather such report as that my lord,
Should keep within doors.
FRANCISCO:                    Have you any children?
CAMILLO: None my lord.
FRANCISCO:                    You are the happier:
I'll tell you a tale.
CAMILLO:          Pray my lord.
FRANCISCO:                    An old tale.
Upon a time Phoebus the god of light,
335    Or him we call the sun, would need be married.
The gods gave their consent, and Mercury
Was sent to voice it to the general world.
But what a piteous cry there straight arose
Amongst smiths, and feltmakers, brewers and cooks,
340    Reapers and butter-women, amongst fishmongers
And thousand other trades, which are annoyed
By his excessive heat; 'twas lamentable.
They came to Jupiter all in a sweat
And do forbid the bans; a great fat cook
345    Was made their speaker, who entreats of Jove
That Phoebus might be gelded, for if now
When there was but one sun, so many men
Were like to perish by his violent heat,
What should they do if he were married
350    And should beget more, and those children
Make fireworks like their father? So say I,

337. *the general world*: the whole world.
351. *fireworks*: sparks of fire; children of fire.

Only I will apply it to your wife:
Her issue, should not providence prevent it,
Would make both nature, time, and man repent it.

MONTICELSO: Look you cousin,                                          355
Go change the air for shame; see if your absence
Will blast your cornucopia; Marcello
Is chosen with you joint commissioner
For the relieving our Italian coast
From pirates.

MARCELLO:        I am much honour'd in't.

CAMILLO:                              But sir               360
Ere I return the stag's horns may be sprouted,
Greater than these are shed.

MONTICELSO:            Do not fear it,
I'll be your ranger.

CAMILLO:        You must watch i'th' nights,
Then's the most danger.

FRANCISCO:            Farewell good Marcello.
All the best fortunes of a soldier's wish                    365
Bring you o' ship-board.

CAMILLO: Were I not best now I am turn'd soldier,
Ere that I leave my wife, sell all she hath
And then take leave of her.

MONTICELSO:            I expect good from you,
Your parting is so merry.                                   370

CAMILLO: Merry my lord, o'th' captain's humour right;
I am resolved to be drunk this night.

*Exit* [CAMILLO; *with* MARCELLO].

FRANCISCO: So, 'twas well fitted: now shall we discern
How his wish'd absence will give violent way
To Duke Brachiano's lust, –

356. *Go change the air:* leave this place.
357. *blast:* destroy; *cornucopia:* 'horn of plenty', ironically the cuckold's
  horn.
363. *ranger:* game-keeper; libertine.          371. *right:* exactly.

71

375 MONTICELSO:                  Why that was it;
     To what scorn'd purpose else should we make choice
     Of him for a sea-captain, and besides,
     Count Lodowick which was rumour'd for a pirate,
     Is now in Padua.
     FRANCISCO:      Is't true?
     MONTICELSO:        Most certain.
380      I have letters from him, which are suppliant
     To work his quick repeal from banishment;
     He means to address himself for pension
     Unto our sister Duchess.
     FRANCISCO:            O 'twas well.
     We shall not want his absence past six days;
385      I fain would have the Duke Brachiano run
     Into notorious scandal, for there's nought
     In such curs'd dotage, to repair his name,
     Only the deep sense of some deathless shame.
     MONTICELSO: It may be objected I am dishonourable,
390      To play thus with my kinsman, but I answer,
     For my revenge I'd stake a brother's life,
     That being wrong'd durst not avenge himself.
     FRANCISCO: Come to observe this strumpet.
     MONTICELSO:                 Curse of greatness,
     Sure he'll not leave her.
     FRANCISCO:          There's small pity in't.
395      Like mistletoe on sere elms spent by weather,
     Let him cleave to her and both rot together.
     *Exeunt.*

---

383. *our sister Duchess:* 'sister' here is a courtesy title given to the
speaker's peer.

## [SCENE TWO]

*Enter* BRACHIANO *with one in the habit of a Conjuror.*

BRACHIANO: Now sir I claim your promise; 'tis dead midnight,
   The time prefix'd to show me by your art
   How the intended murder of Camillo,
   And our loathed Duchess grow to action.
CONJUROR: You have won me by your bounty to a deed    5
   I do not often practise. Some there are,
   Which by sophistic tricks, aspire that name
   Which I would gladly lose, of nigromancer;
   As some that use to juggle upon cards,
   Seeming to conjure, when indeed they cheat;    10
   Others that raise up their confederate spirits,
   'Bout windmills, and endanger their own necks,
   For making of a squib; and some there are
   Will keep a curtal to show juggling tricks
   And give out 'tis a spirit: besides these    15
   Such a whole ream of almanac-makers, figure-flingers,
   Fellows indeed that only live by stealth,
   Since they do merely lie about stol'n goods,
   They'd make men think the devil were fast and loose,
   With speaking fustian Latin. Pray sit down,    20
   Put on this night-cap sir, 'tis charm'd and now
   I'll show you by my strong-commanding art
   The circumstance that breaks your Duchess' heart.

### A DUMB SHOW

*Enter, suspiciously,* JULIO *and* CHRISTOPHERO; *they*

12. *windmills:* fanciful schemes or projects.
16. *ream:* a quibble, ream of paper, realm; *figure-flingers:* those who cast figures or horoscopes.
20. *fustian:* bombastic.

*draw a curtain where* BRACHIANO'*s picture is, they put on spectacles of glass which cover their eyes and noses, and then burn perfumes afore the picture, and wash the lips of the picture; that done, quenching the fire, and putting off their spectacles they depart laughing.*

*Enter* ISABELLA *in her nightgown as to bedward, with lights after her, Count* LODOVICO, GIOVANNI, GUID-ANTONIO *and others waiting on her; she kneels down as to prayers, then draws the curtain of the picture, does three reverences to it, and kisses it thrice, she faints and will not suffer them to come near it, dies; sorrow express'd in* GIOVANNI *and in Count* LODOVICO; *she's convey'd out solemnly.*

BRACHIANO: Excellent, then she's dead –

CONJUROR:                              She's poisoned,
25    By the fum'd picture: 'twas her custom nightly,
      Before she went to bed, to go and visit
      Your picture, and to feed her eyes and lips
      On the dead shadow; Doctor Julio
      Observing this, infects it with an oil
30    And other poison'd stuff, which presently
      Did suffocate her spirits.

BRACHIANO:                        Methought I saw
      Count Lodowick there.

CONJUROR:                      He was, and by my art
      I find he did most passionately dote
      Upon your Duchess. Now turn another way,
35    And view Camillo's far more politic fate:
      Strike louder music from this charmed ground,
      To yield, as fits the act, a tragic sound.

### THE SECOND DUMB SHOW

*Enter* FLAMINEO, MARCELLO, CAMILLO *with four more as Captains, they drink healths and dance; a vaulting-horse is brought into the room,* MARCELLO *and two more whisper'd*

*out of the room, while* FLAMINEO *and* CAMILLO *strip*
*themselves into their shirts, as to vault; compliment who*
*shall begin, as* CAMILLO *is about to vault,* FLAMINEO
*pitcheth him upon his neck, and with the help of the rest,*
*writhes his neck about, seems to see if it be broke, and lays*
*him folded double as 'twere under the horse, makes shows to*
*call for help,* MARCELLO *comes in, laments, sends for the*
*Cardinal and Duke, who comes forth with armed men,*
*wonder at the act; commands the body to be carried home,*
*apprehends* FLAMINEO, MARCELLO, *and the rest, and go*
*as 'twere to apprehend* VITTORIA.

BRACHIANO: 'Twas quaintly done, but yet each circum-
    stance
I taste not fully.

CONJUROR:      O 'twas most apparent,
You saw them enter charged with their deep healths      40
To their boon voyage, and to second that,
Flamineo calls to have a vaulting-horse
Maintain their sport. The virtuous Marcello
Is innocently plotted forth the room,
Whilst your eye saw the rest, and can inform you      45
The engine of all.

BRACHIANO: It seems Marcello and Flamineo
Are both committed.

CONJUROR:        Yes, you saw them guarded,
And now they are come with purpose to apprehend
Your mistress, fair Vittoria; we are now      50
Beneath her roof: 'twere fit we instantly
Make out by some back postern.

BRACHIANO:        Noble friend,
You bind me ever to you; this shall stand

38. *quaintly:* ingeniously.
40. *charged:* filled (with 'deep healths' of wine).
41. *boon voyage:* 'bon voyage'.

As the firm seal annexed to my hand.
It shall enforce a payment.
55 CONJUROR:                    Sir I thank you.
   *Exit* BRACHIANO.
Both flowers and weeds spring when the sun is warm,
As great men do great good, or else great harm.
   *Exit* CONJUROR.

54. *annexed to my hand*: attached to my signature.

# [ACT THREE]

## [SCENE ONE]

*Enter* FRANCISCO, *and* MONTICELSO, *their* CHANCEL-
LOR *and* REGISTER.

FRANCISCO: You have dealt discreetly to obtain the
    presence
Of all the grave lieger ambassadors
To hear Vittoria's trial.

MONTICELSO:         'Twas not ill,
For sir you know we have nought but circumstances
To charge her with, about her husband's death;       5
Their approbation therefore to the proofs
Of her black lust, shall make her infamous
To all our neighbouring kingdoms. I wonder
If Brachiano will be here.

FRANCISCO:         O fie,
'Twere impudence too palpable.            10
    [*Exeunt.*]
    *Enter* FLAMINEO *and* MARCELLO *guarded, and a* LAWYER.

LAWYER: What, are you in by the week? So – I will try now
whether thy wit be close prisoner: methinks none should
sit upon thy sister but old whore-masters –

FLAMINEO: Or cuckolds, for your cuckold is your most
terrible tickler of lechery: whore-masters would serve,    15
for none are judges at tilting, but those that have been old
tilters.

2. *lieger:* resident.
11. *in by the week:* ensnared.
13. *sit upon:* i.e. in judgement.
15. *tickler:* a quibble; punisher, exciter.
16. *tilting . . . tilters:* a double entendre; tilt = copulate.

77

LAWYER: My lord Duke and she have been very private.

FLAMINEO: You are a dull ass; 'tis threat'ned they have been
20 very public.

LAWYER: If it can be proved they have but kiss'd one
another.

FLAMINEO: What then?

LAWYER: My lord cardinal will ferret them –

25 FLAMINEO: A cardinal I hope will not catch conies.

LAWYER: For to sow kisses (mark what I say), to sow kisses,
is to reap lechery, and I am sure a woman that will endure
kissing is half won.

FLAMINEO: True, her upper part by that rule; if you will
30 win her nether part too, you know what follows.

LAWYER: Hark, the ambassadors are lighted.

FLAMINEO [aside]: I do put on this feigned garb of mirth
To gull suspicion.

MARCELLO:           O my unfortunate sister!
I would my dagger's point had cleft her heart
35 When she first saw Brachiano. You 'tis said,
Were made his engine, and his stalking-horse
To undo my sister.

FLAMINEO:           I made a kind of path
To her and mine own preferment.

MARCELLO:                     Your ruin.

FLAMINEO: Hum! thou art a soldier,
40 Followest the great Duke, feedest his victories,
As witches do their serviceable spirits,
Even with thy prodigal blood; what hast got?

18. *private:* intimate; secret.
20. *public:* unchaste; blatant.
24. *ferret:* to catch rabbits with ferrets; to question searchingly.
25. *conies:* (literally) rabbits; colloquially, fools and women.
31. *lighted:* alighted.           33. *gull:* cheat, deceive.
36. *stalking-horse:* a dupe employed to divert suspicion.
41. *serviceable:* ministering.

But, like the wealth of captains, a poor handful,
Which in thy palm thou bear'st, as men hold water;
Seeking to gripe it fast, the frail reward                                45
Steals through thy fingers.

MARCELLO:                        Sir –

FLAMINEO:                                    Thou hast scarce maintenance
To keep thee in fresh chamois.

MARCELLO:                        Brother!

FLAMINEO:                                              Hear me –
And thus when we have even poured ourselves
Into great fights, for their ambition
Or idle spleen, how shall we find reward,                                50
But as we seldom find the mistletoe
Sacred to physic on the builder oak
Without a mandrake by it, so in our quest of gain.
Alas the poorest of their forc'd dislikes
At a limb proffers, but at heart it strikes:                              55
This is lamented doctrine.

MARCELLO:                        Come, come.

FLAMINEO: When age shall turn thee
White as a blooming hawthorn –

MARCELLO:                                    I'll interrupt you.
For love of virtue bear an honest heart,
And stride over every politic respect,                                   60
Which where they most advance they most infect.
Were I your father, as I am your brother,
I should not be ambitious to leave you
A better patrimony.

    *Enter* SAVOY [AMBASSADOR].

FLAMINEO:                        I'll think on't –
The lord ambassadors.                                                    65

47. *chamois*: jerkins of chamois worn under armour.
52. *builder*: used for building.
60. *politic respect*: consideration of policy.

79

*Here there is a passage of the lieger* AMBASSADORS *over the stage severally. Enter* FRENCH AMBASSADOR.

LAWYER: O my sprightly Frenchman, do you know him? He's an admirable tilter.

FLAMINEO: I saw him at last tilting; he showed like a pewter candle-stick fashioned like a man in armour, holding a tilting staff in his hand, little bigger than a candle of twelve i'th'pound.

70

LAWYER: O but he's an excellent horseman.

FLAMINEO: A lame one in his lofty tricks; he sleeps o'horse-back like a poulter.

*Enter* ENGLISH *and* SPANISH [AMBASSADORS].

75 LAWYER: Lo you my Spaniard.

FLAMINEO: He carries his face in's ruff, as I have seen a serving-man carry glasses in a cypress hat-band, mon-strous steady for fear of breaking. He looks like the claw of a blackbird, first salted and then broiled in a candle.

*Exeunt.*

## [SCENE TWO]

### THE ARRAIGNMENT OF VITTORIA

*Enter* FRANCISCO, MONTICELSO, *the six lieger* AM-BASSADORS, BRACHIANO, VITTORIA, [ZANCHE, FLAMINEO, MARCELLO,] LAWYER, *and a guard.*

MONTICELSO: Forbear my lord, here is no place assign'd you.
The business by his holiness is left
To our examination.

BRACHIANO:                May it thrive with you!
*Lays a rich gown under him.*

77. *cypress:* fine lawn or crepe.

FRANCISCO: A chair there for his lordship.

BRACHIANO: Forbear your kindness; an unbidden guest    5
   Should travel as Dutch women go to church:
   Bear their stools with them.

MONTICELSO:              At your pleasure sir.
   Stand to the table gentlewomen. Now signior
   Fall to your plea.

LAWYER: *Domine Judex converte oculos in hanc pestem muli-*    10
   *erum corruptissimam.*

VITTORIA: What's he?

FRANCISCO:          A lawyer, that pleads against you.

VITTORIA: Pray my lord, let him speak his usual tongue.
   I'll make no answer else.

FRANCISCO:            Why you understand Latin.

VITTORIA: I do sir, but amongst this auditory    15
   Which come to hear my cause, the half or more
   May be ignorant in't.

MONTICELSO:       Go on sir.

VITTORIA:              By your favour,
   I will not have my accusation clouded
   In a strange tongue: all this assembly
   Shall hear what you can charge me with.

FRANCISCO:              Signior,    20
   You need not stand on't much; pray change your
     language.

MONTICELSO: O for God sake: gentlewoman, your credit
   Shall be more famous by it.

LAWYER:             Well then have at you.

VITTORIA: I am at the mark sir, I'll give aim to you,
   And tell you how near you shoot.    25

LAWYER: Most literated judges, please your lordships,
   So to connive your judgements to the view

22. *credit:* reputation.
26. *literated:* learned.

Of this debauch'd and diversivolent woman
Who such a black concatenation
30  Of mischief hath effected, that to extirp
The memory of't, must be the consummation
Of her and her projections –

VITTORIA:              What's all this?

LAWYER: Hold your peace.
Exorbitant sins must have exulceration.

35  VITTORIA: Surely my lords this lawyer here hath swallowed
Some pothecary's bills, or proclamations.
And now the hard and undigestible words
Come up like stones we use give hawks for physic.
Why this is Welsh to Latin.

LAWYER:              My lords, the woman
40  Knows not her tropes nor figures, nor is perfect
In the academic derivation
Of grammatical elocution.

FRANCISCO:          Sir your pains
Shall be well spared, and your deep eloquence
Be worthily applauded amongst those
Which understand you.

LAWYER:          My good lord.

45  FRANCISCO *speaks this as in scorn*:      Sir,
Put up your papers in your fustian bag –
Cry mercy sir, 'tis buckram – and accept
My notion of your learn'd verbosity.

28. *diversivolent*: desiring strife.
32. *projections*: projects.
34. *Exorbitant*: anomalous, extraordinary; *exulceration*: (literally) ulceration; here, more generally, 'break out': i.e. Vittoria's secret sins must eventually reveal themselves, as do ulcers inner corruption.
42. *elocution*: expression.
46. *fustian*: coarse cloth; bombast.
47. *Cry mercy*: I cry you mercy; *buckram*: coarse linen traditionally used for lawyers' bags.

LAWYER: I most graduatically thank your lordship.
   I shall have use for them elsewhere.
   [*Exit.*]                                               50
MONTICELSO: I shall be plainer with you, and paint out
   Your follies in more natural red and white
   Than that upon your cheek.
VITTORIA:                 O you mistake.
   You raise a blood as noble in this cheek
   As ever was your mother's.                        55
MONTICELSO: I must spare you till proof cry whore to that;
   Observe this creature here my honoured lords,
   A woman of a most prodigious spirit
   In her effected.
VITTORIA:         Honourable my lord,
   It doth not suit a reverend cardinal
   To play the lawyer thus.                       60
MONTICELSO: O your trade instructs your language!
   You see my lords what goodly fruit she seems,
   Yet like those apples travellers report
   To grow where Sodom and Gomorrah stood        65
   I will but touch her and you straight shall see
   She'll fall to soot and ashes.
VITTORIA:                Your envenom'd
   Pothecary should do't.
MONTICELSO:         I am resolved
   Were there a second paradise to lose
   This devil would betray it.
VITTORIA:              O poor charity!        70
   Thou art seldom found in scarlet.
MONTICELSO: Who knows not how, when several night
   by night

---

49. *graduatically*: in the manner of a graduate; with elaborate courtesy.
71. *scarlet*: the colour both of the cardinal's vestments and the lawyer's
   robes.

Her gates were chok'd with coaches, and her rooms
Outbrav'd the stars with several kind of lights
75   When she did counterfeit a prince's court?
In music, banquets and most riotous surfeits
This whore, forsooth, was holy.

VITTORIA:                 Ha? whore? what's that?

MONTICELSO: Shall I expound whore to you? Sure I shall;
I'll give their perfect character. They are first
80   Sweetmeats which rot the eater: in man's nostril
Poison'd perfumes. They are coz'ning alchemy,
Shipwracks in calmest weather! What are whores?
Cold Russian winters, that appear so barren,
As if that nature had forgot the spring.
85   They are the true material fire of hell,
Worse than those tributes i'th' Low Countries paid,
Exactions upon meat, drink, garments, sleep;
Ay even on man's perdition, his sin.
They are those brittle evidences of law
90   Which forfeit all a wretched man's estate
For leaving out one syllable. What are whores?
They are those flattering bells have all one tune,
At weddings, and at funerals: your rich whores
Are only treasuries by extortion fill'd,
95   And emptied by curs'd riot. They are worse,
Worse than dead bodies, which are begg'd at gallows
And wrought upon by surgeons, to teach man
Wherein he is imperfect. What's a whore?
She's like the guilty counterfeited coin
100   Which whosoe'er first stamps it brings in trouble
All that receive it.

79. *character:* formal character sketch along the lines of the 'characters'
of the Greek writer, Theophrastus.
85. *material fire:* fire formed of matter, as opposed to the other, spiritual
fires of hell.
88. *man's perdition:* prostitution.

VITTORIA:　　　　This character 'scapes me.

MONTICELSO: You gentlewoman?
  Take from all beasts, and from all minerals
  Their deadly poison –

VITTORIA:　　　　Well what then?

MONTICELSO:　　　　　　　I'll tell thee.
  I'll find in thee a pothecary's shop　　　　　　　105
  To sample them all.

FRENCH AMBASSADOR: She hath liv'd ill.

ENGLISH AMBASSADOR: True, but the cardinal's too bitter.

MONTICELSO: You know what whore is; next the devil,
    Adult'ry,
  Enters the devil, Murder.

FRANCISCO:　　　　　Your unhappy
  Husband is dead.

VITTORIA:　　　O he's a happy husband　　　110
  Now he owes nature nothing.

FRANCISCO: And by a vaulting engine.

MONTICELSO:　　　　　　An active plot.
  He jump'd into his grave.

FRANCISCO:　　　　What a prodigy was't,
  That from some two yards' height a slender man
  Should break his neck?

MONTICELSO:　　　I'th'rushes.

FRANCISCO:　　　　　　And what's more,　　115
  Upon the instant lose all use of speech,
  All vital motion, like a man had lain
  Wound up three days. Now mark each circumstance.

MONTICELSO: And look upon this creature was his wife.
  She comes not like a widow: she comes arm'd　120
  With scorn and impudence. Is this a mourning habit?

101. *'scapes:* escapes; Vittoria is punning, meaning both that the
　　'character' is unintelligible and that it is irrelevant.
112. *vaulting engine:* vaulting-horse.
118. *Wound up:* in his shroud.

VITTORIA: Had I foreknown his death as you suggest,
I would have bespoke my mourning.

MONTICELSO:                      O you are cunning.

VITTORIA: You shame your wit and judgement
125    To call it so. What, is my just defence
By him that is my judge call'd impudence?
Let me appeal then from this Christian court
To the uncivil Tartar.

MONTICELSO:            See my lords,
She scandals our proceedings.

VITTORIA:                  Humbly thus,
130    Thus low, to the most worthy and respected
Lieger ambassadors, my modesty
And womanhood I tender; but withal
So entangled in a cursed accusation
That my defence of force like Perseus,
135    Must personate masculine virtue. To the point.
Find me but guilty, sever head from body:
We'll part good friends: I scorn to hold my life
At yours or any man's entreaty, sir.

ENGLISH AMBASSADOR: She hath a brave spirit.

140 MONTICELSO: Well, well, such counterfeit jewels
Make true ones oft suspected.

VITTORIA:               You are deceived.
For know that all your strict-combined heads,
Which strike against this mine of diamonds,
Shall prove but glassen hammers, they shall break;
145    These are but feigned shadows of my evils.
Terrify babes, my lord, with painted devils,

128. *the uncivil Tartar:* the Tartars were at this time a by-word for
barbarity.
134. *of force:* of necessity.
142. *strict-combined:* closely allied; *heads:* military forces; hammer-heads
(Brown).

I am past such needless palsy; for your names
Of whore and murd'ress, they proceed from you,
As if a man should spit against the wind,
The filth returns in's face.                                     150

MONTICELSO: Pray you mistress satisfy me one question:
Who lodg'd beneath your roof that fatal night
Your husband brake his neck?

BRACHIANO:                              That question
Enforceth me break silence: I was there.

MONTICELSO: Your business?

BRACHIANO:                              Why I came to comfort her,   155
And take some course for settling her estate,
Because I heard her husband was in debt
To you my lord.

MONTICELSO:    He was.

BRACHIANO:                        And 'twas strangely fear'd
That you would cozen her.

MONTICELSO:                      Who made you overseer?

BRACHIANO: Why my charity, my charity, which should
    flow                                                            160
From every generous and noble spirit,
To orphans and to widows.

MONTICELSO:                        Your lust.

BRACHIANO: Cowardly dogs bark loudest. Sirrah priest,
I'll talk with you hereafter, – Do you hear?
The sword you frame of such an excellent temper,   165
I'll sheathe in your own bowels:
There are a number of thy coat resemble
Your common post-boys.

MONTICELSO:                        Ha?

BRACHIANO:                              Your mercenary post-boys;

165. *sword:* of justice; *temper:* a pun = (a) anger (b) hardness and
    elasticity imparted to steel by tempering.
167. *coat:* profession.

87

Your letters carry truth, but 'tis your guise
170 To fill your mouths with gross and impudent lies.
    [*He makes for the door.*]
SERVANT: My lord your gown.
BRACHIANO:                   Thou liest, 'twas my stool.
Bestow't upon thy master that will challenge
The rest o'th' household stuff; for Brachiano
Was ne'er so beggarly, to take a stool
175 Out of another's lodging: let him make
Valence for his bed on't, or a demi-foot-cloth,
For his most reverent moil; Monticelso,
*Nemo me impune lacessit.*
   *Exit* BRACHIANO.
MONTICELSO: Your champion's gone.
VITTORIA:              The wolf may prey the better.
180 FRANCISCO: My lord there's great suspicion of the murder,
But no sound proof who did it: for my part
I do not think she hath a soul so black
To act a deed so bloody; if she have,
As in cold countries husbandmen plant vines,
185 And with warm blood manure them, even so
One summer she will bear unsavoury fruit,
And ere next spring wither both branch and root.
The act of blood let pass, only descend
To matter of incontinence.
VITTORIA:           I discern poison
190 Under your gilded pills.
MONTICELSO: Now the Duke's gone, I will produce a letter,
Wherein 'twas plotted he and you should meet,
At an apothecary's summer-house,
Down by the river Tiber – view't my lords –

169. *guise:* custom, habit.     172. *challenge:* lay claim to.
176. *valence:* bed curtains; *demi-foot-cloth:* half-length covering for a horse: cf. note to I, ii, 52.
177. *moil:* mule.     178. 'No one injures me with impunity.'

Where after wanton bathing and the heat 195
Of a lascivious banquet – I pray read it,
I shame to speak the rest.

VITTORIA: Grant I was tempted,
Temptation to lust proves not the act,
*Casta est quam nemo rogavit,*
You read his hot love to me, but you want 200
My frosty answer.

MONTICELSO: Frost i'th' dog-days! strange!

VITTORIA: Condemn you me for that the Duke did love
me?
So may you blame some fair and crystal river
For that some melancholic distracted man,
Hath drown'd himself in't.

MONTICELSO: Truly drown'd indeed. 205

VITTORIA: Sum up my faults I pray, and you shall find,
That beauty and gay clothes, a merry heart,
And a good stomach to a feast, are all,
All the poor crimes that you can charge me with:
In faith my lord you might go pistol flies, 210
The sport would be more noble.

MONTICELSO: Very good.

VITTORIA: But take you your course, it seems you have
beggar'd me first
And now would fain undo me; I have houses,
Jewels, and a poor remnant of crusadoes,
Would those would make you charitable.

MONTICELSO: If the devil 215
Did ever take good shape behold his picture.

VITTORIA: You have one virtue left,
You will not flatter me.

199. 'She is chaste whom no one has solicited.'
201. *dog-days:* evil, lustful, or unhealthy times, associated with hot
weather when Sirius, the dog-star, is high in the sky.
214. *crusadoes:* gold or silver Portuguese coins.

FRANCISCO: Who brought this letter?

VITTORIA: I am not compell'd to tell you.

220 MONTICELSO: My lord Duke sent to you a thousand ducats,
The twelfth of August.

VITTORIA: 'Twas to keep your cousin
From prisón; I paid use for't.

MONTICELSO: I rather think
'Twas interest for his lust.

VITTORIA: Who says so but yourself? If you be my accuser
225 Pray cease to be my judge, come from the bench,
Give in your evidence 'gainst me, and let these
Be moderators. My lord cardinal,
Were your intelligencing ears as long
As to my thoughts, had you an honest tongue
230 I would not care though you proclaim'd them all.

MONTICELSO: Go to, go to.
After your goodly and vain-glorious banquet,
I'll give you a choke-pear.

VITTORIA: O' your own grafting?

MONTICELSO: You were born in Venice, honourably descended
235 From the Vitelli; 'twas my cousin's fate –
Ill may I name the hour – to marry you;
He bought you of your father.

VITTORIA: Ha?

MONTICELSO: He spent there in six months
Twelve thousand ducats, and to my acquaintance
240 Receiv'd in dowry with you not one julio:
'Twas a hard penny-worth, the ware being so light.

222. *use:* interest.          227. *moderators:* judges.
228. *intelligencing:* for discovering secrets.
233. *choke-pear:* rough and unpalatable kind of pear; hence something
   difficult to swallow; *grafting:* a double entendre.
240. *julio:* coin of Pope Julius II (1503–13), worth about sixpence.
241. *light:* a pun; light also means unchaste.

I yet but draw the curtain, now to your picture:
You came from thence a most notorious strumpet,
And so you have continued.

VITTORIA:                  My lord.

MONTICELSO:                      Nay hear me,
    You shall have time to prate. My lord Brachiano –        245
    Alas I make but repetition,
    Of what is ordinary and Rialto talk,
    And ballated, and would be play'd a'th' stage,
    But that vice many times finds such loud friends
    That preachers are charm'd silent.                      250
    You gentlemen Flamineo and Marcello,
    The court hath nothing now to charge you with,
    Only you must remain upon your sureties
    For your appearance.

FRANCISCO:           I stand for Marcello.

FLAMINEO: And my lord Duke for me.                255

MONTICELSO: For you Vittoria, your public fault,
    Join'd to th' condition of the present time,
    Takes from you all the fruits of noble pity.
    Such a corrupted trial have you made
    Both of your life and beauty, and been styl'd          260
    No less in ominous fate than blazing stars
    To princes. Hear your sentence: you are confin'd
    Unto a house of convertites and your bawd –

FLAMINEO [aside]: Who I?

MONTICELSO:             The Moor.

FLAMINEO [aside]:                O I am a sound man again.

VITTORIA: A house of convertites, what's that?

MONTICELSO:                      A house   265
    Of penitent whores.

247. *Rialto talk:* common gossip.
248. *ballated:* balladed.
263. *convertites:* reformed prostitutes.

VITTORIA:    Do the noblemen in Rome
Erect it for their wives, that I am sent
To lodge there?

FRANCISCO: You must have patience.

VITTORIA:     I must first have vengeance.
270 I fain would know if you have your salvation
By patent, that you proceed thus.

MONTICELSO:    Away with her.
Take her hence.

VITTORIA: A rape, a rape!

MONTICELSO:   How?

VITTORIA:    Yes, you have ravish'd justice,
Forc'd her to do your pleasure.

MONTICELSO:    Fie, she's mad –

275 VITTORIA: Die with those pills in your most cursed maw,
Should bring you health, or while you sit o'th' bench,
Let your own spittle choke you.

MONTICELSO:    She's turn'd fury.

VITTORIA: That the last day of judgement may so find you,
And leave you the same devil you were before.
280 Instruct me some good horse-leech to speak treason,
For since you cannot take my life for deeds,
Take it for words. O woman's poor revenge
Which dwells but in the tongue! I will not weep,
No I do scorn to call up one poor tear
285 To fawn on your injustice; bear me hence,
Unto this house of – what's your mitigating title?

MONTICELSO: Of convertites.

VITTORIA: It shall not be a house of convertites.
My mind shall make it honester to me
290 Than the Pope's palace, and more peaceable
Than thy soul, though thou art a cardinal,
Know this, and let it somewhat raise your spite,

271. *patent*: special licence.

Through darkness diamonds spread their richest light.
*Exit* VITTORIA [*with* ZANCHE, *guarded*].
*Enter* BRACHIANO.

BRACHIANO: Now you and I are friends sir, we'll shake
hands,
In a friend's grave, together: a fit place,      295
Being the emblem of soft peace t'atone our hatred.

FRANCISCO: Sir, what's the matter?

BRACHIANO: I will not chase more blood from that lov'd
cheek,
You have lost too much already; fare you well.
[*Exit.*]

FRANCISCO: How strange these words sound? What's the   300
interpretation?

FLAMINEO [*aside*]: Good, this is a preface to the discovery of
the Duchess' death. He carries it well. Because now I
cannot counterfeit a whining passion for the death of my
lady, I will feign a mad humour for the disgrace of my   305
sister, and that will keep off idle questions. Treason's tongue
hath a villainous palsy in't; I will talk to any man, hear no
man, and for a time appear a politic madman.
[*Exit.*]
*Enter* GIOVANNI, *Count* LODOVICO.

FRANCISCO: How now my noble cousin; what, in black?

GIOVANNI: Yes uncle, I was taught to imitate you   310
In virtue, and you must imitate me
In colours for your garments; my sweet mother
Is —

FRANCISCO: How? Where?

GIOVANNI: Is there, no yonder; indeed sir I'll not tell you,
For I shall make you weep.   315

FRANCISCO: Is dead.

GIOVANNI:        Do not blame me now,

307. *palsy:* nervous disease, characterized by involuntary tremors.

I did not tell you so.

LODOVICO: She's dead my lord.

FRANCISCO: Dead?

MONTICELSO: Blessed lady; thou art now above thy woes.

320 Wilt please your lordships to withdraw a little?

[*Exeunt* AMBASSADORS.]

GIOVANNI: What do the dead do, uncle? Do they eat,
Hear music, go a-hunting, and be merry,
As we that live?

FRANCISCO: No coz; they sleep.

GIOVANNI: Lord, Lord, that I were dead,

325 I have not slept these six nights. When do they wake?

FRANCISCO: When God shall please.

GIOVANNI: Good God let her sleep ever.
For I have known her wake an hundred nights,
When all the pillow, where she laid her head,
Was brine-wet with her tears. I am to complain to you sir.

330 I'll tell you how they have used her now she's dead:
They wrapp'd her in a cruel fold of lead,
And would not let me kiss her.

FRANCISCO: Thou didst love her.

GIOVANNI: I have often heard her say she gave me suck,
And it should seem by that she dearly lov'd me,

335 Since princes seldom do it.

FRANCISCO: O, all of my poor sister that remains!
Take him away for God's sake.

[*Exit* GIOVANNI, *attended*.]

MONTICELSO: How now my lord?

FRANCISCO: Believe me I am nothing but her grave,
And I shall keep her blessed memory

340 Longer than thousand epitaphs.

[*Exeunt*.]

## [SCENE THREE]

*Enter* FLAMINEO *as distracted* [MARCELLO *and* LODO-
VICO].

FLAMINEO: We endure the strokes like anvils or hard steel,
Till pain itself make us no pain to feel.
Who shall do me right now? Is this the end of service?
I'd rather go weed garlic; travel through France, and be
mine own ostler; wear sheep-skin linings; or shoes that                  5
stink of blacking; be ent'red into the list of the forty
thousand pedlars in Poland.
*Enter Savoy* [AMBASSADOR].
Would I had rotted in some surgeon's house at Venice,
built upon the pox as well as on piles, ere I had serv'd
Brachiano.                                                               10
SAVOY AMBASSADOR: You must have comfort.
FLAMINEO: Your comfortable words are like honey. They
relish well in your mouth that's whole; but in mine that's
wounded they go down as if the sting of the bee were in
them. O they have wrought their purpose cunningly, as if   15
they would not seem to do it of malice. In this a politician
imitates the devil, as the devil imitates a cannon. Whereso-
ever he comes to do mischief, he comes with his backside
towards you.
*Enter the French* [AMBASSADOR].
FRENCH AMBASSADOR: The proofs are evident.                             20
FLAMINEO: Proof! 'twas corruption. O gold, what a god art
thou! and O man, what a devil art thou to be tempted by
that cursed mineral! Yon diversivolent lawyer; mark him;
knaves turn informers, as maggots turn to flies; you may

5. *linings:* leather drawers.
9. *built upon the pox:* paid for out of fees taken for curing venereal
   disease; *piles:* wooden foundations; haemorrhoids.

25 catch gudgeons with either. A cardinal; – I would he
would hear me, – there's nothing so holy but money will
corrupt and putrify it, like victual under the line.
   *Enter English* [AMBASSADOR].
You are happy in England, my lord; here they sell justice
with those weights they press men to death with. O
30 horrible salary!
ENGLISH AMBASSADOR: Fie, fie, Flamineo.
FLAMINEO: Bells ne'er ring well, till they are at their full
pitch, and I hope yon cardinal shall never have the grace
to pray well, till he come to the scaffold.
   [*Exeunt* AMBASSADORS.]
35 If they were rack'd now to know the confederacy! But
your noblemen are privileged from the rack; and well
may. For a little thing would pull some of them a' pieces
afore they came to their arraignment. Religion; O how it
is commeddled with policy. The first bloodshed in the
40 world happened about religion. Would I were a Jew.
MARCELLO: O, there are too many.
FLAMINEO: You are deceiv'd. There are not Jews enough,
priests enough, nor gentlemen enough.
MARCELLO: How?
45 FLAMINEO: I'll prove it. For if there were Jews enough, so
many Christians would not turn usurers; if priests enough,
one should not have six benefices; and if gentlemen
enough, so many early mushrooms, whose best growth
sprang from a dunghill, should not aspire to gentility.
50 Farewell. Let others live by begging. Be thou one of them;
practise the art of Wolner in England to swallow all's

25. *gudgeons:* small fish; figuratively, simpletons.
27. *under the line:* at the equator.
33. *grace:* God's gift of aid towards salvation.
37. *pull . . . a' pieces:* on the rack; in argument.
39. *commeddled:* mixed together.
48. *mushrooms:* upstarts.

given thee; and let one purgation make thee as hungry
again as fellows that work in a sawpit. I'll go hear the
screech-owl.

    *Exit.*

LODOVICO [*aside*]: This was Brachiano's pander, and 'tis
    strange                                       55
That in such open and apparent guilt
Of his adulterous sister, he dare utter
So scandalous a passion. I must wind him.

    *Enter* FLAMINEO.

FLAMINEO [*aside*]: How dares this banish'd count return to
    Rome,
His pardon not yet purchas'd? I have heard             60
The deceas'd Duchess gave him pension,
And that he came along from Padua
I'th' train of the young prince. There's somewhat in't.
Physicians, that cure poisons, still do work
With counterpoisons.

MARCELLO:               Mark this strange encounter.     65

FLAMINEO: The god of melancholy turn thy gall to poison,
And let the stigmatic wrinkles in thy face,
Like to the boisterous waves in a rough tide
One still overtake another.

LODOVICO:                I do thank thee
And I do wish ingeniously for thy sake            70
The dog-days all year long.

FLAMINEO:              How croaks the raven?
Is our good Duchess dead?

LODOVICO:           Dead.

FLAMINEO:                O fate!
Misfortune comes like the crowner's business,
Huddle upon huddle.

---

58. *wind him:* discover his intentions.     60. *purchas'd:* obtained.
67. *stigmatic:* deformed; ill-favoured.     74. *Huddle upon huddle:* in heaps.

LODOVICO: Shalt thou and I join housekeeping?
75 FLAMINEO: Yes, content.
Let's be unsociably sociable.
LODOVICO: Sit some three days together, and discourse.
FLAMINEO: Only with making faces; lie in our clothes.
LODOVICO: With faggots for our pillows.
FLAMINEO: And be lousy.
80 LODOVICO: In taffeta linings; that's gentle melancholy;
Sleep all day.
FLAMINEO: Yes: and like your melancholic hare
Feed after midnight.
*Enter* ANTONELLI [*and* GASPARO, *laughing*].
We are observed: see how yon couple grieve.
LODOVICO: What a strange creature is a laughing fool,
85 As if a man were created to no use
But only to show his teeth.
FLAMINEO: I'll tell thee what,
It would do well instead of looking-glasses
To set one's face each morning by a saucer
Of a witch's congealed blood.
LODOVICO: Precious rogue!
We'll never part.
90 FLAMINEO: Never: till the beggary of courtiers,
The discontent of churchmen, want of soldiers,
And all the creatures that hang manacled,
Worse than strappado'd, on the lowest felly
Of Fortune's wheel be taught in our two lives
95 To scorn that world which life of means deprives.
ANTONELLI: My lord I bring good news. The Pope on's
death-bed,

80. *taffeta linings:* drawers or underclothes made of taffeta. The point is
that taffeta was popularly held to be louse-proof.
93. *strappado'd:* hung up by the hands, which have been tied behind the
back; *felly:* felloe or section of the rim of a wheel.

At th'earnest suit of the great Duke of Florence,
Hath sign'd your pardon, and restor'd unto you –
LODOVICO: I thank you for your news. Look up again
Flamineo, see my pardon.
FLAMINEO:                      Why do you laugh?     100
There was no such condition in our covenant.
LODOVICO:                            Why?
FLAMINEO: You shall not seem a happier man than I;
You know our vow sir, if you will be merry,
Do it i'th' like posture, as if some great man
Sat while his enemy were executed:             105
Though it be very lechery unto thee,
Do't with a crabbed politician's face.
LODOVICO: Your sister is a damnable whore.
FLAMINEO:                        Ha?
LODOVICO: Look you; I spake that laughing.
FLAMINEO: Dost ever think to speak again?
LODOVICO:                     Do you hear?     110
Wilt sell me forty ounces of her blood,
To water a mandrake?
FLAMINEO:           Poor lord, you did vow
To live a lousy creature.
LODOVICO:           Yes.
FLAMINEO:                Like one
That had for ever forfeited the daylight,
By being in debt –
LODOVICO:       Ha, Ha!                        115
FLAMINEO: I do not greatly wonder you do break:
Your lordship learn't long since. But I'll tell you –
LODOVICO: What?
FLAMINEO:          And't shall stick by you.
LODOVICO:                       I long for it.

116. *break:* go bankrupt; break an oath.
117. *learn't:* learnt it.

FLAMINEO: This laughter scurvily becomes your face;
120    If you will not be melancholy, be angry.
       *Strikes him.*
       See, now I laugh too.
MARCELLO: You are to blame, I'll force you hence.
LODOVICO:                                    Unhand me.
       *Exit* MAR[CELLO] & FLAM[INEO].
       That e'er I should be forc'd to right myself,
       Upon a pander!
ANTONELLI:      My lord.
LODOVICO: H'had been as good meet with his fist a
125    thunderbolt.
GASPARO: How this shows!
LODOVICO:      Ud's death, how did my sword miss him?
       These rogues that are most weary of their lives,
       Still 'scape the greatest dangers.
       A pox upon him: all his reputation,
130    Nay all the goodness of his family,
       Is not worth half this earthquake.
       I learnt it of no fencer to shake thus;
       Come, I'll forget him, and go drink some wine.
       *Exeunt.*

# [ACT FOUR]

## [SCENE ONE]

*Enter* FRANCISCO *and* MONTICELSO.

MONTICELSO: Come, come my lord, untie your folded
   thoughts,
  And let them dangle loose as a bride's hair.
  Your sister's poisoned.

FRANCISCO:          Far be it from my thoughts
  To seek revenge.

MONTICELSO:    What, are you turn'd all marble?

FRANCISCO: Shall I defy him, and impose a war         5
  Most burthensome on my poor subjects' necks,
  Which at my will I have not power to end?
  You know; for all the murders, rapes, and thefts,
  Committed in the horrid lust of war,
  He that unjustly caus'd it first proceed,         10
  Shall find it in his grave and in his seed.

MONTICELSO: That's not the course I'd wish you: pray,
   observe me.
  We see that undermining more prevails
  Than doth the cannon. Bear your wrongs conceal'd,
  And, patient as the tortoise, let this camel       15
  Stalk o'er your back unbruis'd: sleep with the lion,
  And let this brood of secure foolish mice
  Play with your nostrils; till the time be ripe
  For th' bloody audit, and the fatal gripe:

2. In the Jacobean age, brides wore their hair loose as a sign of
   virginity.
16. *your back unbruis'd:* your back being unbruised.
19. *audit:* day when accounts are presented for inspection.

20 Aim like a cunning fowler, close one eye,
That you the better may your game espy.
FRANCISCO: Free me my innocence, from treacherous acts:
I know there's thunder yonder: and I'll stand,
Like a safe valley, which low bends the knee
25 To some aspiring mountain: since I know
Treason, like spiders weaving nets for flies,
By her foul work is found, and in it dies.
To pass away these thoughts, my honour'd lord,
It is reported you possess a book
30 Wherein you have quoted, by intelligence,
The names of all notorious offenders
Lurking about the city.
MONTICELSO:                    Sir I do;
And some there are which call it my black book:
Well may the title hold: for though it teach not
35 The art of conjuring, yet in it lurk
The names of many devils.
FRANCISCO:                    Pray let's see it.
MONTICELSO: I'll fetch it to your lordship.
     *Exit* MONTICELSO.
FRANCISCO:                                   Monticelso,
I will not trust thee, but in all my plots
I'll rest as jealous as a town besieg'd.
40 Thou canst not reach what I intend to act;
Your flax soon kindles, soon is out again,
But gold slow heats, and long will hot remain.
     *Enter* MONT[ICELSO,] *presents* FRAN[CISCO] *with a
     book.*
MONTICELSO: 'Tis here my lord.

30. *by intelligence:* by secret information.
33. *black book:* a list of rogues and villains.
35. *The art of conjuring:* necromancy: cf. II, ii, 8 note, p. 421.
39. *jealous:* vigilant.

FRANCISCO: First your intelligencers, pray let's see.

MONTICELSO: Their number rises strangely,      45
And some of them
You'd take for honest men.
Next are panders.
These are your pirates: and these following leaves,
For base rogues that undo young gentlemen      50
By taking up commodities:
For politic bankrupts:
For fellows that are bawds to their own wives,
Only to put off horses and slight jewels,
Clocks, defac'd plate, and such commodities,      55
At birth of their first children.

FRANCISCO:                    Are there such?

MONTICELSO: These are for impudent bawds,
That go in men's apparel; for usurers
That share with scriveners for their good reportage:
For lawyers that will antedate their writs:      60
And some divines you might find folded there,
But that I slip them o'er for conscience' sake.
Here is a general catalogue of knaves.
A man might study all the prisons o'er,
Yet never attain this knowledge.

FRANCISCO:                    Murderers.      65
Fold down the leaf I pray.
Good my lord let me borrow this strange doctrine.

MONTICELSO: Pray us't my lord.

FRANCISCO:                    I do assure your lordship,
You are a worthy member of the state,

54. *put off:* sell fraudulently.
59. *reportage:* repute.
61. *folded:* included in the fold; ironically, the divines themselves should
be the spiritual shepherds.
67. *doctrine:* information and, punningly, 'religious tenets'.

70 And have done infinite good in your discovery
  Of these offenders.
MONTICELSO:          Somewhat sir.
FRANCISCO:                    O God!
  Better than tribute of wolves paid in England,
  'Twill hang their skins o'th' hedge.
MONTICELSO:                    I must make bold
  To leave your lordship.
FRANCISCO:               Dearly sir, I thank you;
75 If any ask for me at court, report
  You have left me in the company of knaves.
     *Exit* MONT[ICELSO].
  I gather now by this, some cunning fellow
  That's my lord's officer, one that lately skipp'd
  From a clerk's desk up to a justice' chair,
80 Hath made this knavish summons; and intends,
  As th'Irish rebels wont were to sell heads,
  So to make prize of these. And thus it happens,
  Your poor rogues pay for't, which have not the means
  To present bribe in fist: the rest o'th' band
85 Are raz'd out of the knaves' record; or else
  My lord he winks at them with easy will,
  His man grows rich, the knaves are the knaves still.
  But to the use I'll make of it; it shall serve
  To point me out a list of murderers,
90 Agents for any villainy. Did I want
  Ten leash of courtezans, it would furnish me;
  Nay laundress three armies. That in so little paper
  Should lie th'undoing of so many men!
  'Tis not so big as twenty declarations.

91. *leash:* sporting term for a set of three.
92. *laundress:* supply with laundresses, who reputedly doubled as
   prostitutes.
94. *declarations:* official proclamations.

See the corrupted use some make of books: 95
Divinity, wrested by some factious blood,
Draws swords, swells battles, and o'erthrows all good.
To fashion my revenge more seriously,
Let me remember my dead sister's face:
Call for her picture: no; I'll close mine eyes, 100
And in a melancholic thought I'll frame
    *Enter* ISABEL[L]A's *Ghost.*
Her figure 'fore me. Now I ha't – how strong
Imagination works! How she can frame
Things which are not! Methinks she stands afore me;
And by the quick idea of my mind, 105
Were my skill pregnant, I could draw her picture.
Thought, as a subtle juggler, makes us deem
Things supernatural, which have cause
Common as sickness. 'Tis my melancholy.
How cam'st thou by thy death? – How idle am I 110
To question my own idleness – Did ever
Man dream awake till now? – Remove this object,
Out of my brain with't: what have I to do
With tombs, or death-beds, funerals, or tears,
That have to meditate upon revenge? 115
    [*Exit Ghost.*]
So now 'tis ended, like an old wives' story.
Statesmen think often they see stranger sights
Than madmen. Come, to this weighty business.
My tragedy must have some idle mirth in't,
Else it will never pass. I am in love, 120
In love with Corombona, and my suit
Thus halts to her in verse –
    *He writes.*

105. *quick idea:* vivid mental image.
106. *pregnant:* resourceful, inventive.
122. *halts:* limps.

I have done it rarely: O the fate of princes!
I am so us'd to frequent flattery,
125  That being alone I now flatter myself;
But it will serve; 'tis seal'd.
  *[Calls offstage.] Enter* SERVANT.
                              Bear this
To th'house of convertites; and watch your leisure.
To give it to the hands of Corombona,
Or to the matron, when some followers
130  Of Brachiano may be by. Away!
  *Exit* SERVANT.
He that deals all by strength, his wit is shallow:
When a man's head goes through, each limb will follow.
The engine for my business, bold Count Lodowick;
'Tis gold must such an instrument procure,
135  With empty fist no man doth falcons lure.
Brachiano, I am now fit for thy encounter.
Like the wild Irish I'll ne'er think thee dead,
Till I can play at football with thy head.
*Flectere si nequeo superos, Acheronta movebo.*
  *Exit.*

## [SCENE TWO]

*Enter the* MATRON, *and* FLAMINEO.
MATRON: Should it be known the Duke hath such recourse
  To your imprison'd sister, I were like
  T'incur much damage by it.
FLAMINEO:                      Not a scruple.
  The Pope lies on his death-bed, and their heads
5  Are troubled now with other business
  Than guarding of a lady.

3. *damage:* discredit; *scruple:* a minute quantity.
4. Gregory XIII, died 10 April 1585.

*Enter* SERVANT.

SERVANT [*aside*]: Yonder's Flamineo in conference
With the Matrona.
[*To the* MATRON] Let me speak with you.
I would entreat you to deliver for me
This letter to the fair Vittoria.                                    10

MATRON: I shall sir.

*Enter* BRACHIANO.

SERVANT:                    With all care and secrecy;
Hereafter you shall know me, and receive
Thanks for this courtesy.
[*Exit.*]

FLAMINEO:                          How now? What's that?

MATRON: A letter.

FLAMINEO:            To my sister: I'll see't delivered.
[*Exit* MATRON.]

BRACHIANO: What's that you read Flamineo?

FLAMINEO:                                          Look.        15

BRACHIANO: Ha? [*reads*] *To the most unfortunate his best
    respected*
*Vittoria* –
Who was the messenger?

FLAMINEO:                          I know not.

BRACHIANO: No! Who sent it?

FLAMINEO:                          Ud's foot you speak, as if a man
Should know what fowl is coffin'd in a bak'd meat        20
Afore you cut it up.

BRACHIANO: I'll open't, were't her heart. What's here sub-
    scribed –
*Florence?* This juggling is gross and palpable.
I have found out the conveyance; read it, read it.

20. *coffin'd*: enclosed in a coffin, i.e. pie-crust.
24. *conveyance*: means of communication. Brachiano is also playing on
    a second, legal meaning: a document by which property (i.e.
    Vittoria) is transferred from one person to another.

FLAMINEO (*Reads the letter*): *Your tears I'll turn to triumphs,*
25     *be but mine.*
    *Your prop is fall'n; I pity that a vine*
    *Which princes heretofore have long'd to gather,*
    *Wanting supporters, now should fade and wither.*
    Wine i'faith, my lord, with lees would serve his turn.
30     *Your sad imprisonment I'll soon uncharm,*
    *And with a princely uncontrolled arm*
    *Lead you to Florence, where my love and care*
    *Shall hang your wishes in my silver hair.*
    A halter on his strange equivocation.
35     *Nor for my years return me the sad willow:*
    *Who prefer blossoms before fruit that's mellow?*
    Rotten on my knowledge with lying too long i'th' bed-
      straw.
    *And all the lines of age this line convinces:*
    *The gods never wax old, no more do princes.*
40     A pox on't, tear it, let's have no more atheists
    For God's sake.
BRACHIANO: Ud's death, I'll cut her into atomies
    And let th'irregular north-wind sweep her up
    And blow her int' his nostrils. Where's this whore?
FLAMINEO: That! What do you call her?
45 BRACHIANO:               O, I could be mad,
    Prevent the curs'd disease she'll bring me to,
    And tear my hair off. Where's this changeable stuff?

29. *lees:* dregs.
34. *equivocation:* use of words with double meaning in order to deceive;
    Flamineo interprets 'hang' equivocally in his punning reference to
    'halter', i.e. noose.
35. *willow:* emblem of a rejected lover.
37. *bed-straw:* was used instead of mattresses, and to help ripen fruit.
42. *atomies:* fragments of dust.
43. *irregular:* wild.
46-7. i.e. syphilis.
47. *changeable stuff:* watered silk; fickle women.

FLAMINEO: O'er head and ears in water, I assure you,
  She is not for your wearing.

BRACHIANO:                    In you pander!

FLAMINEO: What me, my lord, am I your dog?                    50

BRACHIANO: A blood-hound: do you brave? do you stand
  me?

FLAMINEO: Stand you? Let those that have diseases run;
  I need no plasters.

BRACHIANO:        Would you be kick'd?

FLAMINEO: Would you have your neck broke?
  I tell you Duke, I am not in Russia;                    55
  My shins must be kept whole.

BRACHIANO:                    Do you know me?

FLAMINEO: O my lord! methodically.
  As in this world there are degrees of evils:
  So in this world there are degrees of devils.
  You're a great Duke; I your poor secretary.                    60
  I look now for a Spanish fig, or an Italian sallet daily.

BRACHIANO: Pander, ply your convoy, and leave your
  prating.

FLAMINEO: All your kindness to me is like that miserable
  courtesy of Polyphemus to Ulysses; you reserve me to be
  devour'd last; you would dig turves out of my grave to                    65
  feed your larks: that would be music to you. Come, I'll
  lead you to her.

BRACHIANO: Do you face me?

FLAMINEO: O sir I would not go before a politic enemy with
  my back towards him, though there were behind me a                    70
  whirlpool.

    *Enter* VITTORIA *to* BRACHIANO *and* FLAMINEO.

BRACHIANO: Can you read mistress? Look upon that letter;
  There are no characters nor hieroglyphics.

52. *run:* suppurate.          57. *methodically:* precisely.
64. *Polyphemus:* one of the Cyclops: see *Odyssey*, IX, 369–70.
73. *characters:* ciphers.

You need no comment, I am grown your receiver;
75    God's precious, you shall be a brave great lady,
A stately and advanced whore.

VITTORIA:           Say sir?

BRACHIANO: Come, come, let's see your cabinet, discover
Your treasury of love-letters. Death and furies,
I'll see them all.

VITTORIA:       Sir, upon my soul,
80    I have not any. Whence was this directed?

BRACHIANO: Confusion on your politic ignorance!
    [*Gives her the letter.*]
You are reclaimed, are you? I'll give you the bells
And let you fly to the devil.

FLAMINEO:          Ware hawk, my lord.

VITTORIA [*reads*]: *Florence!* This is some treacherous plot,
    my lord.
85    To me, he ne'er was lovely I protest,
So much as in my sleep.

BRACHIANO:        Right: they are plots.
Your beauty! O, ten thousand curses on't.
How long have I beheld the devil in crystal?
Thou hast led me, like an heathen sacrifice,
90    With music, and with fatal yokes of flowers
To my eternal ruin. Woman to man
Is either a god or a wolf.

VITTORIA:        My lord.

BRACHIANO:           Away.
We'll be as differing as two adamants;
The one shall shun the other. What? dost weep?
95    Procure but ten of thy dissembling trade,
Ye'ld furnish all the Irish funerals
With howling, past wild Irish.

75. *God's precious:* i.e. blood or body.
93. *adamants:* lodestones.

FLAMINEO:                              Fie, my lord.
BRACHIANO: That hand, that cursed hand, which I have
    wearied
    With doting kisses! O my sweetest Duchess
    How lovely art thou now! [to VITTORIA] Thy loose
        thoughts                                                        100
    Scatter like quicksilver; I was bewitch'd;
    For all the world speaks ill of thee.
VITTORIA:                              No matter.
    I'll live so now I'll make that world recant
    And change her speeches. You did name your Duchess.
BRACHIANO: Whose death God pardon.
VITTORIA:                              Whose death God revenge   105
    On thee most godless Duke.
FLAMINEO:                              Now for two whirlwinds.
VITTORIA: What have I gain'd by thee but infamy?
    Thou hast stain'd the spotless honour of my house,
    And frighted thence noble society:
    Like those, which sick o'th' palsy, and retain         110
    Ill-scenting foxes 'bout them, are still shunn'd
    By those of choicer nostrils.
    What do you call this house?
    Is this your palace? Did not the judge style it
    A house of penitent whores? Who sent me to it?         115
    Who hath the honour to advance Vittoria
    To this incontinent college? Is't not you?
    Is't not your high preferment? Go, go brag
    How many ladies you have undone, like me.
    Fare you well sir; let me hear no more of you.          120
    I had a limb corrupted to an ulcer,
    But I have cut it off: and now I'll go
    Weeping to heaven on crutches. For your gifts,

100. *loose:* unconfined; unchaste.
118. *preferment:* advancement in status or position in life.

I will return them all; and I do wish
125 That I could make you full executor
To all my sins. O that I could toss myself
Into a grave as quickly: for all thou art worth
I'll not shed one tear more; – I'll burst first.
*She throws herself upon a bed.*
BRACHIANO: I have drunk Lethe. Vittoria?
130 My dearest happiness! Vittoria!
What do you ail my love? Why do you weep?
VITTORIA: Yes, I now weep poniards, do you see.
BRACHIANO: Are not those matchless eyes mine?
VITTORIA:                                     I had rather
They were not matches.
BRACHIANO:               Is not this lip mine?
135 VITTORIA: Yes: thus to bite it off, rather than give it thee.
FLAMINEO: Turn to my lord, good sister.
VITTORIA:                          Hence you pander.
FLAMINEO: Pander! Am I the author of your sin?
VITTORIA: Yes. He's a base thief that a thief lets in.
FLAMINEO: We're blown up, my lord –
BRACHIANO:                       Wilt thou hear me?
140 Once to be jealous of thee is t'express
That I will love thee everlastingly,
And never more be jealous.
VITTORIA:                    O thou fool,
Whose greatness hath by much o'ergrown thy wit!
What dar'st thou do, that I not dare to suffer,
145 Excepting to be still thy whore? For that,
In the sea's bottom sooner thou shalt make
A bonfire.
FLAMINEO: O, no oaths for God's sake.
BRACHIANO: Will you hear me?

129. *Lethe:* waters of oblivion.      134. *not matches:* squinted.
139. *blown up:* by a mine.

VITTORIA: Never.

FLAMINEO: What a damn'd imposthume is a woman's will?
    Can nothing break it? [*to* BRACHIANO, *aside*] Fie, fie, my
    lord. 150
    Women are caught as you take tortoises,
    She must be turn'd on her back. – Sister, by this hand
    I am on your side. – Come, come, you have wrong'd her.
    What a strange credulous man were you, my lord,
    To think the Duke of Florence would love her? 155
    Will any mercer take another's ware
    When once 'tis tows'd and sullied? And yet, sister,
    How scurvily this frowardness becomes you!
    Young leverets stand not long; and women's anger
    Should, like their flight, procure a little sport; 160
    A full cry for a quarter of an hour;
    And then be put to th' dead quat.

BRACHIANO:               Shall these eyes,
    Which have so long time dwelt upon your face,
    Be now put out?

FLAMINEO:       No cruel landlady i'th' world,
    Which lends forth groats to broom-men, and takes use
      for them 165
    Would do't.
    Hand her, my lord, and kiss her: be not like
    A ferret to let go your hold with blowing.

BRACHIANO: Let us renew right hands.

VITTORIA:                  Hence.

BRACHIANO: Never shall rage, or the forgetful wine, 170
    Make me commit like fault.

149. *imposthume:* abscess.
157. *tows'd:* tousled, dishevelled; also used of a woman who has been
    pulled about in love play.     158. *frowardness:* perversity.
159. *leverets:* young hares; *stand:* hunting term, meaning endure.
162. *quat:* squat (a hunting term).
165. *broom-men:* street-sweepers.

FLAMINEO: Now you are i'th' way on't, follow't hard.

BRACHIANO: Be thou at peace with me; let all the world
Threaten the cannon.

FLAMINEO:                 Mark his penitence.

175   Best natures do commit the grossest faults,
When they're giv'n o'er to jealousy; as best wine
Dying makes strongest vinegar. I'll tell you;
The sea's more rough and raging than calm rivers,
But nor so sweet nor wholesome. A quiet woman

180   Is a still water under a great bridge.
A man may shoot her safely.

VITTORIA: O ye dissembling men!

FLAMINEO:               We suck'd that, sister,
From women's breasts, in our first infancy.

VITTORIA: To add misery to misery.

BRACHIANO:             Sweetest.

185 VITTORIA: Am I not low enough?
Ay, ay, your good heart gathers like a snowball
Now your affection's cold.

BRACHIANO:         Ud's foot, it shall melt
To a heart again, or all the wine in Rome
Shall run o'th' lees for't.

190 VITTORIA: Your hawk or dog should be rewarded better
Than I have been. I'll speak not one word more.

FLAMINEO: Stop her mouth, with a sweet kiss, my lord.
So now the tide's turn'd the vessel's come about.
He's a sweet armful. O we curl'd-hair'd men

195   Are still most kind to women. This is well.

BRACHIANO: That you should chide thus!

FLAMINEO:           O, sir, your little chimneys
Do ever cast most smoke. I sweat for you.
Couple together with as deep a silence
As did the Grecians in their wooden horse.

193. *come about:* reversed its course.     195. *still:* always.

My lord, supply your promises with deeds. 200
*You know that painted meat no hunger feeds.*
BRACHIANO: Stay—ingrateful Rome!
FLAMINEO: Rome! it deserves
To be call'd Barbary, for our villainous usage.
BRACHIANO: Soft; the same project which the Duke of
Florence,
(Whether in love or gullery I know not) 205
Laid down for her escape, will I pursue.
FLAMINEO: And no time fitter than this night, my lord;
The Pope being dead; and all the cardinals ent'red
The conclave for th'electing a new Pope;
The city in a great confusion; 210
We may attire her in a page's suit,
Lay her post-horse, take shipping, and amain
For Padua.
BRACHIANO: I'll instantly steal forth the Prince Giovanni,
And make for Padua. You two with your old mother 215
And young Marcello that attends on Florence,
If you can work him to it, follow me.
I will advance you all: for you Vittoria,
Think of a duchess' title.
FLAMINEO: Lo you sister.
Stay, my lord; I'll tell you a tale. The crocodile, which 220
lives in the river Nilus, hath a worm breeds i'th' teeth of't,
which puts it to extreme anguish: a little bird, no bigger
than a wren, is barber-surgeon to this crocodile; flies into
the jaws of't; picks out the worm; and brings present
remedy. The fish, glad of ease but ingrateful to her that 225
did it, that the bird may not talk largely of her abroad for
non-payment, closeth her chaps intending to swallow

205. *gullery*: trickery.
212. *Lay her post-horse*: provide her with relays of post-horses; *amain*:
full speed. 227. *chaps*: jaws.

her, and so put her to perpetual silence. But nature
loathing such ingratitude, hath arm'd this bird with a
230   quill or prick on the head, top o'th' which wounds the
crocodile i'th' mouth; forceth her open her bloody
prison; and away flies the pretty tooth-picker from her
cruel patient.

BRACHIANO: Your application is, I have not rewarded
  The service you have done me.

235 FLAMINEO:               No my lord;
  You sister are the crocodile: you are blemish'd in your
  fame, my lord cures it. And though the comparison hold
  not in every particle; yet observe, remember, what good
  the bird with the prick i'th' head hath done you; and
240   scorn ingratitude.
  [aside] It may appear to some ridiculous
  Thus to talk knave and madman; and sometimes
  Come in with a dried sentence, stuff'd with sage.
  But this allows my varying of shapes,
245   *Knaves do grow great by being great men's apes.*
    *Exeunt.*

## [SCENE THREE]

*Enter* LODOVICO, GASPARO, *and six* AMBASSADORS.
*At another door* [FRANCISCO] *the Duke of Florence.*

FRANCISCO: So, my lord, I commend your diligence.
  Guard well the conclave, and, as the order is,
  Let none have conference with the cardinals.

LODOVICO: I shall, my lord. Room for the ambassadors!

GASPARO: They're wondrous brave today: why do they
5   wear
  These several habits?

243. *sentence:* maxim.       5. *brave:* finely dressed.
6. *several:* various, diverse.

LODOVICO:        O sir, they're knights
Of several orders.
That lord i'th' black cloak with the silver cross
Is Knight of Rhodes; the next Knight of St Michael;
That of the Golden Fleece; the Frenchman there        10
Knight of the Holy Ghost; my lord of Savoy
Knight of th'Annunciation; the Englishman
Is Knight of th'honoured Garter, dedicated
Unto their saint, St George. I could describe to you
Their several institutions, with the laws        15
Annexed to their orders; but that time
Permits not such discovery.
FRANCISCO:        Where's Count Lodowick?
LODOVICO: Here my lord.
FRANCISCO:        'Tis o'th' point of dinner time;
Marshal the cardinals' service.
LODOVICO:        Sir, I shall.
    *Enter* SERVANTS *with several dishes covered.*
Stand, let me search your dish; who's this for?        20
SERVANT: For my Lord Cardinal Monticelso.
LODOVICO: Who's this?
SERVANT:        For my Lord Cardinal of Bourbon.
FRENCH AMBASSADOR: Why doth he search the dishes? to observe
What meat is dress'd?
ENGLISH AMBASSADOR: No sir, but to prevent
Lest any letters should be convey'd in        25
·To bribe or to solicit the advancement
Of any cardinal. When first they enter
'Tis lawful for the ambassadors of princes
To enter with them, and to make their suit
For any man their prince affecteth best;        30
But after, till a general election,

24. *dress'd:* prepared.

No man may speak with them.

LODOVICO: You that attend on the lord cardinals
Open the window, and receive their viands.

A CONCLAVIST: You must return the service; the lord
35    cardinals
Are busied 'bout electing of the Pope;
They have given o'er scrutiny, and are fallen
To admiration.

LODOVICO:    Away, away.

*[Exeunt* SERVANTS *with dishes.]*

FRANCISCO: I'll lay a thousand ducats you hear news
40    Of a Pope presently. Hark; sure he's elected!

*[The]* Cardinal *[of* ARRAGON *appears] on the terrace.*

Behold! my lord of Arragon appears
On the church battlements.

ARRAGON: *Denuntio vobis gaudium magnum. Reverendissimus*
*Cardinalis Lorenzo de Monticelso electus est in sedem*
45    *apostolicam, et eligit sibi nomen Paulum quartum.*

OMNES: *Vivat Sanctus Pater Paulus Quartus.*

*[Enter* SERVANT.]

SERVANT: Vittoria my lord –
FRANCISCO:    Well: what of her?
SERVANT: Is fled the city –
FRANCISCO:    Ha?
SERVANT:    With Duke Brachiano.
FRANCISCO: Fled? Where's the Prince Giovanni?
SERVANT:    Gone
with his father.

50  FRANCISCO: Let the Matrona of the convertites
Be apprehended. Fled? O damnable!

*[Exit* SERVANT.]

*[Aside]* How fortunate are my wishes. Why? 'Twas this
I only labour'd. I did send the letter

35. *the service:* the dishes.

T'instruct him what to do. Thy fame, fond Duke,
I first have poison'd; directed thee the way                    55
To marry a whore; what can be worse? This follows:
The hand must act to drown the passionate tongue,
I scorn to wear a sword and prate of wrong.
   *Enter* MONTICELSO *in state.*

MONTICELSO: *Concedimus vobis apostolicam benedictionem et
remissionem peccatorum.*                                       60
   [FRANCISCO *whispers to him.*]
My lord reports Vittoria Corombona
Is stol'n from forth the house of convertites
By Brachiano, and they're fled the city.
Now, though this be the first day of our seat,
We cannot better please the divine power,                     65
Than to sequester from the holy church
These cursed persons. Make it therefore known,
We do denounce excommunication
Against them both: all that are theirs in Rome
We likewise banish. Set on.                                    70
   *Exeunt [all except* FRANCISCO *and* LODOVICO].

FRANCISCO: Come dear Lodovico
You have tane the sacrament to prosecute
Th'intended murder.

LODOVICO:         With all constancy.
But, sir, I wonder you'll engage yourself
In person, being a great prince.

FRANCISCO:         Divert me not.      75
Most of this court are of my faction,
And some are of my counsel. Noble friend,
Our danger shall be 'like in this design;
Give leave, part of the glory may be mine.

54. *fond:* foolish.
64. *seat:* 'the technical term for the throne or office of a Pope' (Brown).
78. *'like:* alike.

*Exit* FRAN[CISCO]. *Enter* MONTICELSO.

MONTICELSO: Why did the Duke of Florence with such
80    care
    Labour your pardon? Say.

LODOVICO: Italian beggars will resolve you that
    Who, begging of an alms, bid those they beg of
    Do good for their own sakes; or't may be
85    He spreads his bounty with a sowing hand,
    Like kings, who many times give out of measure;
    Not for desert so much as for their pleasure.

MONTICELSO: I know you're cunning. Come, what devil
    was that
    That you were raising?

LODOVICO:              Devil, my lord?

MONTICELSO:                 I ask you
90    How doth the Duke employ you, that his bonnet
    Fell with such compliment unto his knee,
    When he departed from you?

LODOVICO:                 Why, my lord,
    He told me of a resty Barbary horse
    Which he would fain have brought to the career,
95    The 'sault, and the ring-galliard. Now, my lord,
    I have a rare French rider.

MONTICELSO:           Take you heed:
    Lest the jade break your neck. Do you put me off
    With your wild horse-tricks? Sirrah you do lie.
    O, thou'rt a foul black cloud, and thou dost threat
    A violent storm.

100 LODOVICO:         Storms are i'th' air, my lord;
    I am too low to storm.

MONTICELSO:          Wretched creature!
    I know that thou art fashion'd for all ill,

---

86. *out of measure:* excessively.    93. *resty:* restive, unruly.
97. *jade:* horse; woman.

Like dogs, that once get blood, they'll ever kill.
About some murder? Was't not?

LODOVICO:      I'll not tell you;
And yet I care not greatly if I do;     105
Marry with this preparation. Holy Father,
I come not to you as an intelligencer,
But as a penitent sinner. What I utter
Is in confession merely; which you know
Must never be reveal'd.

MONTICELSO:   You have o'ertane me.   110

LODOVICO: Sir I did love Brachiano's Duchess dearly;
Or rather I pursued her with hot lust,
Though she ne'er knew on't. She was poison'd;
Upon my soul she was: for which I have sworn
T'avenge her murder.

MONTICELSO:   To the Duke of Florence?  115

LODOVICO: To him I have.

MONTICELSO:    Miserable creature!
If thou persist in this, 'tis damnable.
Dost thou imagine thou canst slide on blood
And not be tainted with a shameful fall?
Or, like the black and melancholic yew-tree,  120
Dost think to root thyself in dead men's graves,
And yet to prosper? Instruction to thee
Comes like sweet showers to over-hard'ned ground:
They wet, but pierce not deep. And so I leave thee
With all the Furies hanging 'bout thy neck,  125
Till by thy penitence thou remove this evil,
In conjuring from thy breast that cruel devil.
  *Exit* MON[TICELSO].

LODOVICO: I'll give it o'er. He says 'tis damnable:
Besides I did expect his suffrage,

---

107. *intelligencer:* spy.   110. *o'ertane:* overreached, bested.
129. *suffrage:* approval, sanction.

130 By reason of Camillo's death.

    *Enter* SERVANT *and* FRANCISCO.

FRANCISCO: Do you know that count?

SERVANT:                             Yes, my lord.

FRANCISCO: Bear him these thousand ducats to his lodging;

    Tell him the Pope hath sent them. Happily

    That will confirm more than all the rest.

    [*Exit.*]

SERVANT:                            Sir.

    [SERVANT *delivers purse of money to* LODOVICO.]

135 LODOVICO: To me sir?

SERVANT: His Holiness hath sent you a thousand crowns,

    And wills you, if you travel, to make him

    Your patron for intelligence.

LODOVICO:                  His creature

    Ever to be commanded.

    [*Exit* SERVANT.]

140 Why now 'tis come about. He rail'd upon me;

    And yet these crowns were told out and laid ready,

    Before he knew my voyage. O the art,

    The modest form of greatness! that do sit

    Like brides at wedding dinners, with their looks turn'd

145 From the least wanton jests, their puling stomach

    Sick of the modesty, when their thoughts are loose,

    Even acting of those hot and lustful sports

    Are to ensue about midnight: such his cunning!

    He sounds my depth thus with a golden plummet;

150 I am doubly arm'd now. Now to th'act of blood;

    There's but three Furies found in spacious hell;

    But in a great man's breast three thousand dwell.

    [*Exit.*]

    145. *puling:* sickly.

# [ACT FIVE]

## [SCENE ONE]

*A passage over the stage of* BRACHIANO, FLAMINEO,
MARCELLO, HORTENSIO, [VITTORIA] COROMBONA,
CORNELIA, ZANCHE *and others.*
[*Enter* FLAMINEO *and* HORTENSIO.]

FLAMINEO: In all the weary minutes of my life,
Day ne'er broke up till now. This marriage
Confirms me happy.

HORTENSIO:        'Tis a good assurance.
Saw you not yet the Moor that's come to court?

FLAMINEO: Yes, and conferr'd with him i'th' Duke's closet;   5
I have not seen a goodlier personage,
Nor ever talk'd with man better experienc'd
In state affairs or rudiments of war.
He hath by report serv'd the Venetian
In Candy these twice seven years, and been chief   10
In many a bold design.

HORTENSIO:        What are those two
That bear him company?

FLAMINEO: Two noblemen of Hungary, that living in the
emperor's service as commanders, eight years since,
contrary to the expectation of all the court ent'red into   15
religion, into the strict order of Capuchins: but being not
well settled in their undertaking they left their order and
returned to court: for which being after troubled in
conscience, they vowed their service against the enemies
of Christ; went to Malta; were there knighted; and in   20

8. *rudiments:* principles.
20. *knighted:* in the Order of St John of Jerusalem, the Hospitallers.

their return back, at this great solemnity, they are resolved
for ever to forsake the world, and settle themselves here
in a house of Capuchins in Padua.

HORTENSIO: 'Tis strange.

25 FLAMINEO: One thing makes it so. They have vowed for
ever to wear next their bare bodies those coats of mail
they served in.

HORTENSIO: Hard penance. Is the Moor a Christian?

FLAMINEO: He is.

30 HORTENSIO: Why proffers he his service to our Duke?

FLAMINEO: Because he understands there's like to grow
Some wars between us and the Duke of Florence,
In which he hopes employment.
I never saw one in a stern bold look
35 Wear more command, nor in a lofty phrase
Express more knowing, or more deep contempt
Of our slight airy courtiers. He talks
As if he had travell'd all the princes' courts
Of Christendom; in all things strives t'express
40 That all that should dispute with him may know,
Glories, like glow-worms, afar off shine bright
But look'd to near, have neither heat nor light.
The Duke!

*Enter* BRACHIANO, [FRANCISCO, *Duke of*] *Florence*
*disguised like Mulinassar;* LODOVICO, ANTONELLI,
GASPARO [*disguised,*] FERNESE *having their swords and*
*helmets* [; CARLO *and* PEDRO].

BRACHIANO: You are nobly welcome. We have heard at
full
45 Your honourable service 'gainst the Turk.
To you, brave Mulinassar, we assign
A competent pension: and are inly sorrow,
The vows of those two worthy gentlemen

47. *competent:* sufficient; *inly:* inwardly; *sorrow:* sorry.

Make them incapable of our proffer'd bounty.
Your wish is you may leave your warlike swords          50
For monuments in our chapel. I accept it
As a great honour done me, and must crave
Your leave to furnish out our Duchess' revels.
Only one thing, as the last vanity
You e'er shall view, deny me not to stay          55
To see a barriers prepar'd tonight;
You shall have private standings. It hath pleas'd
The great ambassadors of several princes
In their return from Rome to their own countries
To grace our marriage, and to honour me          60
With such a kind of sport.

FRANCISCO:                    I shall persuade them
To stay, my lord.

BRACHIANO:        Set on there to the presence.
   *Exeunt* BRACHIANO, FLAMINEO *and* [HORTENSIO].

CARLO: Noble my lord, most fortunately welcome.
   *The conspirators here embrace.*
You have our vows seal'd with the sacrament
To second your attempts.

PEDRO:                    And all things ready.          65
He could not have invented his own ruin,
Had he despair'd, with more propriety.

LODOVICO: You would not take my way.

FRANCISCO:                              'Tis better ordered.

LODOVICO: T'have poison'd his prayer book, or a pair of
   beads,
The pommel of his saddle, his looking-glass,          70
Or th'handle of his racket. O that, that!
That while he had been bandying at tennis,

57. *standings:* standing-places.
62. *presence:* presence or audience chamber.
69. *pair:* set.        72. *bandying:* volleying.

He might have sworn himself to hell, and struck
His soul into the hazard! O my lord!
75    I would have our plot be ingenious,
And have it hereafter recorded for example
Rather than borrow example.

FRANCISCO:              There's no way
More speeding than this thought on.

LODOVICO:             On then.

FRANCISCO: And yet methinks that this revenge is poor,
80    Because it steals upon him like a thief;
To have tane him by the casque in a pitch'd field,
Led him to Florence!

LODOVICO:          It had been rare. And there
Have crown'd him with a wreath of stinking garlic,
T'have shown the sharpness of his government,
85    And rankness of his lust. Flamineo comes.

     *Exeunt* [*all save* FRANCISCO].
     *Enter* FLAMINEO, MARCELLO *and* ZANCHE.

MARCELLO: Why doth this devil haunt you? Say.

FLAMINEO:               I know not.
For by this light I do not conjure for her.
'Tis not so great a cunning as men think
To raise the devil: for here's one up already;
90    The greatest cunning were to lay him down.

MARCELLO: She is your shame.

FLAMINEO:           I prithee pardon her.
In faith you see, women are like to burs;
Where their affection throws them, there they'll stick.

ZANCHE: That is my countryman, a goodly person;
95    When he's at leisure I'll discourse with him
In our own language.

FLAMINEO:         I beseech you do.

78. *speeding:* effective.     81. *casque:* helmet.
86. *this devil:* Zanche, the black devil.     88. *cunning:* skill.

*Exit* ZANCHE.

How is't brave soldier? O that I had seen
Some of your iron days! I pray relate
Some of your service to us.

FRANCISCO: 'Tis a ridiculous thing for a man to be his own    100
chronicle; I did never wash my mouth with mine own
praise for fear of getting a stinking breath.

MARCELLO: You're too stoical. The Duke will expect other
discourse from you.

FRANCISCO: I shall never flatter him, I have studied man    105
too much to do that. What difference is between the Duke
and I? No more than between two bricks; all made of one
clay. Only't may be one is plac'd on the top of a turret;
the other in the bottom of a well by mere chance; if I were
plac'd as high as the Duke, I should stick as fast; make as    110
fair a show; and bear out weather equally.

FLAMINEO: If this soldier had a patent to beg in churches,
then he would tell them stories.

MARCELLO: I have been a soldier too.

FRANCISCO: How have you thriv'd?    115

MARCELLO: Faith, poorly.

FRANCISCO: That's the misery of peace. Only outsides are
then respected. As ships seem very great upon the river,
which show very little upon the seas: so some men i'th'
court seem. Colossuses in a chamber, who if they came    120
into the field would appear pitiful pigmies.

FLAMINEO: Give me a fair room yet hung with arras, and
some great cardinal to lug me by th'ears as his endeared
minion.

112. *patent:* licence to beg, obtained from a justice of the peace.
120. *Colossuses:* enormous statues (from the Colossus at Rhodes, one of
the seven wonders of the ancient world).
122. *arras:* a tapestry, often hung sufficiently far from the walls to
enable a spy to hide behind it.

125 FRANCISCO: And thou may'st do – the devil knows what
villainy.

FLAMINEO: And safely.

FRANCISCO: Right; you shall see in the country in harvest
time, pigeons, though they destroy never so much corn,
130 the farmer dare not present the fowling-piece to them!
Why? Because they belong to the lord of the manor;
whilst your poor sparrows that belong to the Lord of
heaven, they go to the pot for't.

FLAMINEO: I will now give you some politic instruction.
135 The Duke says he will give you pension; that's but bare
promise: get it under his hand. For I have known men
that have come from serving against the Turk; for three
or four months they have had pension to buy them new
wooden legs and fresh plasters; but after 'twas not to be
140 had. And this miserable courtesy shows, as if a tormentor
should give hot cordial drinks to one three-quarters dead
o'th' rack, only to fetch the miserable soul again to endure
more dog-days.

*Enter* HORTENSIO, *a* YOUNG LORD, ZANCHE *and two
more.*

How now, gallants; what, are they ready for the barriers?
[*Exit* FRANCISCO.]

145 YOUNG LORD: Yes: the lords are putting on their armour.

HORTENSIO: What's he?

FLAMINEO: A new upstart: one that swears like a falconer,
and will lie in the Duke's ear day by day like a maker of
almanacs; and yet I knew him since he came to th'court
150 smell worse of sweat than an under-tennis-court-keeper.

HORTENSIO: Look you, yonder's your sweet mistress.

FLAMINEO: Thou art my sworn brother; I'll tell thee, I do
love that Moor, that witch, very constrainedly: she knows

---

136. *under his hand:* in writing.
140. *miserable:* miserly, mean.     141. *cordial:* restorative.

some of my villainy; I do love her, just as a man holds a
wolf by the ears. But for fear of turning upon me, and    155
pulling out my throat, I would let her go to the devil.

HORTENSIO: I hear she claims marriage of thee.

FLAMINEO: 'Faith, I made to her some such dark promise,
and in seeking to fly from't I run on, like a frighted dog
with a bottle at's tail, that fain would bite it off and yet    160
dares not look behind him. [to ZANCHE] Now my
precious gipsy!

ZANCHE: Ay, your love to me rather cools than heats.

FLAMINEO: Marry, I am the sounder lover; we have many
wenches about the town heat too fast.    165

HORTENSIO: What do you think of these perfum'd gallants
then?

FLAMINEO: Their satin cannot save them. I am confident
They have a certain spice of the disease.
For they that sleep with dogs, shall rise with fleas.    170

ZANCHE: Believe it! A little painting and gay clothes
Make you loathe me.

FLAMINEO: How? Love a lady for painting or gay apparel?
I'll unkennel one example more for thee. Æsop had a
foolish dog that let go the flesh to catch the shadow. I    175
would have courtiers be better diners.

ZANCHE: You remember your oaths.

FLAMINEO: Lovers' oaths are like mariners' prayers, uttered
in extremity; but when the tempest is o'er, and that the
vessel leaves tumbling, they fall from protesting to    180
drinking. And yet amongst gentlemen protesting and
drinking go together, and agree as well as shoemakers

162. *gipsy:* an allusion to Zanche's dark skin.
168. *satin:* there is a pun on 'satan', which was at this time pronounced
    almost identically.
182-3. 'The shoemaker draws on shoes and salt things induce thirstiness.'
    (Sampson).

and Westphalia bacon. They are both drawers on: for
drink draws on protestation; and protestation draws on
185    more drink. Is not this discourse better now than the
morality of your sunburnt gentleman?

    *Enter* CORNELIA.

CORNELIA: Is this your perch, you haggard? Fly to th'
    stews.

    [*Strikes* ZANCHE.]

FLAMINEO: You should be clapp'd by th'heels now: strike
    i'th'court?

    [*Exit* CORNELIA.]

ZANCHE: She's good for nothing but to make her maids
190    Catch cold o'nights; they dare not use a bedstaff,
    For fear of her light fingers.

MARCELLO:              You're a strumpet.
    An impudent one.

FLAMINEO:       Why do you kick her? Say,
    Do you think that she's like a walnut-tree?
    Must she be cudgell'd ere she bear good fruit?

MARCELLO: She brags that you shall marry her.

195    FLAMINEO:                 What then?

MARCELLO: I had rather she were pitch'd upon a stake
    In some new-seeded garden, to affright
    Her fellow crows thence.

FLAMINEO:          You're a boy, a fool,
    Be guardian to your hound, I am of age.

200    MARCELLO: If I take her near you I'll cut her throat.

FLAMINEO: With a fan of feathers?

MARCELLO:              And for you, I'll whip
    This folly from you.

186. *sunburnt gentleman:* Francisco, disguised as Mulinassar.
187. *haggard:* wild hawk; wanton or intractable woman.
188. *clapp'd by th' heels:* fastened by the ankles in stocks.

FLAMINEO:                    Are you choleric?
  I'll purge't with rhubarb.
HORTENSIO:                    O your brother!
FLAMINEO:                              Hang him.
  He wrongs me most that ought t'offend me least.
  [*to* MARCELLO] I do suspect my mother play'd foul play          205
  When she conceiv'd thee.
MARCELLO:                    Now by all my hopes,
  Like the two slaught'red sons of Œdipus,
  The very flames of our affection
  Shall turn two ways. Those words I'll make thee answer
  With thy heart blood.
FLAMINEO:                    Do; like the gesses in the progress,          210
  You know where you shall find me –
MARCELLO:                              Very good.
    [*Exit* FLAMINEO.]
  And thou beest a noble friend, bear him my sword,
  And bid him fit the length on't.
YOUNG LORD:                    Sir I shall.
    [*Exeunt all but* ZANCHE.]
    *Enter* FRANCISCO *the Duke of Florence.*
ZANCHE [*aside*]: He comes. Hence petty thought of my dis-
    grace!
  I ne'er lov'd my complexion till now,          215
  Cause I may boldly say without a blush,
  I love you.
FRANCISCO: Your love is untimely sown;
  There's a Spring at Michaelmas, but 'tis but a faint one.
  I am sunk in years, and I have vowed never to marry.
ZANCHE: Alas! poor maids get more lovers than husbands.          220

----

202–3. Rhubarb was a recognized antidote for an excess of the choleric
    humour.
210. *gesses*: stopping-places on a royal progress.

Yet you may mistake my wealth. For, as when ambassadors are sent to congratulate princes, there's commonly
sent along with them a rich present; so that though the
prince like not the ambassador's person nor words, yet he
225    likes well of the presentment. So I may come to you in the
same manner, and be better loved for my dowry than my
virtue.

FRANCISCO: I'll think on the motion.

ZANCHE: Do, I'll now detain you no longer. At your better
    leisure
230    I'll tell you things shall startle your blood.
Nor blame me that this passion I reveal;
Lovers die inward that their flames conceal.

FRANCISCO [aside]: Of all intelligence this may prove the
    best,
Sure I shall draw strange fowl, from this foul nest.
    Exeunt.


## [SCENE TWO]

*Enter* MARCELLO *and* CORNELIA [*and a* PAGE, *who
remains in the background*].

CORNELIA: I hear a whispering all about the court,
You are to fight; who is your opposite?
What is the quarrel?

MARCELLO:             'Tis an idle rumour.

CORNELIA: Will you dissemble? Sure you do not well
5    To fright me thus; you never look thus pale,
But when you are most angry. I do charge you
Upon my blessing – nay I'll call the Duke,
And he shall school you.

MARCELLO:          Publish not a fear

228. *motion:* proposal.    8. *school:* punish.

Which would convert to laughter; 'tis not so.
Was not this crucifix my father's?

CORNELIA:            Yes.        10

MARCELLO: I have heard you say, giving my brother suck,
He took the crucifix between his hands,

     *Enter* FLAMINEO.

And broke a limb off.

CORNELIA:          Yes: but 'tis mended.

FLAMINEO: I have brought your weapon back.

     FLAMINEO *runs* MARCELLO *through.*

CORNELIA:              Ha, O my horror!

MARCELLO: You have brought it home indeed.

CORNELIA:              Help! O he's
                       murdered.     15

FLAMINEO: Do you turn your gall up? I'll to sanctuary,
And send a surgeon to you.

     [*Exit.*]

     *Enter* CARL[O,] HORT[ENSIO,] PEDRO.

HORTENSIO:          How? o'th' ground?

MARCELLO: O mother now remember what I told
Of breaking off the crucifix: farewell.
There are some sins which heaven doth duly punish     20
In a whole family. This it is to rise
By all dishonest means. Let all men know
That tree shall long time keep a steady foot
Whose branches spread no wider than the root.

CORNELIA: O my perpetual sorrow!

HORTENSIO:          Virtuous Marcello.     25
He's dead: pray leave him lady; come, you shall.

CORNELIA: Alas he is not dead: he's in a trance.
Why here's nobody shall get anything by his death. Let
me call him again for God's sake.

16. *gall:* the phrase seems here to be used both figuratively of dying;
and literally, because Marcello is vomiting from his wound.

30 CARLO: I would you were deceiv'd.

CORNELIA: O you abuse me, you abuse me, you abuse me.
How many have gone away thus for lack of tendance;
rear up's head, rear up's head. His bleeding inward will
kill him.

35 HORTENSIO: You see he is departed.

CORNELIA: Let me come to him; give me him as he is, if he
be turn'd to earth; let me but give him one hearty kiss, and
you shall put us both into one coffin: fetch a looking-
glass, see if his breath will not stain it; or pull out some
40 feathers from my pillow, and lay them to his lips; will you
lose him for a little pains-taking?

HORTENSIO: Your kindest office is to pray for him.

CORNELIA: Alas! I would not pray for him yet. He may
live to lay me i'th' ground, and pray for me, if you'll let
45 me come to him.

*Enter* BRACHIANO *all armed, save the beaver, with*
FLAMINEO, [FRANCISCO, *disguised as Mulinassar, and*
LODOVICO, *disguised*].

BRACHIANO: Was this your handiwork?

FLAMINEO: It was my misfortune.

CORNELIA: He lies, he lies, he did not kill him: these have
kill'd him, that would not let him be better look'd to.

50 BRACHIANO: Have comfort my griev'd mother.

CORNELIA: O you screech-owl.

HORTENSIO: Forbear, good madam.

CORNELIA: Let me go, let me go.

*She runs to* FLAMINEO *with her knife drawn and coming to*
*him lets it fall.*

The God of heaven forgive thee. Dost not wonder
55 I pray for thee? I'll tell thee what's the reason:
I have scarce breath to number twenty minutes;
I'd not spend that in cursing. Fare thee well –
Half of thyself lies there: and may'st thou live

To fill an hour-glass with his mould'red ashes,
To tell how thou shouldst spend the time to come      60
In blest repentance.

BRACHIANO:      Mother, pray tell me
How came he by his death? What was the quarrel?

CORNELIA: Indeed my younger boy presum'd too much
Upon his manhood; gave him bitter words;
Drew his sword first; and so I know not how,      65
For I was out of my wits, he fell with's head
Just in my bosom.

PAGE:      This is not true madam.

CORNELIA: I pray thee peace.
One arrow's graz'd already; it were vain
T'lose this: for that will ne'er be found again.      70

BRACHIANO: Go, bear the body to Cornelia's lodging:
And we command that none acquaint our Duchess
With this sad accident: for you Flamineo,
Hark you, I will not grant your pardon.

FLAMINEO:      No?

BRACHIANO: Only a lease of your life. And that shall last      75
But for one day. Thou shalt be forc'd each evening
To renew it, or be hang'd.

FLAMINEO:      At your pleasure.

    LODOVICO *sprinkles* BRACHIANO'S *beaver with a poison.*
Your will is law now, I'll not meddle with it.

BRACHIANO: You once did brave me in your sister's lodging;
I'll now keep you in awe for't. Where's our beaver?      80

FRANCISCO [*aside*]: He calls for his destruction. Noble youth,
I pity thy sad fate. Now to the barriers.

---

69. *graz'd*: grassed, lost in the grass.
77. S.D. *beaver*: lower part of the face-guard of a helmet.

This shall his passage to the black lake further,
The last good deed he did, he pardon'd murther.
    *Exeunt.*

## [SCENE THREE]

*Charges and shouts. They fight at barriers; first single pairs,
then three to three.*

*Enter* BRACHIANO *and* FLAMINEO *with others* [*including*
GIOVANNI, VITTORIA, *and* FRANCISCO].

BRACHIANO: An armourer! Ud's death, an armourer!

FLAMINEO: Armourer; where's the armourer?

BRACHIANO: Tear off my beaver.

FLAMINEO:                 Are you hurt, my lord?

BRACHIANO: O my brain's on fire,

    *Enter* ARMOURER.

The helmet is poison'd.

5 ARMOURER:            My lord upon my soul –

BRACHIANO: Away with him to torture.

    [*Exit* ARMOURER, *guarded.*]

There are some great ones that have hand in this,
And near about me.

VITTORIA:          O my loved lord; poison'd?

FLAMINEO: Remove the bar: here's unfortunate revels,

10     Call the physicians; a plague upon you;

    *Ent*[*er*] *two* PHYSICIANS.

We have too much of your cunning here already.
I fear the ambassadors are likewise poisoned.

BRACHIANO: O I am gone already: the infection
Flies to the brain and heart. O thou strong heart!

15     There's such a covenant 'tween the world and it,
They're loth to break.

> 83. *black lake:* the Styx.
> 9. *bar:* either the barriers or a fastening of the beaver.

GIOVANNI:                    O my most loved father!
BRACHIANO: Remove the boy away.
  Where's this good woman? Had I infinite worlds
  They were too little for thee. Must I leave thee?
  What say yon screech-owls, is the venom mortal?          20
PHYSICIANS: Most deadly.
BRACHIANO:               Most corrupted politic hangman!
  You kill without book; but your art to save
  Fails you as oft as great men's needy friends.
  I that have given life to offending slaves
  And wretched murderers, have I not power                 25
  To lengthen mine own a twelvemonth?
  [to VITTORIA] Do not kiss me, for I shall poison thee.
  This unction is sent from the great Duke of Florence.
FRANCISCO: Sir be of comfort.
BRACHIANO: O thou soft natural death, that are joint-twin  30
  To sweetest slumber: no rough-bearded comet
  Stares on thy mild departure: the dull owl
  Beats not against thy casement: the hoarse wolf
  Scents not thy carrion. Pity winds thy corse,
  Whilst horror waits on princes.
VITTORIA:                    I am lost for ever.            35
BRACHIANO: How miserable a thing it is to die
  'Mongst women howling!
      [Enter LODOVICO and GASPARO disguised as Capu-
      chins.]
                              What are those?
FLAMINEO:                           Franciscans.
  They have brought the extreme unction.

22. *without book:* by heart.
28. *unction:* ointment; extreme unction.
31. *rough-bearded comet:* rough-bearded because of its shape; comets
    were believed to presage disasters and evil.
34. *corse:* corpse.

BRACHIANO: On pain of death, let no man name death to me,

40    It is a word infinitely terrible.
Withdraw into our cabinet.

*Exeunt omnes praeter* FRANCISCO *and* FLAMINEO.

FLAMINEO: To see what solitariness is about dying princes. As heretofore they have unpeopled towns; divorc'd friends, and made great houses unhospitable: so now, O
45    justice! where are their flatterers now? Flatterers are but the shadows of princes' bodies, the least thick cloud makes them invisible.

FRANCISCO: There's great moan made for him.

FLAMINEO: 'Faith, for some few hours salt water will run
50    most plentifully in every office o'th' court. But believe it; most of them do but weep over their stepmothers' graves.

FRANCISCO: How mean you?

FLAMINEO: Why? They dissemble, as some men do that live within compass o'th' verge.

55  FRANCISCO: Come you have thriv'd well under him.

FLAMINEO: 'Faith, like a wolf in a woman's breast; I have been fed with poultry: but for money, understand me, I had as good a will to cozen him, as e'er an officer of them all. But I had not cunning enough to do it.

60  FRANCISCO: What did'st thou think of him? 'Faith speak freely.

FLAMINEO: He was a kind of statesman, that would sooner have reckon'd how many cannon-bullets he had discharged against a town, to count his expense that way,
65    than how many of his valiant and deserving subjects he lost before it.

FRANCISCO: O speak well of the Duke.

41. S.D. *Exeunt omnes praeter:* 'All leave except'.
53. *some men:* an ironic understatement (Lucas).
56. *wolf:* ulcer.

FLAMINEO: I have done. Wilt hear some of my court wis-
dom?
    *Enter* LODOVICO.
To reprehend princes is dangerous: and to over-commend
some of them is palpable lying.                                    70
FRANCISCO: How is it with the Duke?
LODOVICO:                                   Most deadly ill.
He's fall'n into a strange distraction.
He talks of battles and monopolies,
Levying of taxes, and from that descends
To the most brain-sick language. His mind fastens           75
On twenty several objects, which confound
Deep sense with folly. Such a fearful end
May teach some men that bear too lofty crest,
Though they live happiest, yet they die not best.
He hath conferr'd the whole state of the dukedom          80
Upon your sister, till the Prince arrive
At mature age.
FLAMINEO:        There's some good luck in that yet.
FRANCISCO: See here he comes.
    *Enter* BRACHIANO, *presented in a bed,* VITTORIA *and
    others [including* GASPARO].
                            There's death in's face already.
VITTORIA: O my good lord!
    *These speeches are several kinds of distractions and in the
    action should appear so.*
BRACHIANO:                          Away, you have abus'd me.
You have convey'd coin forth our territories;                 85
Bought and sold offices; oppress'd the poor,
And I ne'er dreamt on't. Make up your accounts;
I'll now be mine own steward.
FLAMINEO:                          Sir, have patience.
BRACHIANO: Indeed I am too blame.

    89. *too blame:* too blameworthy.

90     For did you ever hear the dusky raven
        Chide blackness? Or was't ever known the devil
        Rail'd against cloven creatures?

VITTORIA:               O my lord!

BRACHIANO: Let me have some quails to supper.

FLAMINEO:                 Sir, you shall.

BRACHIANO: No: some fried dog-fish. Your quails feed on
        poison –

95     That old dog-fox, that politician Florence –
        I'll forswear hunting and turn dog-killer;
        Rare! I'll be friends with him: for mark you, sir, one dog
        Still sets another a-barking: peace, peace,
        Yonder's a fine slave come in now.

FLAMINEO:                Where?

100 BRACHIANO: Why there.
        In a blue bonnet, and a pair of breeches
        With a great codpiece. Ha, ha, ha,
        Look you his codpiece is stuck full of pins
        With pearls o'th' head of them. Do not you know him?

FLAMINEO: No my lord.

105 BRACHIANO:           Why 'tis the devil.
        I know him by a great rose he wears on's shoe
        To hide his cloven foot. I'll dispute with him.
        He's a rare linguist.

VITTORIA:         My lord here's nothing.

BRACHIANO: Nothing? Rare! Nothing! When I want
        money

110     Our treasury is empty; there is nothing.
        I'll not be used thus.

VITTORIA:         O! Lie still my lord –

---

93. *quails:* birds (a delicacy); prostitutes.
94. *dog-fish:* a kind of small shark; but in common use as a term of
    abuse.
106. *rose:* rosette.

BRACHIANO: See, see, Flamineo that kill'd his brother
Is dancing on the ropes there: and he carries
A money-bag in each hand, to keep him even,
For fear of breaking's neck. And there's a lawyer      115
In a gown whipt with velvet, stares and gapes
When the money will fall. How the rogue cuts capers!
It should have been in a halter.
'Tis there; what's she?
FLAMINEO:                     Vittoria, my lord.
BRACHIANO: Ha, ha, ha. Her hair is sprinkled with orris
    powder,                                             120
That makes her look as if she had sinn'd in the pastry.
What's he?
FLAMINEO: A divine my lord.
BRACHIANO: He will be drunk. Avoid him: th'argument is
    fearful when churchmen stagger in't.
Look you; six grey rats that have lost their tails,     125
Crawl up the pillow; send for a rat-catcher.
I'll do a miracle: I'll free the court
From all foul vermin. Where's Flamineo?
FLAMINEO: I do not like that he names me so often,
Especially on's death-bed: 'tis a sign                  130
I shall not live long: see he's near his end.

> BRACHIANO *seems here near his end.* LODOVICO *and*
> GASPARO *in the habit of Capuchins present him in his bed*
> *with a crucifix and hallowed candle.*

LODOVICO: Pray give us leave: *Attende Domine Brachiane.*
FLAMINEO: See, see, how firmly he doth fix his eye
Upon the crucifix.
VITTORIA:              O hold it constant.
It settles his wild spirits; and so his eyes            135
Melt into tears.

116. *whipt:* edged, trimmed.
121. *the pastry:* kitchen where pastry is made.

LODOVICO (*By the crucifix*): *Domine Brachiane, solebas in bello tutus esse tuo clypeo, nunc hanc clypeum hosti tuo opponas infernali.*

140    GASPARO (*By the hallowed taper*): *Olim hasta valuisti in bello; nunc hanc sacram hastam vibrabis contra hostem animarum.*

LODOVICO: *Attende Domine Brachiane si nunc quoque probas ea quae acta sunt inter nos, flecte caput in dextrum.*

GASPARO: *Esto securus Domine Brachiane: cogita quantum*
145    *habeas meritorum, denique memineris meam animam pro tua oppignoratam si quid esse periculi.*

LODOVICO: *Si nunc quoque probas ea quae acta sunt inter nos, flecte caput in laevum.*

He is departing: pray stand all apart,
150    And let us only whisper in his ears
Some private meditations, which our order
Permits you not to hear.

> *Here the rest being departed* LODOVICO *and* GASPARO *discover themselves.*

GASPARO:               Brachiano.

LODOVICO: Devil Brachiano. Thou art damn'd.

GASPARO:                      Perpetually.

LODOVICO: A slave condemn'd, and given up to the gallows
Is thy great lord and master.

155    GASPARO:            True: for thou
Art given up to the devil.

LODOVICO:          O you slave!
You that were held the famous politician;
Whose art was poison.

GASPARO:          And whose conscience murder.

LODOVICO: That would have broke your wife's neck down the stairs
Ere she was poison'd.

160    GASPARO:         That had your villainous sallets —

LODOVICO: And fine embroidered bottles, and perfumes
    Equally mortal with a winter plague –
GASPARO: Now there's mercury –
LODOVICO:                                          And copperas –
GASPARO:                                              And quicksilver –
LODOVICO: With other devilish pothecary stuff
    A-melting in your politic brains: dost hear?                    165
GASPARO: This is Count Lodovico.
LODOVICO:                                   This Gasparo.
    And thou shalt die like a poor rogue.
GASPARO:                                          And stink
    Like a dead fly-blown dog.
LODOVICO: And be forgotten before thy funeral sermon.
BRACHIANO: Vittoria! Vittoria!
LODOVICO:                                O the cursed devil,          17c
    Come to himself again! We are undone.
        *Enter* VITTORIA *and the* ATTEND[ANTS].
GASPARO [*aside to* LODOVICO]: Strangle him in private.
    [*To* VITTORIA] What? Will you call him again
    To live in treble torments? For charity,
    For Christian charity, avoid the chamber.                      175
        *Exeunt* [VITTORIA *and* ATTENDANTS].
LODOVICO: You would prate, sir. This is a true-love knot
    Sent from the Duke of Florence.
        BRACHIANO *is strangled.*
GASPARO:                                What, is it done?
LODOVICO: The snuff is out. No woman-keeper i'th' world,
    Though she had practis'd seven year at the pest-house,
    Could have done't quaintlier.

163. *mercury:* mercuric chloride, or corrosive sublimate, as distinct from
    *quicksilver,* or metallic mercury; *copperas:* copper sulphate. All are
    poisonous, though the last only in large quantities.
180. *quaintlier:* more skilfully.

[*Enter* VITTORIA, FRANCISCO, FLAMINEO, *and*
ATTENDANTS.]

180                                  My lords he's dead.

OMNES: Rest to his soul.

VITTORIA:                    O me! this place is hell.

*Exit* VITTORIA [*with* ATTENDANTS *and* GASPARO].

FRANCISCO: How heavily she takes it.

FLAMINEO:                              O yes, yes;
    Had women navigable rivers in their eyes
    They would dispend them all; surely I wonder
185 Why we should wish more rivers to the city
    When they sell water so good cheap. I'll tell thee,
    These are but moonish shades of griefs or fears,
    There's nothing sooner dry than women's tears.
    Why here's an end of all my harvest, he has given me
        nothing.
190 Court promises! Let wise men count them curs'd
    For while you live he that scores best pays worst.

FRANCISCO: Sure, this was Florence' doing.

FLAMINEO:                                    Very likely.
    Those are found weighty strokes which come from
        th'hand,
    But those are killing strokes which come from th'head.
195 O the rare tricks of a Machivillian!
    He doth not come like a gross plodding slave
    And buffet you to death. No, my quaint knave,
    He tickles you to death; makes you die laughing;
    As if you had swallow'd down a pound of saffron.
200 You see the feat, 'tis practis'd in a trice:
    To teach court-honesty, it jumps on ice.

186. *so good cheap:* at such a bargain price.
187. *moonish:* changeable, like the moon.
195. *a Machivillian:* a Machiavellian, Machiavelli being supposed the
    exemplar of scheming villains.

FRANCISCO: Now have the people liberty to talk
  And descant on his vices.

FLAMINEO:                    Misery of princes,
  That must of force be censur'd by their slaves!
  Not only blam'd for doing things are ill,                        205
  But for not doing all that all men will.
  One were better be a thresher.
  Ud's death, I would fain speak with this Duke yet.

FRANCISCO: Now he's dead?

FLAMINEO: I cannot conjure; but if prayers or oaths               210
  Will get to th'speech of him: though forty devils
  Wait on him in his livery of flames,
  I'll speak to him, and shake him by the hand,
  Though I be blasted.

    *Exit* FLAMINEO.

FRANCISCO:                    Excellent Lodovico!
  What? Did you terrify him at the last gasp?                      215

LODOVICO: Yes; and so idly, that the Duke had like
  T'have terrified us.

FRANCISCO:            How?

    *Enter* [ZANCHE] *the Moor.*

LODOVICO:                    You shall hear that hereafter.
  See! yon's the infernal that would make us sport.
  Now to the revelation of that secret
  She promis'd when she fell in love with you.                    220

FRANCISCO: You're passionately met in this sad world.

ZANCHE: I would have you look up, sir; these court tears
  Claim not your tribute to them. Let those weep
  That guiltily partake in the sad cause.
  I knew last night by a sad dream I had                          225
  Some mischief would ensue; yet to say truth
  My dream most concern'd you.

LODOVICO:                    Shall's fall a-dreaming?

203. *descant*: comment.

FRANCISCO: Yes, and for fashion sake I'll dream with her.

ZANCHE: Methought sir, you came stealing to my bed.

230 FRANCISCO: Wilt thou believe me sweeting? By this light
 I was a-dreamt on thee too: for methought
 I saw thee naked.

ZANCHE:     Fie sir! as I told you,
 Methought you lay down by me.

FRANCISCO:       So dreamt I:
 And lest thou shouldst take cold, I cover'd thee
 With this Irish mantle.

235 ZANCHE:     Verily I did dream,
 You were somewhat bold with me; but to come to't.

LODOVICO: How? how? I hope you will not go to't here.

FRANCISCO: Nay: you must hear my dream out.

ZANCHE:       Well, sir, forth.

FRANCISCO: When I threw the mantle o'er thee, thou didst laugh
 Exceedingly methought.

ZANCHE:    Laugh?

240 FRANCISCO:     And cried'st out,
 The hair did tickle thee.

ZANCHE:    There was a dream indeed.

LODOVICO: Mark her I prithee, she simpers like the suds
 A collier hath been wash'd in.

ZANCHE: Come, sir; good fortune tends you; I did tell you
245  I would reveal a secret: Isabella
 The Duke of Florence' sister was empoison'd,
 By a fum'd picture: and Camillo's neck
 Was broke by damn'd Flamineo; the mischance
 Laid on a vaulting-horse.

FRANCISCO:    Most strange!

235. *Irish mantle:* blanket or plaid worn by Irish peasants till the seventeenth century, often as the only garment.
247. *fum'd:* perfumed.

ZANCHE:                               Most true.
LODOVICO: The bed of snakes is broke.                    250
ZANCHE: I sadly do confess I had a hand
  In the black deed.
FRANCISCO:          Thou kept'st their counsel –
ZANCHE:                               Right.
  For which, urg'd with contrition, I intend
  This night to rob Vittoria.
LODOVICO:                Excellent penitence!
  Usurers dream on't while they sleep out sermons.        255
ZANCHE: To further our escape, I have entreated
  Leave to retire me, till the funeral
  Unto a friend i'th' country. That excuse
  Will further our escape. In coin and jewels
  I shall, at least, make good unto your use             260
  A hundred thousand crowns.
FRANCISCO:              O noble wench!
LODOVICO: Those crowns we'll share.
ZANCHE:                         It is a dowry,
  Methinks, should make that sunburnt proverb false,
  *And wash the Ethiop white.*
FRANCISCO:            It shall, away!
ZANCHE: Be ready for our flight.
FRANCISCO:                     An hour 'fore day.       265
      *Exit* [ZANCHE] *the Moor.*
  O strange discovery! Why till now we knew not
  The circumstance of either of their deaths.
      *Enter* [ZANCHE] *the Moor.*
ZANCHE: You'll wait about midnight in the chapel?
FRANCISCO:                                 There.
LODOVICO: Why now our action's justified.
FRANCISCO:                        Tush for justice.
  What harms it justice? We now, like the partridge       270

250. *bed:* nest.

Purge the disease with laurel: for the fame
Shall crown the enterprise and quit the shame.
    *Exeunt.*

## [SCENE FOUR]

*Enter* FLAM[INEO] *and* GASP[ARO] *at one door, another
way* GIOVANNI *attended.*

GASPARO: The young Duke. Did you e'er see a sweeter
    prince?

FLAMINEO: I have known a poor woman's bastard better
    favour'd. This is behind him. Now, to his face: all com-
5    parisons were hateful. Wise was the courtly peacock,
    that being a great minion, and being compar'd for beauty,
    by some dottrels that stood by, to the kingly eagle, said
    the eagle was a far fairer bird than herself, not in respect
    of her feathers, but in respect of her long tallants. His will
10    grow out in time. My gracious lord.

GIOVANNI: I pray leave me sir.

FLAMINEO: Your Grace must be merry: 'tis I have cause to
    mourn; for wot you what said the little boy that rode
    behind his father on horseback?

15 GIOVANNI: Why, what said he?

FLAMINEO: 'When you are dead father,' said he, 'I hope
    then I shall ride in the saddle.' O 'tis a brave thing for a
    man to sit by himself: he may stretch himself in the
    stirrups, look about, and see the whole compass of the
20    hemisphere; you're now, my lord, i'th'saddle.

GIOVANNI: Study your prayers sir, and be penitent;
    'Twere fit you'd think on what hath former been,
    I have heard grief nam'd the eldest child of sin.
        *Exit* GIOV[ANNI].

7. *dottrels:* dotterels, species of plover; simpletons.
9. *tallants:* talons; talents.

FLAMINEO: Study my prayers? He threatens me divinely;
I am falling to pieces already; I care not, though, like 25
Anacharsis I were pounded to death in a mortar. And yet
that death were fitter for usurers' gold and themselves to
be beaten together, to make a most cordial cullis for the
devil.
He hath his uncle's villainous look already, 30
In *decimo-sexto*. Now sir, what are you?
   *Enter* COURTIER.
COURTIER: It is the pleasure sir, of the young Duke
That you forbear the presence, and all rooms
That owe him reverence.
FLAMINEO:               So, the wolf and the raven
Are very pretty fools when they are young. 35
Is it your office, sir, to keep me out?
COURTIER: So the Duke wills.
FLAMINEO: Verily, master courtier, extremity is not to be
used in all offices. Say that a gentlewoman were taken out
of her bed about midnight, and committed to Castle 40
Angelo, to the tower yonder, with nothing about her,
but her smock: would it not show a cruel part in the
gentleman porter to lay claim to her upper garment, pull
it o'er her head and ears; and put her in naked?
COURTIER: Very good: you are merry. 45
   [*Exit.*]
FLAMINEO: Doth he make a court ejectment of me? A
flaming firebrand casts more smoke without a chimney,
than within 't. I'll smoor some of them.
   *Enter* [FRANCISCO, *Duke of*] *Florence.*
How now? Thou art sad.

28. *cullis:* broth made by bruising meat.
31. *decimo-sexto:* a book of very small pages, each 1/16th of a full sheet
   of paper.
48. *smoor:* smother.

50  FRANCISCO: I met even now with the most piteous sight.
    FLAMINEO: Thou met'st another here, a pitiful
        Degraded courtier.
    FRANCISCO:            Your reverend mother
        Is grown a very old woman in two hours.
        I found them winding of Marcello's corse;
55      And there is such a solemn melody
        'Tween doleful songs, tears, and sad elegies:
        Such as old grandames, watching by the dead,
        Were wont t'outwear the nights with; that believe me
        I had no eyes to guide me forth the room,
        They were so o'ercharg'd with water.
60  FLAMINEO:                        I will see them.
    FRANCISCO: 'Twere much uncharity in you: for your sight
        Will add unto their tears.
    FLAMINEO:            I will see them.
        They are behind the traverse. I'll discover
        Their superstitious howling.
            [Draws the traverse.]
            CORNELIA, [ZANCHE] the Moor and three other Ladies
            discovered, winding MARCELLO'S corse. A song.
65  CORNELIA: This rosemary is wither'd, pray get fresh;
        I would have these herbs grow up in his grave
        When I am dead and rotten. Reach the bays,
        I'll tie a garland here about his head:
        'Twill keep my boy from lightning. This sheet
70      I have kept this twenty year, and every day
        Hallow'd it with my prayers; I did not think
        He should have wore it.
    ZANCHE:                    Look you; who are yonder?
    CORNELIA: O reach me the flowers.

    65. *rosemary:* traditional emblem of remembrance.
    67. *the bays:* a garland of bay leaves such as was used to crown a poet or
        victor.

ZANCHE: Her ladyship's foolish.

WOMAN:                              Alas her grief
    Hath turn'd her child again.

CORNELIA [*to* FLAMINEO]:    You're very welcome.                    75
    There's rosemary for you, and rue for you,
    Heart's-ease for you. I pray make much of it.
    I have left more for myself.

FRANCISCO:                        Lady, who's this?

CORNELIA: You are, I take it, the grave-maker.

FLAMINEO:                                          So.

ZANCHE: 'Tis Flamineo.                                                80
    [CORNELIA *takes his hand.*]

CORNELIA: Will you make me such a fool? Here's a white
    hand:
    Can blood so soon be wash'd out? Let me see:
       CORNELIA *doth this in several forms of distraction.*
    When screech-owls croak upon the chimney tops,
    And the strange cricket i'th' oven sings and hops,
    When yellow spots do on your hands appear,                    85
    Be certain then you of a corse shall hear.
    Out upon't, how 'tis speckled! H'as handled a toad sure.
    Cowslip-water is good for the memory:
    Pray buy me three ounces of't.

FLAMINEO: I would I were from hence.

CORNELIA:                              Do you hear, sir?            90
    I'll give you a saying which my grandmother
    Was wont, when she heard the bell toll, to sing o'er
    Unto her lute –

FLAMINEO:       Do and you will, do.

CORNELIA: *Call for the robin red breast and the wren,*
    *Since o'er shady groves they hover,*                         95
    *And with leaves and flow'rs do cover*
    *The friendless bodies of unburied men.*

    87. *H'as:* he has.

*Call unto his funeral dole*
*The ant, the field-mouse, and the mole*
100 *To rear him hillocks, that shall keep him warm*
*And (when gay tombs are robb'd) sustain no harm,*
*But keep the wolf far thence: that's foe to men,*
*For with his nails he'll dig them up again.*
They would not bury him 'cause he died in a quarrel
105 But I have an answer for them.
*Let holy church receive him duly*
*Since he paid the church tithes truly.*
His wealth is summ'd, and this is all his store:
This poor men get; and great men get no more.
110 Now the wares are gone, we may shut up shop.
Bless you all good people.
        *Exeunt* CORNELIA [ZANCHE] *and Ladies.*
    FLAMINEO: I have a strange thing in me, to the which
        I cannot give a name, without it be
        Compassion; I pray leave me.
            *Exit* FRANCISCO.
115 This night I'll know the utmost of my fate,
        I'll be resolv'd what my rich sister means
        T'assign me for my service. I have liv'd
        Riotously ill, like some that live in court.
        And sometimes, when my face was full of smiles
120 Have felt the maze of conscience in my breast.
        Oft gay and honour'd robes those tortures try,
        *We think cag'd birds sing, when indeed they cry.*
            *Enter* BRACHIA[NO'S] *Ghost. In his leather cassock and*
            *breeches, boots, a cowl [and in his hand] a pot of lily-flowers*
            *with a skull in't.*
        Ha! I can stand thee. Nearer, nearer yet.
        What a mockery hath death made of thee? Thou look'st
        sad.
125 In what place art thou? in yon starry gallery,

Or in the cursed dungeon? No? not speak?
Pray, sir, resolve me, what religion's best
For a man to die in? or is it in your knowledge
To answer me how long I have to live?
That's the most necessary question.                           130
Not answer? Are you still like some great men
That only walk like shadows up and down,
And to no purpose: say:
   *The ghost throws earth upon him and shows him the skull.*
What's that? O fatal! He throws earth upon me.
A dead man's skull beneath the roots of flowers.              135
I pray speak sir; our Italian churchmen
Make us believe, dead men hold conference
With their familiars, and many times
Will come to bed to them, and eat with them.
   *Exit Ghost.*
He's gone; and see, the skull and earth are vanish'd.         140
This is beyond melancholy. I do dare my fate
To do its worst. Now to my sister's lodging,
And sum up all these horrors; the disgrace
The Prince threw on me; next the piteous sight
Of my dead brother; and my mother's dotage;                   145
And last this terrible vision. All these
Shall with Vittoria's bounty turn to good,
Or I will drown this weapon in her blood.
   *Exit.*


## [SCENE FIVE]

*Enter* FRANCISCO, LODOVICO, *and* HORTENSIO
[*over-hearing them*].
LODOVICO: My lord upon my soul you shall no further:

138. *familiars*: familiar spirits; friends or relations.

You have most ridiculously engag'd yourself
Too far already. For my part, I have paid
All my debts, so if I should chance to fall
5    My creditors fall not with me; and I vow
To 'quite all in this bold assembly
To the meanest follower. My lord leave the city,
Or I'll forswear the murder.

FRANCISCO:                         Farewell Lodovico.
If thou dost perish in this glorious act,
10    I'll rear unto thy memory that fame
Shall in the ashes keep alive thy name.

[*Exeunt* FRANCISCO *and* LODOVICO.]

HORTENSIO: There's some black deed on foot. I'll presently
Down to the citadel, and raise some force.
These strong court factions that do brook no checks,
15    In the career oft break the riders' necks.

[*Exit.*]

## [SCENE SIX]

*Enter* VITTORIA *with a book in her hand,* ZANCHE;
FLAMINEO *following them.*

FLAMINEO: What, are you at your prayers? Give o'er.

VITTORIA:                              How ruffin?

FLAMINEO: I come to you 'bout worldly business:
Sit down, sit down. Nay, stay blouze, you may hear it,
The doors are fast enough.

VITTORIA:                         Ha, are you drunk?

FLAMINEO: Yes, yes, with wormwood water; you shall
5    taste
Some of it presently.

6. '*quite:* requite, repay.
1. *ruffin:* devil (slang term).       3. *blouze:* slattern.
5. *wormwood water:* an emblem of spiritual bitterness.

VITTORIA:                    What intends the fury?
FLAMINEO: You are my lord's executrix, and I claim
  Reward, for my long service.
VITTORIA:                    For your service?
FLAMINEO: Come therefore, here is pen and ink, set down
  What you will give me.                                                    10
VITTORIA: There.
  *She writes.*
FLAMINEO:              Ha! have you done already?
  'Tis a most short conveyance.
VITTORIA:                    I will read it.
  [*Reads*] *I give that portion to thee, and no other*
  *Which Cain groan'd under having slain his brother.*
FLAMINEO: A most courtly patent to beg by.
VITTORIA:                              You are a villain.    15
FLAMINEO: Is't come to this? They say affrights cure agues:
  Thou hast a devil in thee; I will try
  If I can scare him from thee. Nay sit still:
  My lord hath left me yet two case of jewels
  Shall make me scorn your bounty; you shall see them.    20
  [*Exit.*]
VITTORIA: Sure he's distracted.
ZANCHE:                    O he's desperate!
  For your own safety give him gentle language.
  *He enters with two case of pistols.*
FLAMINEO: Look, these are better far at a dead lift,
  Than all your jewel house.
VITTORIA:                    And yet methinks,
  These stones have no fair lustre, they are ill set.    25
FLAMINEO: I'll turn the right side towards you: you shall see
  How they will sparkle.
VITTORIA:                    Turn this horror from me:

12. *conveyance*: document by which property is transferred.
23. *at a dead lift*: in a tight corner; but Flamineo is punning on 'dead'.

What do you want? What would you have me do?
Is not all mine, yours? Have I any children?

30 FLAMINEO: Pray thee good woman do not trouble me
With this vain worldly business; say your prayers;
I made a vow to my deceased lord,
Neither yourself, nor I should outlive him,
The numb'ring of four hours.

VITTORIA:        Did he enjoin it?

35 FLAMINEO: He did, and 'twas a deadly jealousy,
Lest any should enjoy thee after him,
That urg'd him vow me to it. For my death,
I did propound it voluntarily, knowing
If he could not be safe in his own court
40 Being a great Duke, what hope then for us?

VITTORIA: This is your melancholy and despair.

FLAMINEO:          Away;
Fool that thou art to think that politicians
Do use to kill the effects of injuries
And let the cause live: shall we groan in irons,
45 Or be a shameful and a weighty burthen
To a public scaffold? This is my resolve:
I would not live at any man's entreaty
Nor die at any's bidding.

VITTORIA:       Will you hear me?

FLAMINEO: My life hath done service to other men,
50 My death shall serve mine own turn; make you ready.

VITTORIA: Do you mean to die indeed?

FLAMINEO:        With as much pleasure
As e'er my father gat me.

VITTORIA [aside to ZANCHE]: Are the doors lock'd?

ZANCHE: Yes madam.

VITTORIA: Are you grown an atheist? Will you turn your
body,
55 Which is the goodly palace of the soul

156

To the soul's slaughter house? O the cursed devil
Which doth present us with all other sins
Thrice candied o'er; despair with gall and stibium,
Yet we carouse it off; [*aside to* ZANCHE] Cry out for help.
Makes us forsake that which was made for man,                    60
The world, to sink to that was made for devils,
Eternal darkness.

ZANCHE:            Help, help!

FLAMINEO:                      I'll stop your throat
With winter plums –

VITTORIA:            I prithee yet remember,
Millions are now in graves, which at last day
Like mandrakes shall rise shrieking.

FLAMINEO:                      Leave your prating,    65
For these are but grammatical laments,
Feminine arguments, and they move me
As some in pulpits move their auditory
More with their exclamation than sense
Of reason, or sound doctrine.

ZANCHE [*aside*]:            Gentle madam          70
Seem to consent, only persuade him teach
The way to death; let him die first.

VITTORIA [*aside*]: 'Tis good, I apprehend it.
To kill oneself is meat that we must take
Like pills, not chew't, but quickly swallow it;            75
The smart o'th' wound, or weakness of the hand
May else bring treble torments.

FLAMINEO:                      I have held it
A wretched and most miserable life,
Which is not able to die.

VITTORIA:            O but frailty!

58. *despair:* see V, iv, 141, note, p. 431; *gall:* bile; bitterness; *stibium:* antimony.
66. *grammatical laments:* laments made according to formal rules.
69. *exclamation:* formal declamation.

80 Yet I am now resolv'd; farewell affliction.
Behold Brachiano, I that while you liv'd
Did make a flaming altar of my heart
To sacrifice unto you; now am ready
To sacrifice heart and all. Farewell Zanche.

85 ZANCHE: How madam! Do you think that I'll outlive you?
Especially when my best self Flamineo
Goes the same voyage.

FLAMINEO:                O most loved Moor!

ZANCHE: Only, by all my love let me entreat you;
Since it is most necessary none of us
90 Do violence on ourselves; let you or I
Be her sad taster, teach her how to die.

FLAMINEO: Thou dost instruct me nobly; take these pistols,
Because my hand is stain'd with blood already:
Two of these you shall level at my breast,
95 Th' other 'gainst your own, and so we'll die,
Most equally contented. But first swear
Not to outlive me.

VITTORIA and ZANCHE: Most religiously.

FLAMINEO: Then here's an end of me: farewell daylight;
And O contemptible physic! that dost take
100 So long a study, only to preserve
So short a life, I take my leave of thee.
    *Showing the pistols.*
These are two cupping-glasses, that shall draw
All my infected blood out.
Are you ready?

VITTORIA and ZANCHE: Ready.

105 FLAMINEO: Whither shall I go now? O Lucian thy ridiculous purgatory! to find Alexander the Great cobbling

---

95. *Th' other:* i.e. the other pair of pistols.
102–3. *cupping-glasses:* surgical vessels used to draw off *infected blood*
    by the creation of a heat-induced vacuum.

shoes, Pompey tagging points, and Julius Caesar making
hair buttons, Hannibal selling blacking, and Augustus
crying garlic, Charlemagne selling lists by the dozen, and
King Pippin crying apples in a cart drawn with one horse. 110
Whether I resolve to fire, earth, water, air,
Or all the elements by scruples, I know not
Nor greatly care. Shoot, shoot,
Of all deaths the violent death is best,
For from ourselves it steals ourselves so fast 115
The pain once apprehended is quite past.
      *They shoot and run to him and tread upon him.*
VITTORIA: What, are you dropp'd?
FLAMINEO: I am mix'd with earth already. As you are noble
Perform your vows, and bravely follow me.
VITTORIA: Whither? to hell?
ZANCHE:                    To most assured damnation. 120
VITTORIA: O thou most cursed devil.
ZANCHE:                           Thou art caught –
VITTORIA: In thine own engine; I tread the fire out
That would have been my ruin.
FLAMINEO: Will you be perjur'd? What a religious oath
was Styx that the gods never durst swear by and violate? 125
O that we had such an oath to minister, and to be so well
kept in our courts of justice.
VITTORIA: Think whither thou art going.
ZANCHE:                                And remember
What villanies thou hast acted.
VITTORIA:                       This thy death
Shall make me like a blazing ominous star, 130
Look up and tremble.

---

107. *tagging points*: 'fixing metal tags on the laces or points which
    largely did the work of buttons in Elizabethan dress' (Lucas).
109. *lists*: strips of cloth.
112. *by scruples*: little by little.

FLAMINEO:          O I am caught with a springe!

VITTORIA: You see the fox comes many times short home,
   'Tis here prov'd true.

FLAMINEO:         Kill'd with a couple of braches.

VITTORIA: No fitter offering for the infernal Furies
135    Than one in whom they reign'd while he was living.

FLAMINEO: O the way's dark and horrid! I cannot see,
   Shall I have no company?

VITTORIA:          O yes thy sins
   Do run before thee to fetch fire from hell,
   To light thee thither.

FLAMINEO:        O I smell soot,
140    Most stinking soot, the chimney is a-fire,
   My liver's parboil'd like Scotch holy-bread;
   There's a plumber, laying pipes in my guts, it scalds;
   Wilt thou outlive me?

ZANCHE:         Yes, and drive a stake
   Through thy body; for we'll give it out,
145    Thou didst this violence upon thyself.

FLAMINEO: O cunning devils! now I have try'd your love,
   And doubled all your reaches. I am not wounded:
      FLAMINEO *riseth.*
   The pistols held no bullets: 'Twas a plot
   To prove your kindness to me; and I live
150    To punish your ingratitude; I knew
   One time or other you would find a way
   To give me a strong potion. O men
   That lie upon your death-beds, and are haunted
   With howling wives, ne'er trust them; they'll remarry
155    Ere the worm pierce your winding sheet; ere the spider
   Make a thin curtain for your epitaphs.
   How cunning you were to discharge! Do you practise at

131. *springe:* snare.     132. *short home:* tailless (and hence, dead).
133. *braches:* bitches.     141. *parboil'd:* partially boiled.
147. *doubled all your reaches:* matched all your scheming.

the Artillery Yard? Trust a woman? Never, never;
Brachiano be my precedent: we lay our souls to pawn to
the devil for a little pleasure, and a woman makes the bill    160
of sale. That ever man should marry! For one Hypermnestra that sav'd her lord and husband, forty-nine of her
sisters cut their throats all in one night. There was a shoal
of virtuous horse-leeches.

Here are two other instruments.

    *Enter* LOD[OVICO], GASP[ARO,] CARLO, PEDRO.

VITTORIA:                       Help, help!    165
FLAMINEO: What noise is that? Hah? False keys i'th' court.
LODOVICO: We have brought you a masque.
FLAMINEO:                 A matachin it seems,
  By your drawn swords. Churchmen turn'd revellers.
CONSPIRATORS: Isabella, Isabella!
  [*They throw off their disguises.*]
LODOVICO: Do you know us now?
FLAMINEO:              Lodovico and Gasparo.    170
LODOVICO: Yes, and that Moor the Duke gave pension to
  Was the great Duke of Florence.
VITTORIA:             O we are lost.
FLAMINEO: You shall not take justice from forth my hands;
  O let me kill her. – I'll cut my safety
  Through your coats of steel. Fate's a spaniel,    175
  We cannot beat it from us. What remains now?
  Let all that do ill take this precedent:
  *Man may his fate forsee, but not prevent.*
  And of all axioms this shall win the prize,
  *'Tis better to be fortunate than wise.*    180
GASPARO: Bind him to the pillar.
VITTORIA:            O your gentle pity!
  I have seen a blackbird that would sooner fly
  To a man's bosom,.than to stay the gripe

183. *stay:* await.

161

Of the fierce sparrow-hawk.

GASPARO:                    Your hope deceives you.

VITTORIA: If Florence be i'th' court, would he would kill
185    me.

GASPARO: Fool! Princes give rewards with their own
          hands,
But death or punishment by the hands of others.

LODOVICO: Sirrah you once did strike me; I'll strike you
Into the centre.

190 FLAMINEO: Thou'lt do it like a hangman; a base hangman;
Not like a noble fellow, for thou seest
I cannot strike again.

LODOVICO:                Dost laugh?

FLAMINEO: Wouldst have me die, as I was born, in whining?

GASPARO: Recommend yourself to heaven.

FLAMINEO: No I will carry mine own commendations
195    thither.

LODOVICO: O could I kill you forty times a day
And use't four year together; 'twere too little:
Nought grieve's but that you are too few to feed
The famine of our vengeance. What dost think on?

200 FLAMINEO: Nothing; of nothing: leave thy idle questions;
I am i'th'way to study a long silence,
To prate were idle; I remember nothing.
There's nothing of so infinite vexation
As man's own thoughts.

LODOVICO:                O thou glorious strumpet,
205 Could I divide thy breath from this pure air
When't leaves thy body, I would suck it up
And breathe't upon some dunghill.

VITTORIA:                          You, my death's-man;
Methinks thou dost not look horrid enough,
Thou hast too good a face to be a hangman;

189. *the centre:* the heart.   198. *grieve's:* grieves us.   202. *idle:* useless.

If thou be, do thy office in right form; 210
  Fall down upon thy knees and ask forgiveness.
LODOVICO: O thou hast been a most prodigious comet,
  But I'll cut off your train: kill the Moor first.
VITTORIA: You shall not kill her first. Behold my breast,
  I will be waited on in death; my servant 215
  Shall never go before me.
GASPARO: Are you so brave?
VITTORIA:                          Yes, I shall welcome death
  As princes do some great ambassadors;
  I'll meet thy weapon half way.
LODOVICO:                          Thou dost tremble,
  Methinks fear should dissolve thee into air. 220
VITTORIA: O thou art deceived, I am too true a woman:
  Conceit can never kill me: I'll tell thee what;
  I will not in my death shed one base tear,
  Or if I look pale, for want of blood, not fear.
CARLO: Thou art my task, black fury.
ZANCHE:                          I have blood 225
  As red as either of theirs: wilt drink some?
  'Tis good for the falling sickness. I am proud
  Death cannot alter my complexion,
  For I shall ne'er look pale.
LODOVICO:                          Strike, strike,
  With a joint motion.
    [*They strike.*]
VITTORIA:                          'Twas a manly blow. 230
  The next thou giv'st, murder some sucking infant,
  And then thou wilt be famous.
FLAMINEO:                          O what blade is't?
  A toledo, or an English fox?
  I ever thought a cutler should distinguish

213. *train:* comet's trail; retinue (here Zanche).
222. *Conceit:* imagination; vanity.

235 The cause of my death, rather than a doctor.
Search my wound deeper: tent it with the steel
That made it.

VITTORIA: O my greatest sin lay in my blood.
Now my blood pays for't.

FLAMINEO:                  Th'art a noble sister,
240 I love thee now; if woman do breed man
She ought to teach him manhood. Fare thee well.
Know many glorious women that are fam'd
For masculine virtue, have been vicious,
Only a happier silence did betide them.
245 She hath no faults, who hath the art to hide them.

VITTORIA: My soul, like to a ship in a black storm,
Is driven I know not whither.

FLAMINEO:                  Then cast anchor.
*Prosperity doth bewitch men seeming clear,*
*But seas do laugh, show white, when rocks are near.*
250 *We cease to grieve, cease to be Fortune's slaves,*
*Nay cease to die by dying.* [*To* ZANCHE] Art thou gone?
[*To* VITTORIA] And thou so near the bottom? False report
Which says that women vie with the nine Muses
For nine tough durable lives. I do not look
255 Who went before, nor who shall follow me;
No, at myself I will begin and end.
*While we look up to heaven we confound*
*Knowledge with knowledge. O I am in a mist.*

VITTORIA: O happy they that never saw the court,
260 *Nor ever knew great man but by report.*

      VITTORIA *dies.*

FLAMINEO: I recover like a spent taper, for a flash
And instantly go out.
Let all that belong to great men remember th'old wives'

236. *tent:* probe.
238–9. *blood . . . blood* (i) passion, sexual appetite; (ii) life-blood.

tradition, to be like the lions i'th' Tower on Candlemas
day, to mourn if the sun shine, for fear of the pitiful re-    265
mainder of winter to come.
'Tis well yet there's some goodness in my death,
My life was a black charnel. I have caught
An everlasting cold. I have lost my voice
Most irrecoverably. Farewell glorious villains,    270
*This busy trade of life appears most vain,*
*Since rest breeds rest, where all seek pain by pain.*
Let no harsh flattering bells resound my knell,
Strike thunder, and strike loud to my farewell.
    *Dies.*
    *Enter* [AMBASSADORS] *and* GIOVANNI. [GUARDS
    *follow.*]
ENGLISH AMBASSADOR: This way, this way, break ope
    the doors, this way.    275
LODOVICO: Ha, are we betray'd?
    Why then let's constantly die all together,
    And having finish'd this most noble deed,
    Defy the worst of fate; not fear to bleed.
ENGLISH AMBASSADOR: Keep back the Prince: shoot,
                                                    shoot –
    [GUARDS *shoot at conspirators.*]
LODOVICO:                                O I am wounded.    280
    I fear I shall be tane.
GIOVANNI:                You bloody villains,
    By what authority have you committed
    This massacre?
LODOVICO:        By thine.
GIOVANNI:                        Mine?
LODOVICO:                                Yes, thy uncle,
    Which is a part of thee enjoin'd us to't:
    Thou know'st me I am sure, I am Count Lodowick,    285
    And thy most noble uncle in disguise

Was last night in thy court.

GIOVANNI: Ha!

CARLO: Yes, that Moor
Thy father chose his pensioner.

GIOVANNI: He turn'd murderer?
Away with them to prison, and to torture;
290 All that have hands in this, shall taste our justice,
As I hope heaven.

LODOVICO: I do glory yet
That I can call this act mine own. For my part,
The rack, the gallows, and the torturing wheel
Shall be but sound sleeps to me; here's my rest:
295 *I limb'd this night-piece and it was my best.*

GIOVANNI: Remove the bodies; see my honoured lord,
What use you ought make of their punishment.
*Let guilty men remember their black deeds*
*Do lean on crutches, made of slender reeds.*
[*Exeunt.*]

300 Instead of an Epilogue only this of Martial supplies me:

*Haec fuerint nobis praemia si placui.*

For the action of the play, 'twas generally well, and I dare
affirm, with the joint testimony of some of their own
quality, (for the true imitation of life, without striving to
305 make nature a monster) the best that ever became them:
whereof as I make a general acknowledgement, so in
particular I must remember the well approved industry
of my friend Master Perkins, and confess the worth of his
action did crown both the beginning and end.

**FINIS**

295. *limb'd:* limned, painted; *night-piece:* painting of a night scene.
304. *quality:* profession.

# THE
# TRAGEDY
## OF THE DVTCHESSE
## Of Malfy.

*As it was Presented priuatly, at the Black-*
*Friers; and publiquely at the Globe, By the*
Kings Maiesties Seruants.

The perfect and exact Coppy, with diuerse
*things Printed, that the length of the Play would*
not beare in the Presentment.

VVritten by *John Webster.*

Hora.——— Si quid——
———Candidus Imperti si non his vtere mecum.

LONDON:

Printed by NICHOLAS OKES, for IOHN
WATERSON, and are to be sold at the
signe of the Crowne, in *Paules*
Church-yard, 1623.

# DRAMATIS PERSONAE

FERDINAND, Duke of Calabria, and twin brother to the DUCHESS.

The CARDINAL, their elder brother.

DANIEL DE BOSOLA, their spy; provisor of the horse to the DUCHESS.

ANTONIO BOLOGNA, Steward of the DUCHESS's household.

DELIO, his friend.

CASTRUCHIO, an elderly courtier, husband to JULIA.

The Marquis of PESCARA, a soldier.

Count MALATESTE, a Roman courtier.

SILVIO
RODERIGO  }Courtiers at Amalfi.
GRISOLAN

The DOCTOR.

*FOROBOSCO, an official at the DUCHESS's court.

The DUCHESS OF MALFI, a widow, afterwards secretly married to ANTONIO.

CARIOLA, her waiting-woman.

JULIA, wife of CASTRUCHIO, and mistress to the CARDINAL.

OLD LADY, a midwife.

Two Pilgrims.

Eight Madmen, comprising an Astrologer, Broker, Doctor, English Tailor, Farmer, Gentleman Usher, Lawyer, and Priest.

Court Officers; Attendants; Servants; Guards; Executioners; Churchmen.

Ladies-in-Waiting.

* a ghost part (see the dramatis personae of *The White Devil*)

*To the Right Honourable* GEORGE HARDING,
BARON BERKELEY, *of Berkeley Castle
and Knight of the Order of the Bath
to the illustrious Prince* CHARLES.

My Noble Lord,                                                        5

   That I may present my excuse why, (being a stranger to your
Lordship), I offer this poem to your patronage, I plead this
warrant; men, who never saw the sea, yet desire to behold that
regiment of waters, choose some eminent river to guide them
thither; and make that as it were, their conduct, or postilion. By    10
the like ingenious means has your fame arrived at my knowledge,
receiving it from some of worth, who both in contemplation, and
practice, owe to your Honour their clearest service. I do not
altogether look up at your title: the ancientest nobility, being but
a relic of time past, and the truest honour indeed being for a man   15
to confer honour on himself, which your learning strives to
propagate, and shall make you arrive at the dignity of a great
example. I am confident this work is not unworthy your Honour's
perusal for by such poems as this, poets have kissed the hands of
great princes, and drawn their gentle eyes to look down upon        20
their sheets of paper, when the poets themselves were bound up in
their winding sheets. The like courtesy from your Lordship, shall
make you live in your grave, and laurel spring out of it; when the
ignorant scorners of the Muses (that like worms in libraries, seem to
live only to destroy learning) shall wither, neglected and forgotten. 25
This work and myself I humbly present to your approved censure.
It being the utmost of my wishes, to have your honourable self my
weighty and perspicuous comment: which grace so done me, shall
ever be acknowledged

                                        By your Lordship's            30
                                        in all duty and
                                        observance,
                                        John Webster.

10. *conduct:* guide.        13. *clearest:* most complete.
26. *approved censure:* experienced judgement.

*In the just worth, of that well deserver*
MR JOHN WEBSTER,
*and upon this masterpiece of tragedy.*

In this thou imitat'st one rich, and wise,
That sees his good deeds done before he dies;
As he by works, thou by this work of fame,
Hast well provided for thy living name;
To trust to others' honourings, is worth's crime,
Thy monument is rais'd in thy life time;
And 'tis most just; for every worthy man
Is his own marble; and his merit can
Cut him to any figure, and express
More art, than Death's cathedral palaces,
Where royal ashes keep their court: thy note
Be ever plainness, 'tis the richest coat:
Thy epitaph only the title be,
Write, *Duchess*, that will fetch a tear for thee,
For who e'er saw this *Duchess* live, and die,
That could get off under a bleeding eye?

                    In Tragaediam.
Ut lux ex tenebris ictu percussa tonantis;
Illa, (ruina malis) claris sit vita poetis.
                              Thomas Middletonus,
                                    Poeta & Chron:
                                        Londinensis.

*To his friend* MR JOHN WEBSTER
*Upon his*
DUCHESS OF MALFI.


I never saw thy Duchess, till the day,
That she was lively body'd in thy play;                          5
Howe'er she answer'd her low-rated love,
Her brothers' anger did so fatal prove,
Yet my opinion is, she might speak more;
But never (in her life) so well before.

                                        WIL: ROWLEY.    10


*To the reader of the author,*
*and his*
DUCHESS OF MALFI.


Crown him a poet, whom nor Rome, nor Greece,
Transcend in all theirs, for a masterpiece:                      15
In which, whiles words and matter change, and men
Act one another; he, from whose clear pen
They all took life, to memory hath lent
A lasting fame, to raise his monument.

                                        JOHN FORD    20

5. *body'd:* embodied.
6. *answer'd:* justified.

# [ACT ONE]

## [SCENE ONE]

[*Enter* ANTONIO *and* DELIO.]

DELIO: You are welcome to your country, dear Antonio,
You have been long in France, and you return
A very formal Frenchman, in your habit.
How do you like the French court?

ANTONIO:               I admire it;
In seeking to reduce both State and people       5
To a fix'd order, their judicious King
Begins at home. Quits first his royal palace
Of flatt'ring sycophants, of dissolute,
And infamous persons, which he sweetly terms
His Master's master-piece, the work of Heaven,     10
Consid'ring duly, that a Prince's court
Is like a common fountain, whence should flow
Pure silver-drops in general. But if't chance
Some curs'd example poison't near the head,
*Death and diseases through the whole land spread.*    15
And what is't makes this blessed government,
But a most provident Council, who dare freely
Inform him, the corruption of the times?
Though some o'th' court hold it presumption
To instruct Princes what they ought to do,       20
It is a noble duty to inform them
What they ought to foresee. Here comes Bosola
     [*Enter* BOSOLA.]
The only court-gall: yet I observe his railing

3. *habit:* dress.        13. *in general:* everywhere.
23. *court-gall:* court sore-spot or source of bitterness.

Is not for simple love of piety:
25 Indeed he rails at those things which he wants,
Would be as lecherous, covetous, or proud,
Bloody, or envious, as any man,
If he had means to be so. Here's the Cardinal.
[*Enter* CARDINAL.]
BOSOLA: I do haunt you still.
30 CARDINAL: So.
BOSOLA: I have done you better service than to be slighted
thus. Miserable age, where only the reward of doing well,
is the doing of it!
CARDINAL: You enforce your merit too much.
35 BOSOLA: I fell into the galleys in your service, where, for
two years together, I wore two towels instead of a shirt,
with a knot on the shoulder, after the fashion of a Roman
mantle. Slighted thus? I will thrive some way: blackbirds
fatten best in hard weather: why not I, in these dog-days?
40 CARDINAL: Would you could become honest –
BOSOLA: With all your divinity, do but direct me the way
to it. I have known many travel far for it, and yet return
as arrant knaves, as they went forth; because they carried
themselves always along with them.
[*Exit* CARDINAL.]
45 Are you gone? Some fellows, they say, are possessed with
the devil, but this great fellow were able to possess the
greatest devil, and make him worse.
ANTONIO: He hath denied thee some suit?
BOSOLA: He and his brother are like plum trees, that grow
50 crooked over standing pools, they are rich, and o'erladen
with fruit, but none but crows, pies, and caterpillars feed
on them. Could I be one of their flatt'ring panders, I

32. *only the reward:* the only reward.
39. *dog-days:* see note to *The White Devil*, III, ii, 201 (p. 89).
50. *standing pools:* stagnant pools.          51. *pies:* magpies.

would hang on their ears like a horse-leech, till I were full, and then drop off. I pray leave me. Who would rely upon these miserable dependences, in expectation to be advanc'd tomorrow? What creature ever fed worse, than hoping Tantalus; nor ever died any man more fearfully, than he that hop'd for a pardon? There are rewards for hawks, and dogs, when they have done us service; but for a soldier, that hazards his limbs in a battle, nothing but a kind of geometry is his last supportation. 55 60

DELIO: Geometry?

BOSOLA: Ay, to hang in a fair pair of slings, take his latter swing in the world, upon an honourable pair of crutches, from hospital to hospital: fare ye well sir. And yet do not you scorn us, for places in the court are but like beds in the hospital, where this man's head lies at that man's foot, and so lower and lower. 65

    [*Exit* BOSOLA.]

DELIO: I knew this fellow seven years in the galleys,
For a notorious murder, and 'twas thought
The Cardinal suborn'd it: he was releas'd
By the French general, Gaston de Foix
When he recover'd Naples. 70

ANTONIO:           'Tis great pity
He should be thus neglected, I have heard
He's very valiant. This foul melancholy
Will poison all his goodness, for, I'll tell you,
If too immoderate sleep be truly said
To be an inward rust unto the soul;
It then doth follow want of action
Breeds all black malcontents, and their close rearing,
Like moths in cloth, do hurt for want of wearing. 75 80

---

55. *dependences:* appointments in reversion.
60–61. *a kind of geometry:* the crutches are being compared to compasses or dividers.

## [SCENE TWO]

[*Enter* CASTRUCHIO, SILVIO, RODERIGO *and*
GRISOLAN.]

DELIO: The presence 'gins to fill. You promis'd me
To make me the partaker of the natures
Of some of your great courtiers.

ANTONIO:            The Lord Cardinal's
And other strangers', that are now in court?

5   I shall. Here comes the great Calabrian Duke.
[*Enter* FERDINAND.]

FERDINAND: Who took the ring oft'nest?

SILVIO: Antonio Bologna, my lord.

FERDINAND: Our sister Duchess' great master of her household? Give him the jewel: when shall we leave this

10   sportive action, and fall to action indeed?

CASTRUCHIO: Methinks, my lord, you should not desire to
go to war, in person.

FERDINAND [*aside*]: Now, for some gravity: why, my lord?

CASTRUCHIO: It is fitting a soldier arise to be a prince, but

15   not necessary a prince descend to be a captain!

FERDINAND: No?

CASTRUCHIO: No, my lord, he were far better do it by a
deputy.

FERDINAND: Why should he not as well sleep, or eat, by a

20   deputy? This might take idle, offensive, and base office
from him, whereas the other deprives him of honour.

CASTRUCHIO: Believe my experience: that realm is never
long in quiet, where the ruler is a soldier.

FERDINAND: Thou told'st me thy wife could not endure

25   fighting.

CASTRUCHIO: True, my lord.

---

1. *presence:* audience chamber.      6. *took the ring:* i.e. jousting.

FERDINAND: And of a jest she broke, of a captain she met full of wounds: I have forgot it.

CASTRUCHIO: She told him, my lord, he was a pitiful fellow, to lie, like the children of Ismael, all in tents. 30

FERDINAND: Why, there's a wit were able to undo all the chirurgeons o' the city, for although gallants should quarrel, and had drawn their weapons, and were ready to go to it; yet her persuasions would make them put up.

CASTRUCHIO: That she would, my lord. 35
How do you like my Spanish jennet?

RODERIGO: He is all fire.

FERDINAND: I am of Pliny's opinion, I think he was begot by the wind; he runs as if he were ballass'd with quick-silver. 40

SILVIO: True, my lord, he reels from the tilt often.

RODERIGO and GRISOLAN: Ha, ha, ha!

FERDINAND: Why do you laugh? Methinks you that are courtiers should be my touchwood, take fire when I give fire; that is, laugh when I laugh, were the subject never so 45 witty –

CASTRUCHIO: True, my lord, I myself have heard a very good jest, and have scorn'd to seem to have so silly a wit, as to understand it.

FERDINAND: But I can laugh at your fool, my lord. 50

CASTRUCHIO: He cannot speak, you know, but he makes faces; my lady cannot abide him.

FERDINAND: No?

CASTRUCHIO: Nor endure to be in merry company: for she

27. *jest she broke:* joke she cracked.
30. *tents:* usual meaning; dressing for wounds.
32. *chirurgeons:* surgeons.
34. *put up:* sheathe their weapons, with a double entendre.
36. *jennet:* a light sporting horse.
39. *ballass'd:* ballasted.

55 says too much laughing, and too much company, fills her
too full of the wrinkle.

FERDINAND: I would then have a mathematical instrument
made for her face, that she might not laugh out of compass.
I shall shortly visit you at Milan, Lord Silvio.

60 SILVIO: Your Grace shall arrive most welcome.

FERDINAND: You are a good horseman, Antonio; you have
excellent riders in France, what do you think of good
horsemanship?

ANTONIO: Nobly, my lord: as out of the Grecian horse
65 issued many famous princes: so out of brave horsemanship, arise the first sparks of growing resolution, that raise
the mind to noble action.

FERDINAND: You have bespoke it worthily.

[*Enter* DUCHESS, CARDINAL, CARIOLA *and* JULIA.]

SILVIO: Your brother, the Lord Cardinal, and sister
70 Duchess.

CARDINAL: Are the galleys come about?

GRISOLAN: They are, my lord.

FERDINAND: Here's the Lord Silvio, is come to take his
leave.

75 DELIO [*aside to* ANTONIO]: Now sir, your promise: what's
that Cardinal? I mean his temper? They say he's a brave
fellow, will play his five thousand crowns at tennis,
dance, court ladies, and one that hath fought single
combats.

80 ANTONIO: Some such flashes superficially hang on him, for
form: but observe his inward character: he is a melancholy
churchman. The spring in his face is nothing but the
engend'ring of toads: where he is jealous of any man, he
lays worse plots for them, than ever was impos'd on

56. *wrinkle:* crease; moral blemish.
58. *out of compass:* immoderately.        71. *come about:* returned to port.
80. *flashes:* ostentatious displays.        82. *spring:* of water, season.

Hercules: for he strews in his way flatterers, panders,   85
intelligencers, atheists: and a thousand such political
monsters: he should have been Pope: but instead of
coming to it by the primitive decency of the Church, he
did bestow bribes, so largely, and so impudently, as if he
would have carried it away without Heaven's knowledge.   90
Some good he hath done.

DELIO: You have given too much of him: what's his
brother?

ANTONIO: The Duke there? a most perverse and turbulent
    nature;
What appears in him mirth, is merely outside,   95
If he laugh heartily, it is to laugh
All honesty out of fashion.

DELIO:                 Twins?

ANTONIO:                     In quality:
He speaks with others' tongues, and hears men's suits
With others' ears: will seem to sleep o'th' bench
Only to entrap offenders in their answers;   100
Dooms men to death by information.
Rewards, by hearsay.

DELIO:               Then the law to him
Is like a foul black cobweb to a spider,
He makes it his dwelling, and a prison
To entangle those shall feed him.

ANTONIO:                  Most true:   105
He nev'r pays debts, unless they be shrewd turns,
And those he will confess, that he doth owe.
Last: for his brother, there, the Cardinal,
They that do flatter him most, say oracles
Hang at his lips: and verily I believe them:   110
For the devil speaks in them.
But for their sister, the right noble Duchess,

86. *intelligencers*: spies. *political*: scheming.

You never fix'd your eye on three fair medals,
Cast in one figure, of so different temper.
115 For her discourse, it is so full of rapture,
You only will begin, then to be sorry
When she doth end her speech: and wish, in wonder,
She held it less vainglory to talk much
Than your penance, to hear her: whilst she speaks,
120 She throws upon a man so sweet a look,
That it were able to raise one to a galliard
That lay in a dead palsy; and to dote
On that sweet countenance: but in that look
There speaketh so divine a continence,
125 As cuts off all lascivious, and vain hope.
Her days are practis'd in such noble virtue,
That, sure her nights, nay more, her very sleeps,
Are more in heaven, than other ladies' shrifts.
Let all sweet ladies break their flatt'ring glasses,
And dress themselves in her.
130 DELIO:                           Fie Antonio,
You play the wire-drawer with her commendations.
ANTONIO: I'll case the picture up: only thus much:
All her particular worth grows to this sum:
She stains the time past: lights the time to come.
135 CARIOLA: You must attend my lady, in the gallery,
Some half an hour hence.
ANTONIO:                           I shall.
   [*Exeunt* ANTONIO *and* DELIO.]
FERDINAND: Sister, I have a suit to you.
DUCHESS:                           To me, sir?
FERDINAND: A gentleman here: Daniel de Bosola:
One, that was in the galleys;

---

114. *figure:* form, shape.          121. *galliard:* a lively dance.
128. *shrifts:* confessions.          131. *play the wire-drawer:* spin out.
134. *stains:* eclipses.

DUCHESS: Yes, I know him.

FERDINAND: A worthy fellow h'is: pray let me entreat for    140
The provisorship of your horse.

DUCHESS: Your knowledge of him
Commends him, and prefers him.

FERDINAND: Call him hither.
[*Exit* ATTENDANT.]
We are now upon parting. Good Lord Silvio
Do us commend to all our noble friends
At the leaguer.

SILVIO: Sir, I shall.    145

DUCHESS: You are for Milan?

SILVIO: I am.

DUCHESS: Bring the caroches: we'll bring you down
to the haven.
[*Exeunt* DUCHESS, CARIOLA, SILVIO, CASTRUCHIO,
RODERIGO, GRISOLAN *and* JULIA.]

CARDINAL: Be sure you entertain that Bosola
For your intelligence: I would not be seen in't.
And therefore many times I have slighted him,    150
When he did court our furtherance: as this morning.

FERDINAND: Antonio, the great master of her household
Had been far fitter.

CARDINAL: You are deceiv'd in him,
His nature is too honest for such business.
He comes: I'll leave you.
[*Enter* BOSOLA.]

BOSOLA: I was lur'd to you.    155
[*Exit* CARDINAL.]

FERDINAND: My brother here, the Cardinal, could never
Abide you.

BOSOLA: Never since he was in my debt.

145. *leaguer*: military camp; siege.
147. *caroches*: large coaches.

FERDINAND: May be some oblique character in your face
    Made him suspect you?

BOSOLA:                   Doth he study physiognomy?
160   There's no more credit to be given to th'face,
    Than to a sick man's urine, which some call
    The physician's whore, because she cozens him.
    He did suspect me wrongfully.

FERDINAND:              For that
    You must give great men leave to take their times:
165   Distrust doth cause us seldom be deceiv'd;
    You see, the oft shaking of the cedar tree
    Fastens it more at root. ˙

BOSOLA:            Yet take heed:
    For to suspect a friend unworthily
    Instructs him the next way to suspect you,
    And prompts him to deceive you.

FERDINAND:           There's gold.
170 BOSOLA:                      So:
    What follows? (Never rain'd such showers as these
    Without thunderbolts i'th' tail of them;)
    Whose throat must I cut?

FERDINAND: Your inclination to shed blood rides post
175   Before my occasion to use you. I give you that
    To live i'th' court, here: and observe the Duchess,
    To note all the particulars of her 'haviour:
    What suitors do solicit her for marriage
    And whom she best affects: she's a young widow,
    I would not have her marry again.

180 BOSOLA:                 No, sir?

FERDINAND: Do not you ask the reason: but be satisfied,
    I say I would not.

BOSOLA:         It seems you would create me
    One of your familiars.

169. *next:* most direct.   174. *post:* in haste.   177. *'haviour:* behaviour.

FERDINAND:     Familiar? what's that?

BOSOLA: Why, a very quaint invisible devil in flesh:
An intelligencer.

FERDINAND:     Such a kind of thriving thing          185
I would wish thee: and ere long, thou mayst arrive
At a higher place by't.

BOSOLA:          Take your devils
Which hell calls angels: these curs'd gifts would make
You a corrupter, me an impudent traitor,
And should I take these they'ld take me to hell.          190

FERDINAND: Sir, I'll take nothing from you that I have
given.
There is a place that I procur'd for you
This morning, the provisorship o'th' horse,
Have you heard on't?

BOSOLA:          No.

FERDINAND:          'Tis yours, is't not worth thanks?

BOSOLA: I would have you curse yourself now, that your
bounty,          195
Which makes men truly noble, e'er should make
Me a villain: O, that to avoid ingratitude
For the good deed you have done me, I must do
All the ill man can invent. Thus the devil
Candies all sins o'er: and what Heaven terms vile,          200
That names he complemental.

FERDINAND:          Be yourself:
Keep your old garb of melancholy: 'twill express
You envy those that stand above your reach,
Yet strive not to come near 'em. This will gain
Access to private lodgings, where yourself          205
May, like a politic dormouse –

---

188. *angels:* gold coins bearing the image of St Michael killing the
dragon.
200. *Candies . . . o'er:* sugars . . . over.          201. *complemental:* accomplished.

BOSOLA:                              As I have seen some,
Feed in a lord's dish, half asleep, not seeming
To listen to any talk: and yet these rogues
Have cut his throat in a dream: what's my place?
210 The provisorship o'th' horse? say then my corruption
Grew out of horse dung. I am your creature.

FERDINAND: Away!

BOSOLA: Let good men, for good deeds, covet good fame,
Since place and riches oft are bribes of shame;
215 Sometimes the devil doth preach.
      *Exit* BOSOLA.
      [*Enter* CARDINAL *and* DUCHESS.]

CARDINAL: We are to part from you: and your own
      discretion
Must now be your director.

FERDINAND:                        You are a widow:
You know already what man is: and therefore
Let not youth, high promotion, eloquence –

CARDINAL: No, nor anything without the addition,
220      Honour,
Sway your high blood.

FERDINAND:                        Marry? they are most luxurious,
Will wed twice.

CARDINAL:                  O fie!

FERDINAND:                        Their livers are more spotted
Than Laban's sheep.

DUCHESS:                        Diamonds are of most value
They say, that have pass'd through most jewellers' hands.

FERDINAND: Whores, by that rule, are precious.

225 DUCHESS:                                    Will you hear me?
I'll never marry –

CARDINAL:              So most widows say:
But commonly that motion lasts no longer

221. *luxurious*: lascivious.          227. *motion*: intention.

Than the turning of an hourglass; the funeral sermon
And it, end both together.
FERDINAND:                    Now hear me:
  You live in a rank pasture here, i'th' court,                          230
  There is a kind of honey-dew that's deadly:
  'Twill poison your fame; look to't; be not cunning:
  For they whose faces do belie their hearts
  Are witches, ere they arrive at twenty years,
  Ay: and give the devil suck.
DUCHESS:                       This is terrible good counsel.   235
FERDINAND: Hypocrisy is woven of a fine small thread,
  Subtler than Vulcan's engine: yet, believe't,
  Your darkest actions: nay, your privat'st thoughts,
  Will come to light.
CARDINAL:           You may flatter yourself,
  And take your own choice: privately be married               240
  Under the eaves of night –
FERDINAND                 Think't the best voyage
  That e'er you made; like the irregular crab,
  Which, though't goes backward, thinks that it goes right,
  Because it goes its own way: but observe:
  Such weddings may more properly be said                      245
  To be executed, than celebrated.
CARDINAL:                    The marriage night
  Is the entrance into some prison.
FERDINAND:                    And those joys,
  Those lustful pleasures, are like heavy sleeps
  Which do forerun man's mischief.
CARDINAL:                    Fare you well.
  Wisdom begins at the end: remember it.                       250
  [Exit CARDINAL.]
DUCHESS: I think this speech between you both was
     studied,
  It came so roundly off.

FERDINAND:                     You are my sister,
This was my father's poniard: do you see,
I'ld be loath to see't look rusty, 'cause 'twas his.
255    I would have you to give o'er these chargeable revels;
A visor and a mask are whispering-rooms
That were nev'r built for goodness: fare ye well:
And women like that part, which, like the lamprey,
Hath nev'r a bone in't.
DUCHESS:                     Fie sir!
FERDINAND:                     Nay,
260    I mean the tongue: variety of courtship;
What cannot a neat knave with a smooth tale
Make a woman believe? Farewell, lusty widow.
         [*Exit* FERDINAND.]
DUCHESS: Shall this move me? If all my royal kindred
Lay in my way unto this marriage:
265    I'ld make them my low foot-steps. And even now,
Even in this hate, (as men in some great battles
By apprehending danger, have achiev'd
Almost impossible actions: I have heard soldiers say so,)
So I, through frights and threat'nings, will assay
270    This dangerous venture. Let old wives report
I winked, and chose a husband.
         [*Enter* CARIOLA.]
                                        Cariola,
To thy known secrecy I have given up
More than my life, my fame.
CARIOLA:                     Both shall be safe:
For I'll conceal this secret from the world
275    As warily as those that trade in poison,
Keep poison from their children.
DUCHESS:                     Thy protestation

255. *chargeable:* expensive.        261. *neat:* finely dressed; healthy.
265. *foot-steps:* stepping stones.

Is ingenious and hearty: I believe it.
Is Antonio come?

CARIOLA:                    He attends you.

DUCHESS:                              Good dear soul,
Leave me: but place thyself behind the arras,
Where thou mayst overhear us: wish me good speed          280
For I am going into a wilderness,
Where I shall find nor path, nor friendly clew
To be my guide.

   [CARIOLA *goes behind the arras; the* DUCHESS *draws the*
   *traverse to reveal* ANTONIO.]
                I sent for you. Sit down:
Take pen and ink, and write. Are you ready?

ANTONIO:                                      Yes.

DUCHESS: What did I say?

ANTONIO:                    That I should write somewhat.          285

DUCHESS: O, I remember:
After these triumphs and this large expense
It's fit, like thrifty husbands, we inquire
What's laid up for tomorrow.

ANTONIO: So please your beautous excellence.

DUCHESS:                              Beauteous?          290
Indeed I thank you: I look young for your sake.
You have tane my cares upon you.

ANTONIO:                              I'll fetch your Grace
The particulars of your revenue and expense.

DUCHESS: O, you are an upright treasurer: but you
   mistook,
For when I said I meant to make inquiry          295
What's laid up for tomorrow: I did mean
What's laid up yonder for me.

---

277. *ingenious:* ingenious; ingenuous.
282. *clew:* thread used as a guide through a labyrinth.
287. *triumphs:* festivities.    288. *husbands:* usual meaning; stewards.

ANTONIO: Where?

DUCHESS: In heaven.
I am making my will, as 'tis fit princes should
In perfect memory, and I pray sir, tell me

300 Were not one better make it smiling, thus?
Than in deep groans, and terrible ghastly looks,
As if the gifts we parted with, procur'd
That violent distraction?

ANTONIO: O, much better.

DUCHESS: If I had a husband now, this care were quit:

305 But I intend to make you overseer;
What good deed shall we first remember? Say.

ANTONIO: Begin with that first good deed, begin i'th'
world,
After man's creation, the sacrament of marriage.
I'ld have you first provide for a good husband,
Give him all.

DUCHESS: All?

310 ANTONIO: Yes, your excellent self.

DUCHESS: In a winding sheet?

ANTONIO: In a couple.

DUCHESS: St Winifred! that were a strange will.

ANTONIO: 'Twere strange
If there were no will in you to marry again.

DUCHESS: What do you think of marriage?

315 ANTONIO: I take't, as those that deny purgatory,
It locally contains or heaven, or hell;
There's no third place in't.

DUCHESS: How do you affect it?

ANTONIO: My banishment, feeding my melancholy,
Would often reason thus:

DUCHESS: Pray let's hear it.

311. *couple:* a pair; marriage; copulation.
315. *those that deny purgatory:* i.e. protestants.     317. *affect:* like.

ANTONIO: Say a man never marry, nor have children, 320
 What takes that from him? only the bare name
 Of being a father, or the weak delight
 To see the little wanton ride a-cock-horse
 Upon a painted stick, or hear him chatter
 Like a taught starling.

DUCHESS:     Fie, fie, what's all this? 325
 One of your eyes is bloodshot, use my ring to't,
 They say 'tis very sovereign: 'twas my wedding ring,
 And I did vow never to part with it,
 But to my second husband.

ANTONIO: You have parted with it now.

DUCHESS:      Yes, to help your eyesight. 330

ANTONIO: You have made me stark blind.

DUCHESS:     How?

ANTONIO: There is a saucy and ambitious devil
 Is dancing in this circle.

DUCHESS:    Remove him.

ANTONIO:     How?

DUCHESS: There needs small conjuration, when your
 finger
 May do it: thus, is it fit?
 [She puts the ring on his finger.] He kneels.

ANTONIO:    What said you?

DUCHESS:     Sir, 335
 This goodly roof of yours, is too low built,
 I cannot stand upright in't, nor discourse,
 Without I raise it higher: raise yourself,
 Or if you please, my hand to help you: so.
 [Raises him.]

ANTONIO: Ambition, Madam, is a great man's madness, 340
 That is not kept in chains, and close-pent rooms,
 But in fair lightsome lodgings, and is girt

327. *sovereign:* efficacious.

191

With the wild noise of prattling visitants,
Which makes it lunatic, beyond all cure.
345  Conceive not, I am so stupid, but I aim
Whereto your favours tend. But he's a fool
That, being a-cold, would thrust his hands i'th' fire
To warm them.

DUCHESS:          So, now the ground's broke,
You may discover what a wealthy mine
I make you lord of.

350  ANTONIO:          O my unworthiness!

DUCHESS: You were ill to sell yourself;
This dark'ning of your worth is not like that
Which tradesmen use i'th' city; their false lights
Are to rid bad wares off: and I must tell you
355  If you will know where breathes a complete man,
(I speak it without flattery), turn your eyes,
And progress through yourself.

ANTONIO:                    Were there nor heaven, nor hell,
I should be honest: I have long serv'd virtue,
And nev'r tane wages of her.

DUCHESS:                    Now she pays it.
360  The misery of us, that are born great,
We are forc'd to woo, because none dare woo us:
And as a tyrant doubles with his words,
And fearfully equivocates: so we
Are forc'd to express our violent passions
365  In riddles, and in dreams, and leave the path
Of simple virtue, which was never made
To seem the thing it is not. Go, go brag
You have left me heartless, mine is in your bosom,
I hope 'twill multiply love there. You do tremble:
370  Make not your heart so dead a piece of flesh

345. *aim*: guess.          352. *dark'ning*: obscuring.
362. *doubles*: acts deceitfully or evasively.

To fear, more than to love me. Sir, be confident,
What is't distracts you? This is flesh, and blood, sir,
'Tis not the figure cut in alabaster
Kneels at my husband's tomb. Awake, awake, man,
I do here put off all vain ceremony,                    375
And only do appear to you, a young widow
That claims you for her husband, and like a widow,
I use but half a blush in't.

ANTONIO:                    Truth speak for me,
I will remain the constant sanctuary
Of your good name.

DUCHESS:                    I thank you, gentle love,    380
And 'cause you shall not come to me in debt,
Being now my steward, here upon your lips
I sign your *Quietus est*. This you should have begg'd now:
I have seen children oft eat sweetmeats thus,
As fearful to devour them too soon.                     385

ANTONIO: But for your brothers?

DUCHESS:                    Do not think of them:
All discord, without this circumference,
Is only to be pitied, and not fear'd.
Yet, should they know it, time will easily
Scatter the tempest.

ANTONIO:                    These words should be mine,    390
And all the parts you have spoke, if some part of it
Would not have savour'd flattery.

DUCHESS:                    Kneel.
    [*Enter* CARIOLA.]

ANTONIO:                    Ha?

DUCHESS: Be not amaz'd, this woman's of my counsel.
I have heard lawyers say, a contract in a chamber,
*Per verba de presenti*, is absolute marriage.           395
Bless, Heaven, this sacred Gordian, which let violence
Never untwine.

ANTONIO: And may our sweet affections, like the spheres,
Be still in motion.

DUCHESS:                    Quick'ning, and make
400   The like soft music.

ANTONIO: That we may imitate the loving palms,
Best emblem of a peaceful marriage,
That nev'r bore fruit divided.

DUCHESS: What can the Church force more?

405   ANTONIO: That Fortune may not know an accident
Either of joy or sorrow, to divide
Our fixed wishes.

DUCHESS:                    How can the Church build faster?
We now are man and wife, and 'tis the Church
That must but echo this. Maid, stand apart,
I now am blind.

410   ANTONIO:            What's your conceit in this?

DUCHESS: I would have you lead your fortune by the hand,
Unto your marriage bed:
(You speak in me this, for we now are one)
We'll only lie, and talk together, and plot
415   T'appease my humorous kindred; and if you please,
Like the old tale, in *Alexander and Lodowick*,
Lay a naked sword between us, keep us chaste.
O, let me shroud my blushes in your bosom,
Since 'tis the treasury of all my secrets.

420   CARIOLA: Whether the spirit of greatness, or of woman
Reign most in her, I know not, but it shows
A fearful madness: I owe her much of pity.

   *Exeunt.*

404. *force:* enforce.
415. *humorous:* ill-humoured.

# [ACT TWO]

## [SCENE ONE]

[*Enter* BOSOLA *and* CASTRUCHIO.]

BOSOLA: You say you would fain be taken for an eminent courtier?

CASTRUCHIO: 'Tis the very main of my ambition.

BOSOLA: Let me see, you have a reasonable good face for't already, and your nightcap expresses your ears sufficient largely; I would have you learn to twirl the strings of your band with a good grace; and in a set speech, at th' end of every sentence, to hum, three or four times, or blow your nose, till it smart again, to recover your memory. When you come to be a president in criminal causes, if you smile upon a prisoner, hang him, but if you frown upon him, and threaten him, let him be sure to 'scape the gallows.

CASTRUCHIO: I would be a very merry president –

BOSOLA: Do not sup a nights; 'twill beget you an admirable wit.

CASTRUCHIO: Rather it would make me have a good stomach to quarrel, for they say your roaring boys eat meat seldom, and that makes them so valiant: but how shall I know whether the people take me for an eminent fellow?

BOSOLA: I will teach a trick to know it: give out you lie a-dying, and if you hear the common people curse you, be sure you are taken for one of the prime nightcaps.

3. *main:* purpose.
5. *nightcap:* white coif worn by sergeants at law; *expresses:* presses out.
6–7. *strings of your band:* white tabs worn by sergeants.
10. *president:* presiding magistrate.
17. *roaring boys:* roistering bullies.     23. *nightcaps:* lawyers.

[*Enter* OLD LADY.]
You come from painting now?

25 OLD LADY: From what?

BOSOLA: Why, from your scurvy face physic: to behold
thee not painted inclines somewhat near a miracle. These
in thy face here, were deep ruts and foul sloughs, the last
progress. There was a lady in France, that having had the
30 smallpox, flayed the skin off her face, to make it more
level; and whereas before she look'd like a nutmeg grater,
after she resembled an abortive hedgehog.

OLD LADY: Do you call this painting?

BOSOLA: No, no, but you call it careening of an old
35 morphew'd lady, to make her disembogue again.
There's rough-cast phrase to your plastic.

OLD LADY: It seems you are well acquainted with my
closet?

BOSOLA: One would suspect it for a shop of witchcraft,
40 to find in it the fat of serpents; spawn of snakes, Jews'
spittle, and their young children's ordure, and all these for
the face. I would sooner eat a dead pigeon, taken from the
soles of the feet of one sick of the plague, than kiss one of
you fasting. Here are two of you, whose sin of your youth
45 is the very patrimony of the physician, makes him renew
his footcloth with the spring, and change his high-priz'd
courtesan with the fall of the leaf: I do wonder you do not
loathe yourselves. Observe my meditation now:
What thing is in this outward form of man
50 To be belov'd? We account it ominous,
If nature do produce a colt, or lamb,
A fawn, or goat, in any limb resembling
A man; and fly from't as a prodigy.
Man stands amaz'd to see his deformity,

28. *sloughs*: bogs; layers of dead tissues.
46. *footcloth*: see *White Devil*, I, ii, note 52 (p. 44).

In any other creature but himself.                                          55
But in our own flesh, though we bear diseases
Which have their true names only tane from beasts,
As the most ulcerous wolf, and swinish measle;
Though we are eaten up of lice, and worms,
And though continually we bear about us                                     60
A rotten and dead body, we delight
To hide it in rich tissue: all our fear,
Nay, all our terror, is lest our physician
Should put us in the ground, to be made sweet.
Your wife's gone to Rome: you two couple, and get you       65
To the wells at Lucca, to recover your aches.
    [*Exeunt* CASTRUCHIO *and* OLD LADY.]
I have other work on foot: I observe our Duchess
Is sick a–days, she pukes, her stomach seethes,
The fins of her eyelids look most teeming blue,
She wanes i'th' cheek, and waxes fat i'th' flank;             70
And, contrary to our Italian fashion,
Wears a loose-bodied gown: there's somewhat in't.
I have a trick, may chance discover it,
A pretty one; I have bought some apricocks,
The first our spring yields.
    [*Enter* ANTONIO *and* DELIO, *talking apart.*]
DELIO:             And so long since married?       75
You amaze me.
ANTONIO:       Let me seal your lips for ever,
For did I think that anything but th' air
Could carry these words from you, I should wish
You had no breath at all.
    [*To* BOSOLA.]
                     Now sir, in your contemplation?

---

58. *ulcerous wolf:* ulcer; *swinish measle:* measle(s), a skin disease in pigs,
    was confused with ordinary measles.
69. *fins:* rims; *teeming:* pregnant.      74. *apricocks:* apricots.

80 You are studying to become a great wise fellow?

BOSOLA: O sir, the opinion of wisdom is a foul tetter, that
runs all over a man's body: if simplicity direct us to have
no evil, it directs us to a happy being. For the subtlest
folly proceeds from the subtlest wisdom. Let me be
85 simply honest.

ANTONIO: I do understand your inside.

BOSOLA: Do you so?

ANTONIO: Because you would not seem to appear to th'
world
Puff'd up with your preferment, you continue
90 This out of fashion melancholy; leave it, leave it.

BOSOLA: Give me leave to be honest in any phrase, in any
compliment whatsoever: shall I confess myself to you? I
look no higher than I can reach: they are the gods, that
must ride on winged horses, a lawyer's mule of a slow pace
95 will both suit my disposition and business. For, mark me,
when a man's mind rides faster than his horse can gallop
they quickly both tire.

ANTONIO: You would look up to Heaven, but I think
The devil, that rules i'th' air, stands in your light.

100 BOSOLA: O, sir, you are lord of the ascendant, chief man
with the Duchess: a duke was your cousin-german,
remov'd. Say you were lineally descended from King
Pippin, or he himself, what of this? Search the heads of the
greatest rivers in the world, you shall find them but
105 bubbles of water. Some would think the souls of princes
were brought forth by some more weighty cause, than
those of meaner persons: they are deceiv'd, there's the
same hand to them: the like passions sway them; the same
reason, that makes a vicar go to law for a tithe-pig, and

81. *tetter*: skin disease.
100. *lord of the ascendant*: dominating influence.
101. *cousin-german*: first cousin.
102-3. *King Pippin*: see *White Devil*, V, vi, 110, additional note.

undo his neighbours, makes them spoil a whole province, 110
and batter down goodly cities with the cannon.

[*Enter* DUCHESS, OLD LADY, LADIES.]

DUCHESS. Your arm Antonio, do I not grow fat?
I am exceeding short-winded. Bosola,
I would have you, sir, provide for me a litter,
Such a one, as the Duchess of Florence rode in. 115

BOSOLA: The duchess us'd one, when she was great with
child.

DUCHESS: I think she did. Come hither, mend my ruff,
Here; when? thou art such a tedious lady; and
Thy breath smells of lemon peels; would thou hadst done;
Shall I sound under thy fingers? I am 120
So troubled with the mother.

BOSOLA [*aside*]:                    I fear too much.

DUCHESS: I have heard you say that the French courtiers
Wear their hats on 'fore the king.

ANTONIO:                              I have seen it.

DUCHESS: In the presence?

ANTONIO:                          Yes.

DUCHESS: Why should not we bring up that fashion? 125
'Tis ceremony more than duty, that consists
In the removing of a piece of felt:
Be you the example to the rest o'th' court,
Put on your hat first.

ANTONIO:                      You must pardon me:
I have seen, in colder countries than in France, 130
Nobles stand bare to th' prince; and the distinction
Methought show'd reverently.

BOSOLA: I have a present for your Grace.

DUCHESS:                                For me sir?

BOSOLA: Apricocks, Madam.

118. *when?*: i.e. 'How long are you going to be?'   120. *sound*: swoon.
121. *mother*: hysteria – with, of course, a pun.   131. *bare*: bare-headed.

DUCHESS:             O sir, where are they?
I have heard of none to-year.

135   BOSOLA [aside]:           Good, her colour rises.

DUCHESS: Indeed I thank you: they are wondrous fair ones.
What an unskilful fellow is our gardener!
We shall have none this month.

BOSOLA: Will not your Grace pare them?

DUCHESS: No, they taste of musk, methinks; indeed they
140   do.

BOSOLA: I know not: yet I wish your Grace had par'd 'em.

DUCHESS: Why?

BOSOLA:         I forgot to tell you the knave gard'ner,
Only to raise his profit by them the sooner,
Did ripen them in horse-dung.

DUCHESS:            O you jest.
[to ANTONIO] You shall judge: pray taste one.

145   ANTONIO:              Indeed Madam,
I do not love the fruit.

DUCHESS:       Sir, you are loth
To rob us of our dainties: 'tis a delicate fruit,
They say they are restorative?

BOSOLA:           'Tis a pretty art,
This grafting.

DUCHESS:     'Tis so: a bett'ring of nature.

150   BOSOLA: To make a pippin grow upon a crab,
A damson on a black-thorn: [aside] How greedily she eats
them!
A whirlwind strike off these bawd farthingales,
For, but for that, and the loose-bodied gown,
I should have discover'd apparently
155   The young springal cutting a caper in her belly.

---

135. *to-year*: this year (cf. to-day).    149. *This grafting*: a double entendre.
150. *a crab*: crab-apple.         152. *farthingales*: hooped petticoats.
154. *apparently*: manifestly.       155. *springal*: stripling.

DUCHESS: I thank you, Bosola: they were right good ones,
 If they do not make me sick.

ANTONIO:       How now Madam?

DUCHESS: This green fruit and my stomach are not friends.
 How they swell me!

BOSOLA [aside]: Nay, you are too much swell'd already.

DUCHESS: O, I am in an extreme cold sweat.     160

BOSOLA: I am very sorry.
 [Exit.]

DUCHESS: Lights to my chamber! O, good Antonio,
 I fear I am undone.
 Exit DUCHESS.

DELIO:      Lights there, lights!

ANTONIO: O my most trusty Delio, we are lost:
 I fear she's fall'n in labour: and there's left   165
 No time for her remove.

DELIO:       Have you prepar'd
 Those ladies to attend her? and procur'd
 That politic safe conveyance for the midwife
 Your Duchess plotted?

ANTONIO:     I have.

DELIO: Make use then of this forc'd occasion:    170
 Give out that Bosola hath poison'd her,
 With these apricocks: that will give some colour
 For her keeping close.

ANTONIO:     Fie, fie, the physicians
 Will then flock to her.

DELIO:     For that you may pretend
 She'll use some prepar'd antidote of her own,   175
 Lest the physicians should repoison her.

ANTONIO: I am lost in amazement: I know not what to
 think on't.
 Ex[eunt].

173. *close:* shut up.

## [SCENE TWO]

[*Enter* BOSOLA *and* OLD LADY.]

BOSOLA: So, so: there's no question but her tetchiness and
most vulturous eating of the apricocks, are apparent signs
of breeding, now?

OLD LADY: I am in haste, sir.

5 BOSOLA: There was a young waiting-woman, had a
monstrous desire to see the glass-house –

OLD LADY: Nay, pray let me go:

BOSOLA: And it was only to know what strange instrument
it was, should swell up a glass to the fashion of a woman's
10 belly.

OLD LADY: I will hear no more of the glass-house, you are
still abusing women!

BOSOLA: Who, I? No, only, by the way now and then,
mention your frailties. The orange tree bears ripe and
15 green fruit and blossoms altogether. And some of you give
entertainment for pure love: but more, for more precious
reward. The lusty spring smells well: but drooping
autumn tastes well. If we have the same golden showers,
that rained in the time of Jupiter the Thunderer: you have
20 the same Danaes still, to hold up their laps to receive them:
didst thou never study the mathematics?

OLD LADY: What's that, sir?

BOSOLA: Why, to know the trick how to make a many lines
meet in one centre. Go, go; give your foster-daughters
25 good counsel: tell them, that the devil takes delight to
hang at a woman's girdle, like a false rusty watch, that she
cannot discern how the time passes.

1. *tetchiness*: irritability.      6. *glass-house*: glass factory.
20. *Danaes*: see note to I, ii, 171–2 (p. 436).

[*Exit* OLD LADY; *enter* ANTONIO, DELIO, RODERIGO, GRISOLAN.]

ANTONIO: Shut up the court gates.

RODERIGO:                  Why sir? what's the danger?

ANTONIO: Shut up the posterns presently: and call
  All the officers o'th' court.

GRISOLAN:            I shall instantly.         30
  [*Exit.*]

ANTONIO: Who keeps the key o'th' park-gate?

RODERIGO:                    Forobosco.

ANTONIO: Let him bring't presently.
  [*Exit* RODERIGO.]
  [*Enter* SERVANTS, GRISOLAN, RODERIGO.]

1 SERVANT: O, gentlemen o'th' court, the foulest treason!

BOSOLA [*aside*]: If that these apricocks should be poison'd
  now;
  Without my knowledge!                 35

1 SERVANT: There was taken even now a Switzer in the
  Duchess' bedchamber.

2 SERVANT: A Switzer?

1 SERVANT: With a pistol in his great cod-piece.

BOSOLA: Ha, ha, ha.                     40

1 SERVANT: The cod-piece was the case for't.

2 SERVANT: There was a cunning traitor. Who would have
  search'd his cod-piece?

1 SERVANT: True, if he had kept out of the ladies' chambers:
  and all the moulds of his buttons were leaden bullets.   45

2 SERVANT: O wicked cannibal: a fire-lock in's cod-piece?

1 SERVANT: 'Twas a French plot upon my life.

2 SERVANT: To see what the devil can do.

ANTONIO: All the officers here?

SERVANTS:                 We are.

---

39. The current pronunciation of 'pistol', without the 't', accentuates
a pun on 'pizzle' = penis.

ANTONIO: Gentlemen,
50 We have lost much plate you know; and but this evening
Jewels, to the value of four thousand ducats
Are missing in the Duchess' cabinet.
Are the gates shut?

I SERVANT: Yes.

ANTONIO: 'Tis the Duchess' pleasure
Each officer be lock'd into his chamber
55 Till the sun-rising; and to send the keys
Of all their chests, and of their outward doors
Into her bedchamber. She is very sick.

RODERIGO: At her pleasure.

ANTONIO: She entreats you take't not ill. The innocent
60 Shall be the more approv'd by it.

BOSOLA: Gentleman o'th' wood-yard, where's your
Switzer now?

I SERVANT: By this hand 'twas credibly reported by one
o'th' black-guard.

[*Exeunt* BOSOLA, RODERIGO *and* SERVANTS.]

DELIO: How fares it with the Duchess?

65 ANTONIO: She's expos'd
Unto the worst of torture, pain, and fear.

DELIO: Speak to her all happy comfort.

ANTONIO: How I do play the fool with mine own danger!
You are this night, dear friend, to post to Rome,
My life lies in your service.

70 DELIO: Do not doubt me.

ANTONIO: O, 'tis far from me: and yet fear presents me
Somewhat that looks like danger.

DELIO: Believe it,
'Tis but the shadow of your fear, no more:
How superstitiously we mind our evils!

52. *cabinet:* private apartment.  60. *approv'd:* commended.
64. *th' black-guard:* scullions.

The throwing down salt, or crossing of a hare,   75
Bleeding at nose, the stumbling of a horse,
Or singing of a cricket, are of power
To daunt whole man in us. Sir, fare you well:
I wish you all the joys of a bless'd father;
And, for my faith, lay this unto your breast,   80
Old friends, like old swords, still are trusted best.
    [*Exit* DELIO.]
    [*Enter* CARIOLA *with a child.*]
CARIOLA: Sir, you are the happy father of a son,
  Your wife commends him to you.
ANTONIO:                 Blessed comfort!
  For heaven' sake tend her well: I'll presently
  Go set a figure for's nativity.   85
    *Exeunt.*


## [SCENE THREE]

    [*Enter* BOSOLA *with a dark lantern.*]
BOSOLA: Sure I did hear a woman shriek: list, ha?
  And the sound came, if I receiv'd it right,
  From the Duchess' lodgings: there's some stratagem
  In the confining all our courtiers
  To their several wards. I must have part of it,   5
  My intelligence will freeze else. List again,
  It may be 'twas the melancholy bird,
  Best friend of silence, and of solitariness,
  The owl, that scream'd so: ha! Antonio?
    [*Enter* ANTONIO *with a candle, his sword drawn.*]
ANTONIO: I heard some noise: who's there? What art
    thou? Speak.   10

85. *figure:* horoscope.
5. *wards:* apartments.

BOSOLA: Antonio! Put not your face nor body
    To such a forc'd expression of fear,
    I am Bosola; your friend.

ANTONIO:                    Bosola!
    [*aside*] This mole does undermine me – heard you not
    A noise even now?

BOSOLA:              From whence?

15  ANTONIO:                        From the Duchess' lodging.

BOSOLA: Not I: did you?

ANTONIO:                I did: or else I dream'd.

BOSOLA: Let's walk towards it.

ANTONIO:                    No. It may be, 'twas
    But the rising of the wind.

BOSOLA:                    Very likely.
    Methinks 'tis very cold, and yet you sweat.
    You look wildly.

20  ANTONIO:          I have been setting a figure
    For the Duchess' jewels.

BOSOLA:                    Ah: and how falls your question?
    Do you find it radical?

ANTONIO:                What's that to you?
    'Tis rather to be question'd what design,
    When all men were commanded to their lodgings,
    Makes you a night-walker.

25  BOSOLA:                    In sooth I'll tell you:
    Now all the court's asleep, I thought the devil
    Had least to do here; I come to say my prayers,
    And if it do offend you, I do so,
    You are a fine courtier.

ANTONIO [*aside*]:            This fellow will undo me.

30  You gave the Duchess apricocks to-day,
    Pray heaven they were not poison'd!

    22. *radical*: fit to be judged.

BOSOLA:                              Poison'd! a Spanish fig
For the imputation.

ANTONIO:             Traitors are ever confident,
Till they are discover'd. There were jewels stol'n too,
In my conceit, none are to be suspected
More than yourself.

BOSOLA:             You are a false steward.                    35

ANTONIO: Saucy slave! I'll pull thee up by the roots.

BOSOLA: May be the ruin will crush you to pieces.

ANTONIO: You are an impudent snake indeed, sir,
Are you scarce warm, and do you show your sting?

BOSOLA: ...

ANTONIO: You libel well, sir.

BOSOLA:             No sir, copy it out:                        40
And I will set my hand to't.

ANTONIO:             My nose bleeds.
One that were superstitious, would count
This ominous: when it merely comes by chance.
Two letters, that are wrought here for my name
Are drown'd in blood!                                          45
Mere accident: for you, sir, I'll take order:
I'th' morn you shall be safe: [aside] 'tis that must colour
Her lying-in: sir, this door you pass not:
I do not hold it fit, that you come near
The Duchess' lodgings, till you have quit yourself;            50
[aside] The great are like the base; nay, they are the same,
When they seek shameful ways to avoid shame.
     Ex[it].

BOSOLA: Antonio here about did drop a paper,

31. a Spanish fig: a contemptuous term, accompanied by an indecent
     gesture.            34. conceit: opinion.
39–40. line(s) omitted – see additional notes.
44. wrought: embroidered (on Antonio's handkerchief).

Some of your help, false friend: oh, here it is.
55 What's here? a child's nativity calculated?
[*Reads*] *The Duchess was deliver'd of a son, 'tween the hours*
*twelve and one, in the night: Anno Dom: 1504. (that's this year)*
*decimo nono Decembris, (that's this night) taken according to*
*the Meridian of Malfi (that's our Duchess: happy discovery).*
60 *The Lord of the first house, being combust in the ascendant,*
*signifies short life: and* Mars *being in a human sign, join'd to*
*the tail of the Dragon, in the eight house, doth threaten a*
*violent death;* Cætera non scrutantur.
Why now 'tis most apparent. This precise fellow
65 Is the Duchess' bawd: I have it to my wish.
This is a parcel of intelligency
Our courtiers were cas'd up for! It needs must follow,
That I must be committed, on pretence
Of poisoning her: which I'll endure, and laugh at.
70 If one could find the father now: but that
Time will discover. Old Castruchio
I'th' morning posts to Rome; by him I'll send
A letter, that shall make her brothers' galls
O'erflow their livers. This was a thrifty way.
75 *Though lust do masque in ne'er so strange disguise*
*She's oft found witty, but is never wise.*
[*Exit.*]


[SCENE FOUR]


[*Enter* CARDINAL *and* JULIA.]
CARDINAL: Sit: thou art my best of wishes; prithee tell me
What trick didst thou invent to come to Rome,
Without thy husband?
JULIA:                          Why, my Lord, I told him

54. *false friend:* the dark lantern.

I came to visit an old anchorite
Here, for devotion.
CARDINAL:   Thou art a witty false one:   5
I mean to him.
JULIA:   You have prevailed with me
Beyond my strongest thoughts: I would not now
Find you inconstant.
CARDINAL:   Do not put thyself
To such a voluntary torture, which proceeds
Out of your own guilt.
JULIA:   How, my Lord?
CARDINAL:   You fear   10
My constancy, because you have approv'd
Those giddy and wild turnings in yourself.
JULIA: Did you e'er find them?
CARDINAL:   Sooth, generally for women:
A man might strive to make glass malleable,
Ere he should make them fixed.
JULIA:   So, my Lord.   15
CARDINAL: We had need go borrow that fantastic glass
Invented by Galileo the Florentine,
To view another spacious world i'th' moon,
And look to find a constant woman there.
JULIA: This is very well, my Lord.
CARDINAL:   Why do you weep?   20
Are tears your justification? The selfsame tears
Will fall into your husband's bosom, lady,
With a loud protestation that you love him
Above the world. Come, I'll love you wisely,
That's jealously, since I am very certain   25
You cannot me make cuckold.
JULIA:   I'll go home
To my husband.
CARDINAL:  You may thank me, lady,

I have taken you off your melancholy perch,
Bore you upon my fist, and show'd you game,
And let you fly at it. I pray thee kiss me.
When thou wast with thy husband, thou wast watch'd
Like a tame elephant: (still you are to thank me.)
Thou hadst only kisses from him, and high feeding,
But what delight was that? 'Twas just like one
That hath a little fing'ring on the lute,
Yet cannot tune it: (still you are to thank me.)

JULIA: You told me of a piteous wound i'th' heart,
And a sick liver, when you wooed me first,
And spake like one in physic.

CARDINAL:                    Who's that?
  [*Enter* SERVANT.]
Rest firm, for my affection to thee,
Lightning moves slow to't.

SERVANT:                    Madam, a gentleman
That's come post from Malfi, desires to see you.

CARDINAL: Let him enter, I'll withdraw.
  *Exit.*

SERVANT:                              He says
Your husband, old Castruchio, is come to Rome,
Most pitifully tir'd with riding post.
  [*Exit* SERVANT; *enter* DELIO.]

JULIA: Signior Delio! [*Aside*] 'tis one of my old suitors.

DELIO: I was bold to come and see you.

JULIA:                    Sir, you are welcome.

DELIO: Do you lie here?

JULIA:                    Sure, your own experience
Will satisfy you no; our Roman prelates
Do not keep lodging for ladies.

DELIO:                    Very well.

28–30. the Cardinal compares Julia to a falcon.
39. *in physic*: under medical treatment.

I have brought you no commendations from your
  husband,
For I know none by him.

JULIA:               I hear he's come to Rome?

DELIO: I never knew man and beast, of a horse and a knight,
  So weary of each other; if he had had a good back,
  He would have undertook to have borne his horse,     55
  His breach was so pitifully sore.

JULIA:              Your laughter
  Is my pity.

DELIO:      Lady, I know not whether
  You want money, but I have brought you some.

JULIA: From my husband?

DELIO:            No, from mine own allowance.

JULIA: I must hear the condition, ere I be bound to take it.   60

DELIO: Look on't, 'tis gold, hath it not a fine colour?

JULIA: I have a bird more beautiful.

DELIO:              Try the sound on't.

JULIA: A lute-string far exceeds it;
  It hath no smell, like cassia or civet,
  Nor is it physical, though some fond doctors     65
  Persuade us, seethe't in cullises. I'll tell you,
  This is a creature bred by –
    [Enter SERVANT.]

SERVANT:          Your husband's come,
  Hath deliver'd a letter to the Duke of Calabria,
  That, to my thinking, hath put him out of his wits.
    [Exit SERVANT.]

JULIA: Sir, you hear,     70
  Pray let me know your business and your suit,
  As briefly as can be.

64. *cassia:* coarser kind of cinnamon; *civet:* a strong musky perfume.
65. *physical:* medicinal.
66. *cullises:* broths made by bruising meat.

DELIO: With good speed. I would wish you,
At such time, as you are non-resident
With your husband, my mistress.

75 JULIA: Sir, I'll go ask my husband if I shall,
And straight return your answer.
*Exit.*

DELIO: Very fine,
Is this her wit, or honesty that speaks thus?
I heard one say the Duke was highly mov'd
With a letter sent from Malfi. I do fear
80 Antonio is betray'd: how fearfully
Shows his ambition now; unfortunate Fortune!
*They pass through whirlpools, and deep woes do shun,*
*Who the event weigh, ere the action's done.*
*Exit.*


[SCENE FIVE]

[*Enter*] CARDINAL, *and* FERDINAND, *with a letter.*

FERDINAND: I have this night digg'd up a mandrake.

CARDINAL: Say you?

FERDINAND: And I am grown mad with't.

CARDINAL: What's the prodigy?

FERDINAND: Read there, a sister damn'd, she's loose
i'th' hilts:
Grown a notorious strumpet.

CARDINAL: Speak lower.

FERDINAND: Lower?
5 Rogues do not whisper't now, but seek to publish't,
As servants do the bounty of their lords,

77. *honesty:* chastity.
1. *mandrake:* see note to *White Devil*, III, i, 53 (p. 421).
3. *loose i'th' hilts:* unreliable (with a double entendre).

Aloud; and with a covetous searching eye,
To mark who note them. O confusion seize her,
She hath had most cunning bawds to serve her turn,
And more secure conveyances for lust,                    10
Than towns of garrison, for service.

CARDINAL:                              Is't possible?
Can this be certain?

FERDINAND:          Rhubarb, O for rhubarb
To purge this choler! Here's the cursed day
To prompt my memory, and here't shall stick
Till of her bleeding heart I make a sponge              15
To wipe it out.

CARDINAL:          Why do you make yourself
So wild a tempest?

FERDINAND:          Would I could be one,
That I might toss her palace 'bout her ears,
Root up her goodly forests, blast her meads,
And lay her general territory as waste,                 20
As she hath done her honour's.

CARDINAL:                              Shall our blood?
The royal blood of Aragon and Castile,
Be thus attainted?

FERDINAND:          Apply desperate physic,
We must not now use balsamum, but fire,
The smarting cupping-glass, for that's the mean         25
To purge infected blood, such blood as hers.
There is a kind of pity in mine eye,
I'll give it to my handkercher; and now 'tis here,
I'll bequeath this to her bastard.

CARDINAL:                              What to do?

FERDINAND: Why, to make soft lint for his mother's

11. *service:* military service; sexual intercourse.
24. *balsamum:* aromatic healing ointment.

30 wounds,
 When I have hewed her to pieces.

CARDINAL:      Curs'd creature!
 Unequal nature, to place women's hearts
 So far upon the left side.

FERDINAND:     Foolish men,
 That e'er will trust their honour in a bark,
35 Made of so slight, weak bulrush, as is woman,
 Apt every minute to sink it!

CARDINAL: Thus ignorance, when it hath purchas'd
 honour,
 It cannot wield it.

FERDINAND:    Methinks I see her laughing,
 Excellent hyena! Talk to me somewhat, quickly,
40 Or my imagination will carry me
 To see her in the shameful act of sin.

CARDINAL: With whom?

FERDINAND: Happily, with some strong-thigh'd barge-
 man;
 Or one o'th' wood-yard, that can quoit the sledge
45 Or toss the bar, or else some lovely squire
 That carries coals up to her privy lodgings.

CARDINAL: You fly beyond your reason.

FERDINAND:      Go to, mistress!
 'Tis not your whore's milk, that shall quench my wild-fire
 But your whore's blood.

50 CARDINAL: How idly shows this rage! which carries you,
 As men convey'd by witches, through the air
 On violent whirlwinds: this intemperate noise
 Fitly resembles deaf men's shrill discourse,
 Who talk aloud, thinking all other men

---

32. *unequal:* unjust.  44. *quoit the sledge:* throw the sledge-hammer.
47. *Go to, mistress:* an expression of disapprobation; also, go to it!
48. *wild-fire:* uncontrollable fire; eruptive skin disease.

To have their imperfection.

FERDINAND:                   Have not you     55
My palsy?

CARDINAL: Yes, I can be angry
Without this rupture; there is not in nature
A thing, that makes man so deform'd, so beastly
As doth intemperate anger. Chide yourself:
You have divers men, who never yet express'd     60
Their strong desire of rest but by unrest,
By vexing of themselves. Come, put yourself
In tune.

FERDINAND: So, I will only study to seem
The thing I am not. I could kill her now,
In you, or in myself, for I do think     65
It is some sin in us, Heaven doth revenge
By her.

CARDINAL: Are you stark mad?

FERDINAND:                   I would have their bodies
Burnt in a coal-pit, with the ventage stopp'd,
That their curs'd smoke might not ascend to Heaven:
Or dip the sheets they lie in, in pitch or sulphur,     70
Wrap them in't, and then light them like a match:
Or else to boil their bastard to a cullis,
And give't his lecherous father, to renew
The sin of his back.

CARDINAL:         I'll leave you.

FERDINAND:               Nay, I have done;
I am confident, had I been damn'd in hell,     75
And should have heard of this, it would have put me
Into a cold sweat. In, in, I'll go sleep:
Till I know who leaps my sister, I'll not stir:
That known, I'll find scorpions to string my whips,
And fix her in a general eclipse.     80
    *Exeunt.*

# [ACT THREE]

## [SCENE ONE]

[*Enter* ANTONIO *and* DELIO.]

ANTONIO: Our noble friend, my most beloved Delio,
  O, you have been a stranger long at court,
  Came you along with the Lord Ferdinand?

DELIO: I did, sir, and how fares your noble Duchess?

5  ANTONIO: Right fortunately well. She's an excellent
  Feeder of pedigrees: since you last saw her,
  She hath had two children more, a son and daughter.

DELIO: Methinks 'twas yesterday. Let me but wink,
  And not behold your face, which to mine eye

10  Is somewhat leaner: verily I should dream
  It were within this half hour.

ANTONIO: You have not been in law, friend Delio,
  Nor in prison, nor a suitor at the court,
  Nor begg'd the reversion of some great man's place,

15  Nor troubled with an old wife, which doth make
  Your time so insensibly hasten.

DELIO:                Pray sir tell me,
  Hath not this news arriv'd yet to the ear
  Of the Lord Cardinal?

ANTONIO:          I fear it hath;
  The Lord Ferdinand, that's newly come to court,
  Doth bear himself right dangerously.

20  DELIO:               Pray why?

ANTONIO: He is so quiet, that he seems to sleep
  The tempest out, as dormice do in winter;
  Those houses, that are haunted, are most still,
  Till the devil be up.

DELIO: What say the common people?

ANTONIO: The common rabble do directly say     25
  She is a strumpet.

DELIO: And your graver heads,
  Which would be politic, what censure they?

ANTONIO: They do observe I grow to infinite purchase
  The left-hand way, and all suppose the Duchess
  Would amend it, if she could. For, say they,     30
  Great princes, though they grudge their officers
  Should have such large and unconfined means
  To get wealth under them, will not complain
  Lest thereby they should make them odious
  Unto the people: for other obligation     35
  Of love, or marriage, between her and me,
  They never dream of.

[*Enter* FERDINAND, DUCHESS *and* BOSOLA.]

DELIO: The Lord Ferdinand
  Is going to bed.

FERDINAND: I'll instantly to bed,
  For I am weary: I am to bespeak
  A husband for you.

DUCHESS: For me, sir! pray who is't?     40

FERDINAND: The great Count Malateste.

DUCHESS: Fie upon him,
  A count? He's a mere stick of sugar-candy,
  You may look quite thorough him: when I choose
  A husband, I will marry for your honour.

FERDINAND: You shall do well in't. How is't, worthy
  Antonio?     45

DUCHESS: But, sir, I am to have private conference with
  you,

27. *censure:* judge, consider.
28. *purchase:* wealth.
29. *left-hand:* sinister.

About a scandalous report is spread
Touching mine honour.

FERDINAND:            Let me be ever deaf to't:
One of Pasquil's paper bullets, court calumny,
50    A pestilent air, which princes' palaces
Are seldom purg'd of. Yet, say that it were true,
I pour it in your bosom, my fix'd love
Would strongly excuse, extenuate, nay deny
Faults were they apparent in you. Go, be safe
In your own innocency.

55 DUCHESS:           O bless'd comfort,
This deadly air is purg'd.
     *Exeunt* [DUCHESS, ANTONIO, DELIO].

FERDINAND:          Her guilt treads on
Hot burning cultures. Now Bosola,
How thrives our intelligence?

BOSOLA:          Sir, uncertainly:
'Tis rumour'd she hath had three bastards, but
By whom, we may go read i'th' stars.

50 FERDINAND:           Why some
Hold opinion, all things are written there.

BOSOLA: Yes, if we could find spectacles to read them;
I do suspect, there hath been some sorcery
Us'd on the Duchess.

FERDINAND:         Sorcery, to what purpose?

65 BOSOLA: To make her dote on some desertless fellow,
She shames to acknowledge.

FERDINAND:         Can your faith give way
To think there's power in potions, or in charms,
To make us love, whether we will or no?

BOSOLA: Most certainly.

70 FERDINAND: Away, these are mere gulleries, horrid things
Invented by some cheating mountebanks

57. *cultures:* coulters, plough-shares.

To abuse us. Do you think that herbs, or charms
Can force the will? Some trials have been made
In the foolish practice; but the ingredients
Were lenative poisons, such as are of force                    75
To make the patient mad; and straight the witch
Swears, by equivocation, they are in love.
The witchcraft lies in her rank blood: this night
I will force confession from her. You told me
You had got, within these two days, a false key            80
Into her bed-chamber.

BOSOLA:                                I have.

FERDINAND:                          As I would wish.

BOSOLA: What do you intend to do?

FERDINAND:                                    Can you guess?

BOSOLA:                                                    No.

FERDINAND: Do not ask then.
He that can compass me, and know my drifts,
May say he hath put a girdle 'bout the world,              85
And sounded all her quick-sands.

BOSOLA:                                        I do not
Think so.

FERDINAND: What do you think then, pray?

BOSOLA:                                            That you
Are your own chronicle too much: and grossly
Flatter yourself.

FERDINAND:      Give me thy hand; I thank thee.
I never gave pension but to flatterers,                          90
Till I entertained thee: farewell,
*That friend a great man's ruin strongly checks,*
*Who rails into his belief all his defects.*
   *Exeunt.*

75. *lenative:* soothing – but dangerous.

# [SCENE TWO]

[*Enter* DUCHESS, ANTONIO *and* CARIOLA.]

DUCHESS: Bring me the casket hither, and the glass;
You get no lodging here to-night, my lord.

ANTONIO: Indeed, I must persuade one.

DUCHESS: Very good:
I hope in time 'twill grow into a custom,
5   That noblemen shall come with cap and knee,
To purchase a night's lodging of their wives.

ANTONIO: I must lie here.

DUCHESS: Must? you are a lord of mis-rule.

ANTONIO: Indeed, my rule is only in the night.

DUCHESS: To what use will you put me?

ANTONIO: We'll sleep together.

10  DUCHESS: Alas, what pleasure can two lovers find in sleep?

CARIOLA: My lord, I lie with her often: and I know
She'll much disquiet you.

ANTONIO: See, you are complain'd of.

CARIOLA: For she's the sprawling'st bedfellow.

ANTONIO: I shall like her the better for that.

15  CARIOLA: Sir, shall I ask you a question?

ANTONIO: I pray thee Cariola.

CARIOLA: Wherefore still, when you lie with my lady
Do you rise so early?

ANTONIO: Labouring men,
Count the clock oft'nest Cariola,
Are glad when their task's ended.

20  DUCHESS: I'll stop your mouth [*kisses him*].

ANTONIO: Nay, that's but one, Venus had two soft doves
To draw her chariot: I must have another [*kisses her*].

5. *with cap and knee:* humbly.
7. *lord of mis-rule:* master of the revels (which took place at night).

When wilt thou marry, Cariola?

CARIOLA:                                             Never, my lord.

ANTONIO: O fie upon this single life: forgo it.
We read how Daphne, for her peevish flight                    25
Became a fruitless bay-tree; Syrinx turn'd
To the pale empty reed; Anaxarete
Was frozen into marble: whereas those
Which married, or prov'd kind unto their friends
Were, by a gracious influence, transhap'd                    30
Into the olive, pomegranate, mulberry:
Became flowers, precious stones, or eminent stars.

CARIOLA: This is vain poetry: but I pray you tell me,
If there were propos'd me wisdom, riches, and beauty,
In three several young men, which should I choose?           35

ANTONIO: 'Tis a hard question. This was Paris' case
And he was blind in't, and there was great cause:
For how was't possible he could judge right,
Having three amorous goddesses in view,
And they stark naked? 'Twas a motion                         40
Were able to benight the apprehension
Of the severest counsellor of Europe.
Now I look on both your faces, so well form'd
It puts me in mind of a question, I would ask.

CARIOLA: What is't?

ANTONIO:                       I do wonder why hard-favour'd ladies   45
For the most part, keep worse-favour'd waiting-women,
To attend them, and cannot endure fair ones.

DUCHESS: O, that's soon answer'd.
Did you ever in your life know an ill painter
Desire to have his dwelling next door to the shop            50
Of an excellent picture-maker? 'Twould disgrace
His face-making, and undo him. I prithee
When were we so merry? My hair tangles.

25. *peevish*: perverse.          40. *motion*: display.

221

ANTONIO [*aside to* CARIOLA]: Pray thee, Cariola, let's steal
    forth the room,
55    And let her talk to herself: I have divers times
    Serv'd her the like, when she hath chaf'd extremely.
    I love to see her angry: softly Cariola.
      *Exeunt* [ANTONIO *and* CARIOLA].
DUCHESS: Doth not the colour of my hair 'gin to change?
    When I wax grey, I shall have all the court
60    Powder their hair with arras, to be like me:
    You have cause to love me, I ent'red you into my heart
      [*Enter* FERDINAND, *unseen.*]
    Before you would vouchsafe to call for the keys.
    We shall one day have my brothers take you napping.
    Methinks his presence, being now in court,
65    Should make you keep your own bed: but you'll say
    Love mix'd with fear is sweetest. I'll assure you
    You shall get no more children till my brothers
    Consent to be your gossips. Have you lost your tongue?
      [*She sees* FERDINAND *holding a poniard.*]
    'Tis welcome:
70    For know, whether I am doom'd to live, or die,
    I can do both like a prince.
      FERDINAND *gives her a poniard.*
FERDINAND:          Die then, quickly.
    Virtue, where art thou hid? What hideous thing
    Is it, that doth eclipse thee?
DUCHESS:            Pray sir hear me –
FERDINAND: Or is it true, thou art but a bare name,
    And no essential thing?
DUCHESS:          Sir –
75 FERDINAND:         Do not speak.
DUCHESS: No sir:

60. *arras:* i.e. orris powder: see note to *White Devil*, V, iii, 120 (p. 429).
68. *gossips:* godparents.

I will plant my soul in mine ears, to hear you.
FERDINAND: O most imperfect light of human reason,
  That mak'st us so unhappy, to foresee
  What we can least prevent. Pursue thy wishes: 80
  And glory in them: there's in shame no comfort,
  But to be past all bounds and sense of shame.
DUCHESS: I pray sir, hear me: I am married –
FERDINAND:                   So.
DUCHESS: Happily, not to your liking: but for that 85
  Alas: your shears do come untimely now
  To clip the bird's wings, that's already flown.
  Will you see my husband?
FERDINAND:             Yes, if I could change
  Eyes with a basilisk.
DUCHESS:          Sure, you came hither
  By his confederacy.
FERDINAND:         The howling of a wolf
  Is music to thee, screech-owl; prithee peace. 90
  Whate'er thou art, that hast enjoy'd my sister,
  (For I am sure thou hear'st me), for thine own sake
  Let me not know thee. I came hither prepar'd
  To work thy discovery: yet am now persuaded
  It would beget such violent effects 95
  As would damn us both. I would not for ten millions
  I had beheld thee; therefore use all means
  I never may have knowledge of thy name;
  Enjoy thy lust still, and a wretched life,
  On that condition. And for thee, vild woman, 100
  If thou do wish thy lecher may grow old
  In thy embracements, I would have thee build
  Such a room for him, as our anchorites
  To holier use inhabit. Let not the sun
  Shine on him, till he's dead. Let dogs and monkeys 105

100. *vild*: vile.

Only converse with him, and such dumb things
To whom nature denies use to sound his name.
Do not keep a paraquito, lest she learn it;
If thou do love him, cut out thine own tongue
Lest it bewray him.

110 DUCHESS:         Why might not I marry?
I have not gone about, in this, to create
Any new world, or custom.

FERDINAND:        Thou art undone:
And thou hast tane that massy sheet of lead
That hid thy husband's bones, and folded it
About my heart.

DUCHESS:      Mine bleeds for't.

115 FERDINAND:          Thine? thy heart?
What should I name't, unless a hollow bullet
Fill'd with unquenchable wild-fire?

DUCHESS:          You are in this
Too strict: and were you not my princely brother
I would say too wilful. My reputation
Is safe.

120 FERDINAND: Dost thou know what reputation is?
I'll tell thee, to small purpose, since th'instruction
Comes now too late:
Upon a time Reputation, Love and Death
Would travel o'er the world: and it was concluded
125 That they should part, and take three several ways.
Death told them, they should find him in great battles:
Or cities plagu'd with plagues. Love gives them counsel
To inquire for him 'mongst unambitious shepherds,
Where dowries were not talk'd of: and sometimes
130 'Mongst quiet kindred, that had nothing left
By their dead parents. 'Stay', quoth Reputation,
'Do not forsake me: for it is my nature

107. *use:* ability.        110. *bewray:* betray, reveal.

If once I part from any man I meet
I am never found again.' And so, for you:
You have shook hands with Reputation,                    135
And made him invisible. So fare you well.
I will never see you more.

DUCHESS:                    Why should only I,
Of all the other princes of the world
Be cas'd up, like a holy relic? I have youth,
And a little beauty.

FERDINAND:          So you have some virgins,          140
That are witches. I will never see thee more.
        *Exit.*
        *Enter* [CARIOLA *and*] ANTONIO *with a pistol.*

DUCHESS: You saw this apparition?

ANTONIO:                          Yes: we are
Betray'd. How came he hither? I should turn
This to thee, for that.
        [*He points the pistol at* CARIOLA.]

CARIOLA:          Pray sir do: and when
That you have cleft my heart, you shall read there,     145
Mine innocence.

DUCHESS:          That gallery gave him entrance.

ANTONIO: I would this terrible thing would come again,
That, standing on my guard, I might relate
My warrantable love. Ha! what means this?

DUCHESS: He left this with me.
        *She shows the poniard.*

ANTONIO:                    And it seems, did wish      150
You would use it on yourself?

DUCHESS:                    His action seem'd
To intend so much.

ANTONIO:          This hath a handle to't,
As well as a point: turn it towards him, and
So fasten the keen edge in his rank gall.

*[Knocking within.]*
How now? Who knocks? More earthquakes?

155 DUCHESS:                              I stand
As if a mine, beneath my feet, were ready
To be blown up.

CARIOLA:                'Tis Bosola.

DUCHESS:                        Away!
O misery, methinks unjust actions
Should wear these masks and curtains; and not we.
You must instantly part hence: I have fashion'd it
160      already.
*Ex[it]* ANT[ONIO]; *enter* BOSOLA].

BOSOLA: The Duke your brother is tane up in a whirlwind;
Hath took horse, and's rid post to Rome.

DUCHESS:                                So late?

BOSOLA: He told me, as he mounted into th' saddle,
You were undone.

DUCHESS:              Indeed, I am very near it.

165 BOSOLA: What's the matter?

DUCHESS: Antonio, the master of our household
Hath dealt so falsely with me, in's accounts:
My brother stood engag'd with me for money
Tane up of certain Neapolitan Jews,
170      And Antonio lets the bonds be forfeit.

BOSOLA: Strange: *[aside]* this is cunning.

DUCHESS:                              And hereupon
My brother's bills at Naples are protested
Against. Call up our officers.

BOSOLA:                I shall.
*Exit.*
*[Enter* ANTONIO.]

DUCHESS: The place that you must fly to, is Ancona,
175      Hire a house there. I'll send after you
My treasure, and my jewels: our weak safety

Runs upon enginous wheels: short syllables
Must stand for periods. I must now accuse you
Of such a feigned crime, as Tasso calls
*Magnanima mensogna:* a noble lie,                    180
'Cause it must shield our honours: hark, they are coming.
   [*Enter* BOSOLA *and* OFFICERS.]
ANTONIO: Will your Grace hear me?
DUCHESS: I have got well by you: you have yielded me
   A million of loss; I am like to inherit
   The people's curses for your stewardship.            185
   You had the trick, in audit time to be sick,
   Till I had sign'd your *Quietus*; and that cur'd you
   Without help of a doctor. Gentlemen,
   I would have this man be an example to you all:
   So shall you hold my favour. I pray let him;         190
   For h'as done that, alas! you would not think of,
   And, because I intend to be rid of him,
   I mean not to publish. Use your fortune elsewhere.
ANTONIO: I am strongly arm'd to brook my overthrow,
   As commonly men bear with a hard year:               195
   I will not blame the cause on't; but do think
   The necessity of my malevolent star
   Procures this, not her humour. O the inconstant
   And rotten ground of service, you may see;
   'Tis ev'n like him that, in a winter night,          200
   Takes a long slumber, o'er a dying fire
   As loth to part from't: yet parts thence as cold,
   As when he first sat down.
DUCHESS:                    We do confiscate,
   Towards the satisfying of your accounts,
   All that you have.
ANTONIO:            I am all yours; and 'tis very fit      205
   All mine should be so.
DUCHESS:                 So sir; you have your pass.

ANTONIO: You may see, gentlemen, what 'tis to serve
A prince with body and soul.
*Exit.*

BOSOLA: Here's an example for extortion; what moisture
210　is drawn out of the sea, when foul weather comes, pours
down, and runs into the sea again.

DUCHESS: I would know what are your opinions
Of this Antonio.

SECOND OFFICER: He could not abide to see a pig's head
215　gaping, I thought your Grace would find him a Jew:

THIRD OFFICER: I would you had been his officer, for your
own sake.

FOURTH OFFICER: You would have had more money.

FIRST OFFICER: He stopp'd his ears with black wool: and to
220　those came to him for money said he was thick of hearing.

SECOND OFFICER: Some said he was an hermaphrodite, for
he could not abide a woman.

FOURTH OFFICER: How scurvy proud he would look,
when the treasury was full. Well, let him go.

225　FIRST OFFICER: Yes, and the chippings of the butt'ry fly
after him, to scour his gold chain.

DUCHESS: Leave us. What do you think of these?
*Exeunt* [OFFICERS].

BOSOLA: That these are rogues, that in's prosperity,
But to have waited on his fortune, could have wish'd
230　His dirty stirrup riveted through their noses:
And follow'd after's mule, like a bear in a ring.
Would have prostituted their daughters to his lust;
Made their first born intelligencers; thought none happy
But such as were born under his bless'd planet;
235　And wore his livery: and do these lice drop off now?

225. *chippings:* bread crumbs.
226. *gold chain:* the steward's badge of office.
231. *in a ring:* with a ring through his nose.

Well, never look to have the like again;
He hath left a sort of flatt'ring rogues behind him,
Their doom must follow. Princes pay flatterers,
In their own money. Flatterers dissemble their vices,
And they dissemble their lies, that's justice.                    240
Alas, poor gentleman!
DUCHESS: Poor! He hath amply fill'd his coffers.
BOSOLA: Sure he was too honest. Pluto the god of riches,
When he's sent, by Jupiter, to any man
He goes limping, to signify that wealth                    245
That comes on God's name, comes slowly; but when he's
    sent
On the devil's errand, he rides post, and comes in by
    scuttles.
Let me show you what a most unvalu'd jewel
You have, in a wanton humour, thrown away,
To bless the man shall find him. He was an excellent                    250
Courtier, and most faithful; a soldier, that thought it
As beastly to know his own value too little,
As devilish to acknowledge it too much;
Both his virtue and form deserv'd a far better fortune:
His discourse rather delighted to judge itself, than show
    itself.                    255
His breast was fill'd with all perfection,
And yet it seem'd a private whisp'ring room:
It made so little noise of't.
DUCHESS:                    But he was basely descended.
BOSOLA: Will you make yourself a mercenary herald,
Rather to examine men's pedigrees, than virtues?                    260
You shall want him:
For know an honest statesman to a prince,
Is like a cedar, planted by a spring,

247. *by scuttles:* scuttling.
248. *unvalu'd:* invaluable, or undervalued.

The spring bathes the tree's root, the grateful tree
265 Rewards it with his shadow: you have not done so.
I would sooner swim to the Bermudas on
Two politicians' rotten bladders, tied
Together with an intelligencer's heart string
Than depend on so changeable a prince's favour.
270 Fare thee well, Antonio, since the malice of the world
Would needs down with thee, it cannot be said yet
That any ill happened unto thee,
Considering thy fall was accomplished with virtue.
DUCHESS: O, you render me excellent music.
BOSOLA:                                        Say you?
275 DUCHESS: This good one that you speak of, is my husband.
BOSOLA: Do I not dream? Can this ambitious age
Have so much goodness in't, as to prefer
A man merely for worth: without these shadows
Of wealth, and painted honours? possible?
DUCHESS: I have had three children by him.
280 BOSOLA:                                        Fortunate lady,
For you have made your private nuptial bed
The humble and fair seminary of peace.
No question but many an unbenefic'd scholar
Shall pray for you, for this deed, and rejoice
285 That some preferment in the world can yet
Arise from merit. The virgins of your land,
That have no dowries, shall hope your example
Will raise them to rich husbands. Should you want
Soldiers, 'twould make the very Turks and Moors
290 Turn Christians, and serve you for this act.
Last, the neglected poets of your time,
In honour of this trophy of a man,
Rais'd by that curious engine, your white hand,
Shall thank you in your grave for't; and make that
295 More reverend than all the cabinets

Of living princes. For Antonio,
His fame shall likewise flow from many a pen,
When heralds shall want coats, to sell to men.

DUCHESS: As I taste comfort, in this friendly speech,
So would I find concealment –

BOSOLA:                              O the secret of my prince,      300
Which I will wear on th'inside of my heart.

DUCHESS: You shall take charge of all my coin, and jewels,
And follow him, for he retires himself
To Ancona.

BOSOLA:      So.

DUCHESS:          Whither, within few days,
I mean to follow thee.

BOSOLA:                     Let me think:                            305
I would wish your Grace to feign a pilgrimage
To Our Lady of Loreto, scarce seven leagues
From fair Ancona, so may you depart
Your country with more honour, and your flight
Will seem a princely progress, retaining                            310
Your usual train about you.

DUCHESS:                          Sir, your direction
Shall lead me, by the hand.

CARIOLA:                         In my opinion,
She were better progress to the baths at Lucca,
Or go visit the Spa
In Germany: for, if you will believe me,                           315
I do not like this jesting with religion,
This feigned pilgrimage.

DUCHESS:                        Thou art a superstitious fool:
Prepare us instantly for our departure.
Past sorrows, let us moderately lament them,                        320
For those to come, seek wisely to prevent them.

        *Exit* [DUCHESS *with* CARIOLA].

298. *coats:* i.e. of arms.

231

BOSOLA: A politician is the devil's quilted anvil,
He fashions all sins on him, and the blows
Are never heard ; he may work in a lady's chamber,
As here for proof. What rests, but I reveal
325     All to my lord? O, this base quality
Of intelligencer ! Why, every quality i'th' world
Prefers but gain, or commendation:
Now for this act, I am certain to be rais'd,
*And men that paint weeds, to the life, are prais'd.*
   *Exit.*

## [SCENE THREE]

[*Enter*] CARDINAL, FERDINAND, MALATESTE,
PESCARA, SILVIO, DELIO.

CARDINAL: Must we turn soldier then?

MALATESTE:             The Emperor,
Hearing your worth that way, ere you attain'd
This reverend garment, joins you in commission
With the right fortunate soldier, the Marquis of Pescara
And the famous Lannoy.

5 CARDINAL:           He that had the honour
Of taking the French king prisoner?

MALATESTE:             The same.
Here's a plot drawn for a new fortification
At Naples.

FERDINAND: This great Count Malateste, I perceive
Hath got employment.

DELIO:          No employment, my lord,
10    A marginal note in the muster book, that he is
A voluntary lord.

FERDINAND:       He's no soldier?

1. *The Emperor:* Charles V (1516–56).     7. *plot:* plan.

DELIO: He has worn gunpowder, in's hollow tooth,
  For the tooth-ache.
SILVIO: He comes to the leaguer with a full intent
  To eat fresh beef, and garlic; means to stay          15
  Till the scent be gone, and straight return to court.
DELIO: He hath read all the late service,
  As the City chronicle relates it,
  And keeps two painters going, only to express
  Battles in model.
SILVIO:              Then he'll fight by the book.          20
DELIO: By the almanac, I think,
  To choose good days, and shun the critical.
  That's his mistress' scarf.
SILVIO:                    Yes, he protests
  He would do much for that taffeta –
DELIO: I think he would run away from a battle          25
  To save it from taking prisoner.
SILVIO:                          He is horribly afraid
  Gunpowder will spoil the perfume on't –
DELIO: I saw a Dutchman break his pate once
  For calling him pot-gun; he made his head
  Have a bore in't, like a musket.          30
SILVIO: I would he had made a touch-hole to't.
  He is indeed a guarded sumpter-cloth
  Only for the remove of the court.
    [*Enter* BOSOLA.]
PESCARA: Bosola arriv'd? What should be the business?
  Some falling out amongst the cardinals.          35
  These factions amongst great men, they are like
  Foxes, when their heads are divided:

17. *service:* military operations.
22. *critical:* related to the crisis or turning point; crucial.
32. *guarded sumpter-cloth:* ornamented saddle cloth used during royal
  progresses.

They carry fire in their tails, and all the country
About them goes to wrack for't.

SILVIO:                                    What's that Bosola?

40  DELIO: I knew him in Padua, a fantastical scholar, like such
who study to know how many knots was in Hercules'
club; of what colour Achilles' beard was, or whether
Hector were not troubled with the toothache. He hath
studied himself half blear-ey'd, to know the true sym-
45  metry of Caesar's nose by a shoeing-horn: and this he did
to gain the name of a speculative man.

PESCARA: Mark Prince Ferdinand,
A very salamander lives in's eye,
To mock the eager violence of fire.

50  SILVIO: That cardinal hath made more bad faces with his
oppression than ever Michael Angelo made good ones: he
lifts up's nose, like a foul porpoise before a storm –

PESCARA: The Lord Ferdinand laughs.

DELIO: Like a deadly cannon, that lightens ere it smokes.

55  PESCARA: These are your true pangs of death,
The pangs of life, that struggle with great statesmen –

DELIO: In such a deformed silence, witches whisper
Their charms.

CARDINAL: Doth she make religion her riding hood
To keep her from the sun and tempest?

60  FERDINAND:                              That:
That damns her. Methinks her fault and beauty
Blended together, show like leprosy,
The whiter, the fouler. I make it a question
Whether her beggarly brats were ever christ'ned.

65  CARDINAL: I will instantly solicit the state of Ancona
To have them banish'd.

FERDINAND:              You are for Loreto?
I shall not be at your ceremony; fare you well:

65. *state:* rulers.

Write to the Duke of Malfi, my young nephew
She had by her first husband, and acquaint him
With's mother's honesty.

BOSOLA:                                  I will.

FERDINAND:                                    Antonio!                    70
A slave, that only smell'd of ink and counters,
And nev'r in's life look'd like a gentleman,
But in the audit time: go, go presently,
Draw me out an hundred and fifty of our horse,
And meet me at the fort-bridge.                                75
    *Exeunt.*

## [SCENE FOUR]

[*Enter*] TWO PILGRIMS *to the Shrine of Our Lady of
Loreto.*

FIRST PILGRIM: I have not seen a goodlier shrine than this,
    Yet I have visited many.

SECOND PILGRIM:          The Cardinal of Aragon
    Is this day to resign his cardinal's hat;
    His sister duchess likewise is arriv'd
    To pay her vow of pilgrimage. I expect                    5
    A noble ceremony.

FIRST PILGRIM:          No question. They come.

*Here the ceremony of the Cardinal's instalment in the habit
of a soldier: perform'd in delivering up his cross, hat, robes,
and ring at the shrine; and investing him with sword, helmet,
shield, and spurs. Then* ANTONIO, *the* DUCHESS *and their
children, having presented themselves at the shrine, are (by a
form of banishment in dumb-show expressed towards them by
the* CARDINAL, *and the state of* ANCONA) *banished.
During all which ceremony this ditty is sung to very solemn
music, by divers churchmen; and then*

71. *counters:* small discs used in accounting.

*[Exeunt all except the two* PILGRIMS.]
*Arms and honours deck thy story,*　　　The Author
*To thy fame's eternal glory,*　　　　　disclaims
*Adverse fortune ever fly thee,*　　　　　this Ditty
10　　*No disastrous fate come nigh thee.*　　to be his.

*I alone will sing thy praises,*
*Whom to honour virtue raises;*
*And thy study that divine is,*
*Bent to martial discipline is:*
15　　*Lay aside all those robes lie by thee,*
*Crown thy arts with arms: they'll beautify thee.*

*O worthy of worthiest name, adorn'd in this manner,*
*Lead bravely thy forces on, under war's warlike banner:*
*O mayst thou prove fortunate in all martial courses,*
20　　*Guide thou still by skill, in arts and forces:*
*Victory attend thee nigh, whilst fame sings loud thy powers,*
*Triumphant conquest crown thy head, and blessings pour down*
*showers.*

FIRST PILGRIM: Here's a strange turn of state: who would
　　have thought
So great a lady would have match'd herself
25　　Unto so mean a person? Yet the Cardinal
Bears himself much too cruel.
SECOND PILGRIM:　　　　　　　They are banish'd.
FIRST PILGRIM: But I would ask what power hath this
　　state
Of Ancona, to determine of a free prince?
SECOND PILGRIM: They are a free state sir, and her brother
　　show'd

---

9. S.D. The authorship of the ditty is unknown.
28. *determine of:* judge.
29. *free state:* Ancona was a semi-independent republic under papal
　　suzerainty.

How that the Pope, forehearing of her looseness,                    30
Hath seiz'd into th' protection of the Church
The Dukedom which she held as dowager.
FIRST PILGRIM: But by what justice?
SECOND PILGRIM:                         Sure I think by none,
Only her brother's instigation.
FIRST PILGRIM: What was it, with such violence he took     35
Off from her finger?
SECOND PILGRIM:      'Twas her wedding-ring,
Which he vow'd shortly he would sacrifice
To his revenge.
FIRST PILGRIM: Alas Antonio!
If that a man be thrust into a well,
No matter who sets hand to't, his own weight                       40
Will bring him sooner to th' bottom. Come, let's hence
Fortune makes this conclusion general,
*All things do help th' unhappy man to fall.*
    *Exeunt.*


## [SCENE FIVE]

[*Enter* ANTONIO, DUCHESS, CHILDREN, CARIOLA,
SERVANTS.]
DUCHESS: Banish'd Ancona?
ANTONIO:                       Yes, you see what power
Lightens in great men's breath.
DUCHESS:                           Is all our train
Shrunk to this poor remainder?
ANTONIO:                         These poor men,
Which have got little in your service, vow
To take your fortune. But your wiser buntings                      5
Now they are fledg'd are gone.

5. *buntings:* family of small birds related to the larks.

237

DUCHESS:                      They have done wisely;
This puts me in mind of death: physicians thus,
With their hands full of money, use to give o'er
Their patients.
ANTONIO:       Right the fashion of the world:
10    From decay'd fortunes every flatterer shrinks,
Men cease to build where the foundation sinks.
DUCHESS: I had a very strange dream tonight.
ANTONIO:                         What was't?
DUCHESS: Methought I wore my coronet of state,
And on a sudden all the diamonds
Were chang'd to pearls.
15  ANTONIO:            My interpretation
Is, you'll weep shortly; for to me, the pearls
Do signify your tears.
DUCHESS:           The birds, that live i'th' field
On the wild benefit of nature, live
Happier than we; for they may choose their mates,
20  And carol their sweet pleasures to the spring.
       [*Enter* BOSOLA *with a letter.*]
BOSOLA: You are happily o'ertane.
DUCHESS:                From my brother?
BOSOLA: Yes, from the Lord Ferdinand; your brother,
All love, and safety –
DUCHESS:           Thou dost blanch mischief;
Wouldst make it white. See, see; like to calm weather
25  At sea before a tempest, false hearts speak fair
To those they intend most mischief.
       [*She reads*] *A Letter.*
*Send* Antonio *to me; I want his head in a business –*
A politic equivocation –
He doth not want your counsel, but your head;
30  That is, he cannot sleep till you be dead.

9. *Right:* exactly.      18. *benefit:* favour.

And here's another pitfall, that's strew'd o'er
With roses: mark it, 'tis a cunning one:
*I stand engaged for your husband for several debts at Naples:*
*let not that trouble him, I had rather have his heart than his*
*money.*                                                                               35
And I believe so too.

BOSOLA:                         What do you believe?

DUCHESS: That he so much distrusts my husband's love,
He will by no means believe his heart is with him
Until he see it. The devil is not cunning enough
To circumvent us in riddles.                                                           40

BOSOLA: Will you reject that noble and free league
Of amity and love which I present you?

DUCHESS: Their league is like that of some politic kings
Only to make themselves of strength and power
To be our after-ruin: tell them so.                                                   45

BOSOLA: And what from you?

ANTONIO:                         Thus tell them: I will not come.

BOSOLA: And what of this?

ANTONIO:                         My brothers have dispers'd
Bloodhounds abroad; which till I hear are muzzl'd
No truce, though hatch'd with ne'er such politic skill
Is safe, that hangs upon our enemies' will.                                            50
I'll not come at them.

BOSOLA:                         This proclaims your breeding.
Every small thing draws a base mind to fear;
As the adamant draws iron: fare you well sir,
You shall shortly hear from's.

DUCHESS:                         I suspect some ambush:
Therefore by all my love, I do conjure you                                             55
To take your eldest son, and fly towards Milan;
Let us not venture all this poor remainder
In one unlucky bottom.

47. *this:* the letter.      53. *adamant:* loadstone.      58. *bottom:* hold, ship·

ANTONIO:      You counsel safely.
Best of my life, farewell. Since we must part
60 Heaven hath a hand in't: but no otherwise
Than as some curious artist takes in sunder
A clock, or watch, when it is out of frame
To bring't in better order.

DUCHESS:     I know not which is best,
To see you dead, or part with you. Farewell boy,
65 Thou art happy, that thou hast not understanding
To know thy misery. For all our wit
And reading brings us to a truer sense
Of sorrow. In the eternal Church, sir,
I do hope we shall not part thus.

ANTONIO:      O be of comfort,
70 Make patience a noble fortitude:
And think not how unkindly we are us'd.
*Man, like to cassia, is prov'd best being bruis'd.*

DUCHESS: Must I like to a slave-born Russian,
Account it praise to suffer tyranny?
75 And yet, O Heaven, thy heavy hand is in't.
I have seen my little boy oft scourge his top,
And compar'd myself to't: nought made me e'er go
 right,
But Heaven's scourge-stick.

ANTONIO:     Do not weep:
Heaven fashion'd us of nothing; and we strive
80 To bring ourselves to nothing. Farewell Cariola,
And thy sweet armful. [*To the* DUCHESS] If I do never see
 thee more,
Be a good mother to your little ones,
And save them from the tiger: fare you well.

DUCHESS: Let me look upon you once more: for that speech
85 Came from a dying father: your kiss is colder

78. *scourge-stick:* whip for a top.

Than I have seen an holy anchorite
Give to a dead man's skull.
ANTONIO: My heart is turn'd to a heavy lump of lead,
With which I sound my danger: fare you well.
*Exit [with elder* SON].
DUCHESS: My laurel is all withered.                               90
CARIOLA: Look, Madam, what a troop of armed men
Make toward us.
*Enter* BOSOLA *with a guard [vizarded]*.
DUCHESS:          O, they are very welcome:
When Fortune's wheel is over-charg'd with princes,
The weight makes it move swift. I would have my ruin
Be sudden. I am your adventure, am I not?                          95
BOSOLA: You are: you must see your husband no more –
DUCHESS: What devil art thou, that counterfeits Heaven's
thunder?
BOSOLA: Is that terrible? I would have you tell me whether
Is that note worse that frights the silly birds
Out of the corn; or that which doth allure them                   100
To the nets? You have heark'ned to the last too much.
DUCHESS: O misery! like to a rusty o'ercharg'd cannon,
Shall I never fly in pieces? Come: to what prison?
BOSOLA: To none.
DUCHESS:          Whither then?
BOSOLA:                          To your palace.
DUCHESS: I have heard that Charon's boat serves to convey    105
All o'er the dismal lake, but brings none back again.
BOSOLA: Your brothers mean you safety and pity.
DUCHESS: Pity!
With such a pity men preserve alive
Pheasants and quails, when they are not fat enough            110
To be eaten.
BOSOLA: These are your children?

95. *adventure*: quarry.

DUCHESS: Yes.

BOSOLA: Can they prattle?

DUCHESS: No:
But I intend, since they were born accurs'd,
Curses shall be their first language.

115 BOSOLA: Fie, Madam!
Forget this base, low fellow.

DUCHESS: Were I a man,
I'ld beat that counterfeit face into thy other –

BOSOLA: One of no birth.

DUCHESS: Say that he was born mean,
Man is most happy, when's own actions
120 Be arguments and examples of his virtue.

BOSOLA: A barren, beggarly virtue.

DUCHESS: I prithee, who is greatest, can you tell?
Sad tales befit my woe: I'll tell you one.
A Salmon, as she swam unto the sea,
125 Met with a Dog-fish; who encounters her
With this rough language: 'Why art thou so bold
To mix thyself with our high state of floods
Being no eminent courtier, but one
That for the calmest and fresh time o'th' year
130 Dost live in shallow rivers, rank'st thyself
With silly Smelts and Shrimps? And darest thou
Pass by our Dog-ship without reverence?'
'O', quoth the Salmon, 'sister, be at peace:
Thank Jupiter, we both have pass'd the Net,
135 Our value never can be truly known,
Till in the Fisher's basket we be shown;
I'th' Market then my price may be the higher,
Even when I am nearest to the Cook, and fire.'
So, to great men, the moral may be stretched.
140 *Men oft are valued high, when th'are most wretch'd.*

117. *counterfeit face*: Bosola is vizarded.

But come: whither you please. I am arm'd 'gainst misery:
Bent to all sways of the oppressor's will.
*There's no deep valley, but near some great hill.*
    *Ex[eunt].*

# [ACT FOUR]

## [SCENE ONE]

[*Enter* FERDINAND *and* BOSOLA.]

FERDINAND: How doth our sister Duchess bear herself
In her imprisonment?

BOSOLA:              Nobly: I'll describe her.
She's sad, as one long us'd to't: and she seems
Rather to welcome the end of misery
5     Than shun it: a behaviour so noble,
As gives a majesty to adversity:
You may discern the shape of loveliness
More perfect in her tears, than in her smiles;
She will muse four hours together: and her silence,
10    Methinks, expresseth more than if she spake.

FERDINAND: Her melancholy seems to be fortifi'd
With a strange disdain.

BOSOLA:             'Tis so: and this restraint
(Like English mastiffs, that grow fierce with tying)
Makes her too passionately apprehend
Those pleasures she's kept from.

15 FERDINAND:            Curse upon her!
I will no longer study in the book
Of another's heart: inform her what I told you.
    *Exit.*

[BOSOLA *draws the traverse to reveal the* DUCHESS,
CARIOLA *and* SERVANTS.]

BOSOLA: All comfort to your Grace –

DUCHESS:              I will have none.
Pray-thee, why dost thou wrap thy poison'd pills
20    In gold and sugar?

BOSOLA: Your elder brother the Lord Ferdinand
　Is come to visit you: and sends you word
　'Cause once he rashly made a solemn vow
　Never to see you more; he comes i'th' night;
　And prays you, gently, neither torch nor taper　　　　25
　Shine in your chamber: he will kiss your hand;
　And reconcile himself: but, for his vow,
　He dares not see you.
DUCHESS:　　　　　　At his pleasure.
　Take hence the lights: he's come.
　　[*Exeunt* SERVANTS *with lights; enter* FERDINAND.]
FERDINAND:　　　　　　　　Where are you?
DUCHESS:　　　　　　　　　　　　Here sir.
FERDINAND: This darkness suits you well.
DUCHESS:　　　　　　　　I would ask your pardon.　　30
FERDINAND: You have it;
　For I account it the honrabl'st revenge
　Where I may kill, to pardon: where are your cubs?
DUCHESS: Whom?
FERDINAND: Call them your children;　　　　　　　35
　For though our national law distinguish bastards
　From true legitimate issue, compassionate nature
　Makes them all equal.
DUCHESS:　　　　　Do you visit me for this?
　You violate a sacrament o'th' Church
　Shall make you howl in hell for't.
FERDINAND:　　　　　　　　It had been well,　　40
　Could you have liv'd thus always: for indeed
　You were too much i'th' light. But no more;
　I come to seal my peace with you: here's a hand,
　　[*He*] *gives her a dead man's hand.*

---

39. *a sacrament o'th' Church:* i.e. marriage.
42. *i'th' light:* in the public eye, unchaste.

To which you have vow'd much love: the ring upon't
You gave.

45 DUCHESS: I affectionately kiss it.

FERDINAND: Pray do: and bury the print of it in your heart.
I will leave this ring with you, for a love-token:
And the hand, as sure as the ring: and do not doubt
But you shall have the heart too. When you need a friend
50 Send it to him that ow'd it: you shall see
Whether he can aid you.

DUCHESS                    You are very cold.
I fear you are not well after your travel:
Ha! Lights! O horrible!

FERDINAND:                  Let her have lights enough.
            *Exit.*
            [*Enter* SERVANTS *with lights.*]

DUCHESS: What witchcraft doth he practise, that he hath
left
55 A dead man's hand here?
            *Here is discover'd, behind a traverse, the artificial figures of*
            ANTONIO *and his children; appearing as if they were dead.*

BOSOLA: Look you: here's the piece from which 'twas tane;
He doth present you this sad spectacle,
That now you know directly they are dead,
Hereafter you may, wisely, cease to grieve
60 For that which cannot be recovered.

DUCHESS: There is not between heaven and earth one wish
I stay for after this: it wastes me more,
Than were't my picture, fashion'd out of wax,
Stuck with a magical needle, and then buried
65 In some foul dunghill: and yond's an excellent property
For a tyrant, which I would account mercy –

44–5. *the ring upon't* / *You gave:* i.e. her wedding ring, torn off by the
    Cardinal (see III, iv, 35–8).
50. *ow'd:* owned.

BOSOLA: What's that?

DUCHESS: If they would bind me to that lifeless trunk,
And let me freeze to death.

BOSOLA:                          Come, you must live.

DUCHESS: That's the greatest torture souls feel in hell,          70
In hell: that they must live, and cannot die.
Portia, I'll new kindle thy coals again,
And revive the rare and almost dead example
Of a loving wife.

BOSOLA:              O fie! despair? remember
You are a Christian.

DUCHESS:              The Church enjoins fasting:          75
I'll starve myself to death.

BOSOLA:                          Leave this vain sorrow;
Things being at the worst, begin to mend:
The bee when he hath shot his sting into your hand
May then play with your eyelid.

DUCHESS:                          Good comfortable fellow
Persuade a wretch that's broke upon the wheel          80
To have all his bones new set: entreat him live,
To be executed again. Who must dispatch me?
I account this world a tedious theatre,
For I do play a part in't 'gainst my will.

BOSOLA: Come, be of comfort, I will save your life.          85

DUCHESS: Indeed I have not leisure to tend so small a
business.

BOSOLA: Now, by my life, I pity you.

DUCHESS:                          Thou art a fool then,
To waste thy pity on a thing so wretch'd
As cannot pity itself. I am full of daggers.
Puff! let me blow these vipers from me.          90
    [Enter SERVANT.]
What are you?

74. despair: see the note to White Devil, V, iv, 141 (p. 431).

247

SERVANT:      One that wishes you long life.

DUCHESS: I would thou wert hang'd for the horrible curse
Thou hast given me: I shall shortly grow one
Of the miracles of pity. I'll go pray. No,
I'll go curse.

BOSOLA:     O fie!

DUCHESS:       I could curse the stars.

95   BOSOLA:                   O fearful!

DUCHESS: And those three smiling seasons of the year
Into a Russian winter: nay the world
To its first chaos.

BOSOLA: Look you, the stars shine still.

DUCHESS:                O, but you must

100   Remember, my curse hath a great way to go:
Plagues, that makes lanes through largest families,
Consume them.

BOSOLA:     Fie lady!

DUCHESS:       Let them like tyrants
Never be rememb'red, but for the ill they have done:
Let all the zealous prayers of mortified
Churchmen forget them –

105   BOSOLA:         O uncharitable!

DUCHESS: Let Heaven, a little while, cease crowning martyrs
To punish them.
Go, howl them this: and say I long to bleed.
*It is some mercy when men kill with speed.*
    *Exit* [*with* SERVANTS].
    [*Enter* FERDINAND.]

110   FERDINAND: Excellent; as I would wish: she's plagu'd in art.
These presentations are but fram'd in wax
By the curious-master in that quality,
Vincentio Lauriola, and she takes them
For true substantial bodies.

BOSOLA:         Why do you do this?

FERDINAND: To bring her to despair.

BOSOLA:                             'Faith, end here;    115
And go no farther in your cruelty,
Send her a penitential garment, to put on
Next to her delicate skin, and furnish her
With beads and prayerbooks.

FERDINAND:                 Damn her! that body of hers,
While that my blood ran pure in't, was more worth    120
Than that which thou wouldst comfort, call'd a soul.
I will send her masques of common courtesans,
Have her meat serv'd up by bawds and ruffians,
And, 'cause she'll needs be mad, I am resolv'd
To remove forth the common hospital    125
All the mad folk, and place them near her lodging:
There let them practise together, sing, and dance,
And act their gambols to the full o'th' moon:
If she can sleep the better for it, let her.
Your work is almost ended.

BOSOLA:                   Must I see her again?    130

FERDINAND: Yes.

BOSOLA:        Never.

FERDINAND:       You must.

BOSOLA:                   Never in mine own shape;
That's forfeited by my intelligence,
And this last cruel lie: when you send me next,
The business shall be comfort.

FERDINAND:               Very likely:
Thy pity is nothing of kin to thee. Antonio    135
Lurks about Milan; thou shalt shortly thither,
To feed a fire as great as my revenge,
Which nev'r will slack, till it have spent his fuel;
*Intemperate agues make physicians cruel.*
   *Exeunt.*

125. *remove forth:* take from.

# [SCENE TWO]

[*Enter* DUCHESS *and* CARIOLA.]

DUCHESS: What hideous noise was that?

CARIOLA:                   'Tis the wild consort
Of madmen, lady, which your tyrant brother
Hath plac'd about your lodging. This tyranny,
I think, was never practis'd till this hour.

5   DUCHESS: Indeed I thank him: nothing but noise, and folly
Can keep me in my right wits, whereas reason
And silence make me stark mad. Sit down,
Discourse to me some dismal tragedy.

CARIOLA: O 'twill increase your melancholy.

DUCHESS:                       Thou art deceiv'd;

10   To hear of greater grief would lessen mine.
This is a prison?

CARIOLA:         Yes, but you shall live
To shake this durance off.

DUCHESS:              Thou art a fool:
The robin red-breast and the nightingale
Never live long in cages.

CARIOLA:            Pray dry your eyes.
What think you of Madam?

15   DUCHESS:                Of nothing:
When I muse thus, I sleep.

CARIOLA: Like a madman, with your eyes open?

DUCHESS: Dost thou think we shall know one another
In th'other world?

CARIOLA:            Yes, out of question.

20   DUCHESS: O that it were possible we might
But hold some two days' conference with the dead,
From them I should learn somewhat, I am sure

1. *consort:* company; group of musicians.

I never shall know here. I'll tell thee a miracle,
I am not mad yet, to my cause of sorrow.
Th'heaven o'er my head seems made of molten brass,    25
The earth of flaming sulphur, yet I am not mad.
I am acquainted with sad misery,
As the tann'd galley-slave is with his oar.
Necessity makes me suffer constantly,
And custom makes it easy. Who do I look like now?    30

CARIOLA: Like to your picture in the gallery,
A deal of life in show, but none in practice:
Or rather like some reverend monument
Whose ruins are even pitied.

DUCHESS:                    Very proper:
And Fortune seems only to have her eyesight,    35
To behold my tragedy.
How now! what noise is that?
    [*Enter* SERVANT.]

SERVANT:                    I am come to tell you,
Your brother hath intended you some sport.
A great physician when the Pope was sick
Of a deep melancholy, presented him    40
With several sorts of madmen, which wild object,
Being full of change and sport, forc'd him to laugh,
And so th'imposthume broke: the selfsame cure
The Duke intends on you.

DUCHESS:                    Let them come in.

SERVANT: There's a mad lawyer, and a secular priest,    45
A doctor that hath forfeited his wits
By jealousy; an astrologian,
That in his works said such a day o'th' month
Should be the day of doom; and, failing of't,

43. *imposthume:* abscess.
45. *secular priest:* one not bound by a vow of poverty, nor a member of
    an order.

50 Ran mad; an English tailor, craz'd i'th' brain
With the study of new fashion; a gentleman usher
Quite beside himself with care to keep in mind
The number of his lady's salutations,
Or 'How do you?' she employ'd him in each morning:
55 A farmer too, an excellent knave in grain,
Mad, 'cause he was hind'red transportation;
And let one broker, that's mad, loose to these,
You'ld think the devil were among them.
DUCHESS: Sit Cariola: let them loose when you please,
60 For I am chain'd to endure all your tyranny.
　　[*Enter* MADMEN.]
*Here, by a madman, this song is sung to a dismal kind of music.*
*O let us howl, some heavy note,*
　*Some deadly-dogged howl,*
*Sounding, as from the threat'ning throat,*
　*Of beasts, and fatal fowl.*
65 *As ravens, screech-owls, bulls, and bears,*
　*We'll bell, and bawl our parts,*
*Till yerksome noise, have cloy'd your ears,*
　*And corrosiv'd your hearts.*
*At last when as our quire wants breath,*
70 　*Our bodies being blest,*
*We'll sing like swans, to welcome death,*
　*And die in love and rest.*
FIRST MADMAN: Doomsday not come yet? I'll draw it
nearer by a perspective, or make a glass, that shall set all the
75 world on fire upon an instant. I cannot sleep, my pillow is
stuff'd with a litter of porcupines.
SECOND MADMAN: Hell is a mere glass-house, where the

---

55. *knave in grain*: a knave in the grain trade; a thorough knave.
56. *transportation*: export.
57. *broker*: pawnbroker, or perhaps a procurer.
74. *perspective*: telescope.

devils are continually blowing up women's souls on hollow irons, and the fire never goes out.

THIRD MADMAN: I will lie with every woman in my 80 parish the tenth night: I will tithe them over like haycocks.

FOURTH MADMAN: Shall my pothecary outgo me, because I am a cuckold? I have found out his roguery: he makes alum of his wife's urine, and sells it to Puritans, that have sore throats with over-straining. 85

FIRST MADMAN: I have skill in heraldry.

SECOND MADMAN: Hast?

FIRST MADMAN: You do give for your crest a woodcock's head, with the brains pick't out on't. You are a very ancient gentleman. 90

THIRD MADMAN: Greek is turn'd Turk; we are only to be sav'd by the Helvetian translation.

FIRST MADMAN: Come on sir, I will lay the law to you.

SECOND MADMAN: O, rather lay a corrosive, the law will eat to the bone. 95

THIRD MADMAN: He that drinks but to satisfy nature is damn'd.

FOURTH MADMAN: If I had my glass here, I would show a sight should make all the women here call me mad doctor. 100

FIRST MADMAN: What's he, a rope-maker?

SECOND MADMAN: No, no, no, a snuffling knave, that while he shows the tombs, will have his hand in a wench's placket.

THIRD MADMAN: Woe to the caroche that brought home 105 my wife from the masque, at three o'clock in the morning; it had a large feather bed in it.

FOURTH MADMAN: I have pared the devil's nails forty

89. the woodcock was reputed brainless.     93. *lay:* expound.
94. *lay:* apply.
101. *rope-maker:* i.e. the hangman's accomplice.

times, roasted them in raven's eggs, and cur'd agues with
110     them.

THIRD MADMAN: Get me three hundred milch bats, to
make possets to procure sleep.

FOURTH MADMAN: All the college may throw their caps
at me, I have made a soap-boiler costive: it was my
115     masterpiece.

*Here the dance consisting of 8 madmen, with music answerable thereunto, after which* BOSOLA, *like an old man, enters.*

DUCHESS: Is he mad too?

SERVANT:                 Pray question him; I'll leave you.

[*Exeunt* SERVANT *and* MADMEN.]

BOSOLA: I am come to make thy tomb.

DUCHESS:                       Ha! my tomb?
Thou speak'st as if I lay upon my death-bed,
Gasping for breath: dost thou perceive me sick?

BOSOLA: Yes, and the more dangerously, since thy sickness
120     is insensible.

DUCHESS: Thou art not mad, sure; dost know me?

BOSOLA: Yes.

DUCHESS: Who am I?

BOSOLA: Thou art a box of worm seed, at best, but a sal-
125     vatory of green mummy: what's this flesh? a little crudded
milk, fantastical puff-paste: our bodies are weaker than
those paper prisons boys use to keep flies in: more contemptible; since ours is to preserve earth-worms: didst
thou ever see a lark in a cage? such is the soul in the body:
130     this world is like her little turf of grass, and the heaven o'er

112. *possets:* hot milk curdled with spiced ale or wine.
113. *throw their caps at:* emulate.     114. *costive:* constipated.
120. *insensible:* imperceptible (because spiritual and not bodily).
124–5. *salvatory:* ointment box.
125. *mummy:* see *White Devil*, I, i, 16 note; *crudded:* curdled.
126. *puff-paste:* light pastry.

our heads, like her looking-glass, only gives us a miserable
knowledge of the small compass of our prison.

DUCHESS: Am not I thy Duchess?

BOSOLA: Thou art some great woman, sure; for riot begins
to sit on thy forehead (clad in grey hairs) twenty years   135
sooner than on a merry milkmaid's. Thou sleep'st worse,
than if a mouse should be forc'd to take up her lodging in a
cat's ear: a little infant, that breeds its teeth, should it lie
with thee, would cry out, as if thou wert the more unquiet
bedfellow.   140

DUCHESS: I am Duchess of Malfi still.

BOSOLA: That makes thy sleeps so broken:
*Glories, like glow-worms, afar off shine bright,*
*But look'd to near, have neither heat nor light.*

DUCHESS: Thou art very plain.   145

BOSOLA: My trade is to flatter the dead, not the living;
I am a tomb-maker.

DUCHESS: And thou com'st to make my tomb?

BOSOLA: Yes.

DUCHESS: Let me be a little merry;   150
Of what stuff wilt thou make it?

BOSOLA: Nay, resolve me first, of what fashion?

DUCHESS: Why, do we grow fantastical in our death-bed?
Do we affect fashion in the grave?

BOSOLA: Most ambitiously. Princes' images on their tombs   155
Do not lie as they were wont, seeming to pray
Up to Heaven: but with their hands under their cheeks,
As if they died of the tooth-ache; they are not carved
With their eyes fix'd upon the stars; but as
Their minds were wholly bent upon the world,   160
The self-same way they seem to turn their faces.

DUCHESS: Let me know fully therefore the effect
Of this thy dismal preparation,

152. *resolve:* explain.

This talk, fit for a charnel.

BOSOLA:                         Now I shall;
    *[Enter* EXECUTIONERS *with] a coffin, cords, and a bell.*
165    Here is a present from your princely brothers,
    And may it arrive welcome, for it brings
    Last benefit, last sorrow.

DUCHESS:                         Let me see it.
    I have so much obedience, in my blood,
    I wish it in their veins, to do them good.

170 BOSOLA: This is your last presence chamber.

CARIOLA: O my sweet lady!

DUCHESS:                         Peace; it affrights not me.

BOSOLA: I am the common bellman,
    That usually is sent to condemn'd persons,
    The night before they suffer.

DUCHESS:                         Even now thou said'st
    Thou wast a tomb-maker?

175 BOSOLA:                         'Twas to bring you
    By degrees to mortification. Listen:
    *[He rings the bell.]*
    *Hark, now every thing is still,*
    *The screech-owl and the whistler shrill*
    *Call upon our Dame, aloud,*
180    *And bid her quickly don her shroud.*
    *Much you had of land and rent,*
    *Your length in clay's now competent.*
    *A long war disturb'd your mind,*
    *Here your perfect peace is sign'd.*
185    *Of what is't fools make such vain keeping?*
    *Sin their conception, their birth, weeping:*
    *Their life, a general mist of error,*
    *Their death, a hideous storm of terror.*

181. *rent:* income.    182. *competent:* sufficient.
184. *peace:* peace treaty.

*Strew your hair with powders sweet:*
*Don clean linen, bathe your feet,*　　　　　　　190
*And, the foul fiend more to check,*
*A crucifix let bless your neck.*
*'Tis now full tide 'tween night and day,*
*End your groan, and come away.*
　　　　[EXECUTIONERS *approach.*]
CARIOLA: Hence villains, tyrants, murderers. Alas!　　195
　　What will you do with my lady? Call for help.
DUCHESS: To whom, to our next neighbours? They are
　　mad-folks.
BOSOLA: Remove that noise.
　　　　[EXECUTIONERS *seize* CARIOLA, *who struggles.*]
DUCHESS:　　　　　　　　Farewell Cariola,
　　In my last will I have not much to give;　　　200
　　A many hungry guests have fed upon me,
　　Thine will be a poor reversion.
CARIOLA:　　　　　　　　　I will die with her.
DUCHESS: I pray thee look thou giv'st my little boy
　　Some syrup for his cold, and let the girl
　　Say her prayers, ere she sleep.
　　　　[CARIOLA *is forced off.*]
　　　　　　　　　　　　Now what you please,　205
　　What death?
BOSOLA: Strangling: here are your executioners.
DUCHESS: I forgive them:
　　The apoplexy, catarrh, or cough o'th' lungs
　　Would do as much as they do.　　　　　210
BOSOLA: Doth not death fright you?
DUCHESS:　　　　　　　Who would be afraid on't?
　　Knowing to meet such excellent company
　　In th'other world.

202. *reversion:* bequest, usually of property or income.
209. *catarrh:* cerebral haemorrhage.

BOSOLA: Yet, methinks,
The manner of your death should much afflict you,
This cord should terrify you?

215 DUCHESS: Not a whit:
What would it pleasure me, to have my throat cut
With diamonds? or to be smothered
With cassia? or to be shot to death, with pearls?
I know death hath ten thousand several doors

220 For men to take their exits: and 'tis found
They go on such strange geometrical hinges,
You may open them both ways: any way, for Heaven
    sake,
So I were out of your whispering. Tell my brothers
That I perceive death, now I am well awake,

225 Best gift is, they can give, or I can take.
I would fain put off my last woman's fault,
I'ld not be tedious to you.

EXECUTIONERS: We are ready.

DUCHESS: Dispose my breath how please you, but my body
Bestow upon my women, will you?

EXECUTIONERS: Yes.

230 DUCHESS: Pull, and pull strongly, for your able strength
Must pull down heaven upon me:
Yet stay, heaven gates are not so highly arch'd
As princes' palaces: they that enter there
Must go upon their knees. Come violent death,

235 Serve for mandragora to make me sleep;
Go tell my brothers, when I am laid out,
They then may feed in quiet.

*They strangle her.*

BOSOLA: Where's the waiting woman?
Fetch her. Some other strangle the children.

[*Exeunt* EXECUTIONERS. *Enter one with* CARIOLA.]

235. *mandragora:* mandrake, used as a narcotic.

Look you, there sleeps your mistress.

CARIOLA:                       O you are damn'd      240
  Perpetually for this. My turn is next,
  Is't not so ordered?

BOSOLA:            Yes, and I am glad
  You are so well prepar'd for't.

CARIOLA:               You are deceiv'd sir,
  I am not prepar'd for't. I will not die,
  I will first come to my answer; and know
  How I have offended.

BOSOLA:            Come, dispatch her.      245
  You kept her counsel, now you shall keep ours.

CARIOLA: I will not die, I must not, I am contracted
  To a young gentleman.

EXECUTIONER:          Here's your wedding-ring.

CARIOLA: Let me but speak with the Duke. I'll discover
  Treason to his person.

BOSOLA:           Delays: throttle her.      250

EXECUTIONER: She bites: and scratches.

CARIOLA:                 If you kill me now
  I am damn'd. I have not been at confession
  This two years.

BOSOLA:    When!

CARIOLA:         I am quick with child.

BOSOLA:                       Why then,
  Your credit's sav'd:
    [CARIOLA *is strangled.*]
                 bear her into th' next room.
  Let this lie still.
    [*Exeunt* EXECUTIONERS *with* CARIOLA's *body.*]
    [*Enter* FERDINAND.]

FERDINAND:    Is she dead?

BOSOLA:              She is what      255
  You'ld have her. But here begin your pity,

*Shows the children strangled.*
Alas, how have these offended?
FERDINAND:                    The death
Of young wolves is never to be pitied.
BOSOLA: Fix your eye here.
FERDINAND:              Constantly.
BOSOLA:                              Do you not weep?
260  Other sins only speak; murder shrieks out:
The element of water moistens the earth,
But blood flies upwards, and bedews the heavens.
FERDINAND: Cover her face. Mine eyes dazzle: she di'd
    young.
BOSOLA: I think not so: her infelicity
Seem'd to have years too many.
265  FERDINAND:                  She and I were twins:
And should I die this instant, I had liv'd
Her time to a minute.
BOSOLA:              It seems she was born first:
You have bloodily approv'd the ancient truth,
That kindred commonly do worse agree
Than remote strangers.
270  FERDINAND:            Let me see her face again;
Why didst not thou pity her? What an excellent
Honest man might'st thou have been
If thou hadst borne her to some sanctuary!
Or, bold in a good cause, oppos'd thyself
275  With thy advanced sword above thy head,
Between her innocence and my revenge!
I bade thee, when I was distracted of my wits,
Go kill my dearest friend, and thou hast done't.
For let me but examine well the cause;
280  What was the meanness of her match to me?
Only I must confess, I had a hope,

268. *approv'd:* confirmed.

Had she continu'd widow, to have gain'd
An infinite mass of treasure by her death:
And that was the main cause; her marriage,
That drew a stream of gall quite through my heart;          285
For thee, (as we observe in tragedies
That a good actor many times is curs'd
For playing a villain's part) I hate thee for't:
And, for my sake, say thou hast done much ill, well.

BOSOLA: Let me quicken your memory: for I perceive          290
You are falling into ingratitude. I challenge
The reward due to my service.

FERDINAND:                    I'll tell thee,
What I'll give thee –

BOSOLA:                  Do.

FERDINAND:                I'll give thee a pardon
For this murder.

BOSOLA:        Ha?

FERDINAND:          Yes: and 'tis
The largest bounty I can study to do thee.                  295
By what authority didst thou execute
This bloody sentence?

BOSOLA:              By yours.

FERDINAND:                    Mine? Was I her judge?
Did any ceremonial form of law
Doom her to not-being? did a complete jury
Deliver her conviction up i'th' court?                      300
Where shalt thou find this judgement register'd
Unless in hell? See: like a bloody fool
Th' hast forfeited thy life, and thou shalt die for't.

BOSOLA: The office of justice is perverted quite
When one thief hangs another: who shall dare               305
To reveal this?

FERDINAND:    O, I'll tell thee:
The wolf shall find her grave, and scrape it up;

    Not to devour the corpse, but to discover
    The horrid murder.

BOSOLA:              You; not I shall quake for't.

FERDINAND: Leave me.

310 BOSOLA:                I will first receive my pension.

FERDINAND: You are a villain.

BOSOLA:                    When your ingratitude
    Is judge, I am so –

FERDINAND:        O horror!
    That not the fear of him which binds the devils
    Can prescribe man obedience.
    Never look upon me more.

315 BOSOLA:                  Why fare thee well:
    Your brother and yourself are worthy men;
    You have a pair of hearts are hollow graves,
    Rotten, and rotting others: and your vengeance,
    Like two chain'd bullets, still goes arm in arm.

320     You may be brothers: for treason, like the plague,
    Doth take much in a blood. I stand like one
    That long hath tane a sweet and golden dream.
    I am angry with myself, now that I wake.

FERDINAND: Get thee into some unknown part o'th' world
    That I may never see thee.

325 BOSOLA:                Let me know
    Wherefore I should be thus neglected? Sir,
    I served your tyranny: and rather strove
    To satisfy yourself, than all the world;
    And though I loath'd the evil, yet I lov'd

330     You that did counsel it: and rather sought
    To appear a true servant than an honest man.

FERDINAND: I'll go hunt the badger by owl-light:
    'Tis a deed of darkness.
      *Exit.*

      321. *take much in a blood*: take a strong hold on a family.

BOSOLA: He's much distracted. Off my painted honour!
  While with vain hopes our faculties we tire,        335
  We seem to sweat in ice and freeze in fire;
  What would I do, were this to do again?
  I would not change my peace of conscience
  For all the wealth of Europe. She stirs; here's life.
  Return, fair soul, from darkness, and lead mine     340
  Out of this sensible hell. She's warm, she breathes:
  Upon thy pale lips I will melt my heart
  To store them with fresh colour. Who's there?
  Some cordial drink! Alas! I dare not call:
  So pity would destroy pity: her eye opes,      345
  And heaven in it seems to ope, that late was shut,
  To take me up to mercy.
DUCHESS:             Antonio!
BOSOLA: Yes, Madam, he is living.
  The dead bodies you saw were but feign'd statues;
  He's reconcil'd to your brothers: the Pope hath wrought  350
  The atonement.
DUCHESS:        Mercy.
   *She dies.*
BOSOLA: O, she's gone again: there the cords of life broke.
  O sacred innocence, that sweetly sleeps
  On turtles' feathers: whilst a guilty conscience
  Is a black register, where is writ        355
  All our good deeds and bad; a perspective
  That shows us hell! That we cannot be suffer'd
  To do good when we have a mind to it!
  This is manly sorrow:
  These tears, I am very certain, never grew     360
  In my mother's milk. My estate is sunk
  Below the degree of fear: where were

341. *sensible:* perceptible.
344. *cordial:* restorative.

These penitent fountains while she was living?
O, they were frozen up! Here is a sight
365 As direful to my soul as is the sword
Unto a wretch hath slain his father. Come,
I'll bear thee hence,
And execute thy last will; that's deliver
Thy body to the reverend dispose
370 Of some good women: that the cruel tyrant
Shall not deny me. Then I'll post to Milan,
Where somewhat I will speedily enact
Worth my dejection.
      *Exit [with the body of the* DUCHESS].

# [ACT FIVE]

## [SCENE ONE]

*[Enter* ANTONIO *and* DELIO.]

ANTONIO: What think you of my hope of reconcilement
    To the Aragonian brethren?

DELIO:                I misdoubt it
    For though they have sent their letters of safe conduct
    For your repair to Milan, they appear
    But nets to entrap you. The Marquis of Pescara,     5
    Under whom you hold certain land in cheat,
    Much 'gainst his noble nature, hath been mov'd
    To seize those lands, and some of his dependants
    Are at this instant making it their suit
    To be invested in your revenues.     10
    I cannot think they mean well to your life,
    That do deprive you of your means of life,
    Your living.

ANTONIO:     You are still an heretic
    To any safety I can shape myself.

DELIO: Here comes the Marquis. I will make myself     15
    Petitioner for some part of your land,
    To know whither it is flying.

ANTONIO:           I pray do.
    *[Enter* PESCARA.]

DELIO: Sir, I have a suit to you.

PESCARA:           To me?

DELIO:                  An easy one:
    This is the citadel of St Bennet,
    With some demesnes, of late in the possession     20

19. *St Bennet:* St Benedict.

265

Of Antonio Bologna; please you bestow them on me?

PESCARA: You are my friend. But this is such a suit
Nor fit for me to give, nor you to take.

DELIO: No sir?

PESCARA: I will give you ample reason for't
Soon, in private. Here's the Cardinal's mistress.
   *[Enter* JULIA.]

JULIA: My lord, I am grown your poor petitioner,
And should be an ill beggar, had I not
A great man's letter here, the Cardinal's
To court you in my favour.
   [*She gives him a letter.*]

PESCARA: He entreats for you
The citadel of St Bennet, that belong'd
To the banish'd Bologna.

JULIA: Yes.

PESCARA: I could not have thought of a friend I could
Rather pleasure with it: 'tis yours.

JULIA: Sir, I thank you:
And he shall know how doubly I am engag'd
Both in your gift, and speediness of giving,
Which makes your grant the greater.
   *Exit.*

ANTONIO [*aside*]: How they fortify
Themselves with my ruin!

DELIO: Sir, I am
Little bound to you.

PESCARA: Why?

DELIO: Because you deni'd this suit to me, and gave't
To such a creature.

PESCARA: Do you know what it was?
It was Antonio's land: not forfeited
By course of law; but ravish'd from his throat
By the Cardinal's entreaty: it were not fit

I should bestow so main a piece of wrong
Upon my friend: 'tis a gratification                          45
Only due to a strumpet; for it is injustice.
Shall I sprinkle the pure blood of innocents
To make those followers I call my friends
Look ruddier upon me? I am glad
This land, tane from the owner by such wrong,                 50
Returns again unto so foul an use,
As salary for his lust. Learn, good Delio,
To ask noble things of me, and you shall find
I'll be a noble giver.
DELIO:                    You instruct me well.
ANTONIO [aside]: Why, here's a man, now, would fright
    impudence                                                 55
From sauciest beggars.
PESCARA:                   Prince Ferdinand's come to Milan
Sick, as they give out, of an apoplexy:
But some say 'tis a frenzy; I am going
To visit him.
    Exit.
ANTONIO:      'Tis a noble old fellow.
DELIO: What course do you mean to take, Antonio?             60
ANTONIO: This night I mean to venture all my fortune,
Which is no more than a poor ling'ring life,
To the Cardinal's worst of malice. I have got
Private access to his chamber: and intend
To visit him, about the mid of night,                         65
As once his brother did our noble Duchess.
It may be that the sudden apprehension
Of danger (for I'll go in mine own shape)
When he shall see it fraught with love and duty,
May draw the poison out of him, and work                      70
A friendly reconcilement: if it fail,
Yet it shall rid me of this infamous calling,

For better fall once, than be ever falling.

DELIO: I'll second you in all danger: and, howe'er,
75    My life keeps rank with yours.

ANTONIO: You are still my lov'd and best friend.
    *Exeunt.*


[SCENE TWO]


[*Enter* PESCARA *and* DOCTOR.]

PESCARA: Now doctor, may I visit your patient?

DOCTOR: If't please your lordship: but he's instantly
    To take the air here in the gallery,
    By my direction.

PESCARA:                Pray thee, what's his disease?

5    DOCTOR: A very pestilent disease, my lord,
    They call lycanthropia.

PESCARA:                What's that?
    I need a dictionary to't.

DOCTOR:                I'll tell you:
    In those that are possess'd with't there o'erflows
    Such melancholy humour, they imagine
10    Themselves to be transformed into wolves,
    Steal forth to churchyards in the dead of night,
    And dig dead bodies up: as two nights since
    One met the Duke, 'bout midnight in a lane
    Behind St Mark's church, with the leg of a man
15    Upon his shoulder; and he howl'd fearfully:
    Said he was a wolf: only the difference
    Was, a wolf's skin was hairy on the outside,
    His on the inside: bade them take their swords,
    Rip up his flesh, and try: straight I was sent for,

And having minister'd to him, found his Grace                    20
Very well recovered.
PESCARA:                    I am glad on't.
DOCTOR: Yet not without some fear
Of a relapse: if he grow to his fit again
I'll go a nearer way to work with him
Than ever Paracelsus dream'd of. If                              25
They'll give me leave, I'll buffet this madness out of him.
Stand aside: he comes.

> [*Enter* CARDINAL, FERDINAND, MALATESTE *and*
> BOSOLA, *who remains in the background.*]

FERDINAND: Leave me.
MALATESTE: Why doth your lordship love this solitariness?
FERDINAND: Eagles commonly fly alone. They are crows,           30
daws, and starlings that flock together. Look, what's that
follows me?
MALATESTE: Nothing, my lord.
FERDINAND: Yes.
MALATESTE: 'Tis your shadow.                                     35
FERDINAND: Stay it; let it not haunt me.
MALATESTE: Impossible, if you move, and the sun shine.
FERDINAND: I will throttle it.

> [*Throws himself upon his shadow.*]

MALATESTE: O, my lord: you are angry with nothing.
FERDINAND: You are a fool. How is't possible I should           40
catch my shadow unless I fall upon't? When I go to hell, I
mean to carry a bribe: for look you, good gifts evermore
make way for the worst persons.
PESCARA: Rise, good my lord.
FERDINAND: I am studying the art of patience.                   45
PESCARA: 'Tis a noble virtue.
FERDINAND: To drive six snails before me, from this town
to Moscow; neither use goad nor whip to them, but let
them take their own time: (the patient'st man i'th' world

50  match me for an experiment!) and I'll crawl after like a
sheep-biter.

CARDINAL: Force him up.

[*They raise* FERDINAND *to his feet.*]

FERDINAND: Use me well, you were best.
What I have done, I have done: I'll confess nothing.

55  DOCTOR: Now let me come to him. Are you mad, my lord?
Are you out of your princely wits?

FERDINAND:                          What's he?

PESCARA: Your doctor.

FERDINAND: Let me have his beard saw'd off, and his
eyebrows
Fil'd more civil.

DOCTOR:                I must do mad tricks with him,
60  For that's the only way on't. I have brought
Your Grace a salamander's skin, to keep you
From sun-burning.

FERDINAND:              I have cruel sore eyes.

DOCTOR: The white of a cocatrice's egg is present remedy.

FERDINAND: Let it be a new-laid one, you were best.
65  Hide me from him. Physicians are like kings,
They brook no contradiction.

DOCTOR:                          Now he begins
To fear me; now let me alone with him.

[FERDINAND *tries to take off his gown; the* CARDINAL
*prevents him.*]

CARDINAL: How now, put off your gown?

DOCTOR: Let me have some forty urinals filled with rose-
70  water: he and I'll go pelt one another with them; now he
begins to fear me. Can you fetch a frisk, sir? [*Aside to*

51. *sheep-biter:* dog that worries sheep.
59. *civil:* becoming.
71. *fetch a frisk:* cut a caper.

270

CARDINAL] Let him go, let him go upon my peril. I find
by his eye, he stands in awe of me: I'll make him as tame
as a dormouse.

[CARDINAL *releases* FERDINAND.]

FERDINAND: Can you fetch your frisks, sir! I will stamp     75
him into a cullis; flay off his skin, to cover one of the
anatomies, this rogue hath set i'th' cold yonder, in
Barber-Chirurgeons' Hall. Hence, hence! you are all of
you like beasts for sacrifice, [*throws the* DOCTOR *down and
beats him*] there's nothing left of you, but tongue and     80
belly, flattery and lechery.

[*Exit.*]

PESCARA: Doctor, he did not fear you throughly.

DOCTOR: True, I was somewhat too forward.

BOSOLA [*aside*]: Mercy upon me, what a fatal judgement
Hath fall'n upon this Ferdinand!

PESCARA:                                    Knows your Grace     85
What accident hath brought upon the Prince
This strange distraction?

CARDINAL [*aside*]: I must feign somewhat. Thus they say it
grew:
You have heard it rumour'd for these many years,
None of our family dies, but there is seen     90
The shape of an old woman, which is given
By tradition, to us, to have been murder'd
By her nephews, for her riches. Such a figure
One night, as the Prince sat up late at's book,
Appear'd to him; when crying out for help,     95
The gentlemen of's chamber found his Grace
All on a cold sweat, alter'd much in face

---

80-81. *tongue and belly:* the tongue and entrails were left for the gods
in ancient sacrifices (Lucas).
82. *throughly:* thoroughly.

And language. Since which apparition
He hath grown worse and worse, and I much fear
100 He cannot live.
BOSOLA: Sir, I would speak with you.
PESCARA:                   We'll leave your Grace,
Wishing to the sick Prince, our noble lord,
All health of mind and body.
CARDINAL:             You are most welcome.
   *[Exeunt* PESCARA, MALATESTE *and* DOCTOR.]
   *[Aside]* Are you come? So: this fellow must not know
105 By any means I had intelligence
In our Duchess' death. For, though I counsell'd it,
The full of all th'engagement seem'd to grow
From Ferdinand. Now sir, how fares our sister?
I do not think but sorrow makes her look
110 Like to an oft-dy'd garment. She shall now
Taste comfort from me – why do you look so wildly?
O, the fortune of your master here, the Prince
Dejects you – but be you of happy comfort:
If you'll do one thing for me I'll entreat,
115 Though he had a cold tombstone o'er his bones,
I'ld make you what you would be.
BOSOLA:                 Any thing;
Give it me in a breath, and let me fly to't:
They that think long, small expedition win,
For musing much o'th' end, cannot begin.
   *[Enter* JULIA.]
JULIA: Sir, will you come in to supper?
120 CARDINAL:            I am busy, leave me.
JULIA *[aside]*: What an excellent shape hath that fellow!
   *Exit.*
CARDINAL: 'Tis thus: Antonio lurks here in Milan;
Inquire him out, and kill him: while he lives

107. *The full of all th'engagement:* the entire business.

Our sister cannot marry, and I have thought
Of an excellent match for her: do this, and style me          125
Thy advancement.

BOSOLA:                    But by what means shall I find him out?

CARDINAL: There is a gentleman, call'd Delio
Here in the camp, that hath been long approv'd
His loyal friend. Set eye upon that fellow,
Follow him to mass; may be Antonio,          130
Although he do account religion
But a school-name, for fashion of the world,
May accompany him: or else go inquire out
Delio's confessor, and see if you can bribe
Him to reveal it: there are a thousand ways          135
A man might find to trace him: as, to know
What fellows haunt the Jews for taking up
Great sums of money, for sure he's in want;
Or else go to th' picture-makers, and learn
Who brought her picture lately: some of these          140
Happily may take –

BOSOLA:                    Well, I'll not freeze i'th' business,
I would see that wretched thing, Antonio,
Above all sights i'th' world.

CARDINAL:                    Do, and be happy.
     *Exit.*

BOSOLA: This fellow doth breed basilisks in's eyes,
He's nothing else but murder: yet he seems          145
Not to have notice of the Duchess' death.
'Tis his cunning: I must follow his example;
There cannot be a surer way to trace,
Than that of an old fox.
     [*Enter* JULIA *with a pistol.*]

JULIA:                    So, sir, you are well met.

BOSOLA: How now?

128. *approv'd:* proved.

150 JULIA: Nay, the doors are fast enough.
Now sir, I will make you confess your treachery.
BOSOLA: Treachery?
JULIA: Yes, confess to me
Which of my women 'twas you hir'd, to put
Love-powder into my drink?
BOSOLA: Love-powder?
155 JULIA: Yes, when I was at Malfi;
Why should I fall in love with such a face else?
I have already suffer'd for thee so much pain,
The only remedy to do me good
Is to kill my longing.
BOSOLA: Sure, your pistol holds
160 Nothing but perfumes or kissing-comfits: excellent lady,
You have a pretty way on't to discover
Your longing. Come, come, I'll disarm you
And arm you thus: yet this is wondrous strange.
JULIA: Compare thy form and my eyes together,
165 You'll find my love no such great miracle.
[Kisses him] Now you'll say
I am a wanton. This nice modesty in ladies
Is but a troublesome familiar
That haunts them.
BOSOLA: Know you me, I am a blunt soldier.
170 JULIA: The better:
Sure, there wants fire where there are no lively sparks
Of roughness.
BOSOLA: And I want compliment.
JULIA: Why, ignorance
In courtship cannot make you do amiss,
If you have a heart to do well.

160. *kissing-comfits:* sweetmeats to sweeten the breath.
163. *arm:* embrace.        168. *familiar:* familiar spirit.
172. *want compliment:* lack finesse.

BOSOLA:                              You are very fair.

JULIA: Nay, if you lay beauty to my charge,                    175
  I must plead unguilty.

BOSOLA:                              Your bright eyes
  Carry a quiver of darts in them, sharper
  Than sunbeams.

JULIA:                    You will mar me with commendation,
  Put yourself to the charge of courting me,
  Whereas now I woo you.                                    180

BOSOLA [*aside*]: I have it, I will work upon this creature,
  Let us grow most amorously familiar.
  If the great Cardinal now should see me thus,
  Would he not count me a villain?

JULIA: No, he might count me a wanton,                        185
  Not lay a scruple of offence on you:
  For if I see, and steal a diamond,
  The fault is not i'th' stone, but in me the thief
  That purloins it. I am sudden with you;
  We that are great women of pleasure, use to cut off       190
  These uncertain wishes and unquiet longings,
  And in an instant join the sweet delight
  And the pretty excuse together: had you been i'th' street,
  Under my chamber window, even there
  I should have courted you.

BOSOLA:                              O, you are an excellent lady.   195

JULIA: Bid me do somewhat for you presently
  To express I love you.

BOSOLA:                    I will, and if you love me,
  Fail not to effect it.
  The Cardinal is grown wondrous melancholy,
  Demand the cause, let him not put you off                 200
  With feign'd excuse; discover the main ground on't.

JULIA: Why would you know this?

BOSOLA:                              I have depended on him,

And I hear that he is fall'n in some disgrace
With the Emperor: if he be, like the mice
205   That forsake falling houses, I would shift
To other dependence.

JULIA: You shall not need follow the wars:
I'll be your maintenance.

BOSOLA: And I your loyal servant;
But I cannot leave my calling.

210   JULIA:                     Not leave
An ungrateful general for the love of a sweet lady?
You are like some, cannot sleep in feather-beds,
But must have blocks for their pillows.

BOSOLA:                       Will you do this?

JULIA: Cunningly.

BOSOLA:        Tomorrow I'll expect th'intelligence.

215   JULIA: Tomorrow? get you into my cabinet,
You shall have it with you: do not delay me,
No more than I do you. I am like one
That is condemn'd: I have my pardon promis'd,
But I would see it seal'd. Go, get you in,
220   You shall see me wind my tongue about his heart
Like a skein of silk.

    [BOSOLA *withdraws; enter* CARDINAL.]

CARDINAL: Where are you?

    [*Enter* SERVANTS.]

SERVANTS:               Here.

CARDINAL:                 Let none upon your lives
Have conference with the Prince Ferdinand,
Unless I know it. [*Aside*] In this distraction
225   He may reveal the murder.

    [*Exeunt* SERVANTS.]

Yond's my ling'ring consumption:
I am weary of her; and by any means
Would be quit of –

JULIA: How now, my Lord?
  What ails you?
CARDINAL: Nothing.
JULIA: O, you are much alter'd:
  Come, I must be your secretary, and remove     230
  This lead from off your bosom; what's the matter?
CARDINAL: I may not tell you.
JULIA: Are you so far in love with sorrow,
  You cannot part with part of it? Or think you
  I cannot love your Grace when you are sad,     235
  As well as merry? Or do you suspect
  I, that have been a secret to your heart
  These many winters, cannot be the same
  Unto your tongue?
CARDINAL: Satisfy thy longing.
  The only way to make thee keep my counsel     240
  Is not to tell thee.
JULIA: Tell your echo this,
  Or flatterers, that, like echoes, still report
  What they hear, though most imperfect, and not me:
  For, if that you be true unto yourself,
  I'll know.
CARDINAL: Will you rack me?
JULIA: No, judgement shall     245
  Draw it from you. It is an equal fault,
  To tell one's secrets unto all, or none.
CARDINAL: The first argues folly.
JULIA: But the last tyranny.
CARDINAL: Very well; why, imagine I have committed
  Some secret deed which I desire the world     250
  May never hear of!
JULIA: Therefore may not I know it?
  You have conceal'd for me as great a sin
  As adultery. Sir, never was occasion

For perfect trial of my constancy
Till now. Sir, I beseech you.

CARDINAL:                          You'll repent it.

255 JULIA:                                  Never.

CARDINAL: It hurries thee to ruin: I'll not tell thee.
Be well advis'd, and think what danger 'tis
To receive a prince's secrets: they that do,
Had need have their breasts hoop'd with adamant

260 To contain them. I pray thee yet be satisfi'd,
Examine thine own frailty; 'tis more easy
To tie knots, than unloose them: 'tis a secret
That, like a ling'ring poison, may chance lie
Spread in thy veins, and kill thee seven year hence.

JULIA: Now you dally with me.

265 CARDINAL:                        No more; thou shalt know it.
By my appointment the great Duchess of Malfi
And two of her young children, four nights since
Were strangled.

JULIA:                  O Heaven! Sir, what have you done?

CARDINAL: How now? How settles this? Think you your
bosom

270 Will be a grave dark and obscure enough
For such a secret?

JULIA:                  You have undone yourself, sir.

CARDINAL: Why?

JULIA:                  It lies not in me to conceal it.

CARDINAL:                                No?
Come, I will swear you to't upon this book.

JULIA: Most religiously.

CARDINAL:              Kiss it.

[*She kisses the book.*]

275 Now you shall never utter it; thy curiosity
Hath undone thee; thou'rt poison'd with that book.

269. *how settles this?*: i.e. in your [Julia's] mind.

Because I knew thou couldst not keep my counsel,
I have bound thee to't by death.
[*Enter* BOSOLA.]
BOSOLA: For pity-sake, hold.
CARDINAL:                    Ha, Bosola!
JULIA:                              I forgive you
This equal piece of justice you have done:          280
For I betray'd your counsel to that fellow;
He overheard it; that was the cause I said
It lay not in me to conceal it.
BOSOLA:                    O foolish woman,
Couldst not thou have poison'd him?
JULIA:                              'Tis weakness,
Too much to think what should have been done. I go,   285
I know not whither.
[*Dies.*]
CARDINAL:          Wherefore com'st thou hither?
BOSOLA: That I might find a great man, like yourself,
Not out of his wits, as the Lord Ferdinand,
To remember my service.
CARDINAL:                    I'll have thee hew'd in pieces.
BOSOLA: Make not yourself such a promise of that life   290
Which is not yours to dispose of.
CARDINAL:                    Who plac'd thee here?
BOSOLA: Her lust, as she intended.
CARDINAL:                    Very well;
Now you know me for your fellow murderer.
BOSOLA: And wherefore should you lay fair marble colours
Upon your rotten purposes to me?                    295
Unless you imitate some that do plot great treasons,
And when they have done, go hide themselves i'th' graves
Of those were actors in't.
CARDINAL: No more: there is a fortune attends thee.

294-5. painting rotten wood to give the appearance of marble.

300 BOSOLA: Shall I go sue to Fortune any longer?
　　　'Tis the fool's pilgrimage.
　CARDINAL:　　　　　　　　I have honours in store for thee.
　BOSOLA: There are many ways that conduct to seeming
　　　Honour, and some of them very dirty ones.
　CARDINAL: Throw to the devil
305　Thy melancholy; the fire burns well,
　　　What need we keep a stirring of't, and make
　　　A greater smother? Thou wilt kill Antonio?
　BOSOLA: Yes.
　CARDINAL:　Take up that body.
　BOSOLA:　　　　　　　　　I think I shall
　　　Shortly grow the common bier for churchyards!
310　CARDINAL: I will allow thee some dozen of attendants,
　　　To aid thee in the murder.
　BOSOLA: O, by no means: physicians that apply horse-
　　　leeches to any rank swelling, use to cut off their tails, that
　　　the blood may run through them the faster. Let me have no
315　train, when I go to shed blood, lest it make me have a
　　　greater, when I ride to the gallows.
　CARDINAL: Come to me after midnight, to help to remove
　　　　that body
　　　To her own lodging. I'll give out she di'd o'th' plague;
　　　'Twill breed the less inquiry after her death.
320　BOSOLA: Where's Castruchio her husband?
　CARDINAL: He's rode to Naples to take possession
　　　Of Antonio's citadel.
　BOSOLA: Believe me, you have done a very happy turn.
　CARDINAL: Fail not to come. There is the master-key
325　Of our lodgings: and by that you may conceive
　　　What trust I plant in you.
　　　　　*Exit.*
　BOSOLA:　　　　　　　　You shall find me ready.
　　　O poor Antonio, though nothing be so needful

To thy estate, as pity, yet I find
Nothing so dangerous. I must look to my footing;
In such slippery ice-pavements men had need                330
To be frost-nail'd well: they may break their necks else.
The precedent's here afore me: how this man
Bears up in blood! seems fearless! Why, 'tis well:
Security some men call the suburbs of hell,
Only a dead wall between. Well, good Antonio,              335
I'll seek thee out; and all my care shall be
To put thee into safety from the reach
Of these most cruel biters, that have got
Some of thy blood already. It may be,
I'll join with thee in a most just revenge.               340
The weakest arm is strong enough, that strikes
With the sword of justice. Still methinks the Duchess
Haunts me: there, there: 'tis nothing but my melancholy.
O penitence, let me truly taste thy cup,
That throws men down, only to raise them up.              345
    *Exit.*


## [SCENE THREE]

[*Enter* ANTONIO *and* DELIO. *There is an*] ECHO (*from
the* DUCHESS' *grave*).
DELIO: Yond's the Cardinal's window. This fortification
  Grew from the ruins of an ancient abbey:
  And to yond side o'th' river lies a wall,
  Piece of a cloister, which in my opinion
  Gives the best echo that you ever heard;                 5
  So hollow, and so dismal, and withal
  So plain in the distinction of our words,

---

333. *bears up in blood:* either 'keeps up his courage' (Lucas) or 'persists
    in shedding blood' (Brown).

That many have suppos'd it is a spirit
That answers.

ANTONIO:     I do love these ancient ruins:
10 We never tread upon them, but we set
Our foot upon some reverend history.
And, questionless, here in this open court,
Which now lies naked to the injuries
Of stormy weather, some men lie interr'd
15 Lov'd the church so well, and gave so largely to't,
They thought it should have canopi'd their bones
Till doomsday. But all things have their end:
Churches and cities, which have diseases like to men
Must have like death that we have.

ECHO:         *Like death that we have.*

DELIO: Now the echo hath caught you.

ANTONIO:     It groan'd,
20 methought, and gave
A very deadly accent!

ECHO:     *Deadly accent.*

DELIO: I told you 'twas a pretty one. You may make it
A huntsman, or a falconer, a musician
Or a thing of sorrow.

ECHO:     *A thing of sorrow.*

ANTONIO: Ay sure: that suits it best.

25 ECHO:     *That suits it best.*

ANTONIO: 'Tis very like my wife's voice.

ECHO:     *Ay, wife's voice.*

DELIO: Come: let's walk farther from't:
I would not have you go to th' Cardinal's tonight:
Do not.

ECHO:  *Do not.*

30 DELIO: Wisdom doth not more moderate wasting sorrow
Than time: take time for't: be mindful of thy safety.

ECHO: *Be mindful of thy safety.*

ANTONIO:                          Necessity compels me:
  Make scrutiny throughout the passages
  Of your own life; you'll find it impossible
  To fly your fate.
ECHO:                    *O fly your fate.*                    35
DELIO: Hark: the dead stones seem to have pity on you
  And give you good counsel.
ANTONIO:                    Echo, I will not talk with thee;
  For thou art a dead thing.
ECHO:                    *Thou art a dead thing.*
ANTONIO: My Duchess is asleep now,
  And her little ones, I hope sweetly: O Heaven          40
  Shall I never see her more?
ECHO:                    *Never see her more.*
ANTONIO: I mark'd not one repetition of the Echo
  But that: and on the sudden, a clear light
  Presented me a face folded in sorrow.
DELIO: Your fancy, merely.
ANTONIO:                    Come: I'll be out of this ague;     45
  For to live thus, is not indeed to live:
  It is a mockery, and abuse of life.
  I will not henceforth save myself by halves;
  Lose all, or nothing.
DELIO:                    Your own virtue save you.
  I'll fetch your eldest son; and second you:              50
  It may be that the sight of his own blood
  Spread in so sweet a figure, may beget
  The more compassion.
ANTONIO:                    However, fare you well.
  Though in our miseries Fortune hath a part
  Yet, in our noble sufferings, she hath none:             55
  Contempt of pain, that we may call our own.
    *Exe[unt].*

## [SCENE FOUR]

*[Enter]* CARDINAL, PESCARA, MALATESTE,
RODERIGO, GRISOLAN.

CARDINAL: You shall not watch tonight by the sick Prince;
His Grace is very well recover'd.

MALATESTE: Good my lord, suffer us.

CARDINAL:                              O, by no means:
The noise and change of object in his eye

5      Doth more distract him. I pray, all to bed,
And though you hear him in his violent fit,
Do not rise, I entreat you.

PESCARA:                              So sir, we shall not –

CARDINAL: Nay, I must have you promise
Upon your honours, for I was enjoin'd to't

10      By himself; and he seem'd to urge it sensibly.

PESCARA: Let our honours bind this trifle.

CARDINAL: Nor any of your followers.

PESCARA:                              Neither.

CARDINAL: It may be to make trial of your promise
When he's asleep, myself will rise, and feign

15      Some of his mad tricks, and cry out for help,
And feign myself in danger.

MALATESTE:                              If your throat were cutting,
I'ld not come at you, now I have protested against it.

CARDINAL: Why, I thank you.

        *[Withdraws.]*

GRISOLAN:                              'Twas a foul storm tonight.

RODERIGO: The Lord Ferdinand's chamber shook like an
osier.

20      MALATESTE: 'Twas nothing but pure kindness in the devil,
To rock his own child.

*Exeunt* [RODERIGO, MALATESTE. PESCARA, GRISOLAN].

CARDINAL: The reason why I would not suffer these
  About my brother, is because at midnight
  I may with better privacy convey
  Julia's body to her own lodging. O, my conscience!    25
  I would pray now: but the devil takes away my heart
  For having any confidence in prayer.
  About this hour I appointed Bosola
  To fetch the body: when he hath serv'd my turn,
  He dies.    30
    *Exit.* [*Enter* BOSOLA.]

BOSOLA: Ha! 'twas the Cardinal's voice. I heard him name
  Bosola, and my death: listen, I hear one's footing.
  [*Enter* FERDINAND.]

FERDINAND: Strangling is a very quiet death.

BOSOLA: Nay then I see, I must stand upon my guard.

FERDINAND: What say' to that? Whisper, softly: do you
  agree to't?    35
  So it must be done i'th' dark: the Cardinal
  Would not for a thousand pounds the doctor should see it.
    *Exit.*

BOSOLA: My death is plotted; here's the consequence of
  murder.
  *We value not desert, nor Christian breath,*
  *When we know black deeds must be cur'd with death.*    40
  [*Withdraws. Enter* ANTONIO *and a* SERVANT.]

SERVANT: Here stay sir, and be confident, I pray:
  I'll fetch you a dark lantern.
    *Exit.*

ANTONIO:                 Could I take him
  At his prayers, there were hope of pardon.

BOSOLA: Fall right my sword:
  [*strikes* ANTONIO *down.*]

45 I'll not give thee so much leisure as to pray.
ANTONIO: O, I am gone. Thou hast ended a long suit,
In a minute.
BOSOLA:          What art thou?
ANTONIO:                         A most wretched thing
That only have thy benefit in death,
To appear myself.
   [*Enter* SERVANT *with a dark lantern.*]
SERVANT:                Where are you sir?
ANTONIO: Very near my home. Bosola?
50 SERVANT:                               O misfortune!
BOSOLA [*to* SERVANT]: Smother thy pity, thou art dead else.
   Antonio!
The man I would have sav'd 'bove mine own life!
We are merely the stars' tennis-balls, struck and banded
Which way please them. O good Antonio,
55 I'll whisper one thing in thy dying ear,
Shall make thy heart break quickly. Thy fair Duchess
And two sweet children –
ANTONIO:                Their very names
Kindle a little life in me.
BOSOLA:             Are murder'd!
ANTONIO: Some men have wish'd to die
60 At the hearing of sad tidings: I am glad
That I shall do't in sadness: I would not now
Wish my wounds balm'd, nor heal'd: for I have no use
To put my life to. In all our quest of greatness,
Like wanton boys, whose pastime is their care,
65 We follow after bubbles, blown in th'air.
Pleasure of life, what is't? Only the good hours
Of an ague: merely a preparative to rest,
To endure vexation. I do not ask

53. *banded:* bandied.
61. *in sadness:* in earnest.

The process of my death: only commend me
To Delio.
BOSOLA:   Break, heart!                                                    70
ANTONIO: And let my son fly the courts of princes.
    [*Dies.*]
BOSOLA: Thou seem'st to have lov'd Antonio?
SERVANT:                                    I brought him hither,
    To have reconcil'd him to the Cardinal.
BOSOLA: I do not ask thee that.
    Take him up, if thou tender thine own life,                     75
    And bear him where the Lady Julia
    Was wont to lodge. O, my fate moves swift.
    I have this Cardinal in the forge already,
    Now I'll bring him to th' hammer. (O direful misprision!)
    I will not imitate things glorious,                             80
    No more than base: I'll be mine own example.
    On, on: and look thou represent, for silence,
    The thing thou bear'st.
    *Exeunt.*


[SCENE FIVE]


[*Enter*] CARDINAL (*with a book*).
CARDINAL: I am puzzl'd in a question about hell:
    He says, in hell there's one material fire,
    And yet it shall not burn all men alike.
    Lay him by. How tedious is a guilty conscience!
    When I look into the fishponds in my garden,                    5
    Methinks I see a thing, arm'd with a rake
    That seems to strike at me. Now? Art thou come?
    [*Enter* BOSOLA *and* SERVANT *with* ANTONIO's *body*.]
    Thou look'st ghastly:

75. *tender:* value.    79. *misprision:* mistake.

There sits in thy face some great determination,
Mix'd with some fear.

10 BOSOLA:                 Thus it lightens into action:
I am come to kill thee.

CARDINAL:          Ha? Help! our guard!

BOSOLA: Thou art deceiv'd:
They are out of thy howling.

CARDINAL: Hold: and I will faithfully divide
Revenues with thee.

15 BOSOLA:               Thy prayers and proffers
Are both unseasonable.

CARDINAL:         Raise the watch:
We are betray'd!

BOSOLA:           I have confin'd your flight:
I'll suffer your retreat to Julia's chamber,
But no further.

CARDINAL:       Help: we are betray'd!
    [*Enter* PESCARA, MALATESTE, RODERIGO *and*
    GRISOLAN, *above.*]

MALATESTE:                Listen.

CARDINAL: My dukedom for rescue!

20 RODERIGO:           Fie upon his counterfeiting.

MALATESTE: Why, 'tis not the Cardinal.

RODERIGO:             Yes, yes, 'tis he:
But I'll see him hang'd, ere I'll go down to him.

CARDINAL: Here's a plot upon me; I am assaulted. I am lost,
Unless some rescue!

GRISOLAN:         He doth this pretty well:

25 But it will not serve to laugh me out of mine honour.

CARDINAL: The sword's at my throat!

RODERIGO:            You would not
bawl so loud then.

   10. *lightens:* flashes.

MALATESTE: Come, come:
  Let's go to bed: he told us thus much aforehand.
PESCARA: He wish'd you should not come at him: but believ't,
  The accent of the voice sounds not in jest.     30
  I'll down to him, howsoever, and with engines
  Force ope the doors.
    [*Exit.*]
RODERIGO:            Let's follow him aloof,
  And note how the Cardinal will laugh at him.
    [*Exeunt above.*]
BOSOLA: There's for you first:
  'Cause you shall not unbarricade the door     35
  To let in rescue.
    *He kills the* SERVANT.
CARDINAL: What cause hast thou to pursue my life?
BOSOLA:               Look there.
CARDINAL: Antonio!
BOSOLA:          Slain by my hand unwittingly.
  Pray, and be sudden: when thou kill'd'st thy sister,
  Thou took'st from Justice her most equal balance,     40
  And left her naught but her sword.
CARDINAL:           O mercy!
BOSOLA: Now it seems thy greatness was only outward:
  For thou fall'st faster of thyself than calamity
  Can drive thee. I'll not waste longer time. There.
    [*Stabs the* CARDINAL.]
CARDINAL: Thou hast hurt me.
BOSOLA:           Again.
    [*Stabs him again.*]
CARDINAL:          Shall I die like a leveret     45
  Without any resistance? Help, help, help!
  I am slain.
    [*Enter* FERDINAND.]

FERDINAND: Th'alarum? give me a fresh horse.
Rally the vaunt-guard; or the day is lost.
Yield, yield! I give you the honour of arms,
50      Shake my sword over you, will you yield?
CARDINAL: Help me, I am your brother.
FERDINAND:            The devil?
My brother fight upon the adverse party?
*He wounds the* CARDINAL *and, in the scuffle, gives*
BOSOLA *his death wound.*
There flies your ransom.
CARDINAL:          O Justice:
I suffer now for what hath former been:
55      *Sorrow is held the eldest child of sin.*
FERDINAND: Now you're brave fellows. Caesar's fortune
was harder than Pompey's: Caesar died in the arms of
prosperity, Pompey at the feet of disgrace: you both died
in the field, the pain's nothing. Pain many times is taken
60      away with the apprehension of greater, as the toothache
with the sight of a barber that comes to pull it out: there's
philosophy for you.
BOSOLA: Now my revenge is perfect: sink, thou main cause
Of my undoing: the last part of my life
65      Hath done me best service.
     *He kills* FERDINAND.
FERDINAND: Give me some wet hay, I am broken winded.
I do account this world but a dog-kennel:
I will vault credit, and affect high pleasures
Beyond death.
BOSOLA:         He seems to come to himself,
70      Now he's so near the bottom.
FERDINAND: My sister. O! my sister, there's the cause on't.
*Whether we fall by ambition, blood, or lust,*
*Like diamonds we are cut with our own dust.*
     [*Dies.*]

CARDINAL: Thou hast thy payment too.

BOSOLA: Yes, I hold my weary soul in my teeth;    75
'Tis ready to part from me. I do glory
That thou, which stood'st like a huge pyramid
Begun upon a large and ample base,
Shalt end in a little point, a kind of nothing.
  [*Enter* PESCARA, MALATESTE, RODERIGO *and*
  GRISOLAN.]

PESCARA: How now, my lord?

MALATESTE:              O sad disaster!

RODERIGO:                   How comes this?   80

BOSOLA: Revenge, for the Duchess of Malfi, murdered
By th' Aragonian brethren; for Antonio,
Slain by this hand; for lustful Julia,
Poison'd by this man; and lastly, for myself,
That was an actor in the main of all,   85
Much 'gainst mine own good nature, yet i'th' end
Neglected.

PESCARA:   How now, my lord?

CARDINAL:               Look to my brother:
He gave us these large wounds, as we were struggling
Here i'th'rushes. And now, I pray, let me
Be laid by, and never thought of.   90
  [*Dies*.]

PESCARA: How fatally, it seems, he did withstand
His own rescue!

MALATESTE:       Thou wretched thing of blood,
How came Antonio by his death?

BOSOLA: In a mist: I know not how;
Such a mistake as I have often seen   95
In a play. O, I am gone:
We are only like dead walls, or vaulted graves
That, ruin'd, yields no echo. Fare you well;
It may be pain: but no harm to me to die

100     In so good a quarrel. O this gloomy world,
In what a shadow, or deep pit of darkness
Doth, womanish, and fearful, mankind live?
Let worthy minds ne'er stagger in distrust
To suffer death or shame for what is just:
105     Mine is another voyage.
       [*Dies.*]
PESCARA: The noble Delio, as I came to th'palace,
Told me of Antonio's being here, and show'd me
A pretty gentleman his son and heir.
    [*Enter* DELIO *with* ANTONIO's *son.*]
MALATESTE: O sir, you come too late.
DELIO:                     I heard so, and
110     Was arm'd for't ere I came. Let us make noble use
Of this great ruin; and join all our force
To establish this young hopeful gentleman
In's mother's right. These wretched eminent things
Leave no more fame behind 'em, than should one
115     Fall in a frost, and leave his print in snow;
As soon as the sun shines, it ever melts
Both form and matter. I have ever thought
Nature doth nothing so great for great men,
As when she's pleas'd to make them lords of truth:
120     *Integrity of life is fame's best friend,*
*Which nobly, beyond death, shall crown the end.*
    *Exeunt.*

**FINIS**

# The Deuils Law-case.

## OR,

### When Women goe to Law, the Deuill is full of Businesse.

*A new Tragecomædy.*

*The true and perfect Copie from the Originall.*

**As it was approouedly well Acted by her Maiesties Seruants.**

*Written by* I O H N  W E B S T E R.

*Non quam diu, sed quam bene.*

**LONDON,**
Printed by *A. M.* for *Iohn Grismand,* and are
to be sold at his Shop in Pauls Alley at the
Signe of the Gunne. **1623.**

# DRAMATIS PERSONAE

ROMELIO, a merchant.

CONTARINO, a nobleman, and suitor to JOLENTA.

ERCOLE, a Knight of Malta, also suitor to JOLENTA.

CRISPIANO, a lawyer.

JULIO, son to CRISPIANO.

PROSPERO, a merchant, and colleague of ROMELIO.

ARIOSTO, a lawyer, and afterwards a judge.

CONTILUPO, a lawyer, representing LEONORA at the trial.

SANITONELLA, a law-clerk, assisting CONTILUPO.

A CAPUCHIN FRIAR.

*BAPTISTA, a merchant.

LEONORA, mother of ROMELIO and of JOLENTA.

JOLENTA, sister of ROMELIO, and sought in marriage by CON-
TARINO and ERCOLE.

WINIFRID, her waiting woman.

ANGIOLELLA, a nun, pregnant by ROMELIO.

Two Surgeons, Judges, Lawyers, Bellmen, Registrar, Marshal,
Herald, and Servants.

*The action takes place at Naples.*

\* 'ghost' character.

Sir, let it not appear strange, that I do aspire to your patronage. Things that taste of any goodness, love to be shelter'd near goodness: nor do I flatter in this (which I hate), only touch at the original copy of your virtues. Some of my other works, as *The White Devil*, *The Duchess of Malfi*, *Guise*, and others, you have formerly seen; I present this humbly to kiss your hands, and to find your allowance. Nor do I much doubt it, knowing the greatest of the *Caesars* have cheerfully entertain'd less poems than this: and had I thought it unworthy, I had not enquir'd after so worthy a patronage. Yourself I understand to be all courtesy. I doubt not therefore of your acceptance, but resolve that my election is happy. For which favour done me, I shall ever rest

*Your worships humbly devoted,*
JOHN WEBSTER.

14 . *election:* choice.

# TO THE JUDICIOUS READER

I hold it, in these kind of poems with that of *Horace; Sapienta prima, stultitia caruisse;* to be free from those vices, which proceed from ignorance; of which I take it this play will ingeniously acquit itself. I do chiefly therefore expose it to the judicious: *Locus est, et pluribus umbris,* others have leave to sit down, and read it, who come unbidden. But to these, should a man present them with the most excellent music, it would delight them no more, than *Auriculas citherae collecta sorde dolentes.* I will not further insist upon the approvement of it, for I am so far from praising myself, that I have not given way to divers of my friends, whose unbegg'd commendatory verses offer'd themselves to do me service in the front of this poem. A great part of the grace of this (I confess) lay in action; yet can no action ever be gracious, where the decency of the language, and ingenious structure of the scene, arrive not to make up a perfect harmony. What I have fail'd of this, you that have approv'd my other works, (when you have read this) tax me of. For the rest, *Non ego ventosae plebis suffragia venor.*

2. *that:* i.e. that saying (a Latinism).
14. *decency:* appropriateness.

# [ACT ONE]

## [SCENE ONE]

*Enter* ROMELIO, *and* PROSPERO.

PROSPERO: You have shown a world of wealth; I did not
    think
    There had been a merchant liv'd in Italy
    Of half your substance.

ROMELIO:                I'll give the King of Spain
    Ten thousand ducats yearly, and discharge
    My yearly custom. The Hollanders scarce trade      5
    More generally than I: my factors' wives
    Wear shaperoons of velvet, and my scriveners
    Merely through my employment, grow so rich,
    They build their palaces and belvederes
    With musical water-works: never in my life     10
    Had I a loss at sea. They call me on th'exchange,
    The fortunate young man, and make great suit
    To venture with me. Shall I tell you sir,
    Of a strange confidence in my way of trading?
    I reckon it as certain as the gain     15
    In erecting a lottery.

PROSPERO:             I pray, sir, what do you think
    Of Signor Baptista's estate?

ROMELIO:               A mere beggar:
    He's worth some fifty thousand ducats.

PROSPERO:                   Is not that well?

---

5. *custom:* i.e. customs duties.       6. *factors:* agents.
7. *shaperoons:* gaily decorated hoods.
9. *belvederes:* turrets built on summer houses and palaces to command
    good views.

ROMELIO: How, well? For a man to be melted to snow-
　　　water,
20　With toiling in the world from three and twenty,
　　　Till threescore, for poor fifty thousand ducats!
PROSPERO: To your estate 'tis little I confess:
　　　You have the spring tide of gold.
ROMELIO:　　　　　　　　　　Faith, and for silver,
　　　Should I not send it packing to th'East Indies,
25　We should have a glut on't.
　　　　　*Enter* SERVANT.
SERVANT: Here's the great Lord Contarino.
PROSPERO:　　　　　　　　　　　O, I know
　　　His business, he's a suitor to your sister.
ROMELIO:　　　　　　　　　Yes sir, but to you –
　　　As my most trusted friend, I utter it –
　　　I will break the alliance.
PROSPERO:　　　　　　You are ill-advis'd then;
30　There lives not a completer gentleman
　　　In Italy, nor of a more ancient house.
ROMELIO: What tell you me of gentry? 'Tis nought else
　　　But a superstitious relic of time past:
　　　And sift it to the true worth, it is nothing
35　But ancient riches: and in him you know
　　　They are pitifully in the wane. He makes his colour
　　　Of visiting us so often, to sell land,
　　　And thinks if he can gain my sister's love,
　　　To recover the treble value.
PROSPERO:　　　　　　　Sure he loves her
　　　Entirely, and she deserves it.
40　ROMELIO:　　　　　　　Faith, though she were
　　　Crook'd-shoulder'd, having such a portion,
　　　She would have noble suitors. But truth is,

36–7. *he makes . . . land:* 'he uses a wish to sell land as an excuse for visiting us'.

I would wish my noble venturer take heed;
It may be whiles he hopes to catch a gilthead,
He may draw up a gudgeon.                                    45
    *Enter* CONTARINO.
PROSPERO: He's come. Sir I will leave you.
    [*Exeunt* PROSPERO *and* SERVANT.]
CONTARINO: I sent you the evidence of the piece of land
    I motioned to you for the sale.
ROMELIO:             Yes.
CONTARINO: Has your counsel perus'd it?
ROMELIO:                  Not yet my
    Lord. Do you
    Intend to travel?
CONTARINO:    No.
ROMELIO:        O then you lose                        50
    That which makes a man most absolute.
CONTARINO:             Yet I have heard
    Of divers, that in passing of the Alps,
    Have but exchang'd their virtues at dear rate
    For other vices.
ROMELIO:        O my Lord, lie not idle;
    The chiefest action for a man of great spirit,        55
    Is never to be out of action. We should think
    The soul was never put into the body,
    Which has so many rare and curious pieces
    Of mathematical motion, to stand still.
    Virtue is ever sowing of her seeds:                  60
    In the trenches for the soldier; in the wakeful study
    For the scholar; in the furrows of the sea
    For men of our profession: of all which

44. *gilthead:* small fish, *Crenilabrus melops*; with a pun on gold coin.
45. *gudgeon:* small fish, *Gobio gobio*, often used for bait.
48. *motioned:* proposed.
51. *absolute:* finished, complete.
59. *mathematical:* precise, intricate.

Arise and spring up honour. Come, I know
65    You have some noble great design in hand,
That you levy so much money.

CONTARINO:            Sir, I'll tell you,
The greatest part of it I mean to employ
In payment of my debts, and the remainder
Is like to bring me into greater bonds,
As I aim it.

ROMELIO:  How sir?

70   CONTARINO:        I intend it
For the charge of my wedding.

ROMELIO:         Are you to be married, my Lord?

CONTARINO: Yes sir; and I must now entreat your pardon,
That I have conceal'd from you a business
Wherein you had at first been call'd to counsel,
75    But that I thought it a less fault in friendship,
To engage myself thus far without your knowledge,
Than to do it against your will: another reason
Was that I would not publish to the world,
Nor have it whisper'd, scarce, what wealthy voyage
80    I went about, till I had got the mine
In mine own possession.

ROMELIO:        You are dark to me yet.

CONTARINO: I'll now remove the cloud. Sir, your sister
    and I
Are vow'd each other's, and there only wants
Her worthy mother's, and your fair consents
85    To style it marriage. This is a way,
Not only to make a friendship, but confirm it
For our posterities. How do you look upon't?

ROMELIO: Believe me sir, as on the principal column
To advance our house: why you bring honour with you,
90    Which is the soul of wealth. I shall be proud

    81. *dark*: obscure.

To live to see my little nephews ride
O'th upper hand of their uncles; and the daughters
Be rank'd by heralds at solemnities
Before the mother: all this deriv'd
From your nobility. Do not blame me sir,                            95
If I be taken with't exceedingly:
For this same honour with us citizens,
Is a thing we are mainly fond of, especially
When it comes without money, which is very seldom.
But as you do perceive my present temper,                         100
Be sure I am yours – [aside] fir'd with scorn and laughter
At your over-confident purpose – and no doubt
My mother will be of your mind.

CONTARINO:                                    'Tis my hope sir.

  Exit ROMELIO.

I do observe how this Romelio
Has very worthy parts, were they not blasted                      105
By insolent vainglory. There rests now
The mother's approbation to the match,
Who is a woman of that state and bearing,
Though she be city-born, both in her language,
Her garments, and her table, she excels                           110
Our ladies of the Court: she goes not gaudy,
Yet I have seen her wear one diamond,
Would have bought twenty gay ones out of their clothes,
And some of them, without the greater grace,
Out of their honesties.

  Enter LEONORA.

                                She comes. I will try              115
How she stands affected to me, without relating
My contract with her daughter.

98. *mainly:* extremely.        105. *blasted:* withered, blighted.
106. *rests:* remains.
114. *without . . . grace:* into the bargain.

LEONORA: Sir, you are nobly welcome, and presume
You are in a place that's wholly dedicated
To your service.

120 CONTARINO: I am ever bound to you
For many special favours.

LEONORA: Sir, your fame
Renders you most worthy of it.

CONTARINO: It could never have got
A sweeter air to fly in, than your breath.

LEONORA: You have been strange a long time; you are
weary

125 Of our unseasonable time of feeding:
Indeed, th'exchange bell makes us dine so late.
I think the ladies of the Court from us
Learn to lie so long abed.

CONTARINO: They have a kind of exchange among them
too.

130 Marry, unless it be to hear of news, I take it,
Theirs is like the New Burse, thinly furnish'd
With tires and new fashions. I have a suit to you.

LEONORA: I would not have you value it the less,
If I say, 'tis granted already.

CONTARINO: You are all bounty.
'Tis to bestow your picture on me.

135 LEONORA: O sir,
Shadows are coveted in summer; and with me,
'Tis fall o'th'leaf.

CONTARINO: You enjoy the best of time:
This latter spring of yours shows in my eye,
More fruitful and more temperate withall,

140 Than that whose date is only limited

118. *presume:* i.e. you must presume.     124. *strange:* a stranger.
125. *unseasonable:* unfashionable.
132. *tires:* dresses.

By the music of the cuckoo.

LEONORA:                    Indeed sir, I dare tell you,
My looking glass is a true one, and as yet
It does not terrify me. Must you have my picture?

CONTARINO: So please you lady, and I shall preserve it
As a most choice object.                              145

LEONORA: You will enjoin me to a strange punishment:
With what a compell'd face a woman sits
While she is drawing! I have noted divers,
Either to feign smiles, or suck in the lips,
To have a little mouth; ruffle the cheeks,            150
To have the dimple seen, and so disorder
The face with affectation, at next sitting
It has not been the same. I have known others
Have lost the entire fashion of their face,
In half an hour's sitting.

CONTARINO:            How?

LEONORA:                       In hot weather,   155
The painting on their face has been so mellow,
They have left the poor man harder work by half,
To mend the copy he wrought by. But indeed,
If ever I would have mine drawn to'th'life,
I would have a painter steal it, at such a time       160
I were devoutly kneeling at my prayers;
There is then a heavenly beauty in't; the soul
Moves in the superficies.

CONTARINO:            Excellent lady,
Now you teach beauty a preservative,
More than 'gainst fading colours; and your judgement  165
Is perfect in all things.

141. *cuckoo:* the emblem of spring; with the implication of cuckoldry.
147. *compell'd:* constrained.
148. *while . . . drawing:* i.e. while she is being drawn.
156. *mellow:* soft (with the implication of rottenness).
163. *Moves in the superficies:* reveals itself in the face.

LEONORA:    Indeed sir, I am a widow,
And want the addition to make it so:
For man's experience has still been held
Woman's best eyesight. I pray sir tell me,
170 You are about to sell a piece of land
To my son, I hear.

CONTARINO: 'Tis truth.

LEONORA:    Now I could rather wish,
That noblemen would ever live i'th'country,
Rather than make their visits up to the city
About such business. O sir, noble houses
175 Have no such goodly prospects any way,
As into their own land: the decay of that,
Next to their begging church land, is a ruin
Worth all men's pity. Sir, I have forty thousand crowns
Sleep in my chest, shall waken when you please,
180 And fly to your commands. Will you stay supper?

CONTARINO: I cannot, worthy lady.

LEONORA: I would not have you come hither sir, to sell,
But to settle your estate. I hope you understand
Wherefore I make this proffer: so I leave you.
  *Exit* LEON[ORA].

185 CONTARINO: What a treasury have I pearch'd! 'I hope
You understand wherefore I make this proffer.'
She has got some intelligence, how I intend to marry
Her daughter, and ingenuously perceiv'd
That by her picture, which I beg'd of her,
190 I meant the fair Jolenta. Here's a letter,
Which gives express charge, not to visit her
Till midnight: [*reads*]
*Fail not to come, for 'tis a business*
*That concerns both our honours.*

167. *the addition*: of a husband's experience.
185. *pearch'd*: pierced, penetrated.

        *Yours in danger to be lost, Jolenta.*   195
'Tis a strange injunction; what should be the business?
She is not chang'd I hope. I'll thither straight:
For women's resolutions in such deeds,
Like bees, light oft on flowers, and oft on weeds.
   *Exit.*

## [SCENE TWO]

*Enter* ERCOLE, ROMELIO, [*and*] JOLENTA.

ROMELIO: O sister, come, the tailor must to work,
  To make your wedding clothes.
JOLENTA:              The tomb-maker,
  To take measure of my coffin.
ROMELIO:             Tomb-maker?
Look you, the King of Spain greets you.
  [*Gives her a paper.*]
JOLENTA:               What does this mean?
Do you serve process on me?
ROMELIO:            Process? Come,   5
You would be witty now.
JOLENTA:        Why, what's this, I pray?
ROMELIO: Infinite grace to you: it is a letter
From his Catholic Majesty, for the commends
Of this gentleman for your husband.
JOLENTA:             In good season:
I hope he will not have my allegiance stretch'd   10
To the undoing of myself.
ROMELIO: Undo yourself? He does proclaim him here –
JOLENTA: Not for a traitor, does he?
ROMELIO:            You are not mad?
For one of the noblest gentlemen.

*5. process:* a summons.      *8. for the commends of:* recommending.

JOLENTA:                        Yet kings many times
15    Know merely but men's outsides. Was this commendation
   Voluntary, think you?

ROMELIO:            Voluntary: what mean you by that?

JOLENTA: Why I do not think but he beg'd it of the King,
   And it may fortune to be out of's way:
   Some better suit, that would have stood his Lordship
20    In far more stead. Letters of commendations;
   Why 'tis reported that they are grown stale,
   When places fall i'th' university.
   I pray you return his pass: for to a widow
   That longs to be a courtier, this paper
25    May do knight's service.

ERCOLE: Mistake not excellent mistress, these commends
   Express, his Majesty of Spain has given me
   Both addition of honour, as you may perceive
   By my habit, and a place here to command
30    O'er thirty galleys: this your brother shows,
   As wishing that you would be partner
   In my good fortune.

ROMELIO:            I pray come hither.
   Have I any interest in you?

JOLENTA:            You are my brother.

ROMELIO: I would have you then use me with that respect
35    You may still keep me so, and to be sway'd
   In this main business of life, which wants
   Greatest consideration, your marriage,
   By my direction. Here's a gentleman –

JOLENTA: Sir: I have often told you,
40    I am so little my own to dispose that way,
   That I can never be his.

ROMELIO:           Come, too much light
   Makes you moon-eyed – are you in love with title?

33. *interest in*: influence with.

I will have a herald, whose continual practice
Is all in pedigree, come a-wooing to you,
Or an antiquary in old buskins.                                    45
ERCOLE: Sir, you have done me the mainest wrong
That e'er was off'red to a gentleman
Of my breeding.
ROMELIO:                    Why sir?
ERCOLE:                                    You have led me
With a vain confidence, that I should marry
Your sister, have proclaim'd it to my friends,           50
Employ'd the greatest lawyers of our state
To settle her a jointure; and the issue
Is, that I must become ridiculous
Both to my friends and enemies: I will leave you
Till I call to you for a strict account                            55
Of your unmanly dealing.
ROMELIO:                                    Stay my Lord!
[*Aside*] Do you long to have my throat cut? Good my
    Lord,
Stay but a little, till I have remov'd
This court-mist from her eyes, till I wake her
From this dull sleep, wherein she'll dream herself     60
To a deformed beggar. [*To* JOLENTA.] You would marry
The great Lord Contarino.
    *Enter* LEONORA.
LEONORA:                              Contarino
Were you talking of? He lost last night at dice
Five thousand ducats; and when that was gone,
Set at one throw a lordship, that twice trebled          65
The former loss.
ROMELIO:                    And that flew after.

46. *mainest*: greatest.
52. *jointure*: marriage settlement providing for joint ownership of
    property.

LEONORA: And most carefully
Carried the gentleman in his caroche
To a lawyer's chamber, there most legally
To put him in possession: was this wisdom?

70 ROMELIO: O yes, their credit in the way of gaming
Is the main thing they stand on; that must be paid,
Though the brewer bawl for's money. And this lord
Does she prefer i'th'way of marriage,
Before our choice here, noble Ercole!

75 LEONORA: You'll be advis'd, I hope. Know for your sakes
I married, that I might have children;
And for your sakes, if you'll be rul'd by me,
I will never marry again. Here's a gentleman
Is noble, rich, well featur'd, but 'bove all,

80 He loves you entirely; his intents are aim'd
For an expedition 'gainst the Turk,
Which makes the contract cannot be delayed.

JOLENTA: Contract? You must do this without my knowledge;
Give me some potion to make me mad,

85 And happily not knowing what I speak,
I may then consent to't.

ROMELIO: Come, you are mad already,
And I shall never hear you speak good sense,
Till you name him for husband.

ERCOLE: Lady, I will do
A manly office for you. I will leave you,

90 To the freedom of your own soul; may it move whither
Heaven and you please.

JOLENTA: Now you express yourself
Most nobly.

ROMELIO: Stay sir, what do you mean to do?

67. *caroche:* large coach.

LEONORA [*kneels*]: Hear me: if ever thou dost marry
    Contarino,
  All the misfortune that did ever dwell
  In a parent's curse, light on thee!               95
ERCOLE: O rise lady, certainly heaven never
  Intended kneeling to this fearful purpose.
JOLENTA: Your imprecation has undone me for ever.
ERCOLE: Give me your hand.
JOLENTA:                No sir.
ROMELIO:                       Giv't me then:
  [*He takes her hand.*]
  O what rare workmanship have I seen this      100
  To finish with your needle, what excellent music
  Have these struck upon the viol! Now I'll teach
  A piece of art.
JOLENTA:       Rather a damnable cunning,
  To have me go about to giv't away,
  Without consent of my soul.
ROMELIO:             Kiss her my lord.     105
  If crying had been regarded, maidenheads
  Had ne'er been lost; at least some appearance of crying
  As an April shower i'th'sunshine.
LEONORA:            She is yours.
ROMELIO: Nay, continue your station, and deal you in
    dumb show;
  Kiss this doggedness out of her.
LEONORA:              To be contracted    110
  In tears, is but fashionable.
ROMELIO:            Yet suppose
  That they were hearty –
LEONORA:          Virgins must seem unwilling.
ROMELIO: O what else? And you remember, we observe
  The like in greater ceremonies than these contracts:

313

115 At the consecration of prelates, they ever use
　　　Twice to say nay, and take it.
　　JOLENTA:　　　　　　　　O brother!
　　　[*He seizes her hand and lays it in* ERCOLE's.]
　　ROMELIO: Keep your possession, you have the door
　　　by'th'ring,
　　　That's livery and seasin in England:
　　　But my lord, kiss that tear from her lip;
120　You'll find the rose the sweeter for the dew.
　　JOLENTA: Bitter as gall.
　　ROMELIO:　　　　　Aye, aye, all you women,
　　　Although you be of never so low stature,
　　　Have gall in you most abundant; it exceeds
　　　Your brains by two ounces. I was saying somewhat:
125　O, do but observe i'th'city, and you'll find
　　　The thriftiest bargains that were ever made,
　　　What a deal of wrangling ere they could be brought
　　　To an upshot!
　　LEONORA:　　Great persons do not ever come together –
　　ROMELIO: With revelling faces, nor is it necessary
130　They should; the strangeness and unwillingness
　　　Wears the greater state, and gives occasion that
　　　The people may buzz and talk of't, though the bells
　　　Be tongue-tied at the wedding.
　　LEONORA:　　　　　　And truly I have heard say,
　　　To be a little strange to one another,
　　　Will keep your longing fresh.
135　ROMELIO:　　　　　Aye, and make you beget
　　　More children when y'are married: some doctors
　　　Are of that opinion. You see, my lord, we are merry
　　　At the contract; your sport is to come hereafter.
　　ERCOLE: I will leave you excellent lady, and withal
140　Leave a heart with you so entirely yours,
　　　That I protest, had I the least of hope

To enjoy you, though I were to wait the time
That scholars do in taking their degree
In the noble arts, 'twere nothing. Howsoe'er,
He parts from you, that will depart from life,                    145
To do you any service, and so humbly
I take my leave.

JOLENTA:          Sir, I will pray for you.

*Exit* ERCOLE.

ROMELIO: Why, that's well; 'twill make your prayer complete,
To pray for your husband.

JOLENTA:               Husband!

LEONORA:                         This is
The happiest hour that I ever arriv'd at.                         150
[*Exit.*]

ROMELIO: Husband, aye, husband! Come you peevish thing,
Smile me a thank for the pains I have tane.

JOLENTA: I hate myself for being thus enforc'd;
You may soon judge then what I think of you
Which are the cause of it.                                        155

*Enter* [WINIFRID, *the*] *waiting woman.*

ROMELIO: You lady of the laundry, come hither.

WINIFRID:                              Sir?

ROMELIO: Look as you love your life, you have an eye
Upon your mistress: I do henceforth bar her
All visitants. I do hear there are bawds abroad,
That bring cut-works, and mantoons, and convey letters            160
To such young gentlewomen, and there are others
That deal in corn-cutting, and fortune-telling:

---

151. *peevish:* obstinate, fretful, querulous.
156. *lady of the laundry:* laundresses were notorious for their easy virtue.
160. *cut-works:* fabric cut in an open-work pattern; *mantoons:* large mantles.

Let none of these come at her on your life,
Nor Deuce-ace the wafer woman, that prigs abroad
165 With musk melons, and malakatoons;
Nor the Scotchwoman with the cittern, do you mark,
Nor a dancer by any means, though he ride on's footcloth,
Nor a hackney coachman, if he can speak French.
WINIFRID: Why sir?
ROMELIO:          By no means: no more words;
Nor the woman with marrow-bone puddings. I have
170    heard
Strange juggling tricks have been convey'd to a woman
In a pudding. You are apprehensive?
WINIFRID: O good sir, I have travell'd.
ROMELIO: When you had a bastard, you travell'd indeed:
175 But, my precious chaperoness,
I trust thee the better for that; for I have heard
There is no warier keeper of a park,
To prevent stalkers, or your night-walkers,
Than such a man, as in his youth has been
A most notorious deer-stealer.
180 WINIFRID:              Very well sir,
You may use me at your pleasure.
ROMELIO: By no means, Winifrid, that were the way
To make thee travel again. Come, be not angry,
I do but jest; thou knowest, wit and a woman
185 Are two very frail things, and so I leave you.

164. *prigs:* thieves' slang meaning (here) haggle.
165. *musk melons:* oriental melons, with a musky flavour; *malakatoons:*
    peaches grafted upon quinces.
166. *cittern:* musical instrument akin to the guitar.
167. *footcloth:* see note to *White Devil*, I, ii, 52 (p. 44).
170. *marrow-bone puddings:* supposed to be aphrodisiac.
172. *apprehensive:* quick-witted.
173-4. *travell'd:* here, and at 183, there is a pun, travel/travail (i.e.
    labour in childbirth).
178. *stalkers, night-walkers:* poachers.

*Exit.*

WINIFRID: I could weep with you, but 'tis no matter,
  I can do that at any time; I have now
  A greater mind to rail a little. Plague of these
  Unsanctified matches: they make us loathe
  The most natural desire our grandame Eve ever left us.    190
  Force one to marry against their will! Why 'tis
  A more ungodly work than enclosing the commons.

JOLENTA: Prithee, peace.
  This is indeed an argument so common,
  I cannot think of matter new enough    195
  To express it bad enough.

WINIFRID:            Here's one, I hope
  Will put you out of 't.
    *Enter* CONTARINO.

CONTARINO:         How now, sweet mistress?
  You have made sorrow look lovely of late,
  You have wept.

WINIFRID: She has done nothing else these three days. Had    200
  you stood behind the arras, to have heard her shed so much
  salt water as I have done, you would have thought she
  had been turn'd fountain.

CONTARINO: I would fain know the cause can be worthy
  this
  Thy sorrow.    205

JOLENTA: Reach me the caskanet. I am studying, sir,
  To take an inventory of all that's mine.

CONTARINO: What to do with it, lady?

JOLENTA:             To make you a deed of gift.

CONTARINO: That's done already. You are all mine.

WINIFRID: Yes, but the devil would fain put in for's share,    210
  In likeness of a separation.

201. *arras:* wall-hanging.
206. *caskanet:* here, a casket.

JOLENTA:                    O sir, I am bewitch'd.
CONTARINO: Ha?
JOLENTA:            Most certain. I am forespoken,
   To be married to another: can you ever think
   That I shall ever thrive in't? Am I not then bewitch'd?
215   All comfort I can teach myself is this:
   There is a time left for me to die nobly,
   When I cannot live so.
CONTARINO: Give me in a word, to whom, or by whose
   means,
   Are you thus torn from me?
220 JOLENTA: By Lord Ercole, my mother, and my brother.
CONTARINO: I'll make his bravery fitter far for a grave,
   Than for a wedding.
JOLENTA:                  So you will beget
   A far more dangerous and strange disease
   Out of the cure. You must love him again
225   For my sake: for the noble Ercole
   Had such a true compassion of my sorrow.
   Hark in your ear, I'll show you his right worthy
   Demeanour to me.
WINIFRID [*aside*]:    O you pretty ones!
   I have seen this lord many a time and oft
230   Set her in's lap, and talk to her of love
   So feelingly, I do protest it has made me
   Run out of my self to think on't.
   O sweet-breath'd monkey; how they grow together!
   Well, 'tis my opinion, he was no woman's friend
235   That did invent a punishment for kissing.
CONTARINO: If he bear himself so nobly,
   The manliest office I can do for him,
   Is to afford him my pity, since he's like

212. *forespoken*: (a) bespoken, (b) bewitched.
221. *bravery*: finery, gay apparel.

To fail of so dear a purchase. For your mother,
Your goodness quits her ill; for your brother,          240
He that vows friendship to a man, and proves
A traitor, deserves rather to be hang'd,
Than he that counterfeits money. Yet for your sake
I must sign his pardon too. Why do you tremble?
Be safe, you are now free from him.

JOLENTA:                                    O but sir,          245
The intermission from a fit of an ague
Is grievous; for indeed it doth prepare us
To entertain torment next morning.

CONTARINO: Why, he's gone to sea.

JOLENTA:                              But he may return too soon.

CONTARINO: To avoid which, we will instantly be married.     250

WINIFRID: To avoid which, get you instantly to bed
    together,
    Do, and I think no civil lawyer for his fee
    Can give you better counsel.

JOLENTA:                              Fie upon thee,
Prithee leave us.

    [*Exit* WINIFRID.]

CONTARINO:        Be of comfort, sweet mistress.

JOLENTA: Upon one condition, we may have no quarrel     255
About this.

CONTARINO: Upon my life, none.

JOLENTA:                              None,
Upon your honour?

CONTARINO:              With whom? With Ercole?
You have delivered him guiltless. With your brother?
He's part of yourself. With your complemental mother?

239. *purchase:* acquisition.
240. *quits her ill:* fails to acquit her (Lucas); but possibly Contarino is
    saying that Jolenta's goodness cancels out her mother's wickedness.
259. *complemental:* courtly, smooth-tongued.

260 I use not fight with women. Tomorrow we'll
Be married. Let those that would oppose this union,
Grow ne'er so subtle, and entangle themselves
In their own work like spiders, while we two
Haste to our noble wishes, and presume
265 The hindrance of it will breed more delight,
As black copartaments shows gold more bright.
    *Exeunt.*

266. *copartaments:* 'Ornamental subdivisions or compartments in a
    larger design' (Lucas).

# [ACT TWO]

## [SCENE ONE]

*Enter* CRISPIANO [*in disguise and*] SANITONELLA

CRISPIANO: Am I well habited?

SANITONELLA: Exceeding well. Any man would take you
for a merchant. But pray sir, resolve me what should be
the reason, that you being one of the most eminent civil
lawyers in Spain, and but newly arriv'd from the East      5
Indies, should take this habit of a merchant upon you?

CRISPIANO: Why my son lives here in Naples, and in's riot
Doth far exceed the exhibition I allow'd him.

SANITONELLA: So then, and in this disguise you mean to
trace him?                                                 10

CRISPIANO: Partly for that, but there is other business
Of greater consequence.

SANITONELLA: Faith, for his expense, 'tis nothing to your
estate. What, to Don Crispiano, the famous Corregidor of
Seville, who by his mere practice of the law, in less time      15
than half a Jubilee, hath gotten thirty thousand ducats a
year!

CRISPIANO: Well, I will give him line,
Let him run on in's course of spending.

SANITONELLA:                              Freely?

CRISPIANO:                                        Freely.

For I protest, if that I could conceive                    20
My son would take more pleasure or content,
By any course of riot, in the expense,

---

1. *habited*: attired.        3. *resolve me*: explain to me.
8. *exhibition*: allowance.
16. *Jubilee*: see additional note to *White Devil*, I, ii, 98 (p. 418).

Than I took joy, nay soul's felicity,
In the getting of it, should all the wealth I have
25 Waste to as small an atomy as flies
I'th' sun, I do protest on that condition,
It should not move me.

SANITONELLA: How's this? Cannot he take more pleasure
in spending it riotously than you have done by scraping
30 it together? O ten thousand times more, and I make no
question, five hundred young gallants will be of my
opinion.
Why all the time of your collectionship,
Has been a perpetual calendar. Begin first
35 With your melancholy study of the law
Before you came to finger the ruddocks; after that,
The tiring importunity of clients,
To rise so early, and sit up so late,
You made yourself half ready in a dream,
40 And never pray'd but in your sleep. Can I think
That you have half your lungs left with crying out
For judgements, and days of trial? Remember sir,
How often have I borne you on my shoulder,
Among a shoal or swarm of reeking night-caps,
45 When that your worship has bepiss'd yourself,
Either with vehemency of argument,
Or being out from the matter. I am merry.

CRISPIANO: Be so.

SANITONELLA: You could not eat like a gentleman, at
leisure;

---

25. *atomy:* tiny particle.
30–31. *I make no question:* I do not doubt.
33–34. *all the time . . . calendar:* i.e. every single day in your career of
accumulating wealth has involved some business.
36. *ruddocks:* slang for gold coin.
44. *night-caps:* lawyers. See note to *Duchess,* II, i, 5 (p. 195).

But swallow'd it like flap-dragons, as if you liv'd          50
With chewing the cud after.

CRISPIANO: No pleasure in the world was comparable to't.

SANITONELLA: Possible?

CRISPIANO:                He shall never taste the like,
Unless he study law.

SANITONELLA:          What, not in wenching, sir?
'Tis a court game believe it, as familiar          55
As gleek, or any other.

CRISPIANO: Wenching? O fie, the disease follows it:
Beside, can the fing'ring taffetas, or lawns,
Or a painted hand, or a breast, be like the pleasure
In taking clients' fees, and piling them          60
In several goodly rows before my desk?
And according to the bigness of each heap,
Which I took by a leer (for lawyers do not tell them)
I vail'd my cap, and withal gave great hope
The cause should go on their sides.

SANITONELLA:                      What think you then          65
Of a good cry of hounds? It has been known
Dogs have hunted lordships to a fault.

CRISPIANO:                Cry of curs?
The noise of clients at my chamber door
Was sweeter music far, in my conceit,
Than all the hunting in Europe.

SANITONELLA:                Pray stay sir,          70
Say he should spend it in good housekeeping?

CRISPIANO: Aye, marry sir, to have him keep a good
house,
And not sell't away; I'd find no fault with that:

---

50. *flap-dragons:* drinks containing small burning objects, drunk out of
   bravado.
56. *gleek:* (a) card-game; (b) ogle, familiar glance.
58. *lawns:* fine linens.          64. *vail'd:* doffed.          69. *conceit:* opinion.

But his kitchen, I'd have no bigger than a sawpit;
75 For the smallness of a kitchen, without question,
Makes many noblemen in France and Spain
Build the rest of the house the bigger.

SANITONELLA: Yes, mock-beggars.

CRISPIANO:                    Some sevenscore chimneys,
But half of them have no tunnels.

80 SANITONELLA: A pox upon them, cuckshaws, that beget
Such monsters without fundaments.

CRISPIANO: Come, come, leave citing other vanities;
For neither wine, nor lust, nor riotous feasts,
Rich clothes, nor all the pleasure that the devil
85 Has ever practis'd with, to raise a man
To a devil's likeness, e'er brought man that pleasure
I took in getting my wealth: so I conclude.
If he can outvie me, let it fly to th' devil.
Yon's my son, what company keeps he?

        *Enter* ROM[ELIO], JULIO, ARIOSTO, [*and*] BAPTISTA.

90 SANITONELLA: The gentleman he talks with, is Romelio
The merchant.

CRISPIANO:      I never saw him till now.
A has a brave sprightly look; I knew his father,
And sojourn'd in his house two years together,
Before this young man's birth. I have news to tell him
95 Of certain losses happened him at sea,
That will not please him.

SANITONELLA:                    What's that dapper fellow
In the long stocking? I do think 'twas he
Came to your lodging this morning.

CRISPIANO:                            'Tis the same.
There he stands, but a little piece of flesh,
100 But he is the very miracle of a lawyer,
One that persuades men to peace and compounds quarrels,

80. *cuckshaws:* quelquechoses, trifles, frivolities.

Among his neighbours, without going to law.

SANITONELLA: And is he a lawyer?

CRISPIANO:                     Yes, and will give counsel
In honest causes gratis, never in his life
Took fee, but he came a spake for't, is a man          105
Of extreme practice, and yet all his longing
Is to become a judge.

SANITONELLA: Indeed, that's a rare longing with men of
his profession. I think he'll prove the miracle of a lawyer
indeed.                                                 110

ROMELIO: Here's the man brought word your father died
i'th' Indies.

JULIO: He died in perfect memory I hope,
And made me his heir.

CRISPIANO:            Yes sir.

JULIO: He's gone the right way then without question.
Friend, in time of mourning we must not use any action,   115
that is but accessory to the making men merry. I do
therefore give you nothing for your good tidings.

CRISPIANO: Nor do I look for it sir.

JULIO: Honest fellow, give me thy hand. I do not think but
thou hast carried New Year's gift to th' Court in thy days,  120
and learned'st there to be so free of thy painstaking.

ROMELIO: Here's an old gentleman says he was chamber-
fellow to your father, when they studied the law together
at Barcelona.

JULIO: Do you know him?                                 125

ROMELIO: Not I, he's newly come to Naples.

JULIO: And what's his business?

ROMELIO: A says he's come to read you good counsel.

CRISPIANO [aside to ARIOSTO]: To him: rate him soundly.

JULIO: And what's your counsel?                         130

106. *Of extreme practice:* either extremely able or extremely hard-
working.

ARIOSTO: Why, I would have you leave your whoring.

JULIO: He comes hotly upon me at first. Whoring?

ARIOSTO: O young quat, incontinence is plagu'd
In all the creatures of the world.

135 JULIO: When did you ever hear that a cock-sparrow
Had the French pox?

ARIOSTO: When did you ever know any of them fat, but
in the nest? Ask all your Cantaride-mongers that question:
remember your self sir.

140 JULIO: A very fine naturalist, a physician, I take you, by
your round slop; for 'tis just of the bigness, and no more,
of the case for a urinal: 'tis concluded, you are a physician.

[ARIOSTO *takes off his hat.*]

What do you mean sir? You'll take cold.

ARIOSTO: 'Tis concluded, you are a fool, a precious one;
145 you are a mere stick of sugar candy, a man may look
quite thorough you.

JULIO: You are a very bold gamester.

[JULIO *takes off his hat.*]

ARIOSTO: I can play at chess, and know how to handle a
rook.

150 JULIO: Pray preserve your velvet from the dust.

ARIOSTO: Keep your hat upon the block sir,
'Twill continue fashion the longer.

JULIO: I was never so abus'd with the hat in the hand
In my life.

ARIOSTO: I will put on; why look you,
155 Those lands that were the client's are now become

---

133. *quat:* pimple, and hence an insignificant individual.
138. *Cantaride-mongers:* on Cantharides, see note to *White Devil*, II, i,
285 (p. 68).
141. *slop:* wide breeches.
149. *rook:* (a) in chess, a castle; (b) a gullible person.
151. *block:* wooden form to preserve the shape of a hat; here, insultingly,
Julio's head.

The lawyer's; and those tenements that were
The country gentleman's, are now grown
To be his tailor's.

JULIO:                    Tailor's?

ARIOSTO: Yes, tailors in France, they grow to great
abominable purchase, and become great officers. How    160
many ducats think you he has spent within a twelvemonth, besides his father's allowance?

JULIO: Besides my father's allowance? Why gentleman,
do you think an auditor begat me? Would you have me
make even at year's end?                               165

ROMELIO: A hundred ducats a month in breaking Venice
glasses.

ARIOSTO: He learnt that of an English drunkard, and a
knight too, as I take it. This comes of your numerous
wardrobe.                                              170

ROMELIO: Aye, and wearing cut-work, a pound a purl.

ARIOSTO: Your dainty embroidered stockings, with
overblown roses, to hide your gouty ankles.

ROMELIO: And wearing more taffeta for a garter, than
would serve the galley dung-boat for streamers.       175

ARIOSTO: Your switching up at the horse-race, with the
Illustrissimi.

ROMELIO: And studying a puzzling arithmetic at the
cock-pit.

ARIOSTO: Shaking your elbow at the Taule-board.       180

ROMELIO: And resorting to your whore in hired velvet,
with a spangled copper fringe at her netherlands.

171. *purl:* pleat, fold.
173. *overblown roses:* oversize silk rosettes on the shoes.
176. *switching:* galloping.          177. *Illustrissimi:* aristocracy.
178. *a puzzling arithmetic:* gambling.
180. *Taule-board:* backgammon board.
182. *spangled copper fringe:* imitation gold lace: *netherlands:* backside; with
a quibble upon the numerous Dutch whores in London.

ARIOSTO: Whereas if you had stay'd at Padua, and fed upon cow-trotters, and fresh beef to supper –

185  JULIO: How I am baited!

ARIOSTO: Nay, be not you so forward with him neither, for 'tis thought, you'll prove a main part of his undoing.

JULIO [aside]: I think this fellow is a witch.

ROMELIO: Who, I sir?

190  ARIOSTO: You have certain rich city choughs, that when they have no acres of their own, they will go and plough up fools, and turn them into excellent meadow; besides some enclosures for the first cherries in the spring, and apricots to pleasure a friend at Court with. You have

195  'pothecaries deal in selling commodities to young gallants, will put four or five coxcombs into a sieve, and so drum with them upon their counter; they'll searse them through like Guinea pepper. They cannot endure to find a man like a pair of tarriers, they would undo him in a

200  trice.

ROMELIO: Maybe there are such.

ARIOSTO: O terrible exactors, fellows with six hands, and three heads.

JULIO: Aye, those are hell-hounds.

205  ARIOSTO: Take heed of them, they'll rend thee like tenter-hooks. Hark in your ear, there is intelligence upon you. The report goes, there has been gold convey'd beyond the sea in hollow anchors. Farewell, you shall know me better, I will do thee more good, than thou art aware of.

    *Exit* AR[IOSTO].

210  JULIO: He's a mad fellow.

190. *choughs*: here, misers; with the additional connotation of 'rook' = swindler.
197. *counter*: there is a play on Counter = debtor's prison; *searse*: sift.
199. *tarriers*: terriers.
205–6. *tenterhooks*: hooks to hold cloth on a 'tenter', or frame, to prevent shrinkage after milling.

328

SANITONELLA: He would have made an excellent barber,
he does so curry it with his tongue.

*Exit* [SANITONELLA].

CRISPIANO: Sir, I was directed to you.

ROMELIO:                 From whence?

CRISPIANO: From the East Indies.

ROMELIO:              You are very welcome.

CRISPIANO: Please you walk apart,                  215
I shall acquaint you with particulars
Touching your trading i'th' East Indies.

ROMELIO: Willingly, pray walk sir.

*Ex[eunt]* CRIS[PIANO *and*] ROM[ELIO]. *Enter* ERCOLE.

ERCOLE: O my right worthy friends, you have stay'd me
long:
One health, and then aboard; for all the galleys      220
Are come about.

*Enter* CONTARINO.

CONTARINO:         Signor Ercole,
The wind has stood my friend sir, to prevent
Your putting to sea.

ERCOLE:             Pray why sir?

CONTARINO: Only love sir;
That I might take my leave sir, and withal         225
Entreat from you a private recommends
To a friend in Malta; 'twould be deliver'd
To your bosom, for I had not time to write.

ERCOLE: Pray leave us gentlemen.

*Exeunt* [JULIO *and* BAPTISTA]. [ERCOLE *and* CON-
TARINO] *sit down.*

                     Wilt please you sit?

CONTARINO: Sir, my love to you has proclaim'd you one,    23c

---

212. *curry:* comb; scratch (as Ariosto's tongue does).
226–7. *Entreat . . . in Malta:* entreat you to deliver a personal message
to a friend in Malta.

Whose word was still lead by a noble thought,
And that thought follow'd by as fair a deed:
Deceive not that opinion. We were students
At Padua together, and have long
235 To'th' world's eye shown like friends;
Was it hearty on your part to me?
ERCOLE: Unfeigned.
CONTARINO:         You are false
To the good thought I held of you, and now
Join the worst part of man to you, your malice,
240 To uphold that falsehood; sacred innocence
Is fled your bosom. Signor, I must tell you,
To draw the picture of unkindness truly,
Is to express two that have dearly lov'd,
And fallen at variance. 'Tis a wonder to me,
245 Knowing my interest in the fair Jolenta,
That you should love her.
ERCOLE: Compare her beauty, and my youth together,
And you will find the fair effects of love
No miracle at all.
CONTARINO:         Yes, it will prove
250 Prodigious to you. I must stay your voyage.
ERCOLE: Your warrant must be mighty.
CONTARINO:                         'T'as a seal
From heaven to do it, since you would ravish from me
What's there entitl'd mine: and yet I vow,
By the essential front of spotless virtue,
255 I have compassion of both our youths:
To approve which, I have not tane the way,
Like an Italian, to cut your throat
By practice, that had given you now for dead,

250. *prodigious:* remarkable, ominous.
254. *essential front:* open forehead (or face).
256. *approve:* demonstrate, prove.
258. *practice:* treachery, deceit.

And never frown'd upon.

ERCOLE: You deal fair, sir.

CONTARINO: Quit me of one doubt, pray sir.                    260

ERCOLE: Move it.

CONTARINO: 'Tis this.
Whether her brother were a main instrument
In her design for marriage.

ERCOLE: If I tell truth,
You will not credit me.

CONTARINO: Why?

ERCOLE: I will tell you truth,
Yet show some reason you have not to believe me:          265
Her brother had no hand in't: is't not hard
For you to credit this? For you may think
I count it baseness to engage another
Into my quarrel; and for that take leave
To dissemble the truth. Sir, if you will fight             270
With any but myself, fight with her mother,
She was the motive.

CONTARINO: I have no enemy
In the world then, but yourself: you must fight
With me.

ERCOLE: I will sir.

CONTARINO: And instantly.

ERCOLE: I will haste before you; point whither.             275

CONTARINO: Why, you speak nobly, and for this fair
    dealing,
Were the rich jewel which we vary for,
A thing to be divided; by my life,
I would be well content to give you half.
But since 'tis vain to think we can be friends,            280
'Tis needful one of us be tane away,
From being the other's enemy.

272. *motive:* instigator.          277. *vary for:* are at variance over.

331

ERCOLE:                                  Yet methinks,
This looks not like a quarrel.
CONTARINO:                        Not a quarrel?
ERCOLE: You have not apparell'd your fury well,
It goes too plain, like a scholar.
285  CONTARINO:                        It is an ornament
Makes it more terrible, and you shall find it
A weighty injury, and attended on
By discreet valour. Because I do not strike you,
Or give you the lie – such foul preparatives
290  Would show like the stale injury of wine –
I reserve my rage to sit on my sword's point,
Which a great quantity of your best blood
Cannot satisfy.
ERCOLE:          You promise well to yourself.
Shall's have no seconds?
CONTARINO:                        None, for fear of prevention.
ERCOLE: The length of our weapons?
295  CONTARINO:                        We'll fit them by the way.
So whether our time calls us to live or die,
Let us do both like noble gentlemen,
And true Italians.
ERCOLE:                  For that let me embrace you.
CONTARINO: Methinks, being an Italian, I trust you
300  To come somewhat too near me:
But your jealousy gave that embrace to try
If I were arm'd, did it not?
ERCOLE:                        No, believe me,
I take your heart to be sufficient proof,
Without a privy coat; and for my part,
305  A taffeta is all the shirt of mail
I am arm'd with.

303. *sufficient proof:* (a) sufficient evidence; (b) sufficiently strong.
304. *privy coat:* an undercoat of mail, illegal in duelling.

CONTARINO:         You deal equally.
   *Exeunt. Enter* JULIO, *and* SERVANT.
JULIO: Where are these gallants, the brave Ercole,
   And noble Contarino?
SERVANT:                They are newly gone, sir,
   And bade me tell you that they will return
   Within this half hour.
   *Enter* ROMELIO.
JULIO:                Met you the Lord Ercole?                      310
ROMELIO: No, but I met the devil in villainous tidings.
JULIO: Why, what's the matter?
ROMELIO:                        O, I am pour'd out
   Like water: the greatest rivers i'th' world
   Are lost in the sea, and so am I. Pray leave me.
   Where's Lord Ercole?
JULIO:                You were scarce gone hence,                   315
   But in came Contarino.
ROMELIO:                Contarino?
JULIO: And entreated some private conference with Ercole,
   And on the sudden they have giv'n's the slip.
ROMELIO: One mischief never comes alone: they are
   Gone to fight.
JULIO:          To fight?
ROMELIO:  -              And you be gentlemen,                      320
   Do not talk, but make haste after them.
JULIO: Let's take several ways then,
   And if't be possible, for women's sakes,
   For they are proper men, use our endeavours,
   That the prick do not spoil them.                               325

   306. *equally:* fairly.
   325. *prick:* the point of the sword; with a double entendre.

## [SCENE TWO]

*Enter* ERCOLE, CONTARINO.

CONTARINO: You'll not forgo your interest in my mistress?

ERCOLE: My sword shall answer that: come, are you ready?

CONTARINO: Before you fight sir, think upon your cause
It is a wondrous foul one, and I wish
5    That all your exercise these four days past
Had been employ'd in a most fervent prayer,
And the foul sin for which you are to fight
Chiefly remembered in't.

ERCOLE:                I'd as soon take
Your counsel in divinity at this present,
10   As I would take a kind direction from you
For the managing my weapon: and indeed,
Both would show much alike.
Come, are you ready?

CONTARINO:         Bethink yourself,
How fair the object is that we contend for.

ERCOLE: O, I cannot forget it.

*They fight.* [ERCOLE] *is wounded.*

15  CONTARINO:            You are hurt.

ERCOLE: Did you come hither only to tell me so,
Or to do it? I mean well, but 'twill not thrive.

CONTARINO: Your cause, your cause, sir:
Will you yet be a man of conscience, and make
20   Restitution for your rage upon your death-bed?

ERCOLE: Never, till the grave father one of us.

[*They*] *fight* [*again*].

CONTARINO: That was fair, and home I think.

[*Wounds* ERCOLE.]

ERCOLE: You prate as if you were in a fence-school.

CONTARINO: Spare your youth, have compassion on yourself.

ERCOLE: When I am all in pieces; I am now unfit     25
For any lady's bed; take the rest with you.
    CONTARINO *wounded, falls upon* ERCOLE.

CONTARINO: I am lost in too much daring: yield your sword.

ERCOLE: To the pangs of death I shall, but not to thee.

CONTARINO: You are now at my repairing, or confusion: Beg your life.

ERCOLE:        O, most foolishly demanded,     30
To bid me beg that which thou canst not give.
    *Enter* ROMELIO, PROS[PERO], BAPT[ISTA], ARI[OSTO],
    [*and*] JULIO.

PROSPERO: See both of them are lost: we come too late.

ROMELIO: Take up the body, and convey it
To Saint Sebastian's monastery.

CONTARINO: I will not part with his sword, I have won't.     35

JULIO: You shall not: take him up gently; so:
And bow his body, for fear of bleeding inward.
Well, these are perfect lovers.

PROSPERO:           Why, I pray?

JULIO: It has ever been my opinion,
That there are none love perfectly indeed,     40
But those that hang or drown themselves for love:
Now these have chose a death next to beheading;
They have cut one another's throats,
Brave valiant lads.

PROSPERO: Come, you do ill, to set the name of valour     45
Upon a violent and mad despair.
Hence may all learn, that count such actions well,

29. *You are now . . . confusion:* you are now at a point where I may either kill or spare you.

The roots of fury shoot themselves to hell.
*Exeunt.*


[SCENE THREE]

*Enter* ROMELIO, ARIOSTO.

ARIOSTO: Your losses, I confess, are infinite,
Yet sir, you must have patience.

ROMELIO:               Sir, my losses
I know, but you I do not.

ARIOSTO:             'Tis most true,
I am but a stranger to you, but am wish'd
5   By some of your best friends, to visit you,
And out of my experience in the world,
To instruct you patience.

ROMELIO: Of what profession are you?

ARIOSTO: Sir I am a lawyer.

ROMELIO:             Of all men living,
10  You lawyers I account the only men
To confirm patience in us; your delays
Would make three parts of this little Christian world
Run out of their wits else. Now I remember,
You read lectures to Julio: are you such a leech
For patience?

15  ARIOSTO:      Yes sir, I have had some crosses.

ROMELIO: You are married then, I am certain.

ARIOSTO:               That I am sir.

ROMELIO: And have you studied patience?

ARIOSTO:            You shall find I have.

ROMELIO: Did you ever see your wife make you cuckold?

ARIOSTO: Make me cuckold?

20  ROMELIO: I ask it seriously: and you have not seen that,
Your patience has not tane the right degree

Of wearing scarlet; I should rather take you
For a Bachelor in the Art, than for a Doctor.

ARIOSTO: You are merry.

ROMELIO:            No sir, with leave of your patience,
I am horrible angry.

ARIOSTO:        What should move you     25
Put forth that harsh interrogatory, if these eyes
Ever saw my wife do the thing you wot of?

ROMELIO: Why, I'll tell you,
Most radically to try your patience,
And the mere question shows you but a dunce in't.   30
It has made you angry; there's another lawyer's beard
In your forehead, you do bristle.

ARIOSTO: You are very conceited:
But come, this is not the right way to cure you.
I must talk to you like a divine.

ROMELIO:         I have heard     35
Some talk of it very much, and many times
To their auditors' impatience; but I pray,
What practice do they make of't in their lives?
They are too full of choler with living honest,
And some of them not only impatient     40
Of their own slightest injuries, but stark mad
At one another's preferment. Now to you sir;
I have lost three goodly carracks.

ARIOSTO:         So I hear.

ROMELIO: The very spice in them,
Had they been shipwreck'd here upon our coast,   45
Would have made all our sea a drench.

ARIOSTO: All the sick horses in Italy
Would have been glad of your loss then.

---

22. *scarlet:* the colour of a doctor's robes (a pun, therefore, on 'degree').
26. *interrogatory:* question.     33. *conceited:* witty.
43. *carracks:* large merchant vessels, galleons.

ROMELIO: You are conceited too.

ARIOSTO: Come, come, come,
50 You gave those ships most strange, most dreadful, and
Unfortunate names: I never look'd they'd prosper.

ROMELIO: Is there any ill omen in giving names to ships?

ARIOSTO: Did you not call one, *The Storm's Defiance*;
Another, *The Scourge of the Sea*; and the third,
*The Great Leviathan*?

55 ROMELIO: Very right, sir.

ARIOSTO: Very devilish names, all three of them:
And surely I think they were curs'd
In their very cradles; I do mean, when they were
Upon their stocks.

ROMELIO: Come, you are superstitious.
60 I'll give you my opinion, and 'tis serious:
I am persuaded there came not cuckolds enough
To the first launching of them, and 'twas that
Made them thrive the worse for't. O, your cuckold's
handsel
Is pray'd for i'th' City.

ARIOSTO: I will hear no more.
65 Give me thy hand. My intent of coming hither,
Was to persuade you to patience: as I live,
If ever I do visit you again,
It shall be to entreat you to be angry; sure it will,
I'll be as good as my word, believe it.
*Exit* [ARIOSTO]. *Enter* LEONORA.

70 ROMELIO: So sir. How now?
Are the screech owls abroad already?

LEONORA: What a dismal noise yon bell makes;
Sure, some great person's dead.

ROMELIO: No such matter,
It is the common bellman goes about,

63. *handsel*: 'first use of a thing; hence, here, inauguration' (Lucas).

To publish the sale of goods.

LEONORA:     Why do they ring  75
Before my gate thus? Let them into'th' court,
I cannot understand what they say.
  *Enter two bellmen and a* CAPUCHIN.

CAPUCHIN: For pity's sake, you that have tears to shed,
Sigh a soft requiem, and let fall a bead
For two unfortunate nobles, whose sad fate  80
Leaves them both dead, and excommunicate:
No churchman's prayer to comfort their last groans,
No sacred sod of earth to hide their bones;
But as their fury wrought them out of breath,
The canon speaks them guilty of their own death.  85

LEONORA: What noblemen, I pray sir?

CAPUCHIN:     The Lord Ercole,
And the noble Contarino, both of them
Slain in single combat.

LEONORA:    O, I am lost forever.

ROMELIO: Denied Christian burial – I pray, what does that,
Or the dead lazy march in the funeral,  90
Or the flattery in the epitaphs, which shows
More sluttish far than all the spider's webs
Shall ever grow upon it: what do these
Add to our well-being after death?

CAPUCHIN: Not a scruple.

ROMELIO:     Very well then,  95
I have a certain meditation,
If I can think of't, somewhat to this purpose;
I'll say it to you, while my mother there

---

79. *bead:* prayer, and hence rosary bead, by which prayers are numbered
  (see II, iii, 99).

85. *canon:* canon law, which treated duelling deaths more or less as
  suicide.

95. *scruple:* minute particle.

Numbers her beads.
You that dwell near these graves and vaults,
Which oft do hide physicians' faults,
Note what a small room does suffice,
To express men's good; their vanities
Would fill more volume in small hand,
Than all the evidence of church land.
Funerals hide men in civil wearing,
And are to the drapers a good hearing,
Make the heralds laugh in their black raiment,
And all die worthies die worth payment
To the altar offerings; though their fame,
And all the charity of their name,
'Tween heaven and this yield no more light,
Than rotten trees, which shine i'th' night.
O look the last act be the best i'th' play,
And then rest gentle bones; yet pray
That when by the precise you are view'd,
A *supersedeas* be not sued,
To remove you to a place more airy,
That in your stead they make keep chary
Stockfish, or sea-coal, for the abuses
Of sacrilege have turn'd graves to viler uses.
How then can any monument say,
Here rest these bones, till the last day,
When time swift both of foot and feather,
May bear them the sexton kens not whither?
What care I then, though my last sleep,
Be in the desert, or in the deep;
No lamp, nor taper, day and night,
To give my charnel chargeable light?

100
105
110
115
120
125

107. *a good hearing:* good news.
109. *all die . . . payment:* i.e. all die worthies who die worth payment.
119. *chary:* charily, carefully.          129. *charnel:* burial vault.

I have there like quantity of ground,     130
And at the last day I shall be found.
Now I pray leave me.
CAPUCHIN:           I am sorry for your losses.
ROMELIO: Um sir, the more spacious that the tennis
Court is, the more large is the hazard.
I dare the spiteful Fortune do her worst,     135
I can now fear nothing.
CAPUCHIN:           O sir, yet consider,
He that is without fear, is without hope,
And sins from presumption. Better thoughts attend you!
    *Exeunt* CAP[UCHIN *and Bellmen*].
ROMELIO: Poor Jolenta, should she hear of this!
She would not after the report keep fresh,     140
So long as flowers in graves.
    *Enter* PROSPERO.
                      How now Prospero?
PROSPERO: Contarino has sent you here his will,
Wherein a has made your sister his sole heir.
ROMELIO: Is he not dead?
PROSPERO:           He's yet living.
ROMELIO: Living? The worse luck.     145
LEONORA: The worse? I do protest it is the best
That ever came to disturb my prayers.
ROMELIO: How?
LEONORA:         Yet I would have him live
To satisfy public justice for the death
Of Ercole. O go visit him for heaven's sake.     150
I have within my closet a choice relic,
Preservative 'gainst swounding, and some earth,
Brought from the Holy Land, right sovereign

133–4. *tennis . . . hazard:* see note to *White Devil*, V, i, 74.
152. *Preservative:* protective, preventative; *swounding:* swooning,
    fainting.     153. *right sovereign:* thoroughly efficacious.

To staunch blood. Has he skilful surgeons, think you?

PROSPERO: The best in Naples.

155 ROMELIO:                     How oft has he been dress'd?

PROSPERO: But once.

LEONORA:         I have some skill this way.
The second or third dressing will show clearly,
Whether there be hope of life. I pray be near him,
If there be any soul can bring me word,
That there is hope of life.

160 ROMELIO:                  Do you prize his life so?

LEONORA: That he may live, I mean, to come to his trial,
To satisfy the law.

ROMELIO:           O, is't nothing else?

LEONORA: I shall be the happiest woman.

    *Exeunt* [LEONORA *and*] PRO[SPERO].

ROMELIO: Here is cruelty apparell'd in kindness.
I am full of thoughts, strange ones, but they're no good
165     ones.
I must visit Contarino; upon that
Depends an engine shall weigh up my losses,
Were they sunk as low as hell: yet let me think,
How I am impair'd in an hour, and the cause of't:
170 Lost in security. O how this wicked world bewitches,
Especially made insolent with riches!
So sails with fore-winds stretch'd, do soonest break,
And pyramids a'th' top are still most weak.

    *Exit.*

## [SCENE FOUR]

*Enter* CAPUCHIN, ERCOLE *led between two.*

CAPUCHIN: Look up, sir, you are preserv'd beyond

---

167. *engine:* device; *weigh up:* offset, counterbalance.
172. *fore-winds:* not head winds, but winds driving the ship forwards.

Natural reason; you were brought dead out a'th' field,
The surgeons ready to have embalm'd you.
ERCOLE: I do look on my action with a thought of terror;
To do ill and dwell in't, is unmanly.                                    5
CAPUCHIN: You are divinely informed sir.
ERCOLE: I fought for one, in whom I have no more right,
Than false executors have in orphans' goods
They cozen them of; yet though my cause were naught,
I rather chose the hazard of my soul,                                    10
Than forgo the compliment of a choleric man.
I pray continue the report of my death, and give out,
'Cause the Church denied me Christian burial,
The vice-admiral of my galleys took my body,
With purpose to commit it to the earth,                                  15
Either in Sicil, or Malta.
CAPUCHIN:                              What aim you at
By this rumour of your death?
ERCOLE:                                      There is hope of life
In Contarino, and he has my prayers,
That he may live to enjoy what is his own,
The fair Jolenta: where, should it be thought                           20
That I were breathing, happily her friends
Would oppose it still.
CAPUCHIN:                         But if you be suppos'd dead,
The law will strictly prosecute his life
For your murder.
ERCOLE:                    That's prevented thus:
There does belong a noble privilege                                      25
To all his family, ever since his father
Bore from the worthy Emperor Charles the Fifth
An answer to the French King's challenge, at such time

1-2. *beyond Natural reason:* miraculously.        5. *dwell:* persist.
16. *Sicil:* Sicily.              21. *happily:* haply, perhaps.
24. *prevented:* forestalled.

343

The two noble princes were engag'd to fight
30 Upon a frontier arm o'th' sea in a flat-bottomed boat,
That if any of his family should chance
To kill a man i'th' field, in a noble cause,
He should have his pardon: now, sir, for his cause,
The world may judge if it were not honest.
35 Pray help me in speech, 'tis very painful to me.

CAPUCHIN: Sir I shall.

ERCOLE:                    The guilt of this lies in Romelio,
And as I hear, to second this good contract,
He has got a nun with child.

CAPUCHIN:                              These are crimes
That either must make work for speedy repentance,
Or for the devil.

40 ERCOLE:                    I have much compassion on him,
For sin and shame are ever tied together,
With Gordian knots, of such a strong thread spun,
They cannot without violence be undone.

       *Exeunt.*

42. *Gordian knots:* see note on *Duchess*, I, ii, 396 (p. 437).

# [ACT THREE]

## [SCENE ONE]

*Enter* ARIOSTO, CRISPIANO.

ARIOSTO: Well sir, now I must claim your promise,
To reveal to me the cause why you live
Thus clouded.

CRISPIANO:     Sir, the King of Spain
Suspects that your Romelio here, the merchant,
Has discover'd some gold mine to his own use,                    5
In the West Indies, and for that employs me
To discover in what part of Christendom
He vents this treasure. Besides, he is inform'd
What mad tricks has been played of late by ladies.

ARIOSTO: Most true, and I am glad the King has heard on't.     10
Why, they use their lords as if they were their wards;
And as your Dutchwomen in the Low Countries,
Take all and pay all, and do keep their husbands
So silly all their lives of their own estates,
That when they are sick, and come to make their will,           15
They know not precisely what to give away
From their wives, because they know not what they are
     worth:
So here should I repeat what factions,
What bat-fowling for offices,
As you must conceive their game is all i'th' night,            20
What calling in question one another's honesties,
Withal what sway they bear i'th' Viceroy's court,
You'd wonder at it: 'twill do well shortly,

---

3. *clouded:* in obscurity, disguised.
8. *vents:* spends.          14. *silly:* ignorant.

Can we keep them off from being of our
Council of War.

25 CRISPIANO:      Well, I have vow'd
That I will never sit upon the bench more,
Unless it be to curb the insolencies
Of these women.

ARIOSTO:      Well, take it on my word then,
Your place will not long be empty.
    *Exeunt.*


## [SCENE TWO]

*Enter* ROMELIO *in the habit of a Jew.*

ROMELIO: Excellently well habited! Why, methinks
That I could play with mine own shadow now,
And be a rare Italianated Jew;
To have as many several change of faces,
5 As I have seen carv'd upon one cherry stone;
To wind about a man like rotten ivy,
Eat into him like quicksilver, poison a friend
With pulling but a loose hair from's beard, or give a
    drench,
He should linger of't nine years, and ne'er complain,
10 But in the spring and fall, and so the cause
Imputed to the disease natural. For slight villainies,
As to coin money, corrupt ladies' honours,
Betray a town to th' Turk, or make a bonfire
A'th' Christian navy, I could settle to't,
15 As if I had eat a politician,
And digested him to nothing but pure blood.
But stay, I lose myself, this is the house.
Within there.

1. *habited:* attired, disguised.

*Enter* TWO SURGEONS.

FIRST SURGEON: Now sir.

ROMELIO: You are the men of art, that as I hear,
Have the Lord Contarino under cure.                    20

SECOND SURGEON: Yes sir, we are his surgeons,
But he is past all cure.

ROMELIO:                    Why, is he dead?

FIRST SURGEON: He is speechless sir, and we do find his
wound
So fester'd near the vitals, all our art
By warm drinks, cannot clear th'imposthumation;       25
And he's so weak, to make [incision]
By the orifix were present death to him.

ROMELIO: He has made a will I hear.

FIRST SURGEON:                    Yes sir.

ROMELIO: And deputed Jolenta his heir.

SECOND SURGEON: He has, we are witness to't.          30

ROMELIO: Has not Romelio been with you yet,
To give you thanks, and ample recompense
For the pains you have tane.

FIRST SURGEON:                    Not yet.

ROMELIO: Listen to me gentlemen, for I protest
If you will seriously mind your own good,             35
I am come about a business shall convey
Large legacies from Contarino's will
To both of you.

SECOND SURGEON: How sir? Why Romelio
Has the will, and in that he has given us nothing.

ROMELIO: I pray attend me: I am a physician.         40

SECOND SURGEON: A physician? Where do you practise?

ROMELIO: In Rome.

FIRST SURGEON:    O then you have store of patients.

25. *imposthumation:* abcess.    27. *orifix:* opening of a wound.
42. *store:* plenty.

347

ROMELIO: Store? Why look you, I can kill my twenty a
    month
    And work but i'th' forenoons: you will give me leave
45    To jest and be merry with you; but as I said,
    All my study has been physic; I am sent
    From a noble Roman that is near akin
    To Contarino, and that ought indeed,
    By the law of alliance, be his only heir,
    To practise his good and yours.
50  BOTH:                         How, I pray sir?
ROMELIO: I can by an extraction which I have,
    Though he were speechless, his eyes set in's head,
    His pulse without motion, restore to him
    For half an hour's space, the use of sense,
55    And perhaps a little speech: having done this,
    If we can work him, as no doubt we shall,
    To make another will, and therein assign
    This gentleman his heir, I will assure you,
    'Fore I depart this house, ten thousand ducats,
60    And then we'll pull the pillow from his head,
    And let him e'en go whither the religion sends him
    That he died in.
FIRST SURGEON: Will you give's ten thousand ducats?
ROMELIO: Upon my Jewism.
    [*The traverse is drawn, revealing*] CONTARINO *in a bed.*
SECOND SURGEON:        'Tis a bargain sir, we are
    yours:
    Here is the subject you must work on.
65  ROMELIO: Well said, you are honest men,
    And go to the business roundly: but gentlemen,
    I must use my art singly.
FIRST SURGEON: O sir, you shall have all privacy.

---

51. *extraction:* extract, essence.
66. *roundly:* promptly, bluntly, briskly.

ROMELIO: And the doors lock'd to me.

SECOND SURGEON:                    At your best pleasure.
   *[aside]* Yet for all this, I will not trust this Jew.                    70

FIRST SURGEON *[aside]*: Faith, to say truth, I do not like
   him neither,
   He looks like a rogue. This is a fine toy,
   Fetch a man to life, to make a new will:
   There's some trick in't. I'll be near you, Jew.
   *Exeunt* SURGEONS.

ROMELIO: Excellent, as I would wish, these credulous fools    75
   Have given me freely what I would have bought
   With a great deal of money. –Softly, here's breath yet;
   Now Ercole, for part of the revenge,
   Which I have vow'd for thy untimely death:
   Besides this politic working of my own,                    80
   That scorns precedent. Why, should this great man live,
   And not enjoy my sister, as I have vow'd
   He never shall? O, he may alter's will
   Every new moon if he please; to prevent which,
   I must put in a strong caveat. Come forth then,           85
   My desperate stiletto, that may be worn
   In a woman's hair, and ne'er discover'd,
   And either would be taken for a bodkin,
   Or a curling iron at most; why 'tis an engine
   That's only fit to put in execution                       90
   Barmotho pigs; a most unmanly weapon,
   That steals into a man's life he knows not how.
   O that great Caesar, he that pass'd the shock
   Of so many armed pikes, and poison'd darts,
   Swords, slings, and battleaxes, should at length,         95

---

85. *caveat:* legal term for a request for a stay in proceedings, pending
   an objection.
91. *Barmotho:* Bermuda, famous for its wild pigs.
93. *great Caesar:* Julius Caesar, assassinated in 44 B.C.

Sitting at ease on a cushion, come to die
By such a shoemaker's awl as this, his soul let forth
At a hole no bigger than the incision
Made for a wheal! 'Uds foot, I am horribly angry
100 That he should die so scurvily: yet wherefore
Do I condemn thee thereof so cruelly,
Yet shake him by the hand? 'Tis to express
That I would never have such weapons us'd,
But in a plot like this, that's treacherous:
105 Yet this shall prove most merciful to thee,
For it shall preserve thee from dying
On a public scaffold, and withal
Bring thee an absolute cure, thus.
        *Stabs* [CONTARINO].
                                So, 'tis done:
And now for my escape.
        *Enter* SURGEONS.
FIRST SURGEON:        You rogue mountebank,
110 I will try whether your inwards can endure
To be wash'd in scalding lead.
ROMELIO:                Hold, I turn
Christian.
SECOND SURGEON: Nay, prithee be a Jew still;
I would not have a Christian be guilty
Of such a villainous act as this is.
ROMELIO: I am Romelio the merchant.
115 FIRST SURGEON:                Romelio!
You have prov'd yourself a cunning merchant indeed.
ROMELIO: You may read why I came hither.
SECOND SURGEON:                Yes,
In a bloody Roman letter.

99. *wheal:* blister.        100. *scurvily:* badly.
110. *inwards:* i.e. 'innards'.
116. *merchant:* a pun, since the word is a slang term for 'fellow'.

ROMELIO:                    I did hate this man,
Each minute of his breath was torture to me.
FIRST SURGEON: Had you forborne this act, he had not
    liv'd                                                                                    120
This two hours.
ROMELIO:          But he had died then,
And my revenge unsatisfied. Here's gold;
Never did wealthy man purchase the silence
Of a terrible scolding wife at a dearer rate,
Than I will pay for yours. Here's your earnest             125
In a bag of double ducats.
SECOND SURGEON: Why look you sir, as I do weigh this
    business,
This cannot be counted murder in you by no means.
Why, 'tis no more than should I go and choke
An Irishman that were three quarters drown'd,             130
With pouring usquebath in's throat.
ROMELIO: You will be secret?
FIRST SURGEON:                As your soul.
ROMELIO: The West Indies shall sooner want gold, than you
    then.
SECOND SURGEON: That protestation has the music of the
    Mint in't.
ROMELIO [aside]: How unfortunately was I surpris'd!       135
I have made myself a slave perpetually
To these two beggars.
    Exit.
FIRST SURGEON:                Excellent.
By this act he has made his estate ours.
SECOND SURGEON: I'll presently grow a lazy surgeon, and
ride on my footcloth. I'll fetch from him every eight     140

125. *earnest:* first instalment of money as a pledge for the remainder.
131. *usquebath:* whiskey.

days a policy for a hundred double ducats; if he grumble,
I'll peach.

FIRST SURGEON: But let's take heed he do not poison us.

SECOND SURGEON: O, I will never eat nor drink with him,
145    Without unicorn's horn in a hollow tooth.

CONTARINO: O!

FIRST SURGEON: Did he not groan?

SECOND SURGEON:          Is the wind in that door still?

FIRST SURGEON: Ha! Come hither, note a strange accident:
His steel has lighted in the former wound,
And made free passage for the congealed blood.
150    Observe in what abundance it delivers
The putrefaction.

SECOND SURGEON: Methinks he fetches
His breath very lively.

FIRST SURGEON:        The hand of heaven is in't,
That his intent to kill him should become
The very direct way to save his life.

SECOND SURGEON: Why this is like one I have heard of in
155    England,
Was cur'd a'th' gout, by being rack'd i'th' Tower.
Well, if we can recover him, here's reward
On both sides. Howsoever, we must be secret.

FIRST SURGEON: We are tied to't.
160    When we cure gentlemen of foul diseases,
They give us so much for the cure, and twice as much
That we do not blab on't. Come, let's to work roundly,
Heat the lotion, and bring the searing.
    *Exeunt.*

142. *peach:* turn informer.
148. *lighted in:* landed in, happened upon.
163. *searing:* cauterizing iron.

## [SCENE THREE]

*A table set forth with two tapers, a death's head, a book.*
JOLENTA *in mourning,* ROMELIO *sits by her.*

ROMELIO: Why do you grieve thus? Take a looking glass,
And see if this sorrow become you; that pale face
Will make men think you us'd some art before,
Some odious painting: Contarino's dead.

JOLENTA: O that he should die so soon!

ROMELIO:                                  Why, I pray tell me,  5
Is not the shortest fever the best? And are not bad plays
The worse for their length?

JOLENTA:                        Add not to'th' ill y'ave done
An odious slander. He stuck i'th' eyes a'th' Court
As the most choice jewel there.

ROMELIO:                          O be not angry.
Indeed the Court to well composed nature  10
Adds much to perfection; for it is, or should be,
As a bright crystal mirror to the world,
To dress itself; but I must tell you sister,
If th'excellency of the place could have wrought salvation,
The devil had ne'er fall'n from heaven; he was proud –  15
[JOLENTA *rises angrily to go away.*]
Leave us, leave us?
Come, take your seat again, I have a plot,
If you will listen to it seriously,
That goes beyond example; it shall breed
Out of the death of these two noblemen,  20
The advancement of our house.

JOLENTA:                          O take heed,
A grave is a rotten foundation.

ROMELIO: Nay, nay, hear me.
'Tis somewhat indirectly, I confess:

353

25 But there is much advancement in the world,
That comes in indirectly. I pray mind me:
You are already made by absolute will,
Contarino's heir: now, if it can be prov'd
That you have issue by Lord Ercole,
30 I will make you inherit his land too.
JOLENTA: How's this?
Issue by him, he dead, and I a virgin?
ROMELIO: I knew you would wonder how it could be done,
But I have laid the case so radically,
35 Not all the lawyers in Christendom
Shall find any the least flaw in't. I have a mistress
Of the Order of St Clare, a beauteous nun,
Who being cloister'd ere she knew the heat
Her blood would arrive to, had only time enough
40 To repent, and idleness sufficient
To fall in love with me; and to be short,
I have so much disorder'd the holy Order,
I have got this nun with child.
JOLENTA: Excellent work, made for a dumb midwife!
45 ROMELIO: I am glad you grow thus pleasant.
Now will I have you presently give out,
That you are full two months quick'ned with child
By Ercole: which rumour can beget
No scandal to you, since we will affirm,
50 The precontract was so exactly done,
By the same words used in the form of marriage,
That with a little dispensation,
A money matter, it shall be register'd
Absolute matrimony.
55 JOLENTA: So, then I conceive you,
My child must prove your bastard.

46. *presently*: immediately.
50. *precontract*: i.e. *per verba de presenti*; cf. *Duchess*, I, ii, 395.

ROMELIO:                           Right;
  For at such time my mistress fall in labour,
  You must feign the like.
JOLENTA:                    'Tis a pretty feat this,
  But I am not capable of it.
ROMELIO:                    Not capable?
JOLENTA: No, for the thing you would have me counter-
    feit,                                                                60
  Is most essentially put in practice: nay, 'tis done,
  I am with child already.
ROMELIO:                    Ha, by whom?
JOLENTA: By Contarino. Do not knit the brow,
  The precontract shall justify it, it shall:
  Nay, I will get some singular fine churchman,                  65
  Or though he be a plural one, shall affirm
  He coupl'd us together.
ROMELIO:                    O misfortune!
  Your child must then be reputed Ercole's.
JOLENTA: Your hopes are dash'd then, since your votary's
    issue
  Must not inherit the land.
ROMELIO:                    No matter for that,                  70
  So I preserve her fame. I am strangely puzzl'd:
  Why, suppose that she be brought abed before you,
  And we conceal her issue till the time
  Of your delivery, and then give out
  That you have two at a birth. Ha, were't not excellent?       75
JOLENTA: And what resemblance think you, would they
    have
  To one another? Twins are still alike:

66. *plural:* i.e. one holding (in defiance of canon law) more than one
    benefice; a pluralist.
69: *votary:* a pun, since the word means both a nun and a 'devout
    worshipper' (here of Romelio).

But this is not your aim; you would have your child
Inherit Ercole's land – O my sad soul,
80     Have you not made me yet wretched enough,
But after all this frosty age in youth,
Which you have witch'd upon me, you will seek
To poison my fame?
ROMELIO:         That's done already.
JOLENTA: No sir, I did but feign it, to a fatal
Purpose, as I thought.
85 ROMELIO:         What purpose?
JOLENTA: If you had lov'd or tend'red my dear honour,
You would have locked your poniard in my heart,
When I nam'd I was with child. But I must live
To linger out, till the consumption
Of my own sorrow kill me.
90 ROMELIO [aside]:         This will not do.
The devil has on the sudden furnish'd me
With a rare charm, yet a most unnatural
Falsehood: no matter, so 'twill take.
Stay sister, I would utter to you a business,
95     But I am very loath: a thing indeed,
Nature would have compassionately conceal'd,
Till my mother's eyes be clos'd.
JOLENTA: Pray what's that sir?
ROMELIO:         You did observe
With what a dear regard our mother tend'red
100     The Lord Contarino, yet how passionately
She sought to cross the match: why this was merely
To blind the eye o'th' world; for she did know
That you would marry him, and he was capable.
My mother doted upon him, and it was plotted
105     Cunningly between them, after you were married,
Living all three together in one house,
A thing I cannot whisper without horror:

Why the malice scarce of devils would suggest
Incontinence 'tween them two.

JOLENTA: I remember since his hurt,                              110
She has been very passionately enquiring
After his health.

ROMELIO:            Upon my soul, this jewel
With a piece of the holy cross in't, this relic,
Valued at many thousand crowns, she would
Have sent him, lying upon his death-bed.                         115

JOLENTA: Professing, as you say, love to my mother:
Wherefore did he make me his heir?

ROMELIO: His will was made afore he went to fight,
When he was first a suitor to you.

JOLENTA: To fight: O well rememb'red!                            120
If he lov'd my mother, wherefore did he lose
His life in my quarrel?

ROMELIO: For the affront sake, a word you understand not;
Because Ercole was pretended rival to him,
To clear your suspicion: I was gulled in't too.                 125
Should he not have fought upon't,
He had undergone the censure of a coward.

JOLENTA: How came you by this wretched knowledge?

ROMELIO: His surgeon overheard it,
As he did sigh it out to his confessor,                          130
Some half hour 'fore he died.

JOLENTA: I would have the surgeon hang'd
For abusing confession, and for making me
So wretched by'th' report. Can this be truth?

ROMELIO: No, but direct falsehood,                               135
As ever was banish'd the Court. Did you ever hear
Of a mother that has kept her daughter's husband
For her own tooth? He fancied you in one kind,
For his lust, and he lov'd our mother

127. *censure of a coward:* condemnation as a coward.

357

140      In another kind, for her money;
     The gallant's fashion right. But come, ne'er think on't,
     Throw the fowl to the devil that hatch'd it, and let this
     Bury all ill that's in't; she is our mother.
     JOLENTA: I never did find anything i'th' world,
145      .Turn my blood so much as this: here's such a conflict
     Between apparent presumption, and unbelief,
     That I shall die in't.
     O, if there be another world i'th' moon,
     As some fantastics dream, I could wish all men,
150      The whole race of them, for their inconstancy,
     Sent thither to people that. Why, I protest
     I now affect the Lord Ercole's memory
     Better than the other's.
     ROMELIO:              But were Contarino
     Living?
     JOLENTA: I do call anything to witness,
155      That the divine law prescrib'd us to strengthen
     An oath, were he living and in health, I would never
     Marry with him. Nay, since I have found the world
     So false to me, I'll be as false to it;
     I will mother this child for you.
     ROMELIO:                    Ha?
160      JOLENTA: Most certainly it will beguile part of my sorrow.
     ROMELIO: O most assuredly; make you smile to think
     How many times i'th'world lordships descend
     To divers men that might, and truth were known,
     Be heir, for anything that belongs to'th' flesh,
165      As well to the Turk's richest eunuch.
     JOLENTA: But do you not think
     I shall have a horrible strong breath now?
     ROMELIO:                    Why?

141. *right*: exactly.
149. *fantastics*: eccentrics.

JOLENTA: O, with keeping your counsel, 'tis so terrible
    foul.

ROMELIO: Come, come, come, you must leave these bitter
    flashes.

JOLENTA: Must I dissemble dishonesty? You have divers     170
    Counterfeit honesty: but I hope here's none
    Will take exceptions; I now must practise
    The art of a great-bellied woman, and go feign
    Their qualms and swoundings.

ROMELIO:               Eat unripe fruit, and oatmeal,
    To take away your colour.

JOLENTA:              Dine in my bed     175
    Some two hours after noon.

ROMELIO:             And when you are up,
    Make to your petticoat a quilted preface,
    To advance your belly.

JOLENTA:           I have a strange conceit now.
    I have known some women when they were with child,
    Have long'd to beat their husbands: what if I,     180
    To keep decorum, exercise my longing
    Upon my tailor that way, and noddle him soundly?
    He'll make the larger bill for't.

ROMELIO: I'll get one shall be as tractable to't as stockfish.

JOLENTA: O my fantastical sorrow! Cannot I now     185
    Be miserable enough, unless I wear
    A pied fool's coat? Nay worse, for when our passions
    Such giddy and uncertain changes breed,
    We are never well, till we are mad indeed.
    *Exit.*

ROMELIO: So, nothing in the world could have done this,     190

---

177–8. *a quilted . . . belly:* a padded forepiece to make J. appear pregnant.
178. *conceit:* notion, idea.       182. *noddle:* beat about the head.
184. *stockfish:* fish dried and beaten to soften them.
187. *pied fool's coat:* i.e. the motley of the court jester.

But to beget in her a strong distaste
Of the Lord Contarino. O jealousy,
How violent, especially in women,
How often has it rais'd the devil up
195 In form of a law-case! My especial care
Must be, to nourish craftily this fiend,
'Tween the mother and the daughter, that the deceit
Be not perceiv'd. My next task, that my sister,
After this suppos'd childbirth, be persuaded
200 To enter into religion: 'tis concluded
She must never marry; so I am left guardian
To her estate: and lastly, that my two surgeons
Be wag'd to the East Indies. Let them prate
When they are beyond the line: the callenture,
205 Or the scurvy, or the Indian pox, I hope,
Will take order for their coming back.
    *Enter* LEON[ORA].
O here's my mother. I ha' strange news for you,
My sister is with child.

LEONORA:           I do look now
For some great misfortunes to follow.
210 For indeed mischiefs are like the visits
Of Franciscan friars, they never come
To prey upon us single. In what estate
Left you Contarino?

ROMELIO:          Strange that you
Can skip from the former sorrow to such a question?
215 I'll tell you: in the absence of his surgeon,

---

204. *line:* equator; *callenture:* tropical disease inducing delirium and
    hallucinations.
205. *Indian pox:* syphilis.
206. *Will take . . . coming back:* will undertake to prevent their return.
210–12. *like the visits . . . us single:* Franciscans habitually travelled in
    pairs. There is a pun on prey/pray.

My charity did that for him in a trice,
They would have done at leisure, and been paid for't.
I have kill'd him.

LEONORA:        I am twenty years elder
Since you last opened your lips.

ROMELIO:             Ha?

LEONORA: You have given him the wound you speak of    220
Quite thorough your mother's heart.

ROMELIO:            I will
Heal it presently mother: for this sorrow
Belongs to your error. You would have him live
Because you think he's father of the child;
But Jolenta vows by all the rights of truth,    225
'Tis Ercole's. It makes me smile to think
How cunningly my sister could be drawn
To the contract, and yet how familiarly
To his bed. Doves never couple without
A kind of murmur.

LEONORA:        O I am very sick.    230

ROMELIO: Your old disease; when you are griev'd, you are
troubl'd
With the mother.

LEONORA [aside]: I am rapt with the mother indeed,
That I ever bore such a son.

ROMELIO:           Pray tend my sister,
I am infinitely full of business.    235

LEONORA: Stay, you will mourn for Contarino?

ROMELIO: O by all means, 'tis fit; my sister is his heir.
Exit.

LEONORA: I will make you chief mourner, believe it.
Never was woe like mine: O that my care
And absolute study to preserve his life,    240
Should be his absolute ruin! Is he gone then?

225. rights: with a pun on rites.

There is no plague i'th' world can be compar'd
To impossible desire, for they are plagu'd
In the desire itself: never, O never
245   Shall I behold him living, in whose life
I liv'd far sweetlier than in mine own.
A precise curiosity has undone me: why did I not
Make my love known directly? 'T had not been
Beyond example, for a matron to affect
250   I'th' honourable way of marriage,
So youthful a person. O I shall run mad:
For as we love our youngest children best,
So the last fruit of our affection,
Wherever we bestow it, is most strong,
255   Most violent, most unresistable,
Since 'tis indeed our latest harvest-home,
Last merriment 'fore winter. And we widows,
As men report of our best picture makers,
We love the piece we are in hand with better
260   Than all the excellent work we have done before:
And my son has depriv'd me of all this. Ha, my son!
I'll be a fury to him; like an Amazon lady,
I'd cut off this right pap, that gave him suck,
To shoot him dead. I'll no more tender him,
265   Than had a wolf stol'n to my teat i'th' night,
And robb'd me of my milk: nay, such a creature
I should love better far. – Ha, ha, what say you?
I do talk to somewhat, methinks: it may be
My evil genius. Do not the bells ring?
270   I have a strange noise in my head. O, fly in pieces!
Come age, and wither me into the malice
Of those that have been happy; let me have
One more property more than the Devil of Hell,
Let me envy the pleasure of youth heartily,

247. *precise curiosity:* overscrupulous nicety.

Let me in this life fear no kind of ill,     275
That have no good to hope for: let me die
In the distraction of that worthy princess,
Who loathed food, and sleep, and ceremony,
For thought of losing that brave gentleman,
She would fain have sav'd, had not a false conveyance     280
Express'd him stubborn-hearted. Let me sink,
Where neither man, nor memory may ever find me.

    [LEONORA] *falls down.* [*Enter* CAPUCHIN *and* ERCOLE.]

CAPUCHIN: This is a private way which I command,
    As her confessor. I would not have you seen yet,
    Till I prepare her.

    [ERCOLE *withdraws.*]

                Peace to you lady.

LEONORA:                   Ha?     285

CAPUCHIN: You are well employ'd, I hope; the best pillow
    I'th' world for this your contemplation,
    Is the earth, and the best object, heaven.

LEONORA: I am whispering to a dead friend.

CAPUCHIN: And I am come     290
    To bring you tidings of a friend was dead,
    Restor'd to life again.

LEONORA:           Say sir?

CAPUCHIN: One whom I dare presume, next to your children,
    You tend'red above life.

LEONORA:            Heaven will not suffer me
    Utterly to be lost.

CAPUCHIN:        For he should have been     295
    Your son-in-law; miraculously sav'd,
    When surgery gave him o'er.

LEONORA:           O may you live
    To win many souls to heaven, worthy sir,

That your crown may be the greater. Why my son
300    Made me believe he stole into his chamber,
And ended that which Ercole began
By a deadly stab in's heart.

ERCOLE [*aside*]:           Alas, she mistakes,
'Tis Contarino she wishes living; but I must fasten
On her last words, for my own safety.

LEONORA:             Where,
O where shall I meet this comfort?

305    ERCOLE [*reveals himself*]: Here in the vow'd comfort of your
daughter.

LEONORA: O I am dead again; instead of the man,
You present me the grave swallowed him.

ERCOLE: Collect yourself, good lady
310    Would you behold brave Contarino living?
There cannot be a nobler chronicle
Of his good than myself: if you would view him dead,
I will present him to you bleeding fresh,
In my penitency.

LEONORA:      Sir, you do only live
315    To redeem another ill you have committed,
That my poor innocent daughter perish not
By your vile sin, whom you have got with child.

ERCOLE [*aside*]: Here begin all my compassion: O poor
soul!
She is with child by Contarino, and he dead;
320    By whom should she preserve her fame to'th' world,
But by myself that lov'd her 'bove the world?
There never was a way more honourable
To exercise my virtue, than to father it,
And preserve her credit, and to marry her.
325    I'll suppose her Contarino's widow, bequeath'd to me

311–12. *a nobler . . . good:* one willing to bear more noble witness to
his qualities.

Upon his death: for sure she was his wife,
But that the ceremony a'th' Church was wanting.
[*To* LEONORA] Report this to her, madam, and withal,
That never father did conceive more joy
For the birth of an heir, than I to understand          330
She had such confidence in me. I will not now
Press a visit upon her, till you have prepar'd her:
For I do read in your distraction,
Should I be brought a'th' sudden to her presence,
Either the hasty fright, or else the shame              335
May blast the fruit within her. I will leave you
To commend as loyal faith and service to her,
As e'er heart harbour'd. By my hope of bliss,
I never liv'd to do good act but this.

CAPUCHIN [*aside to* ERCOLE]: Withal, and you be wise,     340
Remember what the mother has reveal'd
Of Romelio's treachery.

    *Exeunt* ERCOLE, CAPUCHIN.

LEONORA: A most noble fellow! In his loyalty
I read what worthy comforts I have lost
In my dear Contarino, and all adds                      345
To my despair. – Within there!

    *Enter* WINIFRID.

                      Fetch the picture
Hangs in my inner closet.

    *Exit* WIN[IFRID].

              I remember
I let a word slip of Romelio's practice
At the surgeons': no matter, I can salve it,
I have deeper vengeance that's preparing for him:       350
To let him live and kill him, that's revenge
I meditate upon.

    *Enter* WIN[IFRID] *and the picture.*

336. *blast the fruit:* induce a miscarriage.    349. *salve:* salvage, repair.

365

So, hang it up.
I was enjoin'd by the party ought that picture,
Forty years since, ever when I was vex'd,
355   To look upon that. What was his meaning in't,
I know not, but methinks upon the sudden
It has furnish'd me with mischief; such a plot
As never mother dreamt of. Here begins
My part i'th' play: my son's estate is sunk
360   By loss at sea, and he has nothing left
But the land his father left him. 'Tis concluded,
The law shall undo him. Come hither,
I have a weighty secret to impart,
But I would have thee first confirm to me,
365   How I may trust that thou canst keep my counsel
Beyond death.

WINIFRID:        Why mistress, 'tis your only way
To enjoin me first that I reveal to you
The worst act I e'er did in all my life:
So one secret shall bind another.

370   LEONORA: Thou instruct'st me
Most ingeniously, for indeed it is not fit,
Where any act is plotted, that is nought,
Any of counsel to it should be good;
And in a thousand ills have happ'd i'th' world,
375   The intelligence of one another's shame
Have wrought far more effectually than the tie
Of conscience, or religion.

WINIFRID: But think not, mistress,
That any sin which ever I committed
380   Did concern you; for proving false in one thing,
You were a fool if ever you would trust me
In the least matter of weight.

LEONORA:                         Thou hast liv'd with me

353. *ought:* who owned.        372. *nought:* wicked.

These forty years; we have grown old together,
As many ladies and their women do,
With talking nothing, and with doing less:                385
We have spent our life in that which least concerns life,
Only in putting on our clothes. And now I think on't,
I have been a very courtly mistress to thee,
I have given thee good words, but no deeds;
Now's the time to requite all. My son has                390
Six lordships left him.

WINIFRID:                     'Tis truth.

LEONORA:                                   But he cannot
Live four days to enjoy them.

WINIFRID:                              Have you poison'd him?

LEONORA: No, the poison is yet but brewing.

WINIFRID: You must minister it to him with all privacy.

LEONORA: Privacy? It shall be given him                395
In open court. I'll make him swallow it
Before the judge's face. If he be master
Of poor ten arpines of land forty hours longer,
Let the world repute me an honest woman.

WINIFRID: So 'twill I hope.

LEONORA:                          O thou canst not conceive                400
My inimitable plot. Let's to my ghostly father,
Where first I will have thee make a promise
To keep my counsel, and then I will employ thee
In such a subtle combination,
Which will require to make the  practice fit,                405
Four devils, five advocates, to one woman's wit.
　　*Exeunt.*

390. *requite:* repay.
398. *arpines:* Fr. arpent, a land measure equalling 1 to 1½ acres.
401. *ghostly:* spiritual.

# [ACT FOUR]

## [SCENE ONE]

*Enter* LEONORA, SANITONELLA, WINIFRID *and*
REGISTER *at one door: at the other*, ARIOSTO.

SANITONELLA [*to the* REGISTER]: Take her into your office
sir, she has that in her belly will dry up your ink, I can tell
you.
[*Exeunt* WINIFRID, REGISTER.]
[*to* LEONORA]: This is the man that is your learned counsel,

5    A fellow that will trowel it off with tongue:
He never goes without restorative powder
Of the lungs of fox in's pocket, and Malligo raisins
To make him long-winded. Sir, this gentlewoman
Entreats your counsel in an honest cause,

10   Which please you sir, this brief, my own poor labour
Will give you light of.
[*He offers the brief to* ARIOSTO.]

ARIOSTO:              Do you call this a brief?
Here's as I weigh them, some fourscore sheets of paper.
What would they weigh if there were cheese wrap'd in
them,
Or figdates!
[*He reads the brief.*]

SANITONELLA: Joy come to you, you are merry;

15   We call this but a brief in our office.
The scope of the business lies i'th' margent.

S.D. *Register:* registrar.                  5. *trowel it off:* utter volubly.
7. *lungs of fox:* reputed cure for lung diseases; *Malligo:* Malaga.
11. *give you light of:* relieve you of.
14. *figdates:* fig-dote, or wild fig.
16. *scope:* gist, core; *margent:* margin.

368

ARIOSTO: Methinks you prate too much.
　I never could endure an honest cause
　With a long prologue to't.

LEONORA: 　　　　　　　You trouble him.

ARIOSTO: What's here? O strange. I have liv'd this sixty
　　years,　　　　　　　　　　　　　　　　　　　　　　20
　Yet in all my practice never did shake hands
　With a cause so odious. Sirrah, are you her knave?

SANITONELLA: No sir, I am a clerk.

ARIOSTO: Why you whoreson fogging rascal,
　Are there not whores enough for presentations,　　　25
　Of overseers, wrong the will o'th' dead,
　Oppressions of widows, or young orphans,
　Wicked divorces, or your vicious cause
　Of *plus quam satis*, to content a woman,
　But you must find new stratagems, new pursenets?　30
　O woman, as the ballad lives to tell you,
　What will you shortly come to?

SANITONELLA: Your fee is ready sir.

ARIOSTO: 　　　　　　　The devil take such fees,
　And all such suits i'th' tail of them; see the slave
　Has written false Latin: sirrah Ignoramus,　　　　　35
　Were you ever at the university?

SANITONELLA: Never sir: but 'tis well known to divers
　I have commenc'd in a pew of our office.

ARIOSTO: Where? In a pew of your office!

SANITONELLA: I have been dry-found'red in't this four
　　years,　　　　　　　　　　　　　　　　　　　　　　40
　Seldom found non-resident from my desk.

ARIOSTO: Non-resident subsumner!

24. *fogging:* pettifogging.
30. *pursenets:* nets shaped like a bag, with a draw-cord at the neck.
38. *commenc'd:* a technical term meaning to take one's degree at a
　　university.
40. *dry-found'red:* lamed, broken down (a farrier's term).

I'll tear your libel for abusing that word,
By virtue of the clergy.
[*He tears up the brief.*]

SANITONELLA:        What do you mean sir?
It cost me four nights' labour.

45   ARIOSTO:                Hadst thou been drunk
So long, th'adst done our court better service.

LEONORA: Sir, you do forget your gravity, methinks.

ARIOSTO: Cry ye mercy, do I so?
And as I take it, you do very little
50  Remember either womanhood
Or Christianity: why do ye meddle
With that seducing knave, that's good for naught,
Unless 't be to fill the office full of fleas,
Or a winter itch, wears that spacious inkhorn
55  All a vacation only to cure tetters,
And his penknife to weed corns from the splay toes
Of the right worshipful of the office?

LEONORA: You make bold with me sir.

ARIOSTO: Woman, y'are mad, I'll swear it, and have more
    need
60  Of a physician than a lawyer.
The melancholy humour flows in your face,
Your painting cannot hide it. Such vile suits
Disgrace our courts, and these make honest lawyers
Stop their own ears whilst they plead, and that's the
    reason
65  Your younger men that have good conscience,
Wear such large nightcaps. Go old woman, go pray,
For lunacy, or else the devil himself

---

54. *winter itch:* skin disease resulting from exposure to cold.
55. *tetters:* boils and other skin eruptions.
56. *splay:* out-turned, spread.
66. *nightcaps:* satiric term for the white coifs of sergeants at law.

Has tane possession of thee. May like cause
in any Christian court never find name:
Bad suits, and not the law, bred the law's shame.　　70
　　*Exit.*

LEONORA: Sure the old man's frantic.

SANITONELLA: Plague on's gouty fingers.
Were all of his mind, to entertain no suits
But such they thought were honest, sure our lawyers
Would not purchase half so fast. But here's the man,　　75
　　*Enter* CONTILUPO, *a spruce lawyer.*
Learned Signior Contilupo, here's a fellow
Of another piece, believe't; I must make shift
With the foul copy.

CONTILUPO:　　　　　　Business to me?

SANITONELLA: To you sir, from this lady.

CONTILUPO:　　　　　　　　　　　　She is welcome.

SANITONELLA: 'Tis a foul copy sir, you'll hardly read it.　　80
There's twenty double ducats, can you read sir?

CONTILUPO: Exceeding well; very, very exceeding well.

SANITONELLA [*aside*]: This man will be sav'd, he can read.
　　Lord, lord, to see
What money can do! Be the hand never so foul,
Somewhat will be pick'd out on't.

CONTILUPO:　　　　　　　　　　Is not this　　85
*Vivere honeste?*

SANITONELLA: No, that's struck out sir;
And wherever you find *vivere honeste* in these papers,
Give it a dash sir.

CONTILUPO:　　　　I shall be mindful of it.
In truth you write a pretty secretary;

75. *purchase:* make money.
80. *foul copy:* i.e. of the brief; Ariosto having torn up the fair copy.
86. *Vivere honeste:* to live honestly.
88. *give it a dash:* strike it out.
89. *secretary:* kind of handwriting, used chiefly in legal documents.

90 Your secretary hand ever takes best
In mine opinion.

SANITONELLA: Sir, I have been in France,
And there, believe't, your court hand generally,
Takes beyond thought.

CONTILUPO: Even as a man is traded in't.

SANITONELLA [aside]: That I could not think of this virtuous
gentleman

95 Before I went to'th' other hog-rubber!
Why this was wont to give young clerks half fees,
To help him to clients. Your opinion in the case sir?

CONTILUPO: I am struck with wonder, almost extasied,
With this most goodly suit.

LEONORA: It is the fruit
Of a most hearty penitence.

100 CONTILUPO: 'Tis a case
Shall leave a precedent to all the world,
In our succeeding annals, and deserves
Rather a spacious public theatre
Than a pent court for audience: it shall teach

105 All ladies the right path to rectify
Their issue.

SANITONELLA: Lo you, here's a man of comfort.

CONTILUPO: And you shall go unto a peaceful grave,
Discharg'd of such a guilt, as would have lain
Howling for ever at your wounded heart,
And rose with you to Judgement.

110 SANITONELLA: O give me
Such a lawyer, as will think of the day
Of Judgement!

LEONORA: You must urge the business
Against him as spitefully as may be.

92. *court hand*: also used in court work.      93. *traded*: practised.
95. *hog-rubber*: term of abuse.      104. *pent*: narrow, enclosed.

CONTILUPO: Doubt not. What, is he summon'd?

SANITONELLA:                              Yes, and the court
Will sit within this half hour. Peruse your notes,                    115
You have very short warning.

CONTILUPO:                         Never fear you that.
Follow me worthy lady, and make account
This suit is ended already.
     *Exeunt.*


## [SCENE TWO]

*Enter officers preparing seats for the judges; to them* ERCOLE,
*muffled.*

FIRST OFFICER: You would have a private seat sir?

ERCOLE:                                   Yes sir.

SECOND OFFICER: Here's a closet belongs to'th' court,
Where you may hear all unseen.

ERCOLE:                           I thank you;
There's money.

SECOND OFFICER: I give your thanks again sir.
     *Enter* CONTARINO, *the two surgeons, disguised;* [CON-
     TARINO *as a Dane*].

CONTARINO: Is't possible Romelio's persuaded                          5
You are gone to the East Indies?

FIRST SURGEON:               Most confidently.

CONTARINO: But do you mean to go?

SECOND SURGEON: How? Go to the East Indies? And so
many Hollanders gone to fetch sauce for their pickled
herrings: some have been pepper'd there too, lately; but          10
I pray, being thus well recover'd of your wound, why do
you not reveal yourself?

CONTARINO: That my fair Jolenta should be rumour'd
To be with child by noble Ercole,

15 Makes me expect to what a violent issue
These passages will come. I hear her brother
Is marrying the infant she goes with,
'Fore it be born, as, if it be a daughter,
To the Duke of Austria's nephew; if a son,

20 Into the noble ancient family
Of the Palavafini. He's a subtle devil.
And I do wonder what strange suit in law
Has happ'd between him and's mother.

FIRST SURGEON: 'Tis whisper'd 'mong the lawyers, 'twill undo
Him for ever.
*Enter* SANIT[ONELLA], WIN[IFRID].

25 SANITONELLA: Do you hear, officers?
You must take special care, that you let in
No brachigraphy men, to take notes.

FIRST OFFICER: No sir?

SANITONELLA: By no means;
We cannot have a cause of any fame,

30 But you must have scurvy pamphlets, and lewd ballads
Engend'red of it presently. Have you broke fast yet?

WINIFRID: Not I sir.

SANITONELLA: 'Twas very ill done of you:
For this cause will be long a-pleading; but no matter,
I have a modicum in my buckram bag,
To stop your stomach.

35 WINIFRID: What is't? Green ginger?

SANITONELLA: Green ginger, nor pellitory of Spain
Neither, yet 'twill stop a hollow tooth better
Than either of them.

15. *issue:* outcome. 21. *Palavafini:* Pallavicini, a famous Italian family.
34. *buckram bag:* see note to *White Devil*, III, ii, 47 (p 82).
35. *Green ginger:* i.e. the undried root.
36. *pellitory of Spain:* plant with a fiery taste, used as a cure for tooth-ache.

WINIFRID:             Pray what is't?

SANITONELLA:            Look you,
  It is a very lovely pudding-pie,
  Which we clerks find great relief in.               40

WINIFRID: I shall have no stomach.

SANITONELLA: No matter and you have not, I may
  pleasure
  Some of our learned counsel with't; I have done it
  Many a time and often, when a cause
  Has proved like an after-game at Irish.        45

    *Enter* CRISPIANO *like a judge, with another judge;* CON-
    TILUPO *and another lawyer at one bar;* ROMELIO,
    ARIOSTO *at another;* LEONORA *with a black veil over her,*
    *and* JULIO.

CRISPIANO: 'Tis a strange suit; is Leonora come?

CONTILUPO: She's here my lord; make way there for the
  lady.

CRISPIANO: Take off her veil: it seems she is asham'd
  To look her cause i'th' face.

CONTILUPO:             She's sick, my lord.

ARIOSTO: She's mad my lord, and would be kept more
  dark.                                  50
  [*To Romelio*] By your favour sir, I have now occasion
  To be at your elbow, and within this half hour
  Shall entreat you to be angry, very angry.

CRISPIANO: Is Romelio come?

ROMELIO: I am here my lord, and call'd, I do protest,   55
  To answer what I know not, for as yet
  I am wholly ignorant of what the court
  Will charge me with.

CRISPIANO:           I assure you, the proceeding
  Is most unequal then, for I perceive

---

39. *pudding-pie:* meat pudding baked in a dish.    41. *stomach:* appetite.
45. *after-game:* second game; *Irish:* backgammon.    59. *unequal:* unfair.

60 The counsel of the adverse party furnish'd
With full instruction.

ROMELIO:                    Pray my lord,
Who is my accuser?

CRISPIANO:              'Tis your mother.

ROMELIO [*aside*]: She has discover'd Contarino's murder:
If she prove so unnatural, to call
65 My life in question, I am arm'd to suffer
This to end all my losses.

CRISPIANO:                    Sir, we will do you
This favour: you shall hear the accusation,
Which being known, we will adjourn the court
Till a fortnight hence, you may provide your counsel.

70 ARIOSTO: I advise you, take their proffer,
Or else the lunacy runs in a blood,
You are more mad than she.

ROMELIO:                    What are you sir?

ARIOSTO: An angry fellow that would do thee good,
For goodness' sake itself, I do protest,
75 Neither for love nor money.

ROMELIO: Prithee stand further, I shall gall your gout else.

ARIOSTO: Come, come, I know you for an East Indy
merchant,
You have a spice of pride in you still.

ROMELIO:                    My lord,
I am so strength'ned in my innocence,
80 For any the least shadow of a crime,
Committed 'gainst my mother, or the world,
That she can charge me with, here do I make it
My humble suit, only this hour and place
May give it as full hearing, and as free,
85 And unrestrain'd a sentence.

63. *discover'd*: revealed.
71. *runs in a blood*: runs in the blood (i.e. of a family).

CRISPIANO: Be not too confident; you have cause to fear.
ROMELIO: Let fear dwell with earthquakes,
   Shipwrecks at sea, or prodigies in heaven;
   I cannot set myself so many fathom
   Beneath the height of my true heart, as fear.     90
ARIOSTO: Very fine words, I assure you, if they were
   To any purpose.
CRISPIANO:     Well, have your entreaty:
   And if your own credulity undo you,
   Blame not the court hereafter. Fall to your plea.
CONTILUPO: May it please your lordship and the reverend
    court,     95
   To give me leave to open to you a case
   So rare, so altogether void of precedent,
   That I do challenge all the spacious volumes
   Of the whole civil law to show the like.
   We are of counsel for this gentlewoman,     100
   We have receiv'd our fee, yet the whole course
   Of what we are to speak, is quite against her,
   Yet we'll deserve our fee too. There stands one,
   Romelio the merchant; I will name him to you
   Without either title or addition:     105
   For those false beams of his supposed honour,
   As void of true heat as are all painted fires,
   Or glow-worms in the dark, suit him all basely,
   As if he had bought his gentry from the herald,
   With money got by extortion: I will first     110
   Produce this Aesop's crow as he stands forfeit
   For the long use of his gay borrowed plumes,
   And then let him hop naked. I come to'th' point:
   'T'as been a dream in Naples, very near
   This eight and thirty years, that this Romelio     115
   Was nobly descended; he has rank'd himself
   With the nobility, shamefully usurp'd

Their place, and in a kind of saucy pride,
Which like to mushrooms, ever grow most rank
120 When they do spring from dunghills, sought to o'ersway
The Fieschi, the Grimaldi, Doria,
And all the ancient pillars of our state.
View now what he is come to: this poor thing
Without a name, this cuckoo hatch'd i'th'nest
Of a hedge-sparrow.

125 ROMELIO:                Speaks he all this to me?
ARIOSTO: Only to you sir.
ROMELIO:                    I do not ask thee,
Prithee hold thy prating.
ARIOSTO:                     Why very good!
You will be presently as angry as I could wish.
CONTILUPO: What title shall I set to this base coin?
130 He has no name, and for's aspect he seems
A giant in a May-game, that within
Is nothing but a porter: I'll undertake
He had as good have travell'd all his life
With gypsies: I will sell him to any man
135 For an hundred chickeens, and he that buys him of me
Shall lose by'th' hand too.
ARIOSTO:                     Lo, what are you come to:
You that did scorn to trade in anything
But gold or spices, or your cochineal,
He rates you now at poor John.
ROMELIO:                         Out upon thee,
I would thou wert of his side.
140 ARIOSTO:                       Would you so?

121. *Fieschi, the Grimaldi, Doria:* three of the four chief families of
    Genoa, *not* Naples.
130. *aspect:* appearance.
135. *chickeens:* zecchins, Italian coins worth about nine shillings.
136. *by'th' hand:* by the deal.
139. *poor John:* salted fish, hence, something worthless.

ROMELIO: The devil and thee together on each hand,
  To prompt the lawyer's memory when he founders.
CRISPIANO: Signor Contilupo, the court holds it fit,
  You leave this stale declaiming 'gainst the person,
  And come to the matter.
CONTILUPO:              Now I shall my lord.               145
CRISPIANO: It shows a poor malicious eloquence,
  And it is strange men of your gravity
  Will not forgo it. Verily, I presume,
  If you but heard yourself speaking with my ears,
  Your phrase would be more modest.                       150
CONTILUPO: Good my lord, be assured,
  I will leave all circumstance, and come to'th'purpose:
  This Romelio is a bastard.
ROMELIO:                How, a bastard?
  O mother, now the day begins grow hot
  On your side.
CONTILUPO:   Why she is your accuser.                     155
ROMELIO: I had forgot that; was my father married
  To any other woman, at the time
  Of my begetting?
CONTILUPO:       That's not the business.
ROMELIO: I turn me then to you that were my mother,
  But by what name I am to call you now,                  160
  You must instruct me: were you ever married
  To my father?
LEONORA:       To my shame I speak it, never.
CRISPIANO: Not to Francisco Romelio?
LEONORA: May it please your lordships,
  To him I was, but he was not his father.               165
CONTILUPO: Good my lord, give us leave in a few words
  To expound the riddle, and to make it plain
  Without the least of scruple: for I take it,

168. *least of:* slightest; *scruple:* a pun, since the word also means doubt.

  There cannot be more lawful proof i'th' world,
170 Than the oath of the mother.
  CRISPIANO: Well then, to your proofs,
  And be not tedious.
  CONTILUPO:   I'll conclude in a word:
  Some nine and thirty years since, which was the time
  This woman was married, Francisco Romelio,
175 This gentleman's putative father, and her husband,
  Being not married to her past a fortnight,
  Would needs go travel; did so, and continued
  In France and the Low Countries eleven months:
  Take special note o'th' time, I beseech your lordship,
180 For it makes much to'th' business. In his absence
  He left behind to sojourn at his house
  A Spanish gentleman, a fine spruce youth
  By the ladies' confession, and you may be sure
  He was no eunuch neither; he was one
185 Romelio loved very dearly, as oft haps,
  No man alive more welcome to the husband
  Than he that makes him cuckold. This gentleman
  I say, breaking all laws of hospitality,
  Got his friend's wife with child, a full two months
190 'Fore the husband returned.
  SANITONELLA [aside]: Good sir, forget not the lambskin.
  CONTILUPO [aside]: I warrant thee.
  SANITONELLA [aside]:  I will pinch by the buttock,
  To put you in mind of't.
  CONTILUPO [aside]:  Prithee hold thy prating.
  What's to be practis'd now, my lord? Marry this:
195 Romelio being a young novice, not acquainted
  With this precedence, very innocently
  Returning home from travel, finds his wife
  Grown an excellent good huswife, for she had set

  180. *makes much to:* is relevant to. 196. *precedence:* previous goings on.

Her women to spin flax, and to that use,
Had in a study which was built of stone,                              200
Stor'd up at least an hundredweight of flax:
Marry such a thread as was to be spun from the flax,
I think the like was never heard of.
CRISPIANO: What was that?
CONTILUPO: You may be certain, she would lose no time   205
  In bragging that her husband had got up
  Her belly: to be short, at seven months' end,
  Which was the time of her delivery,
  And when she felt her self to fall in travail,
  She makes her waiting woman, as by mischance,        210
  Set fire to the flax, the fright whereof,
  As they pretend, causes this gentlewoman
  To fall in pain, and be delivered
  Eight weeks afore her reckoning.
SANITONELLA [aside]: Now sir, remember the lambskin.   215
CONTILUPO: The midwife straight howls out, there was
    no hope
  Of th'infant's life, swaddles it in a flay'd lambskin,
  As a bird hatch'd too early, makes it up
  With three quarters of a face, that made it look
  Like a changeling, cries out to Romelio             220
  To have it christ'ned, lest it should depart
  Without that it came for: and thus are many serv'd,
  That take care to get gossips for those children,
  To which they might be godfathers themselves,
  And yet be no arch-puritans neither.                225
CRISPIANO: No more!
ARIOSTO:                Pray my lord, give him way, you spoil
  His oratory else: thus would they jest
  Were they feed to open their sister's cases.

220. *changeling*: (a) a child substituted for another, (b) half-wit.
228. *cases*: double entendre.

CRISPIANO: You have urg'd enough; you first affirm,
230    Her husband was away from her eleven
       Months?
CONTILUPO: Yes my lord.
CRISPIANO                    And at seven months' end,
       After his return she was delivered
       Of this Romelio, and had gone her full time?
CONTILUPO: True my lord.
235 CRISPIANO: So by this account this gentleman was begot
       In his suppos'd father's absence.
CONTILUPO:                    You have it fully.
CRISPIANO: A most strange suit this, 'tis beyond example,
       Either time past, or present, for a woman
       To publish her own dishonour voluntarily,
240    Without being call'd in question, some forty years
       After the sin committed, and her counsel
       To enlarge the offence with as much oratory
       As ever I did hear them in my life
       Defend a guilty woman; 'tis most strange:
245    Or why with such a poison'd violence
       Should she labour her son's undoing? We observe
       Obedience of creatures to the Law of Nature
       Is the stay of the whole world: here that Law is broke,
       For though our civil law makes difference
250    'Tween the base, and the legitimate,
       Compassionate Nature makes them equal;
       Nay, she many times prefers them. I pray
       Resolve me sir, have not you and your mother
       Had some suit in law together lately?
255 ROMELIO: None my lord.
CRISPIANO: No? No contention about parting your
       goods?
ROMELIO: Not any.

   256. *parting*: dividing.

CRISPIANO:        No flaw, no unkindness?

ROMELIO: None that ever arriv'd at my knowledge.

CRISPIANO: Bethink yourself, this cannot choose but savour
   Of a woman's malice deeply; and I fear                    260
   Y'are practis'd upon most devilishly.
   How happ'd gentlewoman, you revealed this no sooner?

LEONORA: While my husband lived, my lord, I durst not.

CRISPIANO: I should rather ask you, why you reveal it now?

LEONORA: Because my lord, I loath'd that such a sin            265
   Should lie smother'd with me in my grave; my penitence,
   Though to my shame, prefers the revealing of it
   'Bove worldly reputation.

CRISPIANO:                Your penitence?
   Might not your penitence have been as hearty,
   Though it had never summon'd to the court                 270
   Such a conflux of people?

LEONORA: Indeed, I might have confess'd it,
   Privately to'th' Church, I grant; but you know repentance
   Is nothing without satisfaction.

CRISPIANO: Satisfaction? Why your husband's dead,            275
   What satisfaction can you make him?

LEONORA: The greatest satisfaction in the world, my lord,
   To restore the land to'th' right heir, and that's
   My daughter.

CRISPIANO:        O she's straight begot then?

ARIOSTO: Very well, may it please this honourable court,      280
   If he be a bastard, and must forfeit his land for't,
   She has prov'd herself a strumpet, and must lose
   Her dower; let them go a-begging together.

257. *flaw:* difference of opinion, quarrel.
271. *conflux:* gathering.

SANITONELLA: Who shall pay us our fees then?

CRISPIANO:                                          Most just.

285 ARIOSTO: You may see now what an old house
You are like to pull over your head, dame.

ROMELIO: Could I conceive this publication
Grew from a hearty penitence, I could bear
My undoing the more patiently; but my lord,
290 There is no reason, as you said even now,
To satisfy me but this suit of hers
Springs from a devilish malice, and her pretence,
Of a grieved conscience, and religion,
Like to the horrid powder-treason in England,
295 Has a most bloody unnatural revenge
Hid under it. O the violencies of women!
Why, they are creatures made up and compounded
Of all monsters, poisoned minerals,
And sorcerous herbs that grows.

ARIOSTO:                                          Are you angry yet?

300 ROMELIO: Would man express a bad one, let him forsake
All natural example, and compare
One to another; they have no more mercy
Than ruinous fires in great tempests.

ARIOSTO: Take heed you do not crack your voice sir.

305 ROMELIO: Hard-hearted creatures, good for nothing else,
But to wind dead bodies.

ARIOSTO:                          Yes, to weave seaming lace
With the bones of their husbands that were long since
buried,
And curse them when they tangle.

ROMELIO:                                          Yet why do I

294. *powder-treason in England:* Guy Fawkes's gunpowder plot of 1605.
298. *poisoned:* poisonous.
300–1. *forsake all natural example:* i.e. not try to find parallels in nature.
306. *seaming lace:* lace used for seams.
307. *bones:* bones were used as bobbins in lace-making.

Take bastardy so distastefully, when i'th' world,
A many things that are essential parts                                    310
Of greatness, are but by-slips, and are father'd
On the wrong parties?
Preferment in the world a many times,
Basely begotten? Nay, I have observ'd
The immaculate justice of a poor man's cause,                            315
In such a court as this, has not known whom
To call father, which way to direct itself
For compassion: but I forget my temper:
Only that I may stop that lawyer's throat,
I do beseech the court, and the whole world,                             320
They will not think the baselier of me,
For the vice of a mother: for that woman's sin,
To which you all dare swear when it was done,
I would not give my consent.

CRISPIANO: Stay, here's an accusation,                                   325
But here's no proof; what was the Spaniard's name
You accuse of adultery?

CONTILUPO:                Don Crispiano,
My lord.

CRISPIANO: What part of Spain was he born in?

CONTILUPO: In Castile.

JULIO [aside]:            This may prove my father.

SANITONELLA [aside]: And my master; my client's spoil'd
then.                                                                    330

CRISPIANO: I knew that Spaniard well: if you be a bastard,
Such a man being your father, I dare vouch you
A gentleman; and in that, Signior Contilupo,
Your oratory went a little too far.
When do we name Don John of Austria,                                     335
The Emperor's son, but with reverence?
And I have known in divers families,

335. *Don John of Austria*: illegitimate son of Emperor Charles V.

The bastards the greater spirits. But to'th' purpose;
What time was this gentleman begot? And be sure
You lay your time right.

340 ARIOSTO:                          Now the metal comes
To the touchstone.

CONTILUPO:          In anno seventy-one, my lord.

CRISPIANO: Very well, seventy-one; the battle of Lepanto
Was fought in't – a most remarkable time,
'Twill lie for no man's pleasure. And what proof is there
345 More than the affirmation of the mother,
Of this corporal dealing?

CONTILUPO:                    The deposition
Of a waiting-woman serv'd her the same time.

CRISPIANO: Where is she?

CONTILUPO:                    Where is our solicitor
With the waiting-woman?

ARIOSTO:                        Room for the bag
And baggage!

350 SANITONELLA: Here my lord, *ore tenus*.

CRISPIANO: And what can you say gentlewoman?

WINIFRID: Please your lordship, I was the party that dealt
in the business, and brought them together.

CRISPIANO: Well.

355 WINIFRID: And convey'd letters between them.

CRISPIANO: What needed letters, when 'tis said he lodg'd
in her house?

WINIFRID: A running ballad now and then to her viol, for
he was never well, but when he was fiddling.

342. *Lepanto:* the battle, which ended the Turkish naval threat in Italian
    waters, was fought on 7 October 1571.
343. *remarkable:* notable.
349. *bag and baggage:* i.e. the lawyer (with buckram bag) and Winifrid.
350. *ore tenus:* 'by word of mouth'; Winifrid is to give her testimony
    in person, without a written deposition.
358. *running:* tripping, free-flowing.
359. *fiddling:* a double entendre.

CRISPIANO: Speak to the purpose, did you ever know   360
them bed together?

WINIFRID: No my lord, but I have brought him to the
bed-side.

CRISPIANO: That was somewhat near to the business;
And what, did you help him off with his shoes?   365

WINIFRID: He wore no shoes, an't please you my lord.

CRISPIANO: No? What then, pumps?

WINIFRID: Neither.

CRISPIANO: Boots were not fit for his journey.

WINIFRID: He wore tennis-court woollen slippers, for   370
fear of creaking sir, and making a noise, to wake the rest
o'th' house.

CRISPIANO: Well, and what did he there, in his tennis-
court woollen slippers?

WINIFRID: Please your lordship, question me in Latin, for   375
the cause is very foul; the Examiner o'th' court was fain
to get it out of me alone i'th' counting house, 'cause he
would not spoil the youth o'th' office.

ARIOSTO: Here's a Latin spoon, and a long one, to feed with
the devil.   380

WINIFRID: I'd be loath to be ignorant that way, for I hope
to marry a proctor, and take my pleasure abroad at the
Commencements with him.

ARIOSTO: Come closer to the business.

WINIFRID: I will come as close as modesty will give me   385
leave. Truth is, every morning when he lay with her, I
made a caudle for him, by the appointment of my mistress,
which he would still refuse, and call for small drink.

CRISPIANO: Small drink?

367. *pumps:* light, close-fitting shoes, without heels.
379. *Latin spoon:* there is a pun on lateen = brass.
383. *Commencements:* i.e. of the law terms.
387. *caudle:* hot drink of gruel and wine, with spices.
388. *small drink:* i.e. non-alcoholic.

390   ARIOSTO: For a julep.

WINIFRID: And said he was wondrous thirsty.

CRISPIANO: What's this to the purpose?

WINIFRID: Most effectual, my lord; I have heard them laugh together extremely, and the curtain rods fall from
395   the tester of the bed, and he ne'er came from her, but he thrust money in my hand; and once in truth, he would have had some dealing with me; which I took he thought 'twould be the only way i'th' world to make me keep counsel the better.

400   SANITONELLA [*aside*]: That's a stinger, 'tis a good wench, be not daunted.

CRISPIANO: Did you ever find the print of two in the bed?

WINIFRID: What a question that to be ask'd! May it please your lordship, 'tis to be thought he lay nearer to her
405   than so.

CRISPIANO: What age are you of, gentlewoman?

WINIFRID: About six and forty, my lord.

CRISPIANO:                     Anno seventy-one,
And Romelio is thirty-eight: by that reckoning,
You were a bawd at eight year old: now verily,
You fell to the trade betimes.

410   SANITONELLA [*aside*]:        There y'are from the bias.

WINIFRID: I do not know my age directly: sure I am elder, I can remember two great frosts, and three great plagues, and the loss of Calais, and the first coming up of the breeches with the great codpiece; and I pray what age do
415   you take me of then?

SANITONELLA [*aside*]: Well come off again!

---

390. *julep:* sweetened drink.
393. *effectual:* relevant, significant.
395. *tester:* canopy.
410. *betimes:* early, speedily; *from the bias:* off the rails, off course (the idiom derives from bowls).

ARIOSTO:                      Añ old hunted hare,
  She has all her doubles.
ROMELIO:           For your own gravities,
  And the reverence of the court, I do beseech you,
  Rip up the cause no further, but proceed
  To sentence.
CRISPIANO: One question more and I have done:      420
  Might not this Crispiano, this Spaniard,
  Lie with your mistress at some other time,
  Either áfore or after, than i'th' absence
  Of her husband?
LEONORA:        Never.
CRISPIANO:            Are you certain of that?
LEONORA: On my soul, never.                    425
CRISPIANO: That's well – he never lay with her,
  But in anno seventy-one, let that be remembered.
  Stand you aside a while. Mistress, the truth is,
  I knew this Crispiano, lived in Naples
  At the same time, and loved the geñtleman      430
  As my bosom friend; and as I do remember,
  The gentleman did leave his picture with you,
  If age or neglect have not in so long time ruin'd it.
LEONORA: I preserve it still my lord.
CRISPIANO:              I pray let me see't,
  Let me see the face I then loved so much to look on.    435
LEONORA: Fetch it.
WINIFRID:       I shall, my lord.
CRISPIANO:            No, no, gentlewoman,
  I have other business for you.
    [Exit one for the picture.]
FIRST SURGEON [aside]: Now were the time to cut
    Romelio's throat,
  And accuse him for your murder.

417. *doubles*: doublings back.

CONTARINO [*aside*]: By no means.

SECOND SURGEON [*aside*]: Will you not let us be men of
440       fashion,
And down with him now he's going?

CONTARINO [*aside*]: Peace,
Let's attend the sequel.

CRISPIANO: I commend you lady,
There was a main matter of conscience;
How many ills spring from adultery!
445     First, the supreme law that is violated,
Nobility oft stain'd with bastardy,
Inheritance of land falsely possess'd,
The husband scorn'd, wife sham'd, and babes unbless'd.
     *The picture* [*is brought in*].
So, hang it up i'th' court. You have heard
450     What has been urged 'gainst Romelio.
Now my definitive sentence in this cause,
Is, I will give no sentence at all.

ARIOSTO: No?

CRISPIANO: No, I cannot, for I am made a party.

SANITONELLA [*aside*]: How, a party? Here are fine cross
      tricks,
455     What the devil will he do now?

CRISPIANO: Signior Ariosto, his Majesty of Spain
Confers my place upon you by this patent,
Which till this urgent hour I have kept
From your knowledge: may you thrive in't, noble sir,
460     And do that which but few in our place do;
Go to their grave uncurs'd.

ARIOSTO: This law business
Will leave me so small leisure to serve God,
I shall serve the King the worse.

SANITONELLA [*aside*]: Is he a judge?

443. *main*: major, principal.       454. *cross tricks*: red herrings.

We must then look for all conscience, and no law;
He'll beggar all his followers.

CRISPIANO [*to* ROMELIO]:     Sir,        465
I am of your counsel, for the cause in hand
Was begun at such a time, 'fore you could speak;
You had need therefore have one speak for you.

ARIOSTO: Stay, I do here first make protestation,
I ne'er took fee of this Romelio,     470
For being of his counsel; which may free me,
Being now his judge, for the imputation
Of taking a bribe. Now sir, speak your mind.

CRISPIANO: I do first entreat, that the eyes of all
Here present, may be fixed upon this.     475

LEONORA [*aside*]: O I am confounded: this is Crispiano.

JULIO [*aside*]: This is my father; how the judges have
blear'd him!

WINIFRID [*aside*]: You may see truth will out in spite of the
devil.

CRISPIANO: Behold, I am the shadow of this shadow,
Age has made me so; take from me forty years,     480
And I was such a summer fruit as this,
At least the painter feigned so: for indeed,
Paintings and epitaphs are both alike,
They flatter us, and say we have been thus.
But I am the party here, that stands accus'd     485
For adultery with this woman, in the year
Seventy-one. Now I call you my lord to witness,
Four years before that time I went to'th' Indies,
And till this month, did never set my foot since
In Europe; and for any former incontinence,     490
She has vow'd there was never any. What remains then,
But this is a mere practice 'gainst her son?
And I beseech the court it may be sifted,

477. *blear'd him*: thrown dust in his eyes.

And most severely punish'd.

495 SANITONELLA [*aside*]: 'Uds foot, we are spoiled;
Why my client's proved an honest woman.

WINIFRID [*aside*]: What do you think will become of me
now?

SANITONELLA [*aside*]: You'll be made dance *lachrimae* I
fear
At a cart's tail.

ARIOSTO:  You mistress, where are you now?
500 Your tennis-court slippers, and your tane drink
In a morning for your hot liver; where's the man
Would have had some dealing with you, that you might
Keep counsel the better?

WINIFRID: May it please the court, I am but a young thing,
505 and was drawn arsy-varsy into the business.

ARIOSTO: How young? Of five and forty?

WINIFRID: Five and forty! And shall please you, I am not
five and twenty: she made me colour my hair with bean-
flour, to seem elder than I was; and then my rotten teeth,
510 with eating sweetmeats: why, should a farrier look in
my mouth, he might mistake my age. O mistress,
mistress, you are an honest woman, and you may be
asham'd on't, to abuse the court thus.

LEONORA: Whatso'er I have attempted,
515 'Gainst my own fame, or the reputation
Of that gentleman my son, the Lord Contarino
Was cause of it.

CONTARINO [*aside*]: Who, I?

ARIOSTO: He that should have married your daughter?
It was a plot belike then to confer

---

501. *hot liver:* a pun on (a) one who lives passionately, (b) the liver, as
the seat of the passions.
505. *arsy-varsy:* backside foremost, willy-nilly.
513. *abuse:* deceive.

The land on her that should have been his wife? 520
LEONORA: More than I have said already, all the world
   Shall ne'er extract from me; I entreat from both
   Your equal pardons.
JULIO:             And I from you sir.
CRISPIANO: Sirrah, stand you aside,
   I will talk with you hereafter. 525
JULIO: I could never away with after reckonings.
LEONORA: And now my lords, I do most voluntarily
   Confine myself unto a stricter prison,
   And a severer penance, than this court
   Can impose; I am ent'red into religion. 530
CONTARINO [aside]: I the cause of this practice! This
   ungodly woman
   Has sold herself to falsehood. I will now
   Reveal myself.
ERCOLE [revealing himself]: Stay my lord, here's a window
   To let in more light to the court.
CONTARINO [aside]: Mercy upon me! O that thou art
   living 535
   Is mercy indeed!
FIRST SURGEON [aside]: Stay, keep in your shell
   A little longer.
ERCOLE:         I am Ercole.
ARIOSTO: A guard upon him for the death of Contarino.
ERCOLE: I obey the arrest o'th' court.
ROMELIO: O sir, you are happily restor'd to life, 540
   And to us your friends!
ERCOLE:            Away, thou art the traitor
   I only live to challenge; this former suit
   Touch'd but thy fame; this accusation
   Reaches to thy fame and life: the brave Contarino
   Is generally suppos'd slain by this hand. 545
CONTARINO [aside]: How knows he the contrary?

ERCOLE: But truth is,
Having receiv'd from me some certain wounds,
Which were not mortal, this vile murderer,
Being by will deputed overseer
550 Of the nobleman's estate, to his sister's use,
That he might make him sure from surviving,
To revoke the will, stole to him in's bed,
And kill'd him.

ROMELIO: Strange, unheard of! More practice yet!

ARIOSTO: What proof of this?

555 ERCOLE: The report of his mother deliver'd to me,
In distraction for Contarino's death.

CONTARINO [aside]: For my death? I begin to apprehend,
That the violence of this woman's love to me
Might practise the disinheriting of her son.

560 ARIOSTO: What say you to this, Leonora?

LEONORA: Such a thing I did utter out of my distraction:
But how the court will censure that report,
I leave to their wisdoms.

ARIOSTO: My opinion is,
That this late slander urg'd against her son,
565 Takes from her all manner of credit:
She that would not stick to deprive him of his living,
Will as little tender his life.

LEONORA: I beseech the court,
I may retire myself to my place of penance,
I have vowed myself and my woman.

ARIOSTO: Go when you please. [To ERCOLE] What should
570 move you be thus forward
In the accusation?

ERCOLE: My love to Contarino.

ARIOSTO: O, it bore very bitter fruit at your last meeting.

ERCOLE: 'Tis true: but I begun to love him

556. *In distraction for*: in her unbalanced state of mind over.

394

When I had most cause to hate him; when our bloods
Embrac'd each other, then I pitied                                  575
That so much valour should be hazarded
On the fortune of a single rapier,
And not spent against the Turk.

ARIOSTO:                                        Stay sir,
Be well advis'd, there is no testimony
But your own, to approve you slew him,                               580
Therefore no other way to decide it,
But by duel.

CONTARINO: Yes my lord, I dare affirm
'Gainst all the world, this nobleman speaks truth.

ARIOSTO: You will make yourself a party in the duel.

ROMELIO: Let him, I will fight with them both, sixteen of
   them.                                                            585

ERCOLE: Sir, I do not know you.

CONTARINO:                          Yes, but you have forgot me,
You and I have sweat in the breach together
At Malta.

ERCOLE:    Cry you mercy, I have known
Of your nation brave soldiers.

JULIO [aside]:                          Now if my father
Have any true spirit in him, I'll recover                           590
His good opinion. [To CONTARINO] Do you hear? Do
   not swear sir,
For I dare swear, that you will swear a lie,
A very filthy, stinking, rotten lie:
And if the lawyers think not this sufficient,
I'll give the lie in the stomach,                                   595
That's somewhat deeper than the throat:
Both here, and all France over and over,
From Marseilles, or Bayonne, to Calais sands,

580. *approve*: prove.
589. *your nation*: Contarino is disguised as a Dane.

And there draw my sword upon thee,
600   And new scour it in the gravel of thy kidneys.
ARIOSTO: You the defendant charg'd with the murder,
  And you second there, must be committed
  To the custody of the Knight-Marshal;
  And the court gives charge, they be tomorrow
605   Ready in the lists before the sun be risen.
ROMELIO: I do entreat the court, there be a guard
  Placed o'er my sister, that she enter not
  Into religion: she's rich, my lords,
  And the persuasions of friars, to gain
610   All her possessions to their monasteries,
  May do much upon her.
ARIOSTO:                We'll take order for her.
CRISPIANO: There's a nun too you have got with child,
  How will you dispose of her?
ROMELIO: You question me, as if I were grav'd already,
615   When I have quench'd this wild-fire in Ercole's
  Tame blood, I'll tell you.
    *Exit.*
ERCOLE:              You have judg'd today
  A most confused practice, that takes end
  In as bloody a trial; and we may observe
  By these great persons, and their indirect
620   Proceedings, shadow'd in a veil of state,
  Mountains are deform'd heaps, swell'd up aloft;
  Vales wholesomer, though lower, and trod on oft.
SANITONELLA: Well, I will put up my papers,
  And send them to France for a precedent,
625   That they may not say yet, but, for one strange law-suit,
  We come somewhat near them.
    *Exeunt.*

613. *dispose:* i.e. in his will.

# [ACT FIVE]

## [SCENE ONE]

*Enter* JOLENTA, *and* ANGIOLELLA, *great-bellied.*

JOLENTA: How dost thou friend? Welcome, thou and I
  Were playfellows together, little children,
  So small a while ago, that I presume
  We are neither of us wise yet.

ANGIOLELLA:               A most sad truth
  On my part.

JOLENTA:     Why do you pluck your veil       5
  Over your face?

ANGIOLELLA:    If you will believe truth,
  There's nought more terrible to a guilty heart
  Than the eye of a respected friend.

JOLENTA: Say friend, are you quick with child?

ANGIOLELLA:                  Too sure.

JOLENTA: How could you know [first of your] child    10
  When you quick'ned?

ANGIOLELLA:        How could you know friend?
  'Tis reported you are in the same taking.

JOLENTA: Ha, ha, ha, so 'tis given out:
  But Ercole's coming to life again has shrunk,
  And made invisible my great belly; yes faith,    15
  My being with child was merely in supposition,
  Not practice.

ANGIOLELLA: You are happy; what would I give,
  To be a maid again!

JOLENTA:         Would you? To what purpose?
  I would never give great purchase for that thing
  Is in danger every hour to be lost:    20
  Pray thee laugh. A boy or a girl for a wager?

397

ANGIOLELLA: What heaven please.

JOLENTA: Nay, nay, will you venture
A chain of pearl with me whether?

ANGIOLELLA: I'll lay nothing,
I have ventur'd too much for't already; my fame.
25 I make no question sister, you have heard
Of the intended combat.

JOLENTA: O what else?
I have a sweetheart in't, against a brother.

ANGIOLELLA: And I a dead friend, I fear; what good counsel
Can you minister unto me?

JOLENTA: Faith only this
30 Since there's no means i'th' world to hinder it,
Let thou and I, wench, get as far as we can
From the noise of it.

ANGIOLELLA: Whither?

JOLENTA: No matter,
Any whither.

ANGIOLELLA: Any whither, so you go not
By sea: I cannot abide rough water.

35 JOLENTA: Not endure to be tumbled? Say no more then,
We'll be land-soldiers for that trick: take heart,
Thy boy shall be born a brave Roman.

ANGIOLELLA: O you mean
To go to Rome then.

JOLENTA: Within there!
*Enter a servant.*
Bear this letter
To the Lord Ercole. Now wench, I am for thee
All the world over.

40 ANGIOLELLA: I like your shade pursue you.
*Exeunt.*

35. *tumbled*: (a) by the waves, (b) by a lover.     40. *shade*: shadow.

## [SCENE TWO]

*Enter* PROSPERO *and* SANITONELLA.

PROSPERO: Well, I do not think but to see you as pretty a
piece of law-flesh.

SANITONELLA: In time I may; marry I am resolv'd to take
a new way for't. You have lawyers take their clients'
fees, and their backs are no sooner turn'd, but they call     5
them fools, and laugh at them.

PROSPERO: That's ill done of them.

SANITONELLA: There's one thing too that has a vile abuse
in't.

PROSPERO: What's that?     10

SANITONELLA: Marry this; that no proctor in the term
time be tolerated to go to the tavern above six times
i'th' forenoon.

PROSPERO: Why, man?

SANITONELLA: O sir, it makes their clients overtaken, and     15
become friends sooner than they would be.

*Enter* ERCOLE *with a letter, and* CONTARINO, *coming
in Friars' habits, as having been at the Bathanites, a ceremony
used afore these combats.*

ERCOLE: Leave the room, gentlemen.

*Exeunt* PROSPERO *and* SANITONELLA.

CONTARINO [*aside*]: Wherefore should I with such an
obstinacy,
Conceal myself any longer? I am taught
That all the blood which will be shed tomorrow,     20
Must fall upon my head: one question
Shall fix or untie it. [*to* ERCOLE] Noble brother,
I would fain know how it is possible,

15. *overtaken:* drunk.
22. *it:* i.e. the issue (and hence Contarino's resolvè).

When it appears you love the fair Jolenta
25 With such a height of fervour, you were ready
To father another's child, and marry her,
You would so suddenly engage yourself
To kill her brother, one that ever stood,
Your loyal and firm friend?

ERCOLE:                  Sir, I'll tell you:
30 My love, as I have formerly protested,
To Contarino, whose unfortunate end
The traitor wrought: and here is one thing more,
Dead's all good thoughts of him, which I now receiv'd
From Jolenta.

CONTARINO:   In a letter?

ERCOLE:                Yes, in this letter:
35 For having sent to her to be resolv'd
Most truly, who was father of the child,
She writes back, that the shame she goes withal,
Was begot by her brother.

CONTARINO: O most incestuous villain!

ERCOLE:                    I protest,
40 Before I thought 'twas Contarino's issue,
And for that would have veil'd her dishonour.

CONTARINO: No more. Has the armourer brought the
     weapons?

ERCOLE: Yes sir.

CONTARINO:   I will no more think of her.

ERCOLE: Of whom?

CONTARINO:         Of my mother; I was thinking
45    Of my mother. Call the armourer.
     *Exeunt.*

## [SCENE THREE]

*Enter* [FIRST] SURGEON *and* WINIFRID.

WINIFRID: You do love me sir, you say?

FIRST SURGEON:                    O most entirely.

WINIFRID: And you will marry me?

FIRST SURGEON:            Nay, I'll do more than that.
  The fashion of the world is many times
  To make a woman naught, and afterwards
  To marry her: but I a'th' contrary,                                    5
  Will make you honest first, and afterwards
  Proceed to the wedlock.

WINIFRID: Honest! What mean you by that?

FIRST SURGEON: I mean, that your suborning the late
  law-suit
  Has got you a filthy report. Now there's no way                 10
  But to do some excellent piece of honesty,
  To recover your good name.

WINIFRID:                    How sir?

FIRST SURGEON: You shall straight go, and reveal to your
  old mistress
  For certain truth, Contarino is alive.

WINIFRID: How, living?

FIRST SURGEON:            Yes, he is living.                            15

WINIFRID: No, I must not tell her of it.

FIRST SURGEON:                    No? Why?

WINIFRID: For she did bind me yesterday by oath,
  Never more to speak of him.

FIRST SURGEON:                You shall reveal it then
  To Ariosto the judge.

---

4. *naught:* immoral, wicked, worthless (because a non-virgin).
6. *honest:* virtuous.        9. *suborning:* giving false testimony.
10. *filthy report:* bad name, reputation.

WINIFRID:          By no means, he has heard me
20    Tell so many lies i'th' court, he'll ne'er believe me.
    What if I told it to the Capuchin?
FIRST SURGEON:         You cannot
    Think of a better. [As for] your young mistress,
    Who as you told me, has persuaded you
    To run away with her: let her have her humour.
25    I have a suit Romelio left i'th' house,
    The habit of a Jew, that I'll put on,
    And pretending I am robbed, by break of day
    Procure all passengers to be brought back,
    And by the way reveal myself, and discover
30    The comical event. They say she's a little mad;
    This will help to cure her. Go, go presently,
    And reveal it to the Capuchin.
WINIFRID:             Sir, I shall.
     *Exeunt.*

## [SCENE FOUR]

*Enter* JULIO, PROSPERO, *and* SANITONELLA.

JULIO: A pox on't,
    I have undertaken the challenge very foolishly:
    What if I do not appear to answer it?
PROSPERO: It would be absolute conviction
5    Of cowardice, and perjury; and the Dane
    May to your public shame, reverse your arms,
    Or have them ignominiously fastened
    Under his horse tail.
JULIO:           I do not like that so well.
    I see then I must fight whether I will or no.

---

4. *absolute conviction:* irrefutable proof.
5. *the Dane:* Contarino.

PROSPERO: How does Romelio bear himself? They say     10
   He has almost brain'd one of our cunning'st fencers,
   That practis'd with him.
JULIO: Very certain: and now you talk of fencing,
   Do you not remember the Welsh gentleman,
   That was travelling to Rome upon return?     15
PROSPERO: No, what of him?
JULIO: There was a strange experiment of a fencer.
PROSPERO: What was that?
JULIO: The Welshman in's play, do what the fencer could,
   Hung still an arse; he could not for's life     20
   Make him come on bravely: till one night at supper,
   Observing what a deal of Parma cheese
   His scholar devoured, [a] goes ingeniously
   The next morning, and makes a spacious button
   For his foil, of toasted cheese, and as sure as you live,     25
   That made him come on the braveliest.
PROSPERO:                     Possible!
JULIO: Marry it taught him an ill grace in's play,
   It made him gape still, gape as he put in for't,
   As I have seen some hungry usher.
SANITONELLA: The toasting of it belike,     30
   Was to make it more supple, had he chanc'd
   To have hit him a'th' chaps.
JULIO:               Not unlikely.
   Who can tell me if we may breathe in the duel?
PROSPERO: By no means.
JULIO:            Nor drink?
PROSPERO:                Neither.
JULIO: That's scurvy, anger will make me very dry.     35
PROSPERO: You mistake sir, 'tis sorrow that is very dry.

---

11. *cunning'st:* most skilful.       20. *Hung still an arse:* hung back.
28. *put in for't:* lunged or thrust for it (the cheese).
33. *breathe:* rest to regain breath.

SANITONELLA: Not always sir, I have known sorrow very
   wet.

JULIO: In rainy weather?

SANITONELLA: No, when a woman has come dropping
   wet
Out of a cuckingstool.

40  JULIO:                     Then 'twas wet indeed sir.
   *Enter* ROMELIO, *very melancholy, and the* CAPUCHIN.

CAPUCHIN [*aside*]: Having from Leonora's waiting-woman
   Deliver'd a most strange intelligence
   Of Contarino's recovery, I am come
   To sound Romelio's penitence; that perform'd,

45  To end these errors by discovering
   What she related to me. [*To* ROMELIO] Peace to you sir –
   Pray gentlemen, let the freedom of this room
   Be mine a little – [*to* JULIO] Nay sir, you may stay.
      *Exeunt* PRO[SPERO *and*] SAN[ITONELLA].
   Will you pray with me?

ROMELIO:                  No, no, the world and I

50  Have not made up our accounts yet.

CAPUCHIN: Shall I pray for you?

ROMELIO: Whether you do or no, I care not.

CAPUCHIN: O you have a dangerous voyage to take.

ROMELIO: No matter, I will be mine own pilot:

55  Do not you trouble your head with the business.

CAPUCHIN: Pray tell me, do not you meditate of death?

ROMELIO: Phew, I took out that lesson
   When I once lay sick of an ague: I do now
   Labour for life, for life! Sir, can you tell me

60  Whether your Toledo, or your Milan blade
   Be best temper'd?

CAPUCHIN:            These things you know,
   Are out of my practice.

---

   42. *intelligence:* piece of news.        45. *discovering:* revealing.

404

ROMELIO:             But these are things you know,
I must practise with tomorrow.

CAPUCHIN:             Were I in your case,
I should present to myself strange shadows.

ROMELIO: Turn you, were I in your case, I should laugh    65
At mine own shadow. Who has hired you
To make me coward?

CAPUCHIN:        I would make you
A good Christian.

ROMELIO:       Withal, let me continue
An honest man, which I am very certain,
A coward can never be: you take upon you    70
A physician's place, rather than a divine's.
You go about to bring my body so low,
I should fight i'th' lists tomorrow like a dormouse,
And be made away in a slumber.

CAPUCHIN: Did you murder Contarino?    75

ROMELIO: That's a scurvy question now.

CAPUCHIN:            Why sir?

ROMELIO: Did you ask it as a confessor, or as a spy?

CAPUCHIN: As one that fain would jostle the devil
Out of your way.

ROMELIO:       Um, you are but weakly made for't:
He's a cunning wrestler, I can tell you, and has broke    80
Many a man's neck.

CAPUCHIN:        But to give him the foil
Goes not by strength.

ROMELIO:       Let it go by what it will,

---

63. *'case:* situation, position.
64. *I should . . . shadows:* either 'I should hardly know myself' or 'I would be uncertain of myself'.
65. *Turn you:* either 'To reverse your point' or 'On the other hand, were I you'.
81. *give him the foil:* defeat (a fencing term).

Get me some good victuals to breakfast,
I am hungry.

CAPUCHIN:     Here's food for you.
*Offering him a book.*

85   ROMELIO: Pew, I am not to commence Doctor:
For then the word, devour that book, were proper.
I am to fight, to fight sir, and I'll do't,
As I would feed, with a good stomach.

CAPUCHIN:                         Can you feed,
And apprehend death?

ROMELIO:                   Why sir? Is not Death
90   A hungry companion? Say? Is not the grave
Said to be a great devourer? Get me some victuals.
I knew a man that was to lose his head,
Feed with an excellent good appetite,
To strengthen his heart, scarce half an hour before.
95   And if he did it, that only was to speak,
What should I, that am to do?

CAPUCHIN:                     This confidence,
If it be grounded upon truth, 'tis well.

ROMELIO: You must understand, that resolution
Should ever wait upon a noble death,
100   As captains bring their soldiers out o'th' field,
And come off last: for, I pray, what is death?
The safest trench i'th' world to keep man free
From fortune's gunshot; to be afraid of that
Would prove me weaker than a teeming woman,
105   That does endure a thousand times more pain
In bearing of a child.

CAPUCHIN:             O, I tremble for you:
For I do know you have a storm within you,
More terrible than a sea fight, and your soul

---

85. *commence:* see note to IV, i, 38 (p. 369)
104. *teeming:* pregnant.

Being heretofore drown'd in security,
You know not how to live, nor how to die:       110
But I have an object that shall startle you,
And make you know whither you are going.
ROMELIO: I am arm'd for't.

*Enter* LEONORA *with two coffins borne by her servants, and*
*two winding sheets stuck with flowers; presents one to her*
*son, and the other to* JULIO.

'Tis very welcome, this is a decent garment
Will never be out of fashion. I will kiss it.     115
All the flowers of the spring
Meet to perfume our burying:
These have but their growing prime,
And man does flourish but his time.
Survey our progress from our birth,     120
We are set, we grow, we turn to earth.

*Soft music [is played].*

Courts adieu, and all delights,
All bewitching appetites;
Sweetest breath, and clearest eye,
Like perfumes go out and die;     125
And consequently this is done,
As shadows wait upon the sun.
Vain the ambition of kings,
Who seek by trophies and dead things,
To leave a living name behind,     130
And weave but nets to catch the wind.
O you have wrought a miracle, and melted
A heart of adamant: you have compris'd

109. *security:* the term is being used in both secular and religious senses,
    see note to *Duchess,* V, ii, 334.
113. S.D. *winding sheets:* sheets of linen used to wind the corpse.
126. *consequently:* inevitably.
133. *compris'd:* put together.

In this dumb pageant, a right excellent form
Of penitence.

135 CAPUCHIN:      I am glad you so receive it.

ROMELIO: This object does persuade me to forgive
The wrong she has done me, which I count the way
To be forgiven yonder: and this shroud
Shows me how rankly we do smell of earth
140 When we are in all our glory. Will it please you
Enter that closet, where I shall confer
'Bout matters of most weighty consequence,
Before the duel?

    *Exit* LEONORA [*into the closet*].

JULIO:           Now I am right in the bandoleer
For th' gallows. What a scurvy fashion 'tis,
To hang one's coffin in a scarf!

145 CAPUCHIN:                    Why this is well:
And now that I have made you fit for death,
And brought you even as low as is the grave,
I will raise you up again, speak comforts to you
Beyond your hopes, turn this intended duel
150 To a triumph.

ROMELIO:      More divinity yet?
Good sir, do one thing first, there's in my closet
A prayer book that is cover'd with gilt vellum;
Fetch it, and pray you certify my mother,
I'll presently come to her.

    [*Exit* CAPUCHIN *into the closet.* ROMELIO] *locks him in.*

                  So now you are safe.

JULIO: What have you done?

155 ROMELIO:                    Why I have lock'd them up
Into a turret of the castle, safe enough
For troubling us this four hours; and he please,
He may open a casement, and whistle out to th' sea,

157. *For*: from.

408

Like a bosun, not any creature can hear him.
Wast not thou a-weary of his preaching? 160
JULIO: Yes, if he had had an hour-glass by him,
I would have wish'd he would have jogg'd it a little.
But your mother, your mother's lock'd in too.
ROMELIO: So much the better,
I am rid of her howling at parting. 165
JULIO: Hark, he knocks to be let out and he were mad.
ROMELIO: Let him knock till his sandals fly in pieces.
JULIO: Ha, what says he? Contarino living?
ROMELIO: Aye, aye, he means he would have Contarino's
living
Bestow'd upon his monastery, 'tis that 170
He only fishes for. So, 'tis break of day,
We shall be call'd to the combat presently.
JULIO: I am sorry for one thing.
ROMELIO: What's that?
JULIO: That I made not mine own ballad: I do fear
I shall be roguishly abused in metre, 175
If I miscarry. Well, if the young Capuchin
Does not talk a'th' flesh as fast now to your mother,
As he did to us a'th' spirit! If he do,
'Tis not the first time that the prison royal
Has been guilty of close committing. 180
ROMELIO: Now to'th' combat.
  [*Exeunt.*] *Enter* CAPUCHIN *and* LEONORA *above at a
  window.*
LEONORA: Contarino living?
CAPUCHIN: Yes madam, he is living and Ercole's second.
LEONORA: Why has he lock'd us up thus?
CAPUCHIN: Some evil angel

177. *talk a'th' flesh:* carnal intercourse, as opposed to talk *a'th' spirit.*
180. *close committing:* (a) committing to prison, (b) committing adultery
  or fornication (Lucas).

Makes him deaf to his own safety; we are shut
185   Into a turret, the most desolate prison
Of all the castle, and his obstinacy,
Madness, or secret fate, has thus prevented
The saving of his life.

LEONORA:         O the saving Contarino's,
His is worth nothing: for heaven's sake call louder.

CAPUCHIN: To little purpose.

190 LEONORA:         I will leap these battlements,
And may I be found dead time enough,
To hinder the combat!

CAPUCHIN:       O look upwards rather,
Their deliverance must come thence: to see how heaven
Can invert man's firmest purpose! His intent
195   Of murdering Contarino, was a mean
To work his safety, and my coming hither
To save him, is his ruin: wretches turn
The tide of their good fortune, and being drench'd
In some presumptuous and hidden sins,
200   While they aspire to do themselves most right,
The devil that rules i'th' air, hangs in their light.

LEONORA: O they must not be lost thus: some good
    Christian
Come within our hearing! Ope the other casement
That looks into the city.

CAPUCHIN:       Madam, I shall.
    *Exeunt.*


## [SCENE FIVE]

*The lists set up. Enter the Marshal,* CRISPIANO, *and*
ARIOSTO *as judges, they sit.* [*With them* SANITONELLA.]

MARSHAL: Give the appellant his summons. Do the like
   To the defendant.
   *Two tuckets sounded by several trumpets. Enter at one door,*
   ERCOLE *and* CONTARINO, *at the other,* ROMELIO *and*
   JULIO.
                    Can any of you
   Allege ought, why the combat should not proceed?
COMBATANTS: Nothing.
ARIOSTO:         Have the knights weigh'd and measured
   Their weapons?
MARSHAL:         They have.
ARIOSTO:                    Proceed then to the battle,          5
   And may heaven determine the right.
HERALD: *Soit [la] bataille, et [victoire] a ceux qu[i ont] droit.*
ROMELIO: Stay, I do not well know whither I am going:
   'Twere needful therefore, though at the last gasp,
   To have some churchman's prayer. Run I pray thee,          10
   To Castle Novo; this key will release
   A Capuchin and my mother, whom I shut
   Into a turret; bid them make haste, and pray,
   I may be dead ere he comes.
   [*Exit attendant.*]
   Now, [*Victoire*] *a ceux qu[i ont] droit.*                15
   *The combat continued to a good length, when enters*
   LEONORA, *and the* CAPUCHIN.
LEONORA: Hold, hold, for heaven's sake hold!
ARIOSTO: What are these that interrupt the combat?
   Away to prison with them.
CAPUCHIN: We have been prisoners too long:
   O sir, what mean you? Contarino's living.                  20

   2. S.D. *tuckets:* trumpet calls.
   7. *Soit . . . ont droit:* Let the battle commence, and victory to those in the
      right.

ERCOLE: Living!

CAPUCHIN:       Behold him living.

ERCOLE: You were but now my second, now I make you
   Myself for ever.
   [*They embrace.*]

LEONORA:       O here's one between,
   Claims to be nearer.

CONTARINO:             And to you, dear lady,
   I have entirely vowed my life.

25   ROMELIO:                   If I do not
   Dream, I am happy too.

ARIOSTO:                   How insolently
   Has this high court of honour been abus'd!

   *Enter* ANGIOLELLA, *veil'd, and* JOLENTA, *her face
   colour'd like a Moor, the two* SURGEONS, *one of them like
   a Jew.*

   How now, who are these?

SECOND SURGEON: A couple of strange fowl, and I the
   falconer

30   That have sprung them. This is a white nun,
   Of the Order of Saint Clare; and this a black one,
   You'll take my word for't.
   [*He*] *discovers* JOLENTA.

ARIOSTO:                   She's a black one indeed.

JOLENTA: Like or dislike me, choose you whether;
   The down upon the raven's feather

35   Is as gentle and as sleek,
   As the mole on Venus' cheek.
   Hence vain show! I only care,
   To preserve my soul most fair.
   Never mind the outward skin,

40   But the jewel that's within:
   And though I want the crimson blood,

24. *you, dear lady:* Leonora.          27. *abus'd:* deceived.

412

Angels boast my sisterhood.
Which of us now judge you whiter,
Her whose credit proves the lighter,
Or this black, and ebon hue,                                    45
That unstain'd, keeps fresh and true?
For I proclaim't without control,
There's no true beauty, but i'th' soul.

ERCOLE: O 'tis the fair Jolenta; to what purpose
Are you thus eclips'd?

JOLENTA:                    Sir, I was running away           50
From the rumour of this combat: I fled likewise,
From the untrue report my brother spread
To his politic ends, that I was got with child.

LEONORA: Cease here all further scrutiny, this paper
Shall give unto the court each circumstance,                   55
Of all these passages.

ARIOSTO: No more: attend the sentence of the court.
Rareness and difficulty give estimation
To all things are i'th' world: you have met both
In these several passages: now it does remain,                 60
That these so comical events be blasted
With no severity of sentence. You Romelio,
Shall first deliver to that gentleman,
Who stood your second, all those obligations
Wherein he stands engag'd to you, receiving                    65
Only the principal.

ROMELIO: I shall my lord.

JULIO:                     I thank you,
I have an humour now to go to sea

44. *credit:* character, worth; *lighter:* lesser (with a pun, of course).
45. *ebon:* ebony.
47. *control:* reservation.
56. *passages:* events.        57. *attend:* listen to, wait for.
58. *rareness:* here, the quality of the unusual; *estimation:* value.
61. *blasted:* cursed, ruined.

Against the pirates; and my only ambition
70     Is to have my ship furnish'd with a rare consort
Of music; and when I am pleased to be mad,
They shall play me *Orlando*.

SANITONELLA: You must lay in wait for the fiddlers,
They'll fly away from the press like watermen.

75 ARIOSTO: Next, you shall marry that nun.

ROMELIO: Most willingly.

ANGIOLELLA:          O sir, you have been unkind,
But I do only wish, that this my shame
May warn all honest virgins, not to seek
The way to heaven, that is so wondrous steep,
80     Thorough those vows they are too frail to keep.

ARIOSTO: Contarino, and Romelio, and yourself,
Shall for seven years maintain against the Turk
Six galleys. Leonora, Jolenta,
And Angiolella there, the beauteous nun,
85     For their vows' breach unto the monastery,
Shall build a monastery. Lastly, the two surgeons,
For concealing Contarino's recovery,
Shall exercise their art at their own charge,
For a twelvemonth in the galleys: so we leave you,
90     Wishing your future life may make good use
Of these events, since that these passages,
Which threat'ned ruin, built on rotten ground,
Are with success beyond our wishes crown'd.
    *Exeunt omnes.*

70. *consort:* concert, small orchestra.
72. *Orlando:* i.e. *Orlando Furioso* (Orlando insane); hence the reference to madness.
74. *press:* press-gang.
81. *yourself:* Ercole.
88. *exercise their art:* practise medicine.

# COMMENTARY AND NOTES

*The references are to line numbers*
s.d. *Stage direction.* s.p. *Speech Prefix.*
q. *Quarto.*

## THE WHITE DEVIL

### SOURCES AND INFLUENCES

The events of *The White Devil* are in essence historical, and took place in Italy during the years 1576–85. Whence Webster derived his account of the violent careers of Vittoria Accoramboni and Paulo Giordano Orsini, Duke of Bracciano, is not certain. None of the 109 manuscripts that Professor Gunnar Boklund studied in his work on the play's sources presents the tangle of events as Webster does, and even the one which comes closest to doing so, a letter sent by an Italian agent to the German banking house of Fugger, differs so significantly as to require the theory that other manuscripts, not yet known, played a part in bringing the story from Italy to London, and that London gossip may also have been influential. Not knowing precisely what facts Webster had at his disposal, we cannot always determine where he deliberately altered them for artistic purposes. For discussions of the whole problem, however, see Boklund's *The Sources of The White Devil* and my monograph on the play in the Studies in English Literature Series, listed in the Bibliography.

If the main source is not known, however, two minor sources are. From Hierome Bignon's *A Briefe, but an Effectual Treatise of the Election of Popes* (English version, 1605), Webster certainly derived his account (IV, iii) of the papal election. Equally certainly, he took the Latin litany of damnation which Lodovico and Gasparo intone over the dying Brachiano in V, iii, from one of Erasmus's *Colloquia Familiaria*, 'Funus'.

Dramatic influences are not easy to trace in the work of so assertively individual a genius, but it is generally agreed that the madness of Ophelia lies behind that of Cornelia in V, iv, while Webster's admiration of Chapman and Jonson, expressed in the address 'To the Reader', shows itself in the general attempt to produce a tragedy which is weightily 'sententious' (i.e. full of

# COMMENTARY AND NOTES

'sentences' or apothegms) and conforms to the requirements of tragic writing as they were then understood.

## TITLE PAGE

*White Devil* a common phrase, signifying hypocrisy or evil attractively disguised. A common Elizabethan proverb warned that 'The white devil is worse than the black'.

*The famous Venetian Curtizan* Vittoria Corombona did not, in fact, come from Venice, but from Gubbio, a small town in the Apennines. Webster is merely making his courtesan a citizen of a city famed throughout Europe for its whores.

## DRAMATIS PERSONAE

*Monticelso* the historical Montalto assumed the papal throne 24 April 1585 as Sixtus V.

## TO THE READER

3. *nos . . . nihil* 'we know these things are nothing' (Martial, XIII 2).

5–6. *open and black* the courtyards of public theatres were both unroofed and unlit.

12–13. *Nec . . . molestas* 'you [i.e. my books] shall not fear the snouts of the malicious, nor provide wrapping for mackerel' (Martial, IV, 86).

15–16 *non . . . dixi* 'you cannot say more against my trifles than I have said myself' (Martial, XIII, 2).

22. *O . . . ilia* 'O strong stomachs of harvesters' (Horace, *Epodes*, III, 4, referring to the peasants' fondness for garlic).

26. *Haec . . . relinques* 'what you leave will go to feed the pigs today' (Horace, *Epistles*, I, VII, 19).

49. *non . . . mori* 'these monuments do not know how to die' (Martial, XII, 2).

## ACT ONE

### Scene One

In a masterfully dramatic and economical way, Webster introduces the 'decay'd' Count Lodovico, his friends Gasparo and Antonelli –

416

and, indirectly, Vittoria and Brachiano. Vittoria's standing is unclear: we know she is solicited but not how she responds. Brachiano's position is clearly linked to Lodovico's. Both are transgressors, but only a Duke may offend with impunity: such is Lodovico's bitter conclusion. During the course of the play others, including Flamineo and Mulinassar the Moor, are to make the same complaint. One of the play's principal concerns is to be an examination of the truth of this assertion.

23. *phoenix* a legendary bird, rarest among living creatures since only one existed at any time. The young phoenix arose from the ashes of the old bird, which died in a fire in its nest.

25. *meteor* Elizabethan cosmologists regarded meteors as symbolic of transitoriness, change, decay, and corruption.

51. *Italian cut-works* open-work embroidery made by cutting out or stamping, and popular in Italy in the late sixteenth and early seventeenth centuries.

### Scene Two

Though Vittoria's beauty, intelligence and strength of will quickly establish her ascendancy over Brachiano, it is not she but Flamineo who dominates this first meeting of the lovers. An indefatigable entrepreneur, he is busy throughout, plying his trade of pander, encouraging the hesitant Duke and joining Vittoria in duping the foolish Camillo: all to the accompaniment of a debased and cynical commentary. Crude as they are, his remarks serve as a corrective, preventing us from taking the lovers at their own valuation. Their passion may be real and deep, but it is also adulterous. Their tryst, which began so propitiously, ends in conflict and foreboding. Vittoria's 'dream' spurs Brachiano to plan the deaths of Camillo and Isabella, and so, hopefully, clear the way for their marriage. Cornelia, however, breaks into the lovers' world in the manner of a classical Greek chorus, prophesying early deaths for both of them.

28. *gilder* the gilding process involved drawing mercury off by heat from an amalgam with gold. The vapour was poisonous, and inhaled, led eventually to tremors and insanity.

32. *all downward* testicles, which the Irish, in their gambling fervour, were reputed to put at hazard, i.e. wager upon.

53–60. There is persistent double entendre here: i.e. *travelling* and *travailing* ('working hard', the pun is stressed by the Q reading, 'travailing'). Thus, *count*=tally/cunt; *flaw*=storm/crack/imperfection; *made up*=reconciled/entered.

**63–5.** In conveying his alarm at Brachiano's attentions to Vittoria, Camillo quibbles on bowling terms. To *bowl booty* combine with a second player against a third. *Cheek* rounded surface of the bowl. *Bias* weighted side of a bowl. *Mistress* 'jack', or bowl at which the remainder are aimed. *Jump with* run up against (and, of course, lie with).

**98.** *Jubilee* A year of celebration, during which the faithful might obtain plenary indulgences by certain acts of piety. As originally instituted by Pope Boniface VIII in 1300, years of Jubilee occurred only once a century. By Webster's day the period was twenty-five years. The last Jubilee would have been 1600.

**117.** *Ida* a sacred mountain near Troy, connected with Paris's youth as a shepherd.

**117.** *Corinth* a Greek town famous for its marble and its prostitutes. In the circumstances, both this reference and the preceding are thoroughly ironic.

**150.** *philosopher's stone* the goal of the alchemists, since it would turn base metals to gold, prolong life, and cure disease. Flamineo uses the phrase as a double entendre, as he does 'ring'.

**178–80.** *your silkworm . . . the better* In fact silkworms fast for two days, then spin for up to nine. There was much interest in silkworms in England at this time. James I kept them, but failed in his hopes of establishing a national industry.

**231–53.** An exact explanation of Vittoria's dream is very difficult, since it works more by suggestion than direct statement. However, we may assume the yew to be Brachiano himself, except at line 241, where it is perhaps more specifically his good name, which Vittoria will replace with shame (the withered blackthorn). The crucial point is, of course, that Vittoria expects Brachiano to remove all obstacles (her husband and his wife included) to their union.

**235.** *cross-sticks* meaning uncertain. Perhaps crosses stuck into the grave (Brereton) or osiers used to bind the grave together (Lucas).

**319–21.** *For want of means . . . seven years* poor undergraduates often worked their way by acting as servants to tutors.

**321–2.** *Conspiring . . . graduate.* The meaning is uncertain. Flamineo may mean that he obtained his degree through the passage of time rather than study, or that he did so by conspiracy with an older member of the university.

## ACT TWO

### Scene One

So feeble is Camillo that Vittoria's rejection of him is readily understood, if not applauded. Isabella, on the other hand, is good (without being moralistic), loving and, for all her gentleness, strong, and Brachiano's gratuitously brutal rejection of her love (presented very tellingly by Webster in the form of an inverted sacrament) counts heavily against him, particularly since it is followed by his readiness to let Isabella take the blame for their separation. At first Francisco and Monticelso seem wholly admirable. Their use of Camillo as a pawn in the prosecution of revenge, even a revenge which limits itself to shaming Brachiano into repentance, should, however, make us uneasy.

s.D. *Little Jaques the Moor* is, as Brown points out, a 'ghost' character with nothing to do or say, like 'Christophero' and 'Guid-Antonio' in II, ii. Either the dramatist deleted lines first given such characters or never wrote them.

14. *precious unicorn's horn* unicorn's horns were regarded as a defence or antidote against poison.

38–9. *flower . . . crowns* a quibble, since flower = jewel, and a crown is a garland of flowers.

55. *cloth of tissue* expensive fabrics, into which gold and silver threads were often woven.

111. *Homer's frogs* a reference to *The Battle of Frogs and Mice*, a burlesque epic attributed to Homer. An English translation had been published in 1603.

183–4. *I scorn . . . Polack* Fynes Morrison reports in his *Itinerary* (1617) the Poles' custom of shaving off their hair save for a long forelock, and also the insouciance with which they took human lives.

262. *manet alta mente repostum* 'it remains deep buried in my mind' (Virgil, *Aeneid*, I, 26).

290. *to Candy* Candy was a name for Crete, where the inhabitants were believed to live on serpents and poisonous plants. To Candy therefore = to his death.

292–7. *A poor . . . execution* the quack escaped a whipping for lechery by pretending that he had already been sentenced for debt. However, another rogue, pretending to be the creditor, forced him to pay the 'debt'.

299. *more ventages . . . lamprey* the seventeenth-century cornet closely resembled in appearance the present penny whistle. The lamprey has seven orifices (ventages) on each side to convey water to the gills.

301. *because Ireland . . . poison* the absence of venomous creatures in Ireland is attributed to the intervention of St Patrick.

302–3. *Spaniard's fart . . . Dublin* A certain Don Diego achieved fame, sometime prior to 1598, by farting particularly obnoxiously in St Paul's, London. Flamineo proposes emulating the feat in Dublin both because there are no poisons native to Ireland and because, as Lucas points out, the Irish regarded breaking wind in company as a gross affront.

320–21. *they rise . . . shoulders* Flamineo is thinking of an improvised gallows made by 'placing the condemned man on the shoulders of another man, who then steps aside, leaving the person hanging'. (Sampson.)

326. *Inopem me copia fecit* 'Abundance has left me destitute' (Ovid, *Metamorphoses*, III, 466). This is usually taken to mean that in the richness of Vittoria's beauty, Camillo is poor. The emblem, together with Monticelso's translation of the line, 'Plenty of horns hath made him poor of horns', seems to indicate, however, that Camillo is being taunted for remaining sexually unsatisfied while his wife gratifies her lovers. 'Horn' is a slang term for the phallos.

334–54. *Upon a time . . . repent it* This 'old tale' has been described as inapposite. If, however, we read God for Jove, and Phoebus (the God of light) for Lucifer (light-bearer), we can discover its inner meaning. Men perish in the heat (fires of hell), and these would worsen if Lucifer had children (fireworks) like himself. Likewise, should Vittoria (the white devil) not be prevented by providence from having children, mankind will regret it. She does, of course, die childless.

### Scene Two

For the use of the dumb show Webster has (by some) been taken to task. Yet mime has, here, significant advantages over other techniques he might have used. A report by an eye-witness might have telescoped the action equally conveniently, but only by using the dumb-show and the conjuror's art can Webster juxtapose the deaths and Brachiano's response to them. Having observed the strength of

Isabella's continued love for Brachiano, as demonstrated by her devotions before his portrait, we are the more revolted by his connoisseur's enjoyment of the manner of her death.

8. *nigromancer* necromancer. The Q spelling, retained here, suggests an association with the black arts (Latin *niger* = black).

14. *curtal* a docked horse. The reference is to Morocco, a gelding exhibited by a travelling showman called Banks from 1595 onwards. The horse, which could perform a wide variety of tricks, was commonly regarded as Banks's familiar.

19. *fast and loose* a cheating game in which the victim was asked to say whether a piece of string was knotted (fast) or loose. The nature of the 'knot' ensured that the answer was always wrong.

S.D. *Dumb Show* a medieval device for presenting dramatic action symbolically, valued by Webster and many of his contemporaries as a means of telescoping time, concentrating the action, and, as here, achieving a telling juxtaposition of event and comment. Both Christophero and Guid-Antonio are 'ghost' characters (see note to II, i, S.D.).

## ACT THREE

### Scene One

Set in an ante-chamber adjoining the papal court, III, i, acts as a prologue to the trial, providing us with the terms of reference within which it is to be conducted, and bringing together almost all the participants, indicating briefly what we may expect from each of them. Then Flamineo and Marcello argue over ends and means, and the relative merits of their ways of life. Ironically, all that Flamineo says by way of disparagement about the virtuous life will at last prove relevant to his own amoral existence.

53. *mandrake* a poisonous plant of the genus Mandragora. It has a forked root, and resembles the lower half of the human body. It was believed to grow under gallows, feed on blood (cf. III, iii, 111–12), and shriek when pulled up (cf. V, vi, 65). Because this shriek was reputed to cause madness, dogs were trained to extract the roots.

73–4. *poulter* poulterer. Riding early to market, poulterers often fell asleep on horseback, leaning safely on the baskets they carried in front of them. There is perhaps a quibble on 'palter' and 'palterer'.

### Scene Two

The courage, wit and resourcefulness which Vittoria displays in facing her accusers is such that it is tempting to accept without question her version of events. We feel the more inclined to do so when Brachiano deserts her, and Francisco and Monticelso exceed in their zeal the bounds proper to their offices, with the Cardinal in particular revealing a bitterness which draws comment from the English Ambassador, as always our spokesman. Yet while allowing her to make a bid for our sympathy and allegiance, Webster is careful to show that she is that dangerous mixture of attractiveness and criminality which the epithet 'white devil' comprehends. Some of the pointers are less apparent now than they would have been to a Jacobean audience: e.g. her misuse of rhetoric and the fundamental breach of decorum which leads her, a woman, to 'personate masculine virtue'. Others, such as her attempt to elicit sympathy by giving the impression that she is on trial for her life, when in fact only her liberty and reputation are at stake (though as the instigator of the murders she deserves worse), and her use of lies and evasion, are more obvious to us. Listening attentively, we cannot but condemn Vittoria, however much we admire her courage. The coda to the scene, in which the death of Isabella is announced, underlines, by a telling contrast between Brachiano's hypocrisy and Giovanni's grief, the deeper guilt with which the trial never dealt.

10–11. *Domine . . . corruptissimam* 'Lord Judge, turn your eyes upon this plague, the most corrupt of women.'

24–5. *I am at the mark . . . you shoot* archery terms. Vittoria is sarcastically offering to tell the lawyer how accurately he is shooting, since she is his target.

27. *connive your judgements* the lawyer seems to be trying to exhort the judges to unite their powers of judgement in considering the case. In fact he is asking them to shut their eyes to what Vittoria has done.

36. *pothecary's bills* prescriptions, which were written in tortuous medical Latin. *Proclamations* were, in James I's reign, equally tortuous and longwinded, though in English.

40. *tropes nor figures* rhetorical terms. *Tropes* the use of words or phrases in senses other than those proper to them; more generally,

figures of speech. *Figures* in casual speech, of similar meaning: i.e. 'forms' of expression in which words are used in other than their usual manner.

58–9. *Spirit . . . effected* Effected seems here to mean 'put into effect', 'carried out'. There is, however, a double entendre, since *spirit*= semen and *effected*=ejaculated.

64–7. *like those apples . . . soot and ashes* This legend, much elaborated in the retelling, stems it seems from *Deuteronomy*, xxxii, 32: 'For their vine is of the vine of Sodom, and of the fields of Gomorrah: their grapes are grapes of gall, their clusters are bitter . . .'

86. *tributes i'th' Low Countries paid* basic commodities like food and clothing were proverbially highly taxed in the Low Countries at this time.

89–91. *brittle evidences . . . one syllable* Sir Walter Raleigh's loss of his Sherborne estate, 1608–12, was perhaps the most notable case of the forfeiture of property due to minor scribal errors in the deeds.

96–8. *dead bodies . . . imperfect* the bodies of four felons were allotted to the Company of Barber-Surgeons annually, for purposes of dissection.

134. *Perseus* In Jonson's *Masque of Queenes* (1609), Perseus is presented as a type of heroic and masculine virtue.

234–5. *Vitelli* In real life Vittoria had no connection with this famous Roman family. Interestingly, however, the historical Lodovico was banished for the murder of one Vicenzo Vitelli.

### Scene Three

As Marcello asks us to 'mark this strange encounter', Flamineo and Lodovico, parodying fashionably melancholic attitudes, sound one another out. Then, suddenly, they clash. When Vittoria and Flamineo face their murderers in V, vi, Lodovico will be seeking revenge for himself as well as for his master.

7. *pedlars in Poland* seventeenth-century Poland was reputed full of pedlars, many of them Irish and Scots.

29. *weights . . . to death with* until 1772 those accused who refused to plead were subjected to the torture of having weights laid on them. If they died still refusing to plead, they preserved their goods from confiscation.

39–40. *first bloodshed . . . religion* Cain's murder of Abel; see *Genesis* iv, 3–8.

51. *Wolner* a famous Elizabethan glutton, renowned for his ability to

digest such things as iron, glass, shells, and raw meat and fish. He died of eating a raw eel.

94. *Fortune's wheel* The Goddess Fortuna, or Fortune, directed men's affairs by turning the wheel to which their lives were bound. Thus subjected to mutability, or change, men rose to a peak of good fortune before their inevitable descent into misery. Flamineo is here comparing Fortune's wheel to that of the torturer.

### ACT FOUR

### Scene One

As Flamineo and Lodovico sparred, so do Francisco and Monticelso. In II, i, the Cardinal had seemed the more eager for revenge. Now we are left uncertain about his plans, though Francisco's eagerness to take revenge is apparent. The appearance of Isabella's 'ghost' (if such it be: Webster is careful to leave this an open question) reinforces his determination, and the revenge intrigue is set in motion.

50–51. *base rogues . . . commodities* a reference to the most common of all Jacobean confidence tricks. Loaning goods to young gentlemen, the swindler would demand shortly afterwards a cash payment for them grossly in excess of their value.

52. *politic bankrupts* those who pretended bankruptcy and absconded with their hidden assets.

72. *tribute of wolves* King Edgar (944–75) is reputed to have demanded from the Welsh a tribute of three hundred wolves a year, in order to rid Britain of them. The authenticity of the story is in doubt.

81. *th' Irish rebels . . . sell heads* as part of an energetic 'pacification' programme, English commanders in Ireland offered a bounty for the heads of rebels.

109. *melancholy* Francisco's reaction to the vision as a product of melancholy is in accordance with the Jacobean authority on the subject, Robert Burton. See his *Anatomy of Melancholy* (1621), Part I, Section III, Member 3, Sub-section I.

135. *lure* Francisco is using the word both generally, meaning 'entice' or 'tempt', and in its special sense, involving the recall of a falcon to its owner by means of a bunch of feathers resembling its prey.

139. *Flectere . . . movebo* 'If I cannot prevail upon the Gods above, I

will move the gods of the lower world.' (Virgil, *Aeneid*, VII, 312).
This was a standard villain's tag. In Francisco's case, however, it is
given precise significance as the action proceeds.

### Scene Two

Francisco's letter achieves its purpose when Brachiano abducts
Vittoria from the House of Convertites and flees to his duchy, there
to marry her. It also precipitates a violent quarrel between the lovers,
revealing thereby a mutual distrust and antagonism which, though
the quarrel is, with Flamineo's assistance, made up, permanently
affects our view of their relationship. We may continue to believe in
the passionate intensity of the bond between them, but not that
theirs is love of a quality sufficient to justify Brachiano's rejection of
'dukedom, health, wife, children, friends and all'. At their first
meeting Flamineo's commentary kept us aware that the lovers were
not Romeo and Juliet. The quarrel and Flamineo's commentary
together make it clear that they are not to be compared with Antony
and Cleopatra either.

38. *all the lines . . . convinces* Francisco is quibbling on 'lines' as (a)
lines of verse or prose (b) the lines of age on the face.

55–6. *I am not . . . kept whole* Giles Fletcher's *Russe Commonwealth*
(1591) records this treatment for defaulting debtors as lasting
three hours daily.

61. *a Spanish . . . sallet* poisoned dishes. *sallet* = salad. *A Spanish fig*
was also an indecent expression of contempt, accompanied by
gestures with the fingers.

82. *You are reclaimed . . . the bells* terms in falconry. Brachiano sees
Vittoria as tamed by Francisco, and threatens to provide the bells
fitted to hawks to direct the falconer to her and to frighten her
quarry. His use of 'reclaimed' recalls, ironically, her presence in a
House of Convertites.

83. *Ware hawk, my lord* the hawk, or swindler, is not Vittoria, as
some editors suggest, but Francisco.

88. *devil in crystal* it was widely believed that evil spirits could be
trapped in crystal. This, together with the beauty of crystal, makes
the image singularly appropriate to Vittoria, the white devil.

95–7. *Procure but ten . . . wild Irish* at the funerals of the wealthy,
women were hired to keen, or lament, in traditional Irish fashion.

110–11. *Like those . . . 'bout them* the presence of a fox was supposed
to aid sufferers from palsy, or paralysis.

121–3. *I had a limb . . . on crutches* cf. *Mark*, ix, 45: 'and if thy foot offend thee, cut it off: it is better for thee to enter halt into life, than having two feet to be cast into hell, into the fire that shall never be quenched.'

167–8. *be not like . . . with blowing* the belief is erroneous.

203. *Barbary* the north coast of Africa, present-day Algeria and Morocco. Here, however, the word is being conflated with 'barbarian'.

234–5. *Your application . . . No my lord* for all Flamineo's denial, Brachiano's interpretation of his secretary's tale is undoubtedly correct.

### Scene Three

The ambiguity surrounding his intentions is resolved when Monticelso, newly elected Pope, refuses to take a golden opportunity to revenge himself, and then warns Lodovico to do the same, upon pain of damnation. Having come only jokingly as a 'penitent sinner' to 'confession', Lodovico is impressed both by the Pope's words and by his forbearance. The count's resolve to abandon revenge is, however, nullified by the wiles of Francisco who, like Marlowe's Mephostophilis, is quick to counter any dangerous pangs of conscience. Webster's desire finally to clear Monticelso of suspicion is manifest in the almost antiquarian fidelity to fact displayed in the election, as well as in the choice of Paul IV as the Pope's title. Elected by a vote stressed as free and secret, and given a title carrying none of the opprobrium for patriotic Englishmen that the historically accurate Sixtus V would have done, he stands freed of his past, a model of Christian forbearance against which the actions of the revengers must be read.

9–14. The *Knight of Rhodes* was a member of the order of the Knights of St John of Jerusalem, or Knights Hospitallers. The order, which was founded *c*. 1113, in the period of consolidation following the First Crusade, moved to Cyprus at the fall of the Kingdom of Jerusalem, and then to Rhodes. Later, under pressure from the Turks, they retreated to Crete and finally, in 1530, to Malta. The order of *St Michael* was founded in 1469 by Louis XI. It remained the premier order of chivalry in France until in 1578 Henri III founded the order of the *Holy Ghost*. The order of the *Golden Fleece* was founded by Philip the Good, Duke of Burgundy, in 1430; that of the *Annunciation*, the highest knightly order in Italy, by Amadeus VI of Savoy, in 1362. The order of the *Garter*, premier order in England, was founded *c.* 1346 by Edward III.

38. *admiration* Webster's variant on the technical term, 'adoration', whereby a pope was elected if two thirds of the cardinals present turned towards and made reverence to the candidate they wanted as Pope. The more formal alternative was a 'scrutiny', or vote.

43–5. *Denuntio . . . Paulum quartum* 'I announce to you tidings of great joy. The most reverend Cardinal Lorenzo de Monticelso has been elected to the apostolic see, and chosen for himself the name of Paul IV.' (In fact the historical Cardinal Montalto became Sixtus V.)

46. *Vivat . . . Quartus* 'Long live the Holy Father, Paul IV.'

59–60. *Concedimus . . . peccatorum* 'We grant you the apostolic blessing and remission of sins.'

94–5. *the career . . . ring-galliard* all technical terms concerning the 'manage' of a horse. The *career* involved bringing a horse to a quick and firm halt after galloping him; *the 'sault* was a series of leaps; *the ring-galliard* was, in Lucas's words, 'a mixture of bounding forward, curvetting, and yerking' i.e. lashing out with the heels.

125. *Furies* the three avenging goddesses, Tisiphone, Megaera, and Alecto, sent from Tartarus to avenge wrongs and punish evildoers. By an extension of meaning, a *fury* came to be anyone, particularly female, pursuing revenge in an angry or malicious manner. I follow throughout the convention, established by Elizabeth Brennan in the New Mermaid edition of *The White Devil*, of distinguishing the Furies from furies (cf. IV, iii, 151 and III, ii, 277).

136. *crowns* Webster is not confusing the coinage, simply translating ducats into crowns, whose value was almost the same.

## ACT FIVE

### Scene One

The sense of security which the marriage of Vittoria and Brachiano engenders in Flamineo is ironically undercut by our knowledge that the newcomers he so admires, Mulinassar the Moor and the Hungarian friars, are in fact Francisco, Lodovico and Gasparo. Their plans for murdering Brachiano, made easier by the Duke's generosity, presage the collapse of Flamineo's new world. So, too, does his quarrel with Marcello over Zanche.

16. *Capuchins* originally a splinter group formed within the

Franciscan order, *c.* 1528, to effect a renewed observance of the austerities of St Francis. It became a separate order in 1619.

70. *The pommel of his saddle* in 1598 one Edward Squire was hanged for attempting to murder Queen Elizabeth by poisoning the pommel of her saddle.

74. *hazard* Jacobean tennis was played on an indoor court, on the walls of which were openings, or 'hazards'. To strike the ball into one of these was to win a stroke. The game is now called 'real tennis'.

188. *strike i'th' court* by a law of 1541, blows struck in the royal palace were punishable by fines, imprisonment, and loss of the striker's right hand.

207-9. *two slaught'red sons of Oedipus* legend has it that when the bodies of Eteocles and Polynices, the sons of Oedipus who had slain each other in single combat for the throne of Thebes, were burnt together, the flames on the pyre parted, demonstrating their continuance of the feud beyond death.

### Scene Two

Flamineo's pointless and cowardly murder of Marcello brings him in a moment from success to ruin, leaving him powerless in the hands of an employer who will neither forgive nor forget that his secretary once defied him. But the misery of a daily lease of life is preferable to Brachiano's fate. Even as Flamineo is agreeing that the Duke's 'will is law now', Lodovico is sprinkling poison on his helmet.

16. *sanctuary* according to medieval law, churches and certain other places were designated areas where a fugitive from justice might obtain immunity from arrest.

### Scene Three

That the poisoned Brachiano dare not let Vittoria kiss him – a fact which recalls the manner of Isabella's death and Giovanni's complaint (III, ii, 330-32) as well as Cornelia's prophecy that the Duke would, 'Judas-like, betray in kissing' – is but the first sign of an apt and inexorable pattern of retribution. His vision of the devil and the blasphemous litany the 'friars' recite over him serve to reinforce the conviction that Brachiano is hell-bound. If he is damned, however, so are his murderers, for ignoring the divine injunction, 'Vindicta mihi' and resorting to the 'lex talionis' of 'an eye for an eye, and a tooth for a tooth'. The intrigue between Zanche and Mulinassar, with which the scene concludes, also serves to stress cause and effect. Vittoria, the white devil, 'dreamed' her way to what she wanted. In trying to do the same, Zanche, the black devil, is ensuring Vittoria's destruction and her own.

37. *Franciscans* see V, i, 16 note. Flamineo is, unwittingly, punning. For the 'Capuchins' are in fact the accomplices of Francisco, who is standing quietly by, disguised as Mulinassar.

53–4. *within compass o' th' verge* 'The *verge* was an area extending to a distance of twelve miles round the King's Court, which lay under the jurisdiction of the Lord High Steward' (Lucas).

56–7. Belief that ulcers fed on the sufferer's flesh led physicians to provide raw meat or poultry as food for the ulcer, and hence a cure for the patient.

83. S.D. So that Brachiano may be 'presented in a bed', the traverse is drawn, revealing the inner stage.

94. *feed on poison* the idea, which is erroneous, was common in Elizabethan and Jacobean times.

120. *orris powder* Made from ground orris (or iris) root, the powder smelt of violets and was used as a cosmetic. Vittoria's hair would have been sprinkled with the powder for her wedding earlier in the day.

132. *Attende Domine Brachiane* 'Listen, Lord Brachiano.'

137–48. *Domine Brachiane . . . in laevum* 'Lord Brachiano, you were accustomed, in battle, to be protected by your shield, now you shall oppose *this* shield against your infernal enemy.'

'Once you prevailed in battle with your spear; now you shall wield *this* sacred spear against the enemy of souls.'

'Listen, Lord Brachiano, if you now also approve what has been done between us, turn your head to the right.'

'Rest assured, Lord Brachiano: consider how many good deeds you have done – and lastly remember that my soul is pledged for yours, should there be any peril.'

'If you now also approve what has been done between us, turn your head to the left.'

The passage is taken from Erasmus' colloquy, *Funus*, which compares the deaths of Cornelius Montius, who prepared himself for death in a Christian fashion, and the wealthy Georgius Balearicus, who sought to prepare his way in the after-life by bribes.

When the dying were speechless, it was customary for priests to ask for signs of faith.

159–60. *That would have . . . was poison'd* it was generally believed that the Earl of Leicester killed his wife, Amy Robsart, in just such a fashion (1560).

178. *woman-keeper* female nurse. Nurses were frequently suspected of strangling or smothering plague patients at the *pest house*.

185. *more rivers* built to alleviate a growing shortage of drinking water in London, the New River, running from Ware to Islington, was begun in 1609 and completed in 1613.

264. *And wash the Ethiop white* a popular Elizabethan proverb, derived from Jeremiah xiii, 23: 'Can the Ethiopian change his skin, or the leopard his spots?'

270–71. *like the partridge . . . laurel* on Pliny's authority it was believed that the partridge, along with several other species of birds, purged itself annually with laurel.

### Scene Four

Shaken both by his banishment from court and by Cornelia's madness, Flamineo reveals for the first time an active conscience and a capacity for fellow-feeling. The meeting with Brachiano's ghost, with its emblems of mortality, casts him into the despair which lies 'beyond melancholy', and leaves him no hope of solace save Vittoria's new wealth.

26. *Anacharsis* Webster follows his source, Montreux's *Honour's Academie* (English translation, 1610), in confusing Anacharsis, a Thracian prince of the 6th century B.C., with Anaxarchus, a Scythian philosopher, who was pounded to death in a mortar, on the orders of Nicocreon, tyrant of Cyprus.

40–41. *Castle Angelo* the Castel Sant' Angelo in Rome, where the historical Vittoria was herself imprisoned during 1581–2.

69. *'Twill keep . . . lightning* it is Pliny who records both the exemption of the laurel from being struck by lightning, and the use of a chaplet of laurel leaves as a defence against being so struck.

76–7. *rue, Heart's-ease* these flowers are offered Flamineo chiefly, it seems, for the significance of their names.

83–6. *When screech-owls . . . shall hear* Cornelia here lists a few of the many Elizabethan superstitions about impending death.

88. *Cowslip-water* Gerard's *Herball* makes no claim for this, but does prescribe it for 'frensie'.

94. *the robin red breast and the wren* the robin was widely believed to bury the unburied dead. The wren was equally widely believed to be the robin's wife.

102–3. *wolf . . . dig them up again* the wolf was believed to dig up the bodies of the murdered, in order to expose the crime, c.f. *The Duchess of Malfi*, IV, ii, 307–9.

122. S.D. Brachiano presents himself as a veritable compendium of symbolism concerning death and life after death. The *cowl* suggests the superstition (regarded as such by Protestant Englishmen), that burial in a Friar's cowl brings partial remission of sins. A *pot* of *lily-flowers* served either as an emblem of youth and beauty, or, in a religious context, to denote life. The *skull* is the archetypal memento mori. Brachiano's *cassock* is not a clerical garment, but a gown worn by soldiers.

141. *This is beyond melancholy* Flamineo means that the apparition is more than a mere figment of the melancholic imagination (such as Francisco thought Isabella's ghost). Outside Flamineo's awareness lies a second meaning, however. Beyond melancholy, according to contemporary theology, lay despair, the state of nullity in which men lose all hope of salvation, or even of God's existence. And it is as desperate that Flamineo is presented to us in V, vi, (see lines 4–6, 37–41, and 56–62).

### Scene Five

By the use of verbal and situational parallels, which place Hortensio in a relationship to Lodovico analogous to that of Monticelso in IV, iii, Webster makes the discovery of the revengers' plans by a minor courtier seem not an accident, or an ad hoc solution to a problem inherent in the source material, but part of the play's retributive pattern. For where Monticelso brought penitence, Hortensio brings punishment.

### Scene Six

Given by Vittoria only the fratricide's burden of guilt, Flamineo reveals the despair archetypally identified with Cain. In proving Vittoria's ingratitude, he also associates himself with the other great archetype of despair, Judas. For his mock-death is, unwittingly, a re-enactment of the Duke's last moments, in which Vittoria and Zanche play the parts of Lodovico and Gasparo (and thereby place themselves, morally, on the same level as those who, within moments, will kill them). Alike in viciousness, brother and sister display a like courage in the face of death – and a like degree of spiritual confusion and nullity. This courage of despair is shared equally (if less memorably, poetically) by Lodovico and his accomplices at their capture.

That Francisco remains at large while his accomplices suffer seems to imply that Lodovico's cynical belief in the immunity of great men to punishment is justified. As we ask with Lodovico, however, so we are answered with him. As Brachiano suffered, even at his moment of triumph, so will Francisco. The optimism of the youthful Duke Giovanni is not without foundation.

s.d. *a book* perhaps a bible or prayer book, in view of Flamineo's opening remark. But Webster may simply be employing an established stage convention indicating melancholia.

14. *Which Cain groan'd under* for murdering Abel, God cursed Cain, and decreed that he be an outcast: see *Genesis* iv, 11–15. This comparison of Flamineo with Cain is doubly significant in that the latter was not only the first fratricide, but also regarded as one of the two archetypes of despair (the other being Judas).

105–10. *O Lucian . . . one horse* Lucian's comic purgatory occurs in his *Menippos*. Webster merely varies the list of monarchs and notables to be found there. There is a quibble on *Pippin* (Pepin the Short, King of the Franks, 751–68) as apple-seller.

141. *Scotch holy bread* Cotgrave's *Dictionarie of the French and English Tongues* (1611), defines 'Pain benist d'Escosse' as 'A sodden sheepes liver'.

143–5. *and drive . . . upon thyself* 'the traditional treatment of suicides, who were thus buried at cross-roads.' (Lucas.) The custom became illegal in England only in 1823.

158. *Artillery Yard* the area in Bishopsgate where the Artillery Company carried out its weekly practice. The exercises, which had lapsed after 1588, were revived under royal patronage in 1610.

161. *Hypermnestra* The fifty daughters of Danaus were forced to marry their cousins, the fifty sons of Aegyptus, even though they considered the union incestuous. Warned by an oracle of his impending death at the hands of his nephews, Danaus ordered his daughters to murder their husbands on their wedding night. All did so save Hypermnestra, who spared her husband, Lynceus.

167. *matachin* a sword dance performed by masked dancers, fantas-

tically dressed. An essential element, which may have struck Flamineo as relevant since his confrontation with Vittoria was interrupted by a third party, is a three-sided combat.

181. *the pillar* one of the two columns supporting the 'heavens' above the stage of a public theatre like the Red Bull.

223-5. *I have blood . . . falling sickness* Pliny records the belief that blood sprinkled or smeared on the sufferer's face will cure an epileptic fit.

233. *fox* a common Elizabethan name for a sword, derived either from the brown colour of the steel, or from the figure (in fact a wolf) engraved on the blade of some swords.

264. *lions i'th' Tower* from the time of Henry I kings had kept a small menagerie in the Tower. Occasionally, as in 1609 and 1610, lions were baited for the amusement of the nobility. *Candlemas day* 2 February. Proverbially, the weather on that day forecast that for the remainder of winter.

301. *Haec . . . placui* 'these things will be our reward, if I have pleased' (Martial II, xci, 8).

308. *Master Perkins* Richard Perkins, the most famous 'straight' actor in the Queen's Men, was in 1612 just thirty, yet he had been an actor since at least 1602. The success of his acting at 'both the beginning and end' of the play implies that he played Flamineo.

\*

# THE DUCHESS OF MALFI

## SOURCES AND INFLUENCES

Though the events of *The Duchess of Malfi* have a firm basis in fact, having taken place during the years 1505-13, they reached Webster in a fictional form, and so indirectly that he may well not have known that they were historical. The story had a wide currency in Elizabethan and Jacobean literature – it occurs in George Whetstone's *An Heptameron of Ciuill Discourses* (1582), Thomas Beard's *The Theatre of Gods Iudgements* (1597), and Edward Grimestone's translation of Goulart's *Admirable and Memorable Histories* (1607), to name only works that Webster had read – but the dramatist's primary source seems to have been William Painter's collection of tales, *The Palace of Pleasure* (1566–7). Painter, in turn, derived his account from François de Belleforest, who included the story in the second volume of his *Histoires Tragiques* (1565). Both Painter and Belleforest adopt a sternly moral attitude towards the Duchess, condemning her for lust and for violating the accepted canons of degree. In Belleforest's source, a collection of *Novelle* (1554) by the Italian, Matteo Bandello, this moralizing is, however, notably absent. Instead we have a terse, accurate account, barely disguised as fiction, by one who, as Delio, seems to have been a participant in the tragedy he describes.

Painter provides the main narrative then, and Whetstone, Beard, and Goulart perhaps furnish additional details. From other prose works Webster borrowed sparingly. The device of the dead man's hand may well derive from Barnabe Rich's translation of *The Famous Histories of Herodotus* (1584), while other features of the torturing of the Duchess seem to come from Cinthio's *Ecatommiti* and Sidney's *Arcadia*. The latter is also Webster's richest source of verbal borrowings.

The play's dramatic antecedents are less extensive and less easily defined. Echo-scenes are common during the period. The works most likely to have influenced Webster in this respect include Dekker's *Old Fortunatus*, Jonson's *Cynthia's Revels*, the anonymous *Second Maiden's Tragedy* and George Wither's elegy, *Prince Henry's Obsequies*. For the madmen and their antics, Webster is indebted to the court masque, and works by Campion, Beaumont, and Jonson have been suggested as specific sources, though nothing proved beyond a general relationship.

### TITLE PAGE

5–6. *As it was . . . the Globe* whatever the original distinction between public and private theatres (the question is much debated), by Webster's time it had been reduced to a structural one: the public playhouse was open, and lit by daylight; the private theatre roofed and artificially lit. The King's Men used the open Globe for summer performances, and the Blackfriars for winter.

12–13. *Si quid . . . mecum* the full quotation, taken from Horace's *Epistles*, I, VI, 67–8, reads, in translation, 'If you know wiser precepts than mine, be kind and tell me them; if not, practise mine with me.'

## DEDICATION

1. *George Harding*, thirteenth Baron Berkeley (1601–58), was well-fitted to receive Webster's dedication, his grandfather and father, the first and second Lords Hunsdon, having been patrons of the Lord Chamberlain's Men, whom James I had made the King's Men.

## COMMENDATORY VERSES

Middleton's

*Thomas Middleton* (1580–1627), poet and dramatist, had perhaps collaborated with Webster, *c.* 1621, in the tragicomedy, *Anything for a Quiet Life*.

20–22. *In Tragaediam . . . poetis* 'To Tragedy. / As light is struck from darkness at the blow of the thunderer, / So may it (ruin to the evil) be life to famous poets.'

24–5. *Poeta & Chron: Londinensis* 'Poet and Chronologer of London.' Middleton was appointed City Chronologer in 1620.

Rowley's

*William Rowley* (*c.* 1585–1626), actor, poet and dramatist. The bulk of his dramatic work was done in collaboration, principally with Middleton, but also, in the case of *The Late Murder of the Son upon the Mother* (1624), with Webster and Ford.

Ford's

*John Ford* (1586–?1639), poet and dramatist, after early collaborative work, including that on *The Late Murder* (see above), went on to establish a reputation for himself as a tragic writer.

## ACT ONE

### Scene One

Antonio, newly returned from France, paints a glowingly optimistic picture of a prince's court well-governed. In the railing of the bitter but enigmatic Bosola and his curt dismissal by the Cardinal we sense for the first time a less satisfactory court world, nominally Italian, but also, it may be, English.

57. *Tantalus* the type of the hopeful but disappointed man. Tantalus was punished in Hades by perpetual thirst, though standing up to

his neck in water, and by hunger, though fruit hung just without his grasp.

72. *Gaston de Foix* de Foix (1489–1512), a French general, achieved legendary fame when he was slain at the moment of his greatest triumph, the destruction of the combined Spanish and Papal forces at Ravenna. He was, however, a mere child when Naples was taken by the French in 1501.

*Scene Two*

Antonio's portraits of the cold and taciturn Cardinal and the fiery and voluble Ferdinand arouse suspicions which are confirmed by their conversations with each other and with Bosola. His 'character' of the Duchess involves suspicions of another kind, confirmed when she finds her love reciprocated. In declaring their love for one another, the Duchess and her major-domo use a series of metaphors linking love and death. The violence of her brothers' objections to her re-marriage and the pressure they exert in forcing Bosola to spy for them, make the lovers' conceits seem premonitory and Cariola's final remarks choric.

30. *Ismael* i.e. Ishmael. But some editors? Israel.

38–40. *Pliny's opinion . . . quicksilver* for the belief that Portuguese (not Spanish) mares were impregnated by the west wind, see Pliny's *Natural History* (tr. 1601) VIII, ch. 42.

41. *reels from the tilt* i.e. refuses to run at the ring during jousting. There is, however, a double entendre on 'tilt' (copulate) which makes the ballast of quicksilver significant, mercury being used in the treatment of syphilis.

171–2. *Never rain'd . . . tail of them* Bosola alludes to the shower of gold used by Jupiter as a disguise when visiting Danae.

223. *Laban's sheep* see Genesis xxx, 31–43.

237. *Vulcan's engine* the net, so fine as to be invisible, in which he caught his wife, Venus, and her lover, Mars.

246. *executed . . . celebrated* a play on words. Both words are used in connection with religious service – here the sacrament of marriage – but Ferdinand implies punishment following rejoicing.

258. *lamprey* an eel-like fish, of parasitic habits. Ferdinand is, for all his denial, intending a double entendre: quibbles on *part* and *tail* (penis) emphasize this.

312. *St Winifred* a seventh-century Welsh saint. She was beheaded by Caradoc ap Alauc, whose advances she resisted, but restored to

life by her uncle, St Bueno. But possibly the Q may be right in giving St Winfrid, the seventh-century saint, born in Devon, and famous as Boniface, the apostle of Germany.

332-3. *There is . . . this circle* in raising spirits, magicians protected themselves either by surrounding themselves with a magic circle or by confining the spirits therein.

357. *progress* make a royal tour, or state journey; Antonio is to learn by such a 'journey' that he is ruler of a 'complete man'.

361. *woo . . . woo* the Q. spelling, 'woe . . . woe', emphasizes the pun (derived from the popular etymology, 'woeman'), which is introduced by *misery* in the preceding line.

383. *Quietus est* 'He is discharged of payment due' was a phrase used to indicate that accounts were correct. It is also used of the 'release' of death (as in *Hamlet*, III, i, 75). This allusion to death is only one of many in this part of the scene.

387. *this circumference* either the circumference of the ring or, since they have embraced, of her arms.

395. *Per verba de presenti* a couple could, with or without a witness, and without anything in writing, legally declare themselves married. The church, while recognizing the validity of such unions, was strong in its disapproval of their consummation without ecclesiastical reinforcement.

396. *Gordian* the oracle declared that whoever untied the knot tied by King Gordius of Phrygia would rule Asia. Alexander the Great severed it with his sword.

398. *spheres* the planetary spheres of the pre-scientific Ptolemaic universe were believed, inter alia, to be in perpetual motion, to touch one another, and to generate unheard musical harmonies.

401-3. *That we may . . . fruit divided* derived from Pliny, the belief came to serve as an emblem of marriage.

416. *Alexander and Lodowick* were friends, identical in appearance. Lodowick, marrying in his friend's name, laid a naked sword between himself and his bride nightly, in order not to wrong Alexander.

## ACT TWO

### Scene One

Though Bosola's scheme to prove the Duchess pregnant has a distinctly Machiavellian air, his 'meditation' upon the human condition unites the concerns of the Jacobean malcontent and the medieval *de contemptu mundi* satirist, providing some justification for Antonio's conviction that, freed from the baneful influence of Ferdinand, Bosola would reveal a strong moral sense. When Bosola's stratagem works, and the Duchess falls into premature labour, Antonio panics, but is saved by the resourceful Delio.

34–6. *No, no . . . to your plastic* i.e. 'No, no, but rather scraping clean an old scurfy lady, as if she were the hull of a ship, so that she can put to sea again in search of new adventures. And that's a rough phrase, coarse plaster to use in your fine modelling.'

42–3. *a dead pigeon . . . plague* it was believed that a pigeon or chicken, applied to a plague-sore, represented a cure for the disease.

66. *Lucca* an Italian spa town just north of Pisa, famous as a resort in the sixteenth and seventeenth centuries.

## Scene Two

The confusion with which II, i, ends continues throughout this scene, with the old midwife struggling to get away from the suspicious Bosola, the officers of the court exchanging a grotesque series of rumours, and Antonio shaken by fear and superstition. Only at the last, with Cariola's announcement that the Duchess has given birth to a son, is there a moment of peace.

## Scene Three

During a storm whose rising tumult reflects present confusion and future violence, the prowling Bosola encounters Antonio. Their exchange not only reveals a deep and mutual antipathy, but also underlines the superstitious fears which rack the Duchess's husband. From the horoscope, with its incomplete prediction of a violent death for the new-born child, Bosola learns that the Duchess has a son, but not that Antonio is the father.

39–40. Two successive prefixes for Antonio, as well as a clear break in the sense, indicate an omission in the Qq. What is lost seems to be a retort by Bosola, perhaps involving the term 'slander', which in reply draws a quibble on 'libel'.

56–63. The horoscope, which seems to have been Webster's own invention, is designed to indicate a violent end for the child, though not to confirm it, since *Caetera non scrutantur* ('The rest is not investigated.') i.e. the horoscope is incomplete. In fact the child survives the holocaust of the last act.

### Scene Four

The cold wariness of the Cardinal's relationship with his mistress marks the first of a series of contrasts with the Duchess and her world which Julia serves to provide. Her performance as a 'witty false one', more in keeping with the sententious couplet with which the preceding scene ends than is the Duchess's behaviour, reveals a second. The servant's remarks about the effects of the letter from Malfi, with which the scene ends, alert Delio to the dangers facing Antonio, and us to the frame of mind in which we find Ferdinand in II, v.

### Scene Five

The reactions of Ferdinand and the Cardinal to Bosola's news epitomize the differences between them. The Cardinal, the phlegmatic man of Jacobean humour psychology, is coldly angry that his sister has defiled 'the royal blood of Aragon and Castile'. Ferdinand, on the other hand, displays in his ravings the fiery intemperance of the choleric man and an obsessive concern with sexuality. To him, 'blood' is no synonym for lineage, but literally his sister's blood. Imagining her with a tormenting vividness 'in the shameful act of sin', he conjures up for the lovers a punishment demonic in its implications.

12–13. *Rhubarb . . . choler* an excess of 'bile', one of the four 'humours' believed to determine personality, resulted in a choleric temperament. Rhubarb was generally prescribed as an antidote.

### ACT THREE

### Scene One

That Antonio is right in regarding Ferdinand's unnatural calm as the greatest threat to his domestic happiness is proven when the Duke, alone with Bosola, displays the same violence as in II, v. Any suspicions we by now entertain about his preoccupation with his sister's body are heightened by his refusal to explain to Bosola, or to us, why he means to confront the Duchess in her bed-chamber.

49. *Pasquil's paper bullets* Pasquil, a fifteenth-century cobbler or

schoolmaster renowned for his bitter tongue, had his name given to a statue in Rome, to which, in the sixteenth century, the citizens attached satires and lampoons.

## Scene Two

The warmth and tenderness which Antonio and the Duchess display towards one another make all the more horrific Ferdinand's attack upon her and her love. Though he makes much of reputation and shame in his attempt to 'instruct' her, both his words and his behaviour indi∴ate that his opposition to her liaison is rooted in passion rather than logic. From the phallic symbolism of the poniard (symbolism pointed up when he talks to her about the weapon at I, ii, 253), and his preoccupation with lust, we may legitimately adduce as a motive for his behaviour the unconsciously incestuous passion which critics have suggested.

While the Duchess faces her brother with great courage, Antonio, cautiously returning to the room just after Ferdinand leaves, emerges from the episode with little credit. Nor does what follows restore our waning confidence in him. For though he acts his part well enough, it is the Duchess who plans and carries out the stratagem which covers his flight from court and her pilgrimage to Loreto. Such courage and resourcefulness takes its toll, however. Tired and worried, the Duchess confides her secret to a sympathetic Bosola, and he, in sick self-hatred, prepares to pass it on to his master, Ferdinand.

25–31. *We read . . . mulberry* Daphne was wooed by Apollo, while Pan made his pipe from the reed which *Syrinx* became (see Ovid, *Metamorphoses*, i, 452 & 691). When Iphis hanged himself for love of *Anaxarete*, she was unmoved, and Venus changed her to stone by way of punishment (*Metamorphoses*, xiv, 74). The fruit of the *mulberry* acquired its red colouring when Pyramus slew himself, believing Thisbe dead (*Metamorphoses*, iv, 55–165). No appropriate metamorphoses are known for the *olive* or *pomegranate*.

36. *This was Paris' . . . stark nak'd* brought up by the shepherds on Mt Ida, Paris, the son of King Priam of Troy, was called upon to judge the beauty of three goddesses, Hera, Aphrodite, and Athene. He chose Aphrodite, since she promised him the fairest woman in the world as a bride.

88. *basilisk* a fabulous creature, part cock, part serpent, which killed merely by breathing upon or looking at its victim.

180. *Magnanima mensogna* see Tasso's *Gerusalemne Liberata*, II, 22, where, in order to avoid general persecution of her co-religionists, Soprina admits taking a statute of the Virgin Mary from a mosque.

190–208. Throughout these lines there is, as J. R. Brown pointed out, a series of double entendres, e.g. on *let* (let him go, let him be made an example), *h'as done that . . . I mean not to publish, use, service, I am all yours*, and *to serve/A prince with body and soul*.

243. *Pluto the god of riches*, Plutus, was often confused with the god of the underworld, perhaps because of the subterranean source of gold and silver.

266. *Bermudas* the wreck of Sir George Somers there in 1609 made the island famous for storms, eerie noises and strange creatures.

307. *Loreto* a pilgrimage centre, famous for the Holy House, reputed that of Mary at Nazareth, and supposed to have been transported by angels to Italy (via Dalmatia) when threatened by the Turks.

314. *Spa* a famous Belgian watering place. The Elizabethans tended to use the terms 'German' or 'Dutch' in application to the Low Countries generally.

### Scene Three

Two important items of news reach the brothers. One, which prepares us for the symbolic acts of the next scene, tells the Cardinal that he must temporarily take up arms for the Emperor. The other brings Bosola's discovery that Antonio is the Duchess's husband. Wisely, Webster makes no attempt to repeat the tour-de-force of II, v. Instead we experience the brothers' response to Bosola's announcement indirectly, through Pescara and Delio, and hear from Ferdinand and the Cardinal themselves only a fragmentary account of what they intend.

4. *Marquis of Pescara* Ferdinando Francesco d'Avolos (1489–1525) was, historically, Duke Ferdinand's brother-in-law. Depicted in the play as an old man, he in fact died at thirty-six, shortly after his victory over Francis I of France at Pavia.

5. *Lannoy* Charles de Lannoy, Viceroy of Naples (*c.* 1487–1527), to whom, by choice, Francis I surrendered at Pavia. All this historical detail is anachronistic.

37–9. *Foxes . . . wrack for't* see Samson's device for destroying the Philistines' crops (cf. Judges, xv, 4–5).

### Scene Four

While the two pilgrims offer us a commentary which in its charity and understanding should mould our own, the investiture of the Cardinal and the banishment of the Duchess and her family take place in dumb-show. Though coincidental, the two acts together form a powerful symbolic entity. The participation of the Cardinal in the banishment of his sister and her family from both shrine and state emphasizes the double significance of his investiture. In exchanging his priest's vestments for the arms of the soldier the Cardinal is not merely taking up arms at the Emperor's behest, but also putting off his priestly office in order to persecute his sister the better.

### Scene Five

In their suffering, the Duchess and Antonio find consolation in recognizing the hand of God at work. Captive and alone, the Duchess briefly lapses into hysterical self-pity, but is recalled to a more philosophical frame of mind by Bosola's intervention. The scene ends with one of Webster's much-denigrated tales. The Duchess supplies one reading of it. A deeper one, central to our understanding of the next two scenes, becomes available if we recognize that the Salmon is the Duchess, the Fisher God, the Market the Last Judgement, and the Cook Satan.

105. *Charon's boat* Charon was the ferryman who conveyed the dead over the Styx to Hades.

### ACT FOUR

### Scene One

Enraged by the Duchess's acceptance of her suffering, Ferdinand comes to torment her. Though the vow which is used to explain his preference for darkness has some basis in fact (see III, ii. 141), it rapidly emerges that his choice is symbolically significant, and related to the demonic implications of his use of the wax effigies and severed hand. As a result of these torments the Duchess entertains thoughts of suicide. Finding chaos in her own life, she wishes disorder on the entire universe, cursing the stars. Bosola's reply, 'Look you, the stars shine still', has generally been taken, as by Lucas, to imply 'the insignificance of human agony before the impassive universe'. For Bosola, perhaps, it does mean this. In the light of subsequent events, however, it must also be taken to mean that all is not lost, that divine order still exists despite the suffering of the individual. In one line is announced the double role of comforter and tormentor, minister and scourge, which Bosola is, unwittingly, to play throughout Act Four. Ferdinand's contempt for the soul and his admission that he is tormenting his sister in order to bring her to despair, an admission whose specifically anti-religious significance is pointed up by Bosola's earlier rebuke of the Duchess, 'O fie, despair? / Remember you are a Christian', makes it clear that in IV, ii, we are to be concerned not merely with life and death, but more deeply with salvation and damnation.

21. *elder brother* Though historically Ferdinand was the elder, in the context of the play he is not (see IV, ii, 265–7).
72. *Portia*, the wife of Brutus, choked herself with hot coals after her husband's defeat and death at Philippi.
113. *Vincentio Lauriola* no sculptor of this name has come to light.

### Scene Two

The relationship between love and death, established metaphorically in I, ii, reaches a climax in IV, ii, where the suffering and death of the Duchess are presented through a formal structure resembling that of the court marriage-masque. Thus the madmen, with their pertinently insane chatter and their song and dance, perform an anti-masque, while Bosola, acting as the 'presenter', prepares the 'bride', offering her gifts in the form of 'a coffin, cords and a bell', and in his dirge makes a formal speech, or epithalamion. After which the 'marriage' arranged by Ferdinand is celebrated.

The ironies inherent in the masque-like structure are compounded by the ambiguity surrounding the actions of Bosola. As an 'honest servant' he obeys Ferdinand, even to the point of murder. As a man he does his best to comfort the Duchess, even if only by helping her to face the inevitable. As a providential agent he brings her, un-wittingly, comfort of another kind. For as tomb-maker he makes her see the emptiness of rank, while as the bellman he offers her a heavenly alternative. Brought 'by degrees to mortification', the Duchess dies, not in despair, as Ferdinand planned, but in Christian humility.

Dead, the Duchess works more powerfully upon Ferdinand than she had alive. Unable to face what he has done, or fathom his motives in ordering it, the Duke goes mad. Rejected, unrewarded, Bosola too is tormented by his conscience. With the momentary recovery of the Duchess, he entertains hopes of redeeming himself. Her death confirms his despair, as well as his decision to avenge her and assist Antonio.

73–115. Save for the Fourth Madman, who is clearly the Doctor, there is no wholly consistent identification of individual madmen with the numbered roles. For the rest, the First Madman generally (though not always) sounds like the Astrologer, and the Third the Priest, while the Second is never precisely identifiable. It seems that Webster simply distinguished the speeches by numbering them, and left any further distinctions to be arranged in rehearsal.

172. *common bellman* a charity established in 1605 by Robert Dove, a Merchant Taylor, provided for a bellman to make one speech outside the cell of a condemned felon on the eve of his execution, and another as he left Newgate prison to be hanged at Tyburn. The speeches were to 'put them in minde of their mortalitie' and so of 'securitie, to save their soules from perishing'.

Interestingly, one of the witnesses to this gift was a 'John Webster', a member of the 'Common Council' of the Merchant Taylors' Guild. Whether this was the dramatist or not is impossible to tell (but see the Introduction, p. 10).

176. *mortification* Webster seems to be using the term both medically (indicating the insensibility preceding death) and spiritually (denoting the freedom from earthly concerns encumbent upon Christians at death).

178. *whistler* the ring ouzel, widgeon and lapwing all have a whistling cry, reputed ominous.


### ACT FIVE
#### Scene One

Pescara's willingness to give Antonio's land to Julia, though not to Delio, casts a momentary doubt on his probity. His reasons for doing so establish him firmly as an epitome of right behaviour. Antonio's decision to seek a reconciliation with the Cardinal, on the other hand, further damages our opinion of him.

6. *in cheat* land held of Pescara 'in escheat' would revert to him if Antonio died intestate or committed a felony.

## Scene Two

The form Ferdinand's madness takes is as appropriate as it is extraordinary, since to Webster's contemporaries lycanthropy not only betokened guilt and remorse, but was also associated with witchcraft and love melancholy. A similar rightness about his avoidance of the light and fear of his shadow leads us to endorse Bosola's feeling that 'a fatal judgement hath fall'n upon this Ferdinand'. In the Cardinal we find neither guilt nor fear, only continuing villainy. Yet for all his ruthlessness, his position is weakening. Not trusting Julia, he has to trust Bosola. Murdering her, he provides Bosola with a perfect opportunity for killing him. And these ironies depend upon another, aptly retributive: that just as the Duchess's wooing of Antonio puts her in the hands of her brothers, so Julia's wooing of Bosola puts the Cardinal in the hands of Bosola.

6. *lycanthropia* sufferers from this disease imagined themselves wolves. The doctor's description of Ferdinand's behaviour includes the main forms such a delusion took.

25. *Paracelsus* was the most famous physician of his day (1493–1541). He also had a reputation as a magician.

29. *solitariness* melancholiacs were advised by doctors to seek company and shun solitude.

61. *salamander's skin* the salamander was believed to live in fire.

76-8. *one . . . Hall* the bodies of executed felons, granted to the Guild of Barber-Surgeons, were, after dissection, displayed as specimens (*anatomies*) in the museum in their Hall.

140. *brought* Q Dyce's conjecture, 'bought' has generally been adopted, though Lucas pointed out that *picture-makers* might also be dealers, and that out of need, Antonio might be selling a miniature of his wife.

334. *Security* theologians distinguished between two kinds of security, or over-confidence: 'spiritual' security comprised an undue confidence in the certainty of salvation; 'carnal' security an equally dangerous concentration on this life, and indifference to the next. Bosola detects carnal security in the Cardinal.

## Scene Three

In terms of plot, the echo scene contributes little or nothing. Its value lies rather in the atmosphere it creates; in the elegiac beauty of the verse, and the prefigurative nature of the snatches repeated by the echo. Whether Antonio really sees his wife's face is irrelevant. The point is that he thinks he does.

### Scene Four

The circumstances attending Bosola's accidental slaying of Antonio are a true measure of what both men's lives have come to. Since parting from the Duchess, Antonio has been only half-alive, a pathetic and inglorious figure, sustaining his inactivity with an assortment of neo-Stoic tags and illusory hopes of pardon. Now, equally ingloriously, he is despatched. Bosola, for his part, is spiritually adrift, oppressed since the Duchess's death by the certainty of his damnation. In stabbing the man he longed to help, he reflects the confusion amidst which he lives.

### Scene Five

Gloomily meditating upon hell-fire, and pursued by images of retribution, the Cardinal reveals himself a prey to the despair which he and his brother wished on the Duchess, and which has already overtaken Ferdinand and Bosola. The manner of their deaths reinforces this impression. The Cardinal, having calmly arranged the deaths of others, dies 'like a leveret', in a shockingly craven fashion. His brother, who helped despatch him, insanely imagines 'high pleasures/Beyond death'. Bosola, while triumphing in his revenge, feels he is 'in a mist'. Yet all three acknowledge the rightness of their deaths, and the aptness of the retributive process. After confusion, however, comes calm, and after despair, hope. Pescara, taking charge, deals with the situation as it stands, asking the questions we would ask, and commenting, too, as we would on the carnage. Delio, presenting Antonio's son as a symbol of hope and regeneration, expresses a larger view. Using what is, significantly, the only sun image in a dark play, he points to the negativity and futility of evil and expresses his conviction (one which, in the light of what the play has revealed, we must surely share) that 'integrity of life' is rewarded beyond the grave.

s.d. *Enter . . . a book.* The book is clearly a work of theology. The mere possession of the book indicates, however, that the Cardinal is a prey to melancholy. (cf. *White Devil*, V, vi, s.d. note, p. 432).

47–53. In his madness, Ferdinand imagines he is doing battle with an enemy when he is attacking his brother. Hence the military terminology: *vaunt-guard* = vanguard; *the honour of arms* = the right to retain one's arms when surrendering. *There flies your ransom*: dead, the Cardinal will be worth nothing to Ferdinand in ransom money.

\*

# THE DEVIL'S LAW-CASE

## SOURCES AND INFLUENCES

No source for the plot of *The Devil's Law-Case* as a whole has been traced, and it is generally assumed, as by F. L. Lucas, that it is of Webster's own invention. Such an assumption is strengthened by the impression the play creates of having been written, in part at least, as a corrective for prevalent social ills, notably duelling, malevolent law-suits and the failure of arrogant and domineering women to observe their proper place in society.

For a few incidents, however, sources may be suggested. Romelio's unintentional cure of the dying Contarino seems to have been drawn by Webster from the account of 'An Extraordinarie Cure' in Simon Goulart's *Admirable and Memorable Histories* (English translation by E. Grimeston, 1607). For Leonora's unsuccessful attempt to prove Romelio a bastard, several sources are possible, the most likely being either Bernardo Giustiniani's *De Origine Urbis Gestisque Venetorum* (1492) or Joannes Magnus' *De Omnibus Gothorum Sueonumque Regibus* (1554). Since neither appeared in English until after the play was published, however, and since neither offers more than a general parallel, no firm conclusions can be drawn. No certainty exists, either, concerning Winifrid and her part in the law-suit, but it is possible, as Lucas suggests, that she was modelled upon a certain Sarah Swarton, who gave perjured evidence on behalf of her mistress, Lady Lake, during the notorious Lake-Roos trial of 1618–19.

Among literary influences, two stand out. The first is Marlowe's *The Jew of Malta*, which supplies in Barabbas, the Machiavellian Jew, a prototype for Romelio's italianate villainies in III, ii. The second, not surprisingly when one considers the dramatist's predilection for re-working his material, is *The Duchess of Malfi*. From it Webster took not merely general features such as Romelio's

447

career, which like the Duchess's moves from pride through humility to consolation, but also a number of individual incidents. Of these the most notable involve the activities of Bosola in IV, ii; his successive disguises as tomb-maker and bellman and his dirge. Re-worked, they are to be found in the entry of the Capuchin and bellmen in II, iii, the entry of Leonora and the servants, carrying coffins and winding sheets in V, iv, and the meditations of Romelio in response to these two events.

## TITLE PAGE

10. *Non . . . bene* an abbreviated quotation from Seneca, *Epistles*, 77. Translated, it reads in full: '[With life, as with a play, it matters] not how long, but how good the performance is.'

12. *A.M.* Augustine Matthews, in business as a printer, 1619–53. *John Grismand* was both a printer and bookseller, active 1618–38.

## DEDICATION

1–3. *Sir Thomas Finch* the second son of Sir Moyle Finch and grandson of Sir Thomas Heneage (d. 1595), Vice-Chamberlain of Queen Elizabeth's household. He was M.P. for Winchelsea 1621–2, and for Kent 1628–9. Succeeding to the Earldom of Winchilsea in 1633, on the death of his mother, he died in 1639. It is not clear why Webster chose him as dedicatee, though Finch obviously knew the dramatist and his earlier works.

8. *Guise* little is known of this play, now lost. Seemingly written after *The Duchess of Malfi* and before *The Devil's Law-Case*, it is tentatively dated *c.* 1616–17. From late seventeenth-century play-lists we learn both that it was printed and (inconclusively) that it was a comedy.

10–11. *the greatest of the Caesars* Gaius Julius Caesar Octavianus, named 'Augustus' (63 B.C. – A.D. 14), nephew of Julius Caesar, and first Emperor (27 B.C.). The Augustan age is generally regarded as the high point of Latin literature.

## TO THE JUDICIOUS READER

1–2. *Sapienta prima, stultitia caruisse* from Horace, *Epistles*, I, 1, 41–2, 'the beginning of wisdom is freedom from folly'.

5–6. *Locus est, et pluribus umbris* 'there is room also for a number of unbidden guests' (Horace, *Epistles*, I, 5, 28).

9. *Auriculas . . . dolentes* an abbreviated quotation ·from Horace, it reads, in full: '[it would give no more pleasure to them than] the music of lyres to ears afflicted with the dirt of ages' (*Epistles*, I, 2,. 53).

18. *Non ego . . . venor* 'I do not pursue the approbation of the fickle populace' (Horace, *Epistles*, I, 19, 37).

## ACT ONE

### Scene One

By his conversation with Prospero, Romelio's wealth is demonstrated, as well as his pride and arrogant self-assurance. His encounter with Contarino shows him to be intelligent but also unscrupulous. Contarino, for his part, emerges as likeable but naïve, since he fails entirely to perceive Romelio's heavy ironies, or to see that Leonora has taken literally his conceit about her 'picture'. Unaware of Romelio's fierce opposition to his request for Jolenta's hand, Contarino takes her note less seriously than we do, and appears complacent, and even condescending, in his suspicion that she may be proving fickle.

10. *musical water-works* in the sixteenth and seventeenth centuries the gardens of the wealthy were often adorned with fountains, cascades and the like; these contrived to play instruments or make imitation birds sing.

16. *lottery* the first in England was conducted in 1569, while a major one, to benefit the Virginia settlement, was drawn in 1612. By a law of 1620 they were declared illegal.

52. *Alps* the setting being Italy, Contarino must be talking of travel to Northern Europe. The audience would, however, see the comment in the context of English warnings against travel south of the Alps, to Italy.

126. *the Exchange bell* the morning hours at the Old Exchange were eleven to twelve. The merchants dined thereafter, whereas the nobility dined at eleven.

131. *New Burse* built by the Earl of Salisbury in 1609, as a rival to the Old Exchange built by Sir Thomas Gresham in 1566–7, the New Burse contained numerous milliner's and draper's shops. At first it did badly, hence the reference here.

135. *picture* Contarino uses 'picture' to mean Jolenta, who resembles her mother. Leonora, of course, takes the request literally.

171-8. *Now I could . . . men's pity* Leonora here voices widely felt disapprobation on two public issues: the movement of the aristocracy from their country estates to London, and the attempts of land-hungry laymen to appropriate church estates, either by threat or persuasion. James I tried to prevent both, without success.

188. *ingenuously* Q. The Q spelling is retained here, though it should be noted, as apposite here, that the Jacobeans did not generally distinguish orthographically between 'ingenuously' and 'ingeniously'.

### Scene Two

The gentleness and consideration Ercole accords the distressed Jolenta contrast sharply with the attempts of Romelio and Leonora to bully or cajole her into accepting him. Yet despite Ercole's nobility of soul, and despite, too, any reservations we may have about Contarino, particularly concerning his prodigality, we remain sufficiently convinced of his deserts to endorse Winifrid's enthusiasm over the lovers' happiness. Only at the last, faced with Contarino's naïve optimism, do our doubts reassert themselves.

41-2. *too much . . . moon-eyed* 'too much gazing on the glitter of worldly greatness has dazzled and half-blinded you' (Lucas).

109. *continue . . . dumb show* the metaphor, as Lucas points out, is drawn from the moveable pageants of the medieval mystery cycles. The stations were the stopping-places of the moveable stages in their progress through a town. Ercole is, therefore, to stay where he is, but continue in dumb show, kissing rather than talking.

115-16. *At the consecration . . . take it* it was apparently usual for clerics offered bishoprics to reply in the negative twice before accepting.

117-18. *the door . . . livery and seasin* an allusion to a feudal land-holding practice, involving 'feoffment with livery and seisin'. On the transfer of land, the feoffee gave the feoffer a token of allegiance; in the case of a house, the door latch.

164. *Deuce-ace* a 'deuce ace' is a poor throw in dice, ace on one side, deuce on the other. Here it is a derogatory term. A *wafer-woman* sold thin cakes and confectionery, and apparently often acted as a go-between.

192. *A more ungodly work . . . commons* the enclosure by wealthy landowners of common pasturage, frequent at this time, brought both criticism and local peasant revolts.

## ACT TWO

### Scene One

The scene falls into two main segments and a brief coda. In the first, the arrival of the disguised Judge, Crispiano, in search of his spendthrift son, Julio, provides an opportunity for satiric comment upon the greed and dishonesty of lawyers. Ariosto, on the other hand, is presented as a 'very miracle of a lawyer', a peacemaker and altruist, though his first task is to administer a stinging rebuke to the cheerfully unrepentant Julio. In the second section Contarino, breaking his vow to Jolenta, engineers a quarrel, and thence a duel, with Ercole. The coda is primarily concerned with efforts to prevent the duel from taking place, but it also shows Romelio reeling under the first setback he has ever suffered, the loss of some of his ships.

14. *Corregidor of Seville* Corregidor was normally a title meaning Chief Justice of a town. Here, however, it seems to mean simply an advocate. There is a play here, perhaps, as at line 5, on Seville/civil.

63. *I took by a leer* i.e. assessed by a stealthy glance, since lawyers do not demean themselves by counting their fees.

66-7. *a good cry . . . to a fault* A *cry* is a pack; a *fault* a break in the scent. But Webster is also punning on *fault* = ruin; i.e. he is saying that by their passion for hunting, landowners have ruined their estates.

75-81. *For the smallness . . . without fundaments* Webster is alluding to the practice of building mock-chimneys for effect, but also, like Tourneur in *The Revenger's Tragedy*, to the decline in aristocratic hospitality.

175. *the galley dung-boat for streamers* a *galley* was a large rowing-boat. Romelio compares Julio in taffeta to a dung-boat decked out for a festival.

195. *commodities* concerning this commonest of Jacobean swindles, see the note to *White Devil*, IV, i, 50-51 (p. 424).

202-3. *three heads . . . hell-hounds* Cerberus, who guarded the gates of Hell in Roman mythology, had three heads.

### Scene Two

The duel between Contarino and Ercole results in serious, and perhaps fatal, wounds for each. Admiring the extraordinary volitesse with which the duel has been conducted, we need the corrective of Prospero's reproof of Julio for setting 'the name of palour / Upon a violent and mad despair'.

### Scene Three

Counselling patience in the face of adversity, and implying that the loss of Romelio's ships is a direct result of spiritual pride, Ariosto appears in a curiously prophetic light, only later understood as part of a providentially guided attempt to reclaim the merchant. The Capuchin and bellmen, soliciting prayers for the dead duellers, serve the same end, shocking Romelio into an awareness of death which offers hope for his soul, despite his mood of angry despair. Prospero's news that Contarino is still clinging to life brings in its train Leonora's suspiciously strong concern for his well-being, as well as Romelio's determination to use the nobleman's death for his own purposes.

44–7. *The very spice . . . sick horses* spices such as myrrh, pepper, and aloes were used in farriers' remedies at this time.

74–5. *common bellman . . . sale of goods* the bellman acted as town-crier, making announcements of civic events, sales, etc. For his more serious role, see the note to *Duchess*, IV, ii, 172 (p. 444).

117. *supersedeas* technically, a supersedeas was a writ superseding another, and requiring a stay in the action which the first provided for. Here the inference is that the Puritans (*the precise*), wanting a charnel-vault for business purposes, will not hesitate to take legal action to achieve their ends.

170. *security* see note to *Duchess*, V, ii, 334 (p. 445).

### Scene Four

Ercole's narrow escape from death, which the Capuchin sees as miraculous, shocks him into penitence and abnegation. Bitterly regretting his part in the duel, he hopes, by giving out that he is dead, to leave Contarino free to marry Jolenta. His goodness contrasts with the news that Romelio 'has got a nun with child', and the Friar's prediction of dire results if the merchant does not speedily change his ways.

27–30. *the worthy Emperor . . . flat-bottomed boat* Webster is referring, in conflation, to two occasions upon which Charles V and Francis I of France exchanged challenges to single combat. Neither combat took place.

## ACT THREE

### Scene One

In telling Ariosto why he is disguised, Crispiano goes beyond the explanation he gave Sanitonella in II, i – that of checking up on his son – to reveal one of the play's *raisons d'être*, that of curbing the arrogant claims of domineering women. That the heart of the play lies deeper still, in the reclamation of the proud sinner, Romelio, is gradually to be revealed as the 'other business / Of greater consequence' so cryptically alluded to in II, i.

19. *bat-fowling* not bat-catching, but catching roosting birds at night by dazzling them with torches, then striking them down with bats, or clubs.

### Scene Two

Posing as a doctor, and consciously imitating that 'rare Italianated Jew', Marlowe's Barabbas, Romelio gains access to the dying Contarino, in order to ensure his death. By an irony which the First Surgeon immediately claims as providential, however, he assures the survival of his victim, and at the same time puts himself at the mercy of the surgeons.

3. *Italianated Jew* Romelio seems clearly to be thinking of Marlowe's Barabbas, the Machiavellian hero-villain in *The Jew of Malta*.
118. *in a bloody Roman letter* the metaphor is drawn from Roman type in printing. Romelio is pretending he is a Roman physician.

### Scene Three

In a long and complex scene, the tangle of intrigue is greatly enlarged. To gain his sister's acquiescence in his scheme to get control of Ercole's lands as well as Contarino's, Romelio invents a liaison between Contarino and Leonora. Unaware that on Leonora's side there *is* love, he then boasts to his mother of Contarino's murder, and so fosters a hatred far more violent than the jealousy he has aroused in Jolenta. When Leonora unintentionally reveals

Romelio's secret to Ercole and the Capuchin, however, she is laying the basis for moves against Romelio far more efficacious than the poisonous law-suit she is planning.

37. *Order of St Clare* the Order of Poor Clares, formerly known as Poor Ladies and (in England) the Minoresses, was founded *c.* 1215 by St Clare of Assisi (*c.* 1194–1253). The Order was characterized by poverty and austerity.

262. *Amazon lady* the legendary Amazons appear first in Homer. In late medieval legends, a distinction is made between noble Amazons, who have the left breast removed in order to use a shield, and the lower orders, who lose the right to facilitate their archery.

276–81. *let me die . . . stubborn-hearted* a reference to the tale (unsubstantiated) that the Earl of Essex sent a ring, given him by Queen Elizabeth, to the Queen as a token of former love and of hope of pardon. The ring miscarried, by a *false conveyance* (messenger) the Countess of Nottingham, and the Queen was unable to exercise clemency. According to the tale, the Countess made a death-bed confession, whereupon the Queen too took to her bed, and shortly died.

## ACT FOUR
### Scene One

While Winifrid is questioned offstage by the Registrar, Sanitonella offers Leonora's case to Ariosto. Unabashed by the latter's disgusted rejection of the brief, the clerk finds in the 'spruce' but unscrupulous Contilupo an advocate fitted to the task of teaching 'All ladies the right path to rectify / Their issue'.

25–9. *Are there not ₁ . . . content a woman* a confusingly elliptical passage. Its meaning is, 'Are there not enough whores for presentations, enough executors (*overseers*) who wrong the dead by failing to observe the terms of their wills, enough cases involving the oppression of widows or young orphans, enough wicked divorces, or vicious law-cases based on *plus quam satis*, to satisfy a woman?' The meaning of *presentations* and *plus quam satis* remain obscure. The first is a technical term relating to the placing of clergy in livings; the second (so Lucas conjectures) is a comic variant on *nunquam satis*, a legal tag in suits for annulment of marriage on grounds of impotence.

35–44. The basis of this passage is Sanitonella's use of university and ecclesiastical language (*commenc'd* and *non-resident*) to describe his humble occupation of law-clerk, and Ariosto's angry response to this self-satisfaction and ignorance. He abuses Sanitonella by calling him a *subsumner*, i.e. a deputy to the most menial of court officials, the summoner, then tears up the *libel*, or statement of the plaintiff's case, to the accompaniment of an ironic version of the phrase 'benefit of clergy'; ironic both because non-residence was a cause of scandal within the church, and because Sanitonella is not qualified to such a legal exemption (see below).

83. *This man . . . can read* a reference to benefit of clergy, whereby a man convicted of a capital offence might escape death by reading a 'neck-verse' from the Bible, so proving himself a 'clerk' (i.e. able to read).

84–5. *Be the hand . . . pick'd out on't* Webster puns, meaning (a) 'However bad the handwriting, something of the meaning will be made out'; (b) 'However dirty the hand, some gain will be forthcoming'.

### Scene Two

Though, by a coincidence clearly providential, Leonora fails in her attempt to disinherit Romelio as a bastard, the devil's law-case is not without effect upon those present. Leonora herself is shocked into an awareness of what she has done, and vows a life of penitence in a nunnery for herself and (ironically) Winifrid. In Romelio such repentance is not to be expected, but the shocks of the trial do break the shell of cold indifference with which he has surrounded himself (as Ariosto predicted they would), while the prospect of trial by combat leaves him melancholy and reflective. On the lesser figures, too, some effects are seen. Contarino, for instance, realizes for the first time the strength of Leonora's feelings for him, while Julio, in a desperate attempt to regain his father's favour, volunteers to act as Romelio's second.

8–10. *Go to the East Indies . . . pepper'd there too, lately* an allusion to conflicts between the English and Dutch over trade. Particularly violent clashes occurred in 1619–20.

131. *giant in a May-game* Jack in the Green, a giant figure, probably in origin a vegetation-spirit, was a central feature of May-Day celebrations.

222–5. *and thus are . . . arch-puritans neither* A Church of England canon forbade parents to be godparents (*gossips*) to their own children. The Puritan wing of the Church, inclined to the Genevan view which permitted this, objected strenuously.

382. *proctor* the equivalent in courts administering civil or canon law of the attorney or solicitor in courts of equity and common law.

412–14. *I can remember . . . great codpiece* in her efforts to prove herself an old woman, Winifrid gradually remembers earlier and earlier events. The *two great frosts* were those of 1564 and 1607–8; the *three great plagues* probably of 1563, 1592–4 and 1603; the *loss of Calais* occurred in January 1558, while the *great codpiece* first appeared in English fashions *c.* 1515.

498. *dance lachrimae . . . At a cart's tail* Lachrimae (Tears) was a set of seven pavanes written by John Dowland in 1608. The inference here is that Winifrid will dance tearfully as she is whipped through the city at a cart's tail – this being the punishment for a bawd.

548–53. *this vile murderer . . . And kill'd him* another highly elliptical passage: 'this vile murderer, being appointed, in Contarino's will, executor of his estate, which his [Romelio's] sister is to inherit, in order to ensure that he [Contarino] did not live to revoke the will, went secretly to his bedside and killed him'.

587–8. *sweat in the breach together / At Malta* almost certainly a reference to the defence of Malta against the Turks by the Knights of St John in 1565. (See note to *White Devil*, IV, iii, 9.)

595. *give the lie in the stomach* for effect, Julio improves upon the usual charge, 'You lie in the throat' – which is itself an intensification of a simple charge of lying.

598. *Calais sands* duelling was illegal in England, and as the closest place outside the jurisdiction of English law, Calais was a popular resort for Englishmen intent on settling differences with the sword.

603. *Knight-Marshal* an officer of the English royal household, with jurisdiction 'within the verge' of the court, i.e. for twelve miles round it (Lucas).

ACT FIVE

*Scene One*

The meeting between Jolenta and Angiolella seems, at first, to dwell on the different ways the two have taken since their childhood friendship. In the event it is the similarities which are most striking.

For each is with child by Romelio – one in fact, the other by repute – and each, fearing to lose the man she loves, is planning to flee from the outcome of the trial by combat.

### Scene Two

The two women wronged by Romelio met as nuns. The two men he has betrayed are dressed in the friars' habit in which they have just kept vigil. Where Jolenta and Angiolella are frank with each other, however, Contarino is deterred from revealing his identity to Ercole by their joint misunderstanding of Jolenta's quibbling reference to her 'shame'.

16. S.D. *the Bathanites* obscure, though probably a corruption of Bethanites (i.e. the Order of St Mary or St Lazarus of Bethany). There is no connection, however, between this order and special customs preceding duels, if indeed such existed.

38. *begot* Jolenta equivocates. She appears to mean incest; in fact she means that Romelio begot the rumour of her pregnancy, and hence her 'shame'.

### Scene Three

Where Contarino's conscience fails to persuade him to reveal his identity, the Second Surgeon prompts Winifrid to do so. Were his suggestion that she tell Leonora or Ariosto followed, the duel would immediately have been called off. As it is, with the Capuchin perhaps bound to maintain the secrecy of the confessional, suspense is maintained.

### Scene Four

Julio's uneasiness over the duel contrasts with the cold determination Romelio displays in his discussion with the Capuchin. Recognizing the dangerously negative outlook upon which this confidence is based, the friar tries to alert the merchant to the dangers of security. Though the emblems of mortality with which he confronts Romelio bring him to an awareness of the transitoriness of human existence and aspirations, however, they do not provide a concomitant moral change. Outwitted by Romelio, and unable to prevent a duel she knows to be unnecessary, Leonora finds her faith in a positive outcome severely tried. Recalling the providential reversals which have already occurred, however, the Capuchin convinces her – and us – that all is not lost.

15. *upon return* So great were the perils involved in overseas travel at this time that travellers gambled on the risks to their lives, putting down a deposit with an agent prior to their departure, and claiming, *upon return*, a sum up to five times that amount.

40. *cuckingstool* 'a stool on the end of a swinging pole by means of which scolds were ducked in the village-pond' (Lucas).

143–5. *Now I am right ... in a scarf* A *bandoleer* is a scarf. Julio's comment is best explained if we imagine, as Lucas suggests, 'some by-play in which he takes the winding-sheet from the coffin and puts it over his shoulder like a scarf; in this pose he wryly compares himself to a felon bound for the gallows and wearing his halter (as in pictures of the Burgesses of Calais)'.

174. *I made not mine own ballad* on the way to execution condemned felons were commonly subjected to ballads written for the occasion.

### Scene Five

Considered realistically, V, v, is disappointing, with Romelio's sudden failure of nerve out of keeping with the splendid, if negative, courage he has displayed hitherto, Jolenta's disguise preposterous, and the pairing of Leonora and Contarino grotesque. Seen symbolically, however, as so much in the play must be, these events fall neatly into place. Romelio's volte-face is not cowardice but wisdom, a product of the persistent efforts of Ariosto and the Capuchin to reclaim him, and a providential reversal towards which all the earlier ones have been building. Likewise Jolenta, the black nun to Angiolella's white, brings us a visual reinforcement to her lyric invitation to meditate the nature of guilt and innocence, appearance and reality. As for Contarino's dedication to Leonora, it is but a variant on the traditional comic purgation administered to the likeable but fallible young hero. Ercole deserves Jolenta, and wins her. Contarino, likeable but feckless, deserves Leonora – and needs her thousand crowns. Her age is irrelevant: it is her standing within the play's moral structure which is the determinant. To ask more is as pointless as to ask whether Angiolella will be happy with Romelio, or (in another problem play with which *The Devil's Law-Case* has much in common) whether, in *Measure for Measure*, Mariana should be wed to Angelo and Isabella to the Duke. What threatened tragedy has ended well: that is what we are left with. That, and Ariosto's injunction, shared with the penitents on stage, to take what we have just witnessed to heart.

85. *their vows' breach unto the monastery* Angiolella's broken vow is obvious; Leonora's is that she did not enter a nunnery, as she intended (see IV, ii, 567-9); Jolenta's is obscure, presumably no more than that she disguised herself as a nun.

# FOR THE BEST IN PAPERBACKS, LOOK FOR THE

In every corner of the world, on every subject under the sun, Penguin represents quality and variety – the very best in publishing today.

For complete information about books available from Penguin – including Puffins, Penguin Classics and Arkana – and how to order them, write to us at the appropriate address below. Please note that for copyright reasons the selection of books varies from country to country.

**In the United Kingdom:** Please write to *Dept JC, Penguin Books Ltd, FREEPOST, West Drayton, Middlesex, UB7 0BR.*

If you have any difficulty in obtaining a title, please send your order with the correct money, plus ten per cent for postage and packaging, to *PO Box No 11, West Drayton, Middlesex*

**In the United States:** Please write to *Dept BA, Penguin, 299 Murray Hill Parkway, East Rutherford, New Jersey 07073*

**In Canada:** Please write to *Penguin Books Canada Ltd, 2801 John Street, Markham, Ontario L3R 1B4*

**In Australia:** Please write to the *Marketing Department, Penguin Books Australia Ltd, P.O. Box 257, Ringwood, Victoria 3134*

**In New Zealand:** Please write to the *Marketing Department, Penguin Books (NZ) Ltd, Private Bag, Takapuna, Auckland 9*

**In India:** Please write to *Penguin Overseas Ltd, 706 Eros Apartments, 56 Nehru Place, New Delhi, 110019*

**In the Netherlands:** Please write to *Penguin Books Netherlands B.V., Postbus 3507, NL–1001 AH, Amsterdam*

**In West Germany:** Please write to *Penguin Books Ltd, Friedrichstrasse 10–12, D–6000 Frankfurt/Main 1*

**In Spain:** Please write to *Alhambra Longman S.A., Fernandez de la Hoz 9, E–28010 Madrid*

**In Italy:** Please write to *Penguin Italia s.r.l., Via Como 4, I-20096 Pioltello (Milano)*

**In France:** Please write to *Penguin France S.A., 17 rue Lejeune, F-31000 Toulouse*

**In Japan:** Please write to *Longman Penguin Japan Co Ltd, Yamaguchi Building, 2–12–9 Kanda Jimbocho, Chiyoda-Ku, Tokyo 101*

# FOR THE BEST IN PAPERBACKS, LOOK FOR THE 🐧

## PENGUIN CLASSICS